Housing Finance Policy
in Emerging Markets

Housing Finance Policy in Emerging Markets

Edited by

Loïc Chiquier
and Michael Lea

NON-BANK FINANCIAL
INSTITUTIONS GROUP

GLOBAL CAPITAL MARKETS
DEVELOPMENT DEPARTMENT

FINANCIAL AND PRIVATE SECTOR
DEVELOPMENT VICE PRESIDENCY

 **THE WORLD BANK**

Contents

Foreword xix

Acknowledgments xxi

Abbreviations xxiii

Introduction xxix
    Introduction xxix
    Objectives... xxix
    Evolution of Housing Finance Systems............................. xxxi
    Policy Recommendations xxxiv
    Impact and Lessons of the U.S. Subprime Crisis xxxvii
    Housing Finance Is Interrelated with the Broader Economy....... xxxviii
    Structure of the Book xxxix
    Summary Conclusions xliv

CHAPTER 1
Housing Finance and the Economy... 1
    Developed Economies.. 1
    Emerging Economies 3
    The Importance of Housing Finance.................................... 5
    The Demand for Housing Finance 11
        Macroeconomic Factors 11
        Financial Liberalization 13

Technological Change..13
Concerns and Opportunities..14
The Effect of Mortgage Finance on Savings 14
The Effect of Mortgage Finance on Investment.................15
Mortgage Finance and Growth...15
Housing Finance, Business Cycles, and Economic Fragility...........17
Mortgage Finance and the Distribution of Risk................20
House Prices, Housing Finance, and Economic Activity 22
Lessons for Emerging Markets...24

CHAPTER 2
Structure and Evolution of Housing Finance Systems 29
Mortgage Lending Models..30
Building Societies/Savings & Loans.....................................30
Commercial Banks..33
Contract Saving Schemes 35
Specialist Mortgage Banks..36
Combining Different Systems..37
Secondary Mortgage Markets 39
Introducing New Lending Models: Mexico and India.......................40
Unbundling of Mortgage Value Chain....................................42
State-owned Lenders 46
Conclusions 47

CHAPTER 3
Mortgage Instruments 49
Fixed-Rate Mortgages 50
Adjustable-Rate Mortgages..52
Indexed Mortgages 56
Interest-Only Mortgages..60
Reverse Mortgages..62
Lessons for Emerging Markets...63

CHAPTER 4
Primary Mortgage Market Infrastructure 65
Appraisal 68
The Importance of Sound Appraisal.....................................68
Developing an Appraisal Industry 69

International Standardization of Appraisal Methodology 69
Appraiser Qualifications, Appraisal Associations,
    Independence, and Ethics 72
Quantitative Appraisal Models and Real Estate Data......................73
The Challenges of Establishing an Appraisal Industry in
    Emerging Markets 74
Mortgage-Related Insurance Products...76
    Property Insurance..76
    Mortgage Life Insurance...78
    Catastrophic Insurance...80
    Title Insurance 83
Credit Information Bureaus 85
    The Importance of Credit Information in Mortgage Finance 85
    Credit Bureaus in Developed Markets...86
    Credit Bureaus in Emerging Markets 88
    Membership 90
    Ownership 91
    Management and Development 91
    Data 91
    Consumer Protection...92

CHAPTER 5

Enforcement of Mortgage Rights... 93
    Does Mortgage Collateral Matter?..95
    Differences between Legal Systems 97
    Forms of Mortgage and Mortgage Documentation 100
        Alternative Security Devices...100
        The Land Charge 102
        The Mortgage Certificate..102
        Mortgage Documentation...102
        Secondary Mortgage Markets...103
    Procedural Issues in Mortgage Enforcement 104
        Non-judicial Enforcement...106
        Negotiated versus Auction Sale 112
        Responsibility for Sale...112
        Auction Sale Prices...113
        Creditor's Right to Acquire the Mortgaged Property 113
        Notice, Cure, Rights of Redemption, and Stays of Execution........114
        Bankruptcy and Other Preferences..116

Appeals...116
Eviction..117
Distributions 118
Alternatives to Mortgage Enforcement................................118
Forbearance...119
Alternatives to Mortgage Collateral................................120
Common Property Mortgage 122
Minimizing Enforcement Actions....................................123

CHAPTER 6
Consumer Information and Protection 125

Defining the Consumer...127
Developed Markets...127
Emerging Markets 127
Consumer Protection Objectives...128
Information Asymmetry between Lenders and Consumers.........129
Consumer Heterogeneity 130
Transaction Cost Asymmetries during the Going Concern.........131
Vulnerability of the Consumer to Market Risks...............131
Protecting the Consumer through the Loan Life Cycle 133
Before Borrowing 133
The Loan Offer and Closing...137
The Ongoing Concern 139
The Back End: Default 147
The Costs of Consumer Protection 150
Opportunity Costs of Regulation 150
Alternative Implementation Forms, Costs.......................151
Enforcement Costs 152
Is Consumer Protection a Luxury Good for Emerging Markets? 153
Emerging Markets Are Part of the Global Consumer
Protection Trend...153
Appropriate Regulations May Support FinancialSector
Development..153
Conclusions 156

CHAPTER 7
Construction Finance in Emerging Economies 159

Real Estate Development Process and Risks 162

Financing by Buyers 163
Financing by Banks...167
Funding from Capital Markets..170
Financing of Buyers...171
Other Regulatory Aspects..173

CHAPTER 8
Risk Management and Regulation..175
The Risks of Housing Finance..176
Credit Risk..178
Other Risks 182
 Liquidity Risk...182
 Market Risk 183
 Agency Risk...186
 Operational Risk..187
 Systemic Credit Risk 188
 Political Risk..189
The Role and Tools of Regulation 189
International Standards for Reporting and Capital 192
Provisions...193
Capital Requirements for Primary Lenders 196
Basel II Capital Standards and Mortgage Lending................197
Capital Requirements—Supervisory Standards.....................200
 Credit Concentration Risk 201
 Market and Liquidity Risk...201
 Mortgage Loan Design..203
Other Regulator Actions..203
 Real Estate Market Information 204
 Management and Reporting Standards..............................204
 Taking Corrective Actions...205
Financial Reporting and Disclosures by Primary Lenders.....206
Regulation of Secondary Mortgage Institutions 207
Case Study: The U.S. Subprime Crisis....................................207
 The Property Boom and Loose Credit Underwriting.........208
 Reduced Reliance on Credit Enhancements......................209
 Risky Loan Design...209
 Lack of Consumer Information 210
 Breakdowns in the Behavior of Participants in the
  Securitization Value Chain...210

The Influence of Trends in International Capital Markets.............211
Reduced Transparency Resulting from Complex Security
    Structures and Incomplete Information on Exposures...............211
Regulatory Failures in the United States Contributed to the
    Growth of Risky Subprime Lending Practices............................212
The Risks of Subprime Practices and Those of Lending to
    Moderate- and Low-income Households Should Not Be
    Confused..212
The Subprime Crisis Was Avoidable 213

CHAPTER 9

Contractual Savings for Housing 215

Key Features of a Contractual Savings Scheme for Housing 216
    General Character 216
    Basic Structure of a CSH Contract...216
    Open and Closed CSH Schemes..217
    Financing Function of CSH 219
    CSH and Other Housing Finance Products 219
Historical Development of CSH Schemes...220
    Developed Mortgage Markets..220
    CSH in Emerging Markets 222
Managing Risk under a CSH Scheme 223
    Risk Profile of CSH Contracts 223
    Demand Fluctuations...225
    Inflation Risk..227
    Contract Design Flaws 228
    Misallocation of Excess Liquidity 230
CSHs as a Policy Choice in Emerging Markets................................232
    Mobilization of Savings 233
    Lack of Long-Term Funding 234
    Credit Risk Mitigation and Financial Stability 235
    Stimulation of Modernization and Small Transactions
        Lending Market 238
Institutional Requirements for CSH Lenders 239
    Regulation of CSH Schemes 239
Subsidies for CSHs 241
    CSH Subsidies in Emerging Markets..241
    Guiding Principles 244
Conclusions for Emerging Markets 244

CHAPTER 10
State Housing Banks..**247**
A Brief Overview of State Housing Banks..248
Definition and Classification 248
Types of State Housing Banks..249
The Rationale for Creating a State Housing Bank.........................250
The Model Failed in Many Countries 251
State Housing Bank Failings...254
Weak Corporate Governance...254
Lax Management of Credit Risk..255
Assets/Liability Mismatches...256
Misallocation of Subsidies and Rent-Seeking Policies...................257
SHB as Obstacles to the Growth of Housing Finance Markets? ...258
Available Safeguards and Alternative Options....................................258
Good Governance 259
Autonomy of Funding..260
Alignment of Corporate Interest with Market Development........260
Examples of SHBs Meeting These Conditions..............................261
Policy Alternatives 263
Regulatory or Contractual Credit Orientation.............................264
Second-Tier Institutions..264
Public-Private Partnerships...265
"Double Bottom Line"—Social and Commercial—
    Private-Sector Lenders..266
Exit Strategies 267
Enable a "Corporatization Process" to Create a Commercially
    Run Institution..267
Partial or Full Privatization 269
Conversion of an SHB into a Second-Tier Refinance Institution .271
State Support to Private Sector 271
Conclusion: A Decision Tree for Policy Makers..............................274

CHAPTER 11
Housing Provident Funds **277**
Description of HPF...277
Subsidies 278
Governance 280
Development of an HPF 281

International Experience...282
  China...282
  Singapore 284
  Mexico...285
  Brazil 287
  Philippines...289
  Nigeria National Housing Fund 290

CHAPTER 12
Mortgage Securities in Emerging Markets 293
  Why Are Mortgage Securities Important?.......................295
  What Are the Prerequisites for Issuing Mortgage Securities?...........297
  What Has Been the Experience in Emerging Markets?.....................301
    Covered Bond Issuers 302
    MBS Issuers 304
    Liquidity Facilities 306
  Safety and Soundness Regulation in Mortgage Capital Markets.......308
    Mortgage-Backed Securities....................................308
    Mortgage Bonds...310
    Reporting for Secondary Market Instruments 312
    The Role of the Credit Rating Agencies...................315
  Lessons Learned 317
  The Basics...317
  Market Demand 319
  Simplicity 319
  Role of Government 321

CHAPTER 13
Mortgage Insurance 325
  Definition and Unique Features of MI...............................326
  Purposes of MI 326
  Countries that Have MI Today.......................................327
  Prerequisite Conditions for MI Success.........................327
  Key Program Characteristics...330
    Individual Loan Coverage 331
    Premium Rates...332
    Eligible Loans..334
    Underwriting Method 335

Meeting Social Objectives..338
Special MI Products for Mortgage-Backed Securities (MBS)/
    Structured Finance..339
    Mortgage Pool Insurance..340
    Timely Payment and Cash-flow Protection 340
Credit Risk Management 341
Regulatory Issues 341
Bank Risk-Based Capital Rules 345
Consumer Issues...347
Information Technology 349
Public-Private MI Partnerships...350
    Public MI Provider Supported by Private Reinsurer(s)..............351
    Government Backup for Private MI Provider 352
    Government-Sponsored Enterprises (GSEs), Privately Insured ...354
Public-Private MI Competition 355
Lessons Learned..358
Conclusion...360

CHAPTER 14

Residential Rental Housing Finance.. 363

Introduction 363
The Rental Sector in Housing Policy..364
    The Importance of Enabling a Vibrant Rental Sector....................364
    Imbalance between Rental and Homeownership.............................366
    Rental Housing as an Investment..367
The Challenges of Developing Rental Housing in Emerging
    Economies 369
    Rights of Landlords and Tenants...371
    Rent Control..372
    Unfavorable Tax Regimes...374
    Social Rental Housing 375
Some Market Financing Models for Rental Housing.........................377
    All-Equity Based...377
    Real Estate Investment Trusts (REIT)................................378
    Bank-Supplied Credit for Residential Rental Investment 380
    Capital Market Financing 382
    Credit Enhancements and Insurance Products..............................385
Country Examples 387

The Low-Income Housing Tax Credit (LIHTC) in the
United States 388
Brazil: the Residential Leasing Program (PAR)..............................389
Poland: the TBS Experience...391
Conclusions 393

CHAPTER 15

Housing Microfinance...**395**
The Rise of Housing Microfinance 395
An Overview of Housing Microfinance......................................398
Potential Size of HMF Markets: The Cases of Peru and
Guatemala..399
Financial Performance of HMF 402
Other Opportunities for Housing Microfinance 404
Limited Potential for Linking HMF and Housing Subsidies.........404
Linkages between Commercial Banks and Housing
Microfinance 407
The Limitations of Housing Microfinance..................................409
Market Size...409
Pricing and Access...410
Refinancing and Other Microfinance Limitations.........................412
Potential to Contribute to Entrenchment of Informality..............414
Conclusion..414

CHAPTER 16

Housing Finance Subsidies **417**
Where to Start? Linking Housing Problems to Subsidy Policy..........420
Analyzing the Causes of the Housing Problems 420
Subsidies and Other Types of Government Intervention 426
Why Subsidize Housing? 428
Subsidies and the Expansion of Housing Finance Systems 429
Housing Finance Sector Problems, Causes, and Subsidies 429
Housing Finance Subsidies, Market Structure, andVested
Interests..432
Housing Finance Subsidies to Alleviate Funding Constraints 434
Subsidies to Address Lending Risks and High Transaction
Costs..436
Problems with Subsiding a Housing Finance System...................439

Subsidies for the Financing of Rental Housing.....................440
    The Rental Market...440
    Rental Sector Regulations, Taxation, and Subsidies 441
    Subsidies to the Rental Sector...443
    Project Finance for Ownership Housing.........................447
    Public-Private Partnerships for the Provision of Affordable
        Rental Housing 447
    Making Rental Subsidies Work...................................448
Housing Finance Subsidies to Households.........................449
    Household Problems and Subsidies.............................449
    Lower-Middle Income Households 453
    Low-Income Households: Subsidies When Housing Supply
        Markets Do Not Work 458
Conclusions 460

Bibliography

Bibliography...463

Contributors

Contributors..485

Figures

1. Selected Housing Loan to GDP Ratios xxxii
2. Share of Urban Slum Dwellers and Housing Loan to GDP
    Ratio, Asia and Latin America, 2001 xxxv
1.1. Mortgage Debt/GDP—Developed Markets 2
1.2. Mortgage Debt/GDP—Emerging Markets........................3
1.3. Correlation of Private Consumption Growth with Real House
    Price Changes...7
1.4. Marginal Propensities to Consume Out-of-Housing Wealth
    and Mortgage Market Indicators...............................8
1.5. Mortgage Rates in Developed Countries.........................12
1.6. Mortgage Rates in Emerging Markets............................12
2.1. Depository and Direct Lending.....................................31
2.2. Mortgage Bank System..36
2.3. Mortgage Lenders by Type 37
2.4. Emerging Market Mortgage Funding 38
2.5. Housing Finance with a Secondary Mortgage Market 39
2.6. The Bundled Home Mortgage Delivery..........................43
2.7. Unbundled Mortgage Delivery 43

2.8. Mortgage Distribution Channels.......................................44
3.1. Instrument Alternatives 50
3.2. Cost of the Danish Prepayment Option 52
3.3. Mortgage Products: Percentage of Adjustable Rate Loans...........53
3.4. Mexican Mortgage Instrument Payment Performance 56
3.5. Mexican Mortgage Instrument Balance Performance..................57
3.6. Amortization by Interest Rate Type in the United States
(U.S. H1 2006)..61
3.7. Method of Repayment United Kingdom 61
7.1. Basic Construction Finance Model..............................168
9.1. Basic Structure of a CSH Contract............................217
9.2. Origins of Building Societies, Savings & Loans, and
Bausparkassen..221
9.3. Closed System CSH Contract Demand and Capital Market
Rates, Germany, 1973–2007......................................226
9.4. Role of CSH Deposits for the Financing Structure of
Monetary Financial Institutions, Czech Republic, 2002–07...........233
15.1. Government and Banking Association Charter Target Group
in South Africa..397
15.2. Effective Interest Rates (inclusive of fees) for MFIs in 2004.....410

Tables

1.1. Real Estate and Banking Crises—Selected Cases...........................23
5.1. Enforcing Mortgage Collateral...94
9.1. Main Differences between Open and Closed CSH Schemes......218
9.2. CSH Subsidies in Central and Eastern Europe Compared.........241
12.1. Capital Market Finance of Housing in Emerging Economies..302
12.2. Basel II Standardized Risk Weights for Long-Term Bonds.......314
13.1. Selected Countries with MI Programs, 2008 328
13.2. MI Prerequisite Conditions for Success..................................329
13.3. LTV Correlates Strongly with Default Risk and Losses.............330
13.4. Insurable Loans, Selected Countries......................................335
13.5. Credit Risk Management Tools 342
13.6. Advantages and Disadvantages of Public and Private MI
Schemes 350
13.7. MI Program Reversals and Resolutions—Selected Cases.........357
15.1. HMF Performance Indicators for Six MFIs in Latin America .403
16.1. Potential Access to Housing Finance in Mexico, 2006 423
16.2. Affordable Loan/House Price Scenario 424

16.3. Examples of System Subsidies..431
16.4. Examples of Housing Finance Subsidies to Households...........452

Boxes

1.1. Real Estate and Financial Crises: Thailand.......................19
1.2. Mexican Past Crises and the Role of Housing Finance 21
2.1. SOFOLs—Mexican Mortgage Companies 41
2.2. HDFC—Creating a Market 42
3.1. The Limits of Adjustable-Rate Mortgages (ARMs)......................55
3.2. Colombia: Difficulties with Indexed Mortgages...........................58
4.1. Developing the Appraisal Industry 75
4.2. Examples of Property and Disaster Insurance................................82
4.3. Croatian Credit Bureau Development: HROK...............................89
5.1. The Crisis of Mortgage Markets in Colombia................................96
5.2. Judicial Enforcement of Mortgages in West Africa......................105
5.3. Judicial Enforcement in Mexico 106
5.4. Non-judicial Enforcement of Mortgage Rights in Croatia..........107
5.5. Non-judicial Enforcement of Mortgage Rights in Sri Lanka......108
5.6. Time in Foreclosure in Power of Sale and Judicial Procedure
States in the United States 109
5.7. Non-judicial Enforcement of Mortgage Rights in India.............109
5.8. Reforms of Mortgage Rights in Pakistan.................................110
5.9. France: Guarantees as a Substitute for Mortgages.......................121
5.10. Housing Lending in Indonesia 122
6.1. "High" and "Low" Levels of Consumer Protection—
The Clash of Approaches in Europe.................................132
6.2. Defining the Annual Percentage Rate of Charge..........................135
6.3. Prepayment Indemnities—How Much is Too Much? 139
6.4. Foreign Currency Mortgages—Low Rates, High Risk.................142
6.5. Consumer Protection in the United States and the Subprime
Market...144
6.6. The Legacy of Brazil's Old Housing Finance System 146
6.7. A New Consumer Protection Framework for Mexico.................155
8.1. Innovative Underwriting in Thailand 181
8.2. Proactive Servicing in Mexico 182
8.3. Managing Market Risk...184
8.4. Polish Foreign Exchange Lending Requirements....................185
8.5. Keystone Bank...190
8.6. Spain's Statistical Provision...195

8.7. Colombia Crisis 198

9.1. CSH—an Islamic Finance Product in Iran...................223

9.2. Prepayment Risk in the Austrian Market......................227

9.3. Illiquidity of the Iranian Housing Savings Scheme......................229

9.4. Liquidity Fluctuations and Disconnect from the Housing
Finance System in Tunisia...231

9.5. CSH System Choice in Transition Countries in the 1990s..........236

9.6. Attempts to Introduce CSH in India 238

9.7. CSH Subsidies in Hungary...242

9.8. Planned CSH Law and Subsidies in Russia 242

10.1. The Fiscal Cost of Bailing Out State Housing Banks.................252

10.2. The Case of BancoEstado (Chile)................................261

10.3. The Case of the Government Housing Bank (GHB) of
Thailand...262

10.4. The Case of the Federal Mortgage Bank of Nigeria 272

11.1. The Reforms of INFONAVIT in Mexico......................286

14.1. Returns on Formal Rental Housing in São Paulo, Brazil 371

14.2. Underwriting Criteria for Multifamily Rental Loans 381

14.3. Securitization of Multifamily Rental Loans and Social
Housing Loans 383

14.4. Bond Enhancement Products for Multifamily Rental
Housing..387

16.1. Example of Income and Finance Affordability...........................425

16.2. Defining Subsidies 426

y20

Main BK t:

Foreword

au on pg xx

This book is a magnificent effort to pull together both knowledge and experiences from advanced and emerging markets to help policy makers in all markets establish sound housing finance policies.

The book covers all the important aspects of housing finance. Having been actively involved in this topic as a policy maker in the past, I can say this book would have made our options more clear, our thinking more focused, and our decision-making faster, if we could have had this publication at that time.

It will be a very valuable tool for policy makers going forward.

This volume could not be more timely. The debacle of the U.S. subprime mortgage market is distorting the discussion around housing finance in emerging markets. To cut through the maze, this book offers insights around all the building blocks of a housing finance system—including mortgage securitization—and guides the reader through the different policy options available in each case and the most common mistakes policy makers must avoid.

The vastness of the experiences related from around the globe, and the cross-cutting perspective of the World Bank technical experts, will surely enable the reader to relate the topics discussed with the situation faced in his or her country. While reading it, I understood that the problems we face in the Mexican housing market are strikingly similar to those of other emerging economies. There is a lot we may learn from each other, and this book just made that so much easier.

Guillermo Babatz
President
Comisión Nacional Bancaria y de Valores, Mexico

NA

Acknowledgments

We would like to express our immense gratitude to the authors and co-authors of the chapters in this book. Their contributions have been of the upmost professional quality, and reflect decades of international exposure and experience as well as a capacity to synthesize their unbiased and in-depth knowledge. We take also this opportunity to thank them for their incredible support and patience. A special thanks is given to Roger Blood, Robert Buckley, Steve Butler, Franck Daphnis, Hans-Joachim Dübel, Richard Green, Britt Gwinner, Olivier Hassler, Marja Hoek-Smit, David Le Blanc, Sally Merrill, Bertrand Renaud, Claude Taffin, and Simon Walley. Many more in developed and emerging economies should be thanked for their direct and indirect contributions. As the list would simply be too long, we can only sincerely and collectively thank all of those we have had the privilege to work with throughout these past years.

This book represents a pioneering effort to fill a very large knowledge gap in this important but poorly understood area of housing finance in emerging economies. This publication should be improved through subsequent versions. As markets and policies keep changing rapidly, we can only encourage all contributors to keep updating the collective knowledge and wisdom by taking further initiatives to share their experiences.

A fantastic effort was deployed by the GCMNB Department of the World Bank, spearheaded by Olivier Hassler, Colleen Mascenik and Simon Walley in order to update, adjust, edit and assemble the various part of this book, including updates related to the crisis. Without their tenacious and professional involvement, this book would have not become a reality. A special thanks as well to Patricia Braxton and Megan Gerrard of the World Bank, and Mellen Candage of Grammarians for their superb editorial contribution. James Quigley has done a highly professional job designing and laying out the book.

As authors and editors of the book, we are also especially thankful to our great peer reviewers, Guillermo Babatz and Mila Freire, who made the time to provide us with detailed and constructive comments, which have been critical to improve the quality of the book.

Last but not the least, we would like to thank Rodney Lester and Bertrand Renaud for their inspirational, intellectual and managerial support. This book is also largely theirs.

Loïc Chiquier and Michael Lea

NA

Abbreviations

ABS	asset backed securities
AIDS	acquired immune deficiency syndrome
ANIL	L'Agence Nationale pour Information sur Logement (National Agency for Housing Information, France)
APR	annual percentage rate
ARA	Housing Finance and Development Centre of Finland
ARM	adjustable (or variable) rate mortgages
AVM	automated valuation model
BAFIN	Bundesanstalt für Finanzdienstleistungsaufsicht (Federal Financial Supervisory Authority, Germany)
BHSA	Banco Hipotecario SA (Argentina)
BHU	Banco Hipotecario del Uruguay
BIS	Bank for International Settlements
BKN	Statens bostadskreditnämnd (National Housing Credit Guarantee Board, Sweden)
CAMEL	capital, assets, management, earnings, liquidity
CEE	Central and Eastern Europe
CEF	Caixa Econômica Federal (Federal Housing Bank, Brazil)
CFR	Code of Federal Regulations
CMBS	Commercial Mortgage-Backed Securities
CMHC	Canada Mortgage and Housing Corporation

CNEP	Caisse Nationale d'Epargne et de Prévoyance
CPF	Central Provident Fund (Singapore)
CSH	Contractual Saving Schemes for Housing
DIM	dual index mortgage
EBRD	European Bank for Reconstruction and Development
ECA	Europe and Central Asia
EMF	European Mortgage Federation
EU	European Union
FAMA	Fundación para el Apoyo a la Microempresa, Acción Investments (Nicaragua)
FGHM	Fonds de Garantie Hypothécaire du Mali (Mortgage Guarantee Fund of Mali)
FGTS	Fundo de Garantia do Tempo de Serviço (Peru)
FHA	U.S. Federal Housing Administration; Instituto de Fomento de Hipotecas Aseguradas (Guatemala)
FICO	Fair, Isaac and Company
FMBN	Federal Mortgage Bank of Nigeria
FMO	Financierings-Maatschappij voor Ontwikkelingsladen (Netherlands Development Finance Company)
FOVI	Fondo de Operación y Financiamiento Bancario a la Vivienda (Mexico)
FOVISSTE	Fondo de Vivienda para los Trabajadores al Servicio del Estado (Mexico)
FRM	fixed-rate mortgages
FSA	Financial Services Authority
FTT	fiduciary transfer of title
FX	foreign exchange
GBP	United Kingdom Pound Sterling
GDP	gross domestic product
GHB	Government Housing Bank (Thailand)
GHLC	Government Housing Loan Corporation
GNMA	Government National Mortgage Association
GNP	gross national product

GSE	government-sponsored enterprise
HBFC	House Building Finance Corporation
HDB	Housing Development Board
HDFC	Housing Development Finance Corporation
HEW	housing equity withdrawal
HFCs	Housing Finance Companies
HKMC	Hong Kong, China Mortgage Corporation
HLGC	Home Loan Guarantee Company (South Africa)
HGC	Home Guaranty Corporation (Philippines)
HMF	Housing Microfinance
HPF	Housing Provident Fund
HPI	House Price Index
HROK	Croatian Registry of Credit Obligations
HUD	U.S. Housing and Urban Development Department
HUF	Hungarian Forint
IADB	Inter-American Development Bank
IAS	International Accounting Standards
ICICI	Industrial Credit and Investment Corporation of India
IFC	International Finance Corporation
IMF	International Monetary Fund
INFONAVIT	Instituto del Fondo Nacional de Vivienda para los Trabajadores (Mexico)
IRB	internal-ratings-based (approach)
IT	information technology
IUHF	International Union for Housing Finance
IVSC	International Valuation Standards Committee
JMRC	Jordan Mortgage Refinance Corporation
KFM	National Housing Fund (Poland)
KH&CB	Korea Housing and Commercial Bank
KHB	Korea Housing Bank
KMGF	Kazakhstan Mortgage Guarantee Fund
LAC	Latin America and the Caribbean
LIHTC	low-income housing tax credit

LMI	lenders mortgage insurance
LTV	loan-to-value
MBA	Mortgage Bankers Association (United States)
MBS	mortgage-backed security
MDG	Millennium Development Goal
MENA	Middle East and North Africa
MFI	microfinance institution
MI	mortgage default insurance
MIF	Mortgage Insurance Fund
MLS	multiple listing service
MLV	mortgage lLending value
MMIF	Mutual Mortgage Insurance Fund
MPC	marginal propensity to consume
MV	market value
NGO	non-government organization
NHF	National Housing Fund
NPL	non-performing loan
OECD	Organisation for Economic Co-operation and Development
PAG-IBIG	Filipino Development Housing Fund (Philippines)
PAR	Programa de Arrendamento Residencial (Residential Leasing Program, Brazil)
PBoC	People's Bank of China
PLAM	price-level adjusted mortgage
PLN	Polish Zloty New
PMI	Primary Mortgage Institution
PT	pass-through
RBA	Reserve Bank of Australia
REIT	Real Estate Investment Trust
ROA	return on assets
ROE	return on equity
RSL	registered social landlord
S&L	savings & loan

SCHUFA   Schutzgemeinschaft für Allgemeine Kreditsicherung (German Credit Protection Association)

SCPI   Société Civile de Placement Immobilier (Real Estate Investment Trust, France)

SEC   Securities and Exchange Commission

SGCI   Système de Gestion Centralisée des Impressions

SHB   State Housing Banks

SHF   Sociedad Hipotecaria Federal (Mexico)

SIDA   Swedish International Development Cooperation Agency

SOFOL   Sociedad Financiera de Objecto Limitado (Mexico)

SPV   special purpose vehicle

TBS   Nonprofit Landlord Associations (Poland)

TC   Titularizadora Colombiana (Colombia)

THFC   The Housing Finance Corporation Limited

UPAC   Unidad de Poder Adquisitivo Constante (Constant Purchasing Power Unit of Exchange, Colombia)

UVR   Unidad de Valor Real (Colombia)

VAT   value added tax

WEW   Homeownership Guarantee Fund (Netherlands)

Note: All dollar amounts are U.S. dollars unless otherwise indicated.

y 20

Main Bk tis

Introduction

Loïc Chiquier and Michael Lea

Objectives

In 1993, the World Bank published an influential report on housing policy, "Housing: Enabling Markets to Work." This report documented the importance of housing in the economy while at the same time providing governments with guidelines on how best to design policy to create efficient housing markets. A section of that report already focused on housing finance and its importance in the effective operation of housing markets.

There have been numerous publications focusing on the evolution of housing finance systems, but most focus on developed economies where large markets have been built over several decades. Few publications describe the features and challenges of developing housing finance in emerging economies. There are some common features between developed and emerging markets, but the overall environment, in particular for housing and financial services, presents greater challenges. These include less favorable financial and economic conditions; greater range and quantum risks to manage; limited fiscal space, which can constrain government policy; and, importantly, emerging markets, which often suffer from shortages of housing in terms of both quantity and quality.

The purpose of this book is to provide fact-based information and guidance to policy makers concerned with housing finance in emerging markets. An overarching goal is to improve the understanding of the importance of housing finance to the economy. This includes covering the prerequisites for an effective housing finance system together with the main characteristics of such a system. The book continues by laying out some of the policy alternatives and models of housing finance (products, infrastructure, risk management, regulations, funding). In line with the priorities of many governments, the book is focused on solutions; in particular the role of government in contributing to the growth of housing finance and in increasing access to housing finance for lower and informal income households. The way taken to achieve these objectives is of the essence: they cannot be achieved, at least in a sustainable manner, by involving the creation of undue additional risks for the financial sector or eventually unbearable fiscal liabilities.

Housing finance brings together complex and multi-sector issues that are driven by constantly changing local features, such as a country's legal environment or culture, economic makeup, regulatory environment, or political system. This examination of housing finance policy highlights some general lessons for policy makers and regulators. It does not, however, provide an exhaustive review of all developments across the housing finance world. It is worth stating at the outset that there is no "best" model set out in this book. The aim is to provide a developmental roadmap that can be tailored and sequenced to each country's situation and timing.

The book is focused on housing finance policy and takes into account only broader housing-policy considerations where it directly relates to housing finance. For instance, the book does not discuss many other fundamental aspects of a comprehensive housing policy, such as title registration, urban development rules, management of public land, access to land for development, slum upgrading tools, non-finance subsidies, the relationship between national and local authorities, and so forth.

Neither would the book represent a technical guide or a handbook for lenders. Many in-depth publications can provide the reader with detailed accounts of developing mortgage markets at a country level or of different products, funding models, or types of reform. There is a detailed bibliography with this book that interested readers are invited to consult.

This publication seeks to stimulate a debate among the public- and private-sector players in this rapidly evolving industry. It should be seen as a first edition, which can be greatly enhanced by adding experiences, case studies, and corrections in subsequent editions. This book also represents the starting point of a dialogue with readers who are welcome to contribute their input for future editions.

The book is based on the experience accumulated by the Housing Finance Team of the World Bank (composed of L. Chiquier, O. Hassler, B. Gwinner, and S. Walley), which has been in the privileged position of working in more than 30 countries. The team also follows closely developments in the housing finance systems of other countries, including developed economies. The book was co-edited by Dr. Michael Lea, who is one of the most active international experts in housing finance. Several chapters were drafted by recognized experts in their field who also worked in many emerging economies.

Evolution of Housing Finance Systems

Since 1993, the penetration of housing finance has increased dramatically in developed economies. In the United States, in European countries, Australia, or Japan, residential mortgage markets represent between 50 and 100 percent of the gross domestic product (GDP).

Housing finance has also been developing in more emerging markets, albeit at a different pace and with different outcomes and impacts across countries (figure 1). Over the last 20 years, housing finance has also reached significant levels in a few middle-income countries (the Republic of Korea, South Africa, Malaysia, Chile, Baltic countries), with residential mortgage debt amounting to 20–35 percent of GDP. Over the past five years, housing finance has also made inroads in several other "latecomer" countries (China, India, Thailand, Mexico, most of the new European Union [EU] countries, Morocco, Jordan, and even more recently in many more countries, including Brazil, Turkey, Peru, Kazakhstan, and Ukraine) where mortgage markets stand at 6–17 percent of GDP. This expansion is impressive and seen by most as irreversible ("The housing finance genie is out of the bottle," Buckley,

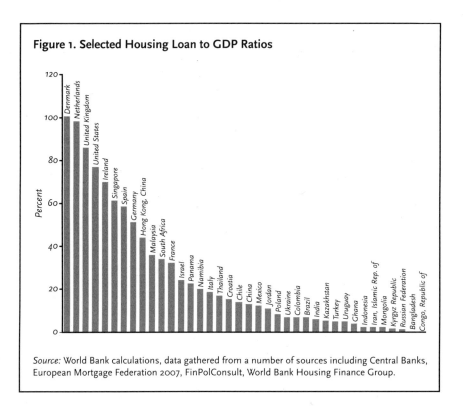

Figure 1. Selected Housing Loan to GDP Ratios

Source: World Bank calculations, data gathered from a number of sources including Central Banks, European Mortgage Federation 2007, FinPolConsult, World Bank Housing Finance Group.

World Bank 2006). Progress is also observed in a few lower–income economies, including Indonesia, Egypt, Ghana, Pakistan, Senegal, Uganda, Mali,
Mongolia, and Bangladesh, but not on a large-enough scale to address some
of the chronic housing issues they face.

This book focuses mostly on residential mortgage finance (for home
acquisition). There is recognition of other relevant forms of housing finance,
such as developer finance, rental finance, or microfinance applied to housing.
Developer finance is often in the form of unregulated advance payments
by buyers, and developers sometimes provide long-term finance to buyers
through installment sales when mortgage markets are not accessible. Microfinance for housing is typically used for home improvement or progressive
housing purposes. Loans are typically granted without pledging properties.
Although the overall impact of microfinance in housing remains limited,
this activity can represent an important source of funding for those in the
informal sector.

In the last decade, a few far-reaching trends have been significant drivers for the expansion of housing finance in emerging economies. These include the following:

- *Favorable macro conditions, notably in terms of falling inflation and mortgage rates (both in nominal and real terms).* Many emerging economies have experienced GDP growth, which is partly converted into rising incomes of households. These conditions have favored the expansion of mortgage markets. Conversely, many of the historical failures of housing finance are linked to macroeconomic instability, often combined with an inadequate regulatory and risk-management environment. This is particularly the case in Latin America, where the model of savings and loans was devastated by hyperinflation. Macro instability increases the risk and cost of providing long-term loans. While indexed mortgage instruments can facilitate housing finance in inflationary environments, they require advanced risk management skills and prudential regulations that often remain amiss.
- *Increasing housing demand linked to long-term urbanization and demographic forces.* A total of 91 percent of the net increase of the world population between 2000 and 2030 will be located in cities of emerging economies (Population Division of the Department of Economic and Social Affairs of the United Nations Secretariat, 2005). Africa and Asia in particular are likely to face increasing urbanization pressure over the next decade. Similar trends are observed in many countries in other regions (Turkey, Mexico, Iran, and so on). Demand is also fueled by strong aspirations for better housing conditions. In addition, housing increasingly forms part of a household's savings strategy for investment and as security for old age. In many cases, real estate is one of the asset classes available when financial investment instruments and government debt markets are underdeveloped.
- *Financial liberalization,* with the ending of closed public housing finance circuits (earmarked housing funds, state-owned housing banks, and so forth) can be an important stimulant for housing finance. The housing sector is too large for any government to finance it alone. Liberalization is a universal trend that mobilizes savings from the public through banks and, in later stages of development, through

capital markets, as long as housing loans can offer an attractive risk-adjusted rate of return for investors. Housing finance has become an area of increasing importance for many institutions (linked to retail finance and construction finance), including liquid banks and finance and specialist mortgage companies. Their access to private bond markets is a key ingredient, inextricably linked to other reforms (public debt management, development of capital markets, pension funds, and insurance). The growth of the financial sector has led to lower operational costs, improved information technology, and better risk-management tools.

The role of the state has evolved from direct lending and housing construction to regulation, policy development, building market infrastructure, and more efficient assistance for low-income groups.

Policy Recommendations

Although the importance of the housing sector in social and economic development is widely accepted, the role of housing finance has gained prominence in the last decade. This shift has mirrored the rise in importance accorded to the development of the financial sector. The 2002 World Bank Development report emphasized the importance of growing the financial sector as part of a development strategy. Housing finance is often seen as critical both to the housing sector and to the development of the financial sector (banks, non-banking financial institutions, and bond markets).

Housing has risen up the policy and political agendas with many governments. This is in part because of the significant contribution that housing and housing construction can make to GDP growth. There is also an important human dimension, where the need for public shelter programs is also increasingly recognized. This was made explicit in the Millennium Development Goals (MDG), where a reduction in the number of people forced to live in slums was one of the key targets under MDG 7, which covers environmental sustainability. This point is clearly illustrated in figure 2, which shows the correlation between developing a housing finance system and the number of slum dwellers. Lastly, the importance of housing and

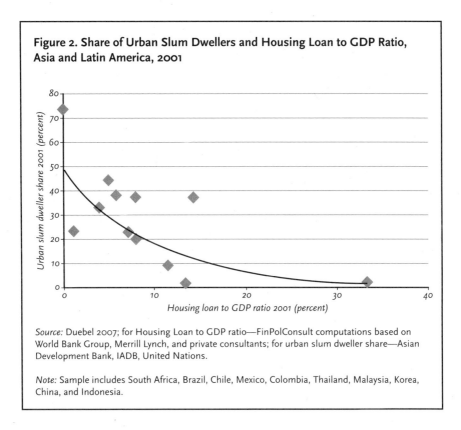

Figure 2. Share of Urban Slum Dwellers and Housing Loan to GDP Ratio, Asia and Latin America, 2001

Source: Duebel 2007; for Housing Loan to GDP ratio—FinPolConsult computations based on World Bank Group, Merrill Lynch, and private consultants; for urban slum dweller share—Asian Development Bank, IADB, United Nations.

Note: Sample includes South Africa, Brazil, Chile, Mexico, Colombia, Thailand, Malaysia, Korea, China, and Indonesia.

its associated finance as a development catalyst for the broader financial sector should not be underestimated despite the subprime market debacle. A number of countries have successfully developed capital markets with significant volumes coming from the refinancing of mortgage debt.

Sound regulation and infrastructure are needed to build a sustainable housing finance system. The imperatives for developing a housing finance system can be set out as 12 Herculean tasks for policy makers:

1. Enforceable property rights and effective registration system.
2. Enforceable foreclosure for mortgage lenders (collateralized lending is superior to uncollateralized lending in cost and availability).
3. Access for all lenders to diversified funding (including mortgage securities).
4. Comprehensive credit information systems.

5. Strong prudential regulations that encourage responsible lending and adequate consumer information (avoid abusive or unfair lending).
6. Level playing field among lenders to encourage competition.
7. Credit products adjusted to economic and financial realities, different consumer needs, and sound risk-management practices.
8. Accessible and reliable information on house transactions and prices.
9. Professional real estate intermediaries, including developers, appraisers, insurers, and realtors.
10. Urban development regulations adapted to economic realities to encourage the production of formal affordable housing.
11. Comprehensive national housing policy, including socially and economically efficient subsidies, slum upgrading, and title regularization programs.
12. Access to titled land for developers.

Many studies demonstrate the correlation between implementing these policy recommendations and a subsequent growth in housing finance markets. Rapid and sustainable expansion has been observed in countries that have managed to get high marks on most of these factors (as in Chile, Mexico, and Malaysia).

In most emerging economies, housing finance remains available only to the middle and upper echelons of the salaried income-distribution structure of households. With a few important exceptions (like Malaysia or Mexico), other low and informal income households have yet to see any mass-scale development of housing finance. In addition to formidable urbanization and demographic forces, this situation favors the proliferation of slums. On one hand, lenders already face difficulties in managing their additional risks and extend smaller loans in a cost-effective way. On the other hand, households may be confronted by expensive formal housing markets resulting from an inadequate housing policy. Key factors relate to obtaining ownership titles, adequate urban planning and development regulations, infrastructure for real estate intermediaries, resale procedures, rental laws, access to land for developers, and the way subsidies are designed and implemented. The adequacy of government policy is critical to expand the outreach of housing finance.

Impact and Lessons of the U.S. Subprime Crisis

As this book goes to print, world attention is focused on the U.S. subprime crisis. Although subprime adjustable rate mortgages (ARMs) only make up 8 percent of U.S. mortgage debt, a large amount of credit risks is now held by global investors through the debt leverage of securitization and complex financial structures. The fall in the quality of these securities, and the difficulty to value them, have precipitated large losses, as well as distrust throughout financial markets and a liquidity squeeze. The magnitude of the global crisis has been a surprise for most experts.

Some financial investors have suffered from direct losses, but most housing finance markets in emerging economies have not been contaminated. The structure and performance of mortgage markets in emerging economies are different, smaller, and more conservative. The mortgage markets are typically funded by domestic deposits that reduce the global contagion via capital market flows. Emerging mortgage markets that have made heaviest use of global securitization look likely to be most affected (the Russian Federation, Kazakhstan, Korea). In non-contaminated and high-quality mortgage markets, domestic residential mortgage-backed security markets remain active, albeit with slightly higher spreads (by 20–40 basis points in Mexico).

Whereas the leverage effect on global financial markets is a new element, this crisis displays many of the conventional features seen during other real estate finance crises, as analyzed in greater detail in several chapters of the book, including:

- poor credit underwriting coupled with higher-risk products for riskier borrowers, where lenders have used continuing house-price appreciation as a safety net;
- poor levels of disclosure and consumer protection;
- unregulated originators having no incentive to preserve the portfolio quality;
- inadequate incentives to manage credit risks;
- funding models that have proved too complex and too heavily reliant on short-term debt to satisfy the appetite of investors for higher yields; and

- inadequate and weak regulatory response from a multitude of fragmented regulators.

The subprime market crisis does not contradict the goal of expanding the access to housing finance, but shows what happens when this expansion is done with no consideration for the specificities of this market segment. The purpose of the book is to provide guidelines for emerging markets on how they might avoid such issues through setting up a sound regulatory regime supported by the necessary risk-management infrastructure.

Housing Finance Is Interrelated with the Broader Economy

Wider access to housing finance has a significant impact on construction, economic growth, and urban development (see Renaud 1999). In countries with underdeveloped housing finance systems, households incrementally self-build their house over long periods of time, or settle for a low-quality structure that does not comply with planning and building regulations, which contributes to the proliferation of slums. Under these circumstances, formal construction may not develop and a vicious circle is created, leading to further housing shortages. Also, the lack of housing finance for resale markets prevents the recovery of costs of housing assets and hinders labor mobility. This is particularly true for affordable housing markets, which prevents investment to improve the quality of housing, reduces labor mobility, and reduces net tax receipts raised from real estate transactions.

A well-functioning housing finance system contributes to the expansion of home ownership with key externalities for growth, job creation, neighborhood development, fiscal returns, and last, but not least, social and political stability. A well-functioning housing finance system is an important contributor to household wealth accumulation and retirement strategy, with spillover effects on the broader economy. For example, a large portion of the capital for start-up businesses in the United States comes from housing finance. The work by de Soto on housing wealth in emerging economies confirms the true cost of informality (economically "dead" housing assets) to emerging economies. He sets out the formidable value of these unsecured housing assets, which provide very little return given that they cannot be used as collateral for economic investments. Excessive emphasis on asset-based lending can prove destabilizing, however. The subprime crisis in the United States is a clear example of this, where home ownership was pushed to groups that did not have the required loan repayment capacity.

Structure of the Book

Chapter 1 reviews the macroeconomic significance of housing finance, noting possible benefits but also costs. There are key links between housing finance, the financial sector, economic growth, and, ultimately, poverty alleviation. Housing has always played a role in larger business cycles because it is an interest-sensitive asset, as seen during crises both in developed markets (United Kingdom, Japan, Scandinavia) and emerging markets (Mexico, Argentina, Brazil). The recent experience of Australia, the United Kingdom and the United States suggests that equity extracted from housing assets can finance an excessive level of consumption debt and engender macroeconomic instability. Likewise, the U.S. subprime crisis is interlinked with an adverse cycle of real estate markets that now affects both the U.S. and world economy.

Chapter 2 discusses the different ways in which housing finance can be delivered. Historically, in developed economies, specialist lenders such as building societies or mortgage banks provided housing finance. These institutions were often part of special circuits of finance that were dismantled or lost market share to commercial banks. In some developed markets, some functions associated with mortgage lending have been unbundled through various specialists (for example, intermediaries, third-party servicers, insurers). So far, this has been less the case in emerging economies, except for mortgage brokers (Poland) and mortgage insurers (Mexico, South Africa). In most countries, housing finance is mostly provided by banks, but competition may come from specialized finance companies (Mexico, Egypt, UAE, India), housing provident funds (Mexico, China, Colombia), credit cooperatives (Burkina Faso, Rwanda), and micro-lenders (Peru).

Chapter 3 focuses on how proper credit design is a key ingredient for a successful housing finance system to allocate risk between consumers, lenders, and investors. In most emerging markets, variable or adjustable rate mortgages remain the prevailing and sole products available, offered by depository-based lenders to manage their interest-rate risk. Unfortunately, borrowers then bear most of the interest-rate risk passed through additional credit risks.[1] Most of the U.S. subprime defaults relate to adjustable rate loans with lower initial "teaser" rates that can show significant increases once past the initial period and in a rising interest rate environment. It is possible to protect the consumer by offering long-term fixed-rate mortgages (FRMs) that grant the borrower the right of early repayment. These, however, require lenders to access advanced capital markets or derivative-market products in order to manage their cash-flow risks. Hence, in most emerging markets FRMs remain inappropriate for lenders or too expensive for borrowers. Indexed credits developed for inflationary economies have had some success (Chile) but also problems (Colombia, Brazil, Mexico).

Any effective housing finance system requires a sound primary market infrastructure. Chapter 4 describes some of the essential building blocks, with particular emphasis placed on home appraisal practices, insurance products related to mortgage lending, and credit information systems.

Many countries have improved the judicial enforcement procedures for creditors or developed non-judicial mechanisms to foreclose on a property. Chapter 5 sets out some of the key elements required for the creation of a sound legal basis for mortgage lending. A complementary pillar would be an effective system of enforceable and registered property rights, but this vast theme is beyond the scope of this book.

Chapter 6 discusses the importance of adequate consumer information to help households take and refinance a mortgage loan. Households should compare loan offers and make an educated decision when taking and repaying a loan. The issue exists in both developed countries and emerging countries. In emerging markets, mortgage consumer information rarely exists (Mexico and South Africa represent exceptions). When loans go bad, the judiciary and political systems are often less inclined to defend the rights of lenders and investors, where the consumer has been inadequately informed. This can be detrimental to future lending activities.

Another critical, yet often overlooked, element in the housing chain consists of providing finance to real estate developers. Without adequate

---

1. Remedies include a proper selection of the index used to periodically adjust the rates and caps on these rate adjustments provided at least during the first years of the loan.

financing in place, it falls to the households to provide larger amounts of unsecured deposits during the construction phase. This practice reduces a household's ability to leverage and exposes it to a high level of risk associated with fraud or problems during the construction phase. Construction finance remains constrained in some countries, where lenders do not have sufficient expertise to manage such types of risky project finance. It is also important to develop systems that better protect consumers against construction risks. Chapter 7 provides an overview of these issues together with some policy solutions.

As housing finance markets expand, a larger range of players, including non-banks, may get involved and be exposed to various risks that may be spread quite differently. Chapter 8 provides a review of the risks and of the regulatory frameworks in place to deal with these risks. Risks come in many forms, and regulators face many new challenges arising from financial innovation, complex instruments to spread risks, the cyclical nature of real estate markets, and the long-term nature of housing debt. Most crises in real estate finance correspond to failures in both market discipline and regulation.[2]

Chapter 9 reviews contractual housing savings schemes. Under these schemes, households lock in a future housing loan at a predetermined interest rate, but only after they have completed a period of savings. The credit conditions are contractually correlated to the accrued savings in order to limit liquidity risks. A key attribute is reduced credit risk, notably for lower-income households that need to build a down payment and their credit score before accessing home ownership. This model was exported from Germany to several countries in Eastern and Central Europe, where contracts have become very popular through subsidized saving rates. The aggregate impact on the housing finance system is delayed, and fiscal costs are significant, but if properly implemented, this system can play an important complementary role to the main mortgage markets.

Special public circuits for housing finance still exist in some emerging economies, notably where private lenders have not yet entered housing finance. Housing banks are common examples of such circuits. Unfortu-

---

2. The subprime crisis has been worsened by the unregulated nature of intermediaries, the global leverage of debt through complex securitization, and balkanized U.S. regulatory agencies (if measures had been taken in 2005 when the toxicity of these loans was apparent, the magnitude of the crisis would have been reduced).

xlii HOUSING FINANCE POLICY IN EMERGING MARKETS

nately, the experience with them has been mostly unsatisfactory. Most have been plagued with high levels of defaults, non-targeted lending crowding out private sector competitors, ineffective and regressive subsidies, inefficiency, and politically motivated lending. Many have disappeared, others were restructured. The few thriving ones went through changes to comply with private banking standards, as presented in chapter 10.

Housing provident funds (HPFs) may also be significant providers of finance in a number of countries. While they mobilize large sums of money for housing through recurrent wage taxes, they share many of the problems of housing banks. Furthermore, their dual responsibilities of providing affordable mortgage finance and providing an acceptable return for retirees present conflicting objectives. In countries like Mexico, Brazil, Singapore, or China, they play an important role that needs to be better understood. Chapter 11 provides an assessment of their role in the provision of housing finance.

The use of mortgage-related securities to fund housing has a long history in developed countries, and mortgage securities are second only to government securities in importance in the United States and Europe. Chapter 12 shows how they have been introduced in a growing number of emerging markets, in order for lenders to diversify their funding strategy, raise longer-term resources, and manage their cash-flow risks. Housing finance can also help to develop long-term private debt markets (Chile, Malaysia, or Mexico). So far, results have been mixed, as only in about a dozen countries mortgage-related securities finance 5–20 percent of the mortgage debt (including Chile, Malaysia, Colombia, Czech Republic, South Africa, Jordan, Mexico, Hungary, and India), but remain underdeveloped or absent in most other countries. The regulatory infrastructure may not be developed to support such products, or banks may find core deposits to be a cheaper funding. Investor demand may be lacking, particularly if institutional investors are not yet in place or reluctant to take prepayment risks. Covered bonds and liquidity facilities can also represent effective alternative or transition models to securitization. It is important to diversify funding instruments for lenders; keep them exposed to part of the credit risk; and design simple, secure, and transparent bond products for domestic investors.

Mortgage loss insurance is a growing business worldwide. Such products were instituted in the United States at the beginning of the 20th century and are now available in more than 30 countries worldwide, offered by both privately and publicly owned companies. Chapter 13 points out how mortgage default insurance (MI) can improve the affordability of housing finance by lowering the down payment. MI facilitates the transfer of mortgage credit risk from the banking sector to companies specializing in risk management. MI provides tools for and encourages responsible lending practices, thus supplementing supervisory resources and reducing overall risk exposures. For MI to be successful, however, there must be a relatively strong legal and regulatory framework, as well as a history of mortgage lending. The chapter analyzes key success and failure factors.

Rental housing is often overlooked, although it represents a critical part of any housing market. Finance can expand the supply of affordable rental stock and facilitate greater mobility on the part of the population, as discussed in chapter 14. The risks, underwriting and institutional mechanisms for providing rental finance differ from owner-occupied finance. While the finance of affordable rental housing is well established in developed markets, it is more scarce and problematic in developing countries because of legal difficulties (for example, rent control), instability, and affordability problems for tenants.

Chapter 15 considers the development of the microfinance industry, which has gained credibility and scale in recent years. It has achieved this by demonstrating its financial sustainability, and by accessing a large number of low and informal income households. One of its key advantages is that it provides a wider range of financial services than traditional lenders are able to provide. This chapter reviews the main features and challenges of housing microfinance, as well as providing an assessment of the limits of this new class of lending.

Countries intervene in housing markets through an array of policies and subsidies intended to stimulate housing production or consumption by various groups. Chapter 16 details the myriad of housing finance subsidies offered on the demand side (for example, interest-rate subsidies, housing-savings subsidies, mortgage-interest tax deduction) and supply side (subsidized funding for lenders, state guarantees for insurance, securities or secondary market institutions). There is a rich experience on the effectiveness of subsidies, some of it positive and some negative. In general, subsidies should be transparent, targeted, and efficient in terms of providing incentives for market forces to deliver and finance affordable housing, but also in terms of cost of delivery and minimized distortions.

Summary Conclusions

What are the lessons to be learned from the development of housing finance in different markets? There is no magic cure that can create an effective housing finance system overnight. The basics have to be in place before a market can grow and flourish. This means achieving relative macroeconomic stability, creating the necessary legal and regulatory infrastructure to back collateralized lending, encouraging competition among housing finance institutions, and ensuring that the appropriate risk-management frameworks are in place. The specific model implemented does not matter as long as the infrastructure is in place and competition between lenders is not distorted. The secondary mortgage market depends on a healthy and developed primary market. Securitization is a powerful tool for lenders but is not the way to build the market, nor is it the only bond-market instrument available to mortgage lenders. Simpler, low-risk, and transparent bond products may be more attractive for domestic investors.

What should be the role of government in developing an effective housing finance system? Its primary role should be to enable the development of mortgage markets through the creation of the lending infrastructure and elimination of barriers to lending. Historical experience suggests that the development of mortgage lending follows a sequence starting with financial liberalization and sector development, followed by the expansion of the primary market and then the creation of mortgage capital markets. The state can accelerate this development by improving the liquidity of mortgage assets and reducing the costs of credit-risk underwriting for investors. Government also has a role to play in helping lower-income households obtain adequate-quality housing. Experience has shown that targeted demand-side subsidies such as housing allowances and interest-rate buy-downs can offer an effective way to reach lower-income groups and help them meet their housing needs.

LDCp, MDCp
selected countries

G21 R31
    R21 G01
016 E32

CHAPTER 1

Housing Finance and the Economy

Robert Buckley, Loïc Chiquier, and Michael Lea

On a worldwide basis, housing finance is growing at an unprecedented rate. In the last decade, outstanding mortgage debt has increased by more than $7 trillion. Figure 1.1 suggests that the majority of developed economies have experienced a strong surge in debt levels used to finance housing. This is also the case for a significant number of emerging markets, such as China, India, and Mexico, although housing finance remains underdeveloped in many parts of the developing world. This chapter provides an overview of this experience and shows the various linkages between housing finance and the broader economy, in order to identify some of the opportunities and challenges when developing a housing finance system.

Developed Economies

Housing finance was once an underdeveloped segment of domestic financial markets. It now occupies a very significant place, not only in the financial system of individual economies, but as part of the global financial system as

Figure 1.1. Mortgage Debt/GDP—Developed Markets

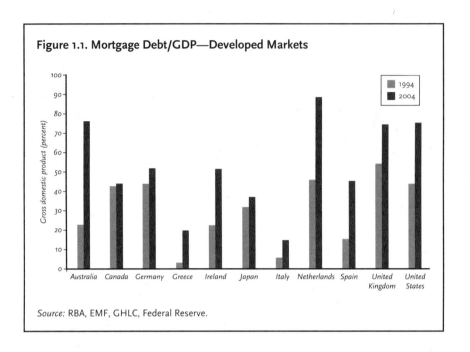

Source: RBA, EMF, GHLC, Federal Reserve.

well. For example, U.S. mortgages are now financed through securitization on a significant scale by Chinese and Indian savers, among others.[1]

The size of residential mortgage markets has been growing in developed economies relative to the overall economy (at least one-third of their GDP, and often considerably more). For example, as recently as 1984, residential mortgage debt was one-third of U.S. GDP, but this ratio increased to 74 percent by 2005. In recent years, Australia, Netherlands, Ireland, and Spain have seen annual growth rates in excess of 20 percent per year, fueled by strong economic growth and lower market interest rates.

Improved macroeconomic circumstances have played a big role in the emergence of housing finance. Over a longer historical perspective, however, another crucial factor has been the ongoing and seemingly relentless liberalization of financial markets, including of housing finance.[2] Instead of specialized,

---

1. The U.S. Treasury estimates that nearly 15 percent of U.S.-agency securities were held by overseas investors in 2005.
2. Abiad and Mody (2005) measured the financial liberalization of 35 countries between 1972 and 1996. Until 1982, liberalization in developed countries was modest and, in emerging markets, almost nonexistent. Over the next 14 years, liberalization increased rapidly and continuously in all developed markets. A similar pattern characterizes liberalization in less-developed

frequently publicly owned lenders providing limited amounts of often-subsidized credit to a similarly limited number of borrowers, new lenders using new kinds of instruments coupled with new ways of accessing finance and managing risks have emerged in both developed and emerging markets.

Emerging Economies

In contrast to the situation in developed countries, the size of the mortgage market in most emerging markets is still small, often accounting for less than 10 percent of GDP, as shown in figure 1.2. Despite starting from such a low base, the pace of growth has often been considerably faster. For example, the Chinese mortgage market, which only started in the early 1990s, has been growing at an annual pace of more than 40 percent since 2000, reaching 11 percent of GDP in less than 10 years. Similarly, the Indian market has

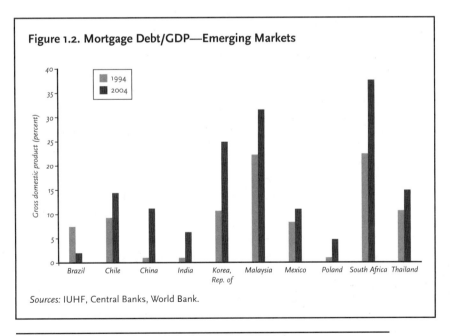

Figure 1.2. Mortgage Debt/GDP—Emerging Markets

Sources: IUHF, Central Banks, World Bank.

---

countries. By 1996, however, despite significant improvements, low-income developing countries had not yet reached the level of liberalization achieved by developed economies in the early 1970s.

been growing at 30 percent per year, and some transition countries such as Hungary, the Baltic countries, and Kazakhstan have seen growth of more than 20 percent per year. Once again, the common factors in these countries are a growing economy, low inflation, interest rates, and most importantly, liberalizing financial sectors. This has permitted a growing number of households in these countries to invest in better housing.

There are a number of reasons for the relatively small size of housing finance systems in developing countries. They include a history of macroeconomic instability with high and volatile inflation and interest rates, low growth rates, weak legal systems that do not adequately protect the interests of lenders, and, more broadly, an underdeveloped infrastructure for housing and housing finance markets, as well as some underdeveloped and poorly regulated banking and capital markets.

A significant reason for the lack of development in housing finance was the widespread reliance on the directed credit systems and public banks to finance development policy. This view of the public role in allocating credit toward strategic sectors was not unusual and was held by many leading scholars. This view was predominant despite the empirically documented weaknesses of the public role in generating either financial sector development or growth. This approach continued to be a commonly used approach, particularly in low-income countries, up to the mid-1990s. The "market failure" argument is more appealing for some policy makers than the inability of this approach to mobilize sufficient resources and manage risks related to housing lending.

While the drivers of growth in institutional mortgage finance are clear, questions remain about how and why housing finance fits into the economy and the financial system. For example, how does growth (or lack thereof) in the housing finance system relate to the performance of the economy and to housing market and financial system policies? What are the costs and consequences of a poorly performing housing finance system in exacerbating economic instability or misallocating resources? This chapter will explore these issues in order to create a context for the broader housing finance book.

The Importance of Housing Finance

One of the main reasons why housing finance is important is that the asset it finances, housing, is such a significant part of wealth and the fixed capital stock, as documented in Goldsmith's seminal works on *Comparative National Balance Sheets* (1984), for example. When a good accounts for 50 percent of national wealth, a majority of the fixed capital stock, and for more than 80 percent of the wealth of most households in almost all economies, the way that it is financed clearly has significant effects on the economy.[3]

Housing also represents a large proportion of most households' consumption. In the United States, for example, housing rent and utility expenses account for 25–30 percent of personal expenditures Residential investment is a major component of GDP, typically amounting to 4–8 percent of GDP and 20–30 percent of total investment. In rapidly growing countries, the share going to housing can be much higher (for example, Spain and Ireland in recent years). Therefore, the ability to efficiently finance such an important component of the economic system will have a significant effect on overall levels of investment and growth.

Despite its importance, the use of institutional mortgage finance for housing is a rather recent phenomenon. Until well into the 20th century, such finance was the exception rather than the rule. The use of mortgage debt was limited. Up to the 1920s, the majority of U.S. homes were self-financed (out of savings accumulations) or financed outside of formal financial-sector channels.[4] At that time, the urban population of the world only accounted for about 15 percent of world population, around 250 million people, with the resulting lower demand for mortgage credit.[5]

---

3. Real estate represents the great majority of the tangible capital stock, and housing is the great majority of the stock of real estate. Real estate accounts for approximately 50 percent of world wealth, of which one-quarter is commercial and three-quarters residential (Source: 1993 study by Ibbotson and Associates).
4. Including construction companies, real estate bond companies, fraternal organizations, developers, or previous owners of properties (see Ratcliff 1949). In 1925, these non-institutional sources were nearly as important as savings and loan associations and mutual savings banks, from which the majority of institutional mortgage borrowing occurred.
5. The U.S. experience is by no means unusual, as Boleat (1985) relates. The U.S. savings and loans followed a similar development path as the U.K. building societies as did the Swedish co-ops and non-bank institutions in a number of other European countries. Neither, however, was it universal. Many of the housing finance systems in place today in developed economies bear the hallmark of path-dependent reactions to shocks. For example, the destruction of Copenhagen by fire in 1795 was instrumental in developing the Danish mortgage bond system, as was

In much the same way, housing remains mostly self-financed by households' equity in many emerging economies. This limits access to home ownership and leads to expanding incremental construction and informal housing. Frequently, the only alternative is finance provided by developers through deferred installment sales. The major difference, however, from the historical experience comes from today's increased urbanization, which requires extraordinary levels of housing investment. Urban population growth between 2000 and 2030 will exceed 2 billion people; that is more than eight times the total urban population at the beginning of the 20th century. In 1950, there was one city, New York, with a population in excess of 10 million. By 2015, there will be 21 of these cities, 17 of which will be in developing countries. By 2030, Asia alone will have to house 2.7 billion people in cities. This inexorable demographic trend means housing demand must be met through significant improvements in housing finance systems.

Mortgage finance improves the operation of the housing market and the economy in a number of ways, both directly by facilitating transactions and indirectly by improving the environments in which transactions take place. Consider first the direct effects.

The use of debt allows households to better match the timing of their housing expenditures with the flow of services they receive. Housing is a long-lived, durable asset that provides a flow of services over a long period (frequently outliving its occupants). A household can purchase more housing at an earlier stage in the life cycle using debt, as opposed to paying for it all at once through accumulated savings. Furthermore, because housing provides such good collateral, mortgages are usually the lowest-cost way for households to finance general borrowing for consumption, non-housing investment, or business formation. Housing investors (for example, for rental housing) use leverage to increase the returns on investment, as well as to expand and diversify their investment opportunities. In sum, for a number of reasons, housing finance can help smooth consumption expenditures and help households flexibly adjust their wealth.

---

the effect of destruction of the Seven Years' War on the German system. Baron Haussmann's redevelopment of Paris in the mid-19th century created the French system, and the Great Depression created many of the housing finance institutions observed in the United States.

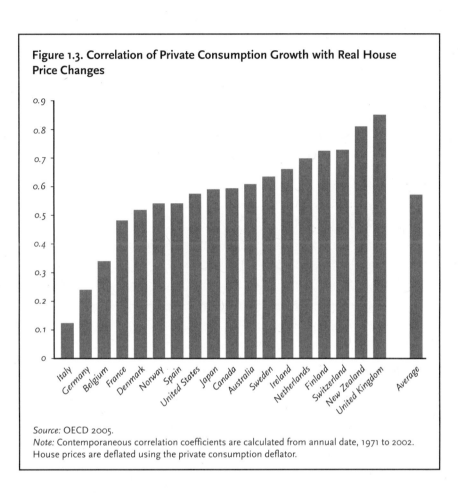

Figure 1.3. Correlation of Private Consumption Growth with Real House Price Changes

Source: OECD 2005.
Note: Contemporaneous correlation coefficients are calculated from annual date, 1971 to 2002. House prices are deflated using the private consumption deflator.

Housing finance also affects the economy in indirect ways that go beyond the specific transaction. For instance, a number of studies have suggested that housing wealth has a stronger effect on consumption expenditures than do other forms of savings. If this is so, then house-price increases can lead to stronger increases in consumer demand than do rising stock markets, with the result that housing market trends may be more closely related to overall macroeconomic cycles. As mortgage markets deepen, there are greater opportunities for households to access this wealth. In particular, the ability to

Figure 1.4. Marginal Propensities to Consume Out-of-Housing Wealth and Mortgage Market Indicators

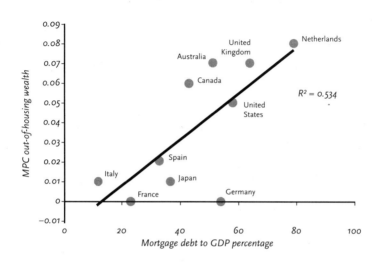

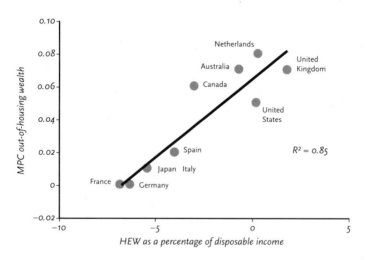

Source: OECD 2005.
Note: MPC = marginal propensity to consume; HEW = home equity withdrawal.

refinance allows families to spend the capital gains realized on rapid house-price increases.[6]

Organisation for Economic Co-ordination and Development (OECD) research confirms the existence of significant housing wealth effects on consumption in the United States, United Kingdom, Canada, Netherlands, and Australia, as shown in figure 1.3. In France, Germany, and Italy, however, the association has been weaker. The estimated long-run marginal propensity to consume out-of-housing wealth is in the range of 0.05 to 0.08 for the first group of countries.

The size and direction of the consumption effect appears to be positively correlated with mortgage-debt ratios across countries, suggesting that the mortgage market is pivotal in translating house-price changes into spending responses (figure 1.4). This effect depends on the extent to which housing wealth can be accessed; in particular, through the ability of homeowners to borrow against housing wealth through mortgage equity withdrawal. The OECD finds that the size of housing equity withdrawal is correlated with the impact of housing wealth on consumption. In turn, the degree of mortgage market completeness plays an important role in housing-equity withdrawal through the ability to serve a broader range of borrowers, offer a greater variety of mortgage products and higher loan-to-value (LTV) loans, and pass on lower mortgage interest-rate spreads (Mercer Oliver Wyman 2003).

Two important constraints emerged from the OECD analysis. Higher administrative costs and greater amounts of time required to realize collateral in the event of default significantly reduced the completeness of the market and the house-price consumption nexus. Additionally, regulatory constraints on LTV ratios also reduced this effect.

A number of factors are likely to have contributed to this trend. The shift to a low-interest-rate environment over the past decade or so gave households an enhanced capacity to service any given level of debt, allowing the

6. A number of studies have highlighted the role of equity withdrawal in consumption. While this ability undoubtedly provides households with considerably more flexibility in arranging their expenditures over time, there are also problems that can arise with widespread equity withdrawals. This concern has led the European Central Bank (2003) to examine the implications of this phenomenon for the development of the single currency market. In Australia, housing equity went from positive (accumulation) to negative (withdrawal) during the late 1990s and early 2000s. Mortgage debt rose sharply; however, residential investment recorded only a modest gain. Rather, the increase in indebtedness went to consumption that fueled growth in the macro economy. Similar results were recorded in the United States and United Kingdom.

household sector in aggregate to carry a higher level of debt in relation to income. In addition, most countries where equity withdrawal took place had experienced an increase in the relative price of housing, sometimes of a substantial amount. A period of equity withdrawal might be viewed as part of the process of shifting from relatively low to higher levels of debt over time, or a rearranging of a household's portfolio in line with increased wealth.

While there are a number of undesirable features of such increases in indebtedness, including higher default rates, there are also a number of significant advantages as well. For example, in the wake of the 9/11 attack, *The Economist* described the U.S. housing market as the vehicle that saved the world from depression in 2001 and 2002. Similarly, in a review of the *2005 Economic Report of the President*, Martin Feldstein (2006) argues that the household expenditures, which were enabled by mortgage refinancing, kept the U.S. economy going strongly in 2005. Therefore, in many ways, the accessibility of mortgage finance adds flexibility to consumer choices. Whether or not that increased flexibility is or (as we will discuss) can be used effectively is an important issue that the chapters in this book address.

A broadened access to housing finance can also have a strong impact on urban development, as suggested by Renaud's (1990) aphorism that "cities are built the way they are financed." In countries with underdeveloped housing finance systems, most households either build their house individually over long periods or settle for a low-quality structure that does not comply with planning and building regulations. This leads to poorly planned and serviced urban areas. Moreover, the lack of housing finance for resale markets prevents the recovery of costs of housing assets; hinders mobility, particularly in low- and moderate-income housing markets; and negatively affects the quality of urban neighborhoods, hence the fiscal situation of cities. Consequently, the lack of effective housing finance hinders both local-government service provision and labor markets.

Housing finance can also have desirable spillover effects on both the financial system and social cohesion. With respect to the latter, it has been shown that ownership, which is made more accessible by housing finance, has positive externalities for neighborhood development, empowerment of households through communities, and children's educational achievements.

As for the financial sector, because housing is so durable and provides good collateral for developed countries and for developing countries, it can be important in promoting long-term bond markets. And it is also important as a source of innovation for different financing techniques. In the United States, for instance, housing finance began the move toward securitization and improved efficiency of bond markets. It was instrumental in developing some financial derivative markets. Financial innovations, however, are not always unequivocal gains. The ability to move money into a country or a sector is matched by the ability to move it out quickly; hence, if not done prudently, mortgage market development, like other financial development, may fuel instability. Before discussing the potentially destabilizing role of housing finance, we first provide a perspective on the prospects for housing finance development.

The Demand for Housing Finance

Macroeconomic Factors

What is behind the significant growth in housing finance in recent years? Clearly, the growth in overall income and wealth has been a major contributing factor. It is perhaps not surprising that countries such as Germany and Japan, which have exhibited slower growth and, in the latter case, considerably slower financial liberalization, have also experienced reduced expansions of housing finance. Once again, stable and low interest rates and stable growth appear to be the key factors in mortgage market expansion.

Over the past decade, interest rates in most countries have fallen significantly with a parallel increase in mortgage debt outstanding (figure 1.5 and figure 1.6) a longer trend would show greater change. Mortgage rates, although falling, remain high in a number of emerging markets, thereby accounting for the relatively slower growth in their mortgage markets (for example, Brazil and Colombia). In such countries, the combined effect of lower market rates, liquid banks, and an improved regulatory environment for lenders can result in an effective kick-start of residential mortgage markets, as has been seen in India. A stable, benign macroeconomic environment is a prerequisite for the expansion of sustainable housing finance, but other conditions are also required. Two other factors that come into play are financial liberalization and technological innovation.

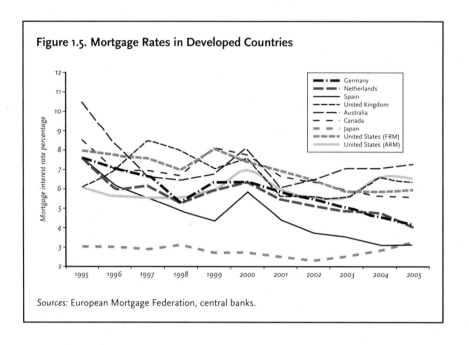

Figure 1.5. Mortgage Rates in Developed Countries

Sources: European Mortgage Federation, central banks.

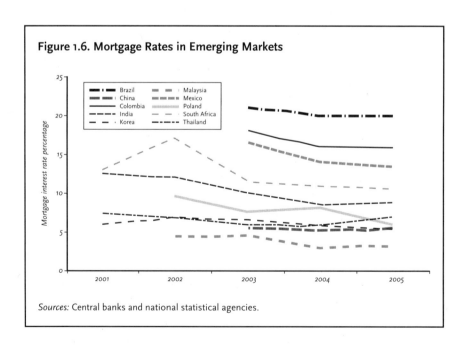

Figure 1.6. Mortgage Rates in Emerging Markets

Sources: Central banks and national statistical agencies.

Financial Liberalization

Financial liberalization is the most fundamental factor in housing finance's growth. As noted earlier, throughout the developed world, the 1980s was a period of substantial liberalization of the financial markets, including (and often specifically focused on) housing finance. The financial architecture of the postwar period was one of financial control, interest rates ceilings, and limited competition. But this paradigm broke down and has been increasingly replaced by a more competitive and integrated world financial system. In their study of the provision of mortgage finance in five major developed markets in 1993, Diamond and Lea chronicled the breakdown of special circuits for housing finance and the resultant integration of housing finance into the broader financial markets in five major developed markets.

Technological Change

At the same time that the world was innovating in its financial delivery systems, the innovations in technology were driving down the costs of intermediation and, particularly, mortgage intermediation. No longer was it necessary to have a depository institution to be able to underwrite and monitor mortgage loans. It has been documented that some of the significant cost savings have been realized through automated underwriting and servicing. These changes mean that mortgage lending no longer has to rely simply on the costly collection of small deposits for repackaging in larger mortgage loans. Now, small mortgage loans can be repackaged in large and diversified mortgage-backed securities (MBSs), which can access large investors with appetites for non-recourse, long-term investments (such as pension funds) and life insurance companies.

In sum, financial liberalization and technology improvements have had an important effect on the growth of the demand for housing finance. Furthermore, if one argues that the underlying financial-sector institutional development and macroeconomic stability are increasingly being achieved in emerging economies—as suggested by the growth rate of more than 7 percent for developing countries (the highest in more than 30 years) and a median inflation rate of less than 7 percent (less than half that of a decade earlier)—then one can expect a rapid growth rate in the supply of housing finance going forward. Indeed, with housing finance in China and India, which together account for more than one-third of the world's population, growing at compound annual rates in excess of 35 percent per year; and in Europe, where it has been growing at more than 8 percent a year, it is clear that the growth of housing finance still has substantial momentum.

Concerns and Opportunities

Even under conservative assumptions, it is reasonable to expect that in emerging economies, housing finance should grow rapidly in the coming years. What risks and opportunities are associated with such a trend? What steps can be taken so that the benefits realized by the 20 or so rapidly growing emerging systems can be not only sustained, but also prudently extended to the far larger number of countries where growth remains stagnant?

The Effect of Mortgage Finance on Savings

Jappeli argues that increased access to housing finance can have a negative effect on saving and investment. Financial repression in the form of borrowing constraints on young borrowers can force them to borrow less than they would otherwise. This clearly has a negative effect in terms of intertemporal management of consumption, inducing suboptimal timing of consumption. But it also increases saving, which may be welcome in some markets where there is too little saving and investment. Furthermore, an argument can be made that improved housing finance can actually increase rather than decrease savings. For instance, new financial instruments, such as mortgage securities (safe, but also providing better returns than government bonds), that provide a relatively attractive financial instrument can stimulate saving, contributing to the development of a sustainable pension and life insurance industry.

The Effect of Mortgage Finance on Investment

Mortgage finance could also have an effect on the structure of capital formation, moving it toward housing and away from other investments. The effects of a change in portfolio composition, however, are difficult to infer. Among other things, the degree to which the shift occurs ultimately depends on the extent to which mortgage markets are integrated with the broader capital markets, as well as, importantly, on factors such as the elasticity of savings with respect to interest rates.[7] In a highly developed financial system such as in the United States, it has been argued that increases in the supply of mortgage funds have little to no effect on the amount of housing investment. In other words, in their view, mortgage debt is simply the lowest-cost way for households to issue the fungible debt that is used to finance relatively constant investment demands.

On the other hand, one study of the welfare costs attributable to the existence of an inadequate mortgage financing system has been undertaken by Kim (1990) for Seoul, Korea. Using a long-run equilibrium model that compares returns to housing and non-housing capital, Kim found that Korea's housing finance system—or lack thereof—skewed investment away from housing sufficiently to engender significant welfare losses. Point estimates varied with assumptions, but his estimates of the equivalent variation of losses because of this inadequacy could be 10 percent of household income or more.

Mortgage Finance and Growth

As has been shown by Levine and Demırguç-Kunt (2003) and others, financial systems promote economic growth by channeling capital to its most productive use. That is, deeper financial systems lead to higher levels of growth. As financial systems grow and become deeper, housing finance emerges as an

---

7. For example, Van Order (2006) shows that with a positive elasticity of savings with respect to interest rates, tax subsidies for housing may increase, rather than decrease, total savings, as the increase in total savings more than offsets the portfolio shifts toward housing. The point is not that we know the effects of such policies; rather, it is to suggest how difficult it is to infer such impacts and how closely such results are linked to quite specific and often intractable assumptions about behavior.

increasingly important part of the financial system. In other words, housing finance tends to account for an increasing share of the financial system as it matures and provides a broader range of financial services. From this perspective, the process of maturation of financial systems appears to lead to the development of housing finance, and this deeper, more extensive financial system, in turn, contributes to higher rates of growth.

While difficult to quantify, as are sources of growth generally, this result has a good deal of intuitive appeal for two reasons:

- First, the provision of finance only allows, not mandates, specific investments. As a result, the growth in the supply of housing finance should largely be self-limiting by the value consumers place on housing investments relative to other assets. In urbanizing countries where the development process generates sharp increases in the demands for mobility and relocation, empirical evidence shows that housing investment increases as a share of GDP until middle-income status is achieved. In these countries, it is reasonable to expect that the demand for mortgage credit would therefore also rise.
- Second, denying small businesses and households access to the lowest-cost source of funds through liquefying savings they have accumulated in housing—by restricting their access to market-rate mortgage finance—seems to be a remarkably ineffective locus for government policy. In many ways, it mimes an intellectual vein developed by Hernando de Soto (2002), who has emphasized the importance of unlocking wealth through mortgages. He argues that in this way low-income borrowers, who have few prospects for borrowing in the formal financial sector, can raise money for businesses by pledging their property as collateral.

In sum, it is conceivable that the increased ability of households to become indebted can have some undesirable side macroeconomic effects. But it is also important to keep in mind that the instruments used to offset or discourage this sort of behavior have usually had much worse effects on savings, investment, and economic growth.

Housing Finance, Business Cycles, and Economic Fragility

The experience of the 1990s suggests that increased attention should be given to helping countries avoid some of the precipitous drops in income that were experienced during that period.[8] The achievement of higher growth by itself is no longer the unambiguous target of macroeconomic management, as the welfare costs of macroeconomic instability are far higher than was thought to be the case. The effects that the provision of housing finance can have on contributing to or exacerbating macro volatility is an important dimension of housing finance's broader effects on the economy.

Housing has always played a role in business cycles, as suggested long ago by Keynes (1937) in his Great Depression advice to President Roosevelt, and subsequently by Harberger (1974), who labeled the housing sector "the handmaiden of monetary policy."[9] This is primarily because it is a very interest-sensitive asset, so that changes in interest rates have big effects on housing demand and production. These kinds of shifts can either help or hurt in terms of stabilizing. They can hurt because increases in interest rates lower housing production. This might not be such a bad thing.[10] If business cycles come from the "real side" (for example, fluctuations in demand for capital goods), then housing can be an "automatic stabilizer," falling in expansions and rising in contractions. This seems to have been the case recently. For example, in the United States, declining interest rates resulting from a combination of central bank policy and lower demand for funds by businesses caused the housing demand to increase, partially offsetting output declines in other sectors. On the other hand, if a decline comes from the financial side, such as a loss of confidence in the financial sector and a "liquidity crunch," leading to higher rates and/or less availability of funds, then housing contractions will exacerbate the contraction. This process may be under way in the United States today (mid-2008).

---

8. The IMF's increased emphasis on financial-sector assessments for all developing countries reflects the increased policy interest in the costs of macro volatility.
9. Keynes' recommendation to Roosevelt was in an open letter to him in which he called for Roosevelt's focus on housing as a means of stimulating the Depression-constrained economy.
10. We are explicitly *not* considering the role of housing as a provider of jobs. In the long run, there is nothing special about construction as a form of employment, and markets tend to clear. Instead, we focus on cyclical elements where housing is important, and on the role of housing in resource allocation.

Improving the housing finance system may or may not make much difference in volatility. In the United States, removing deposit-rate ceilings probably diminished the effects of interest rate increases on housing. Nevertheless, housing is likely to be cyclical in any system simply because it is so durable. The durability implies that annual housing production is typically on the order of 4 percent of the housing stock. Hence, if there is a 1 percent change in housing demand and adjustment to this lower demand is made in one year, then housing production will fall by 25 percent (from 4 percent to 3 percent of the stock). This change suggests that under any circumstances, housing output will be more volatile than that of other goods.

Regular business cycles, however, are not the only cyclical problem. A major part of the relationship between housing and the macro economy has been its negative role in affecting macro stability through major financial instability (for example, through bubbles in asset prices affecting collateral value and inducing rapid changes in financial structure and interest rates). In many emerging economies, housing finance systems remain too underdeveloped to fuel the creation of any real estate bubble. Yet, the real estate sector has been an important part of the financial fragility seen in Asia and other places in the past few decades. The instability related to real estate lending has been greater in some emerging markets relative to the size of their economies. In Thailand, real estate lending was a major contributing factor in the 1997 "Asian crisis." Quigley (2001) and Mera and Renaud (2004) trace the channels by which housing finance problems helped to propagate the financial crises. China's central bank has instituted controls on mortgage lending (maximum LTV ratios, restrictions on lending against speculative investment) in order to slow the pace of house-price increase and reduce the likelihood of a destabilizing bursting of any possible bubble.

Thus, precautions are essential, but a case can also be made for local-currency residential mortgage markets—to the extent that they attract longer-term funds and mitigate the risk of financial fragility. For instance, bond or secondary markets might be a particularly good way of tapping international capital markets for long-term loans, because the collateral is, with the right legal structure, both good and long-lived. This can be a significant contribution to emerging markets. Mortgage-backed securities have been developed in many countries not only to improve the housing finance system, but also to help develop resilient private bond markets for institutional investors, as

Box 1.1. Real Estate and Financial Crises: Thailand

The performance of Thailand's economy was remarkable during the 1965–95 period; however, the economy suffered a major setback with the currency devaluation in 1997. Poor credit risk management and excessive lending to the real estate sector played a major role in the financial sector crisis in the late 1990s.

The property boom started in the late 1980s, when Thailand was enjoying double-digit growth. With that kind of growth rate, there was indeed a shortage of office and residential space, particularly in Bangkok. The resulting construction spree was only to be expected and, in the beginning, justified by demand, at least until about 1992–93 (Renaud, Zhang, and Koeberle 1998). By 1994, it was becoming obvious that supply was overshooting requirements. By the mid-1990s, the level of oversupply and vacancy rates in Bangkok became among the highest on record.

Lenders collaborated closely in fueling the property boom. Bank of Thailand data indicate that the bank's share of real estate lending in their overall portfolio went up from 6.3 percent at the end of 1988 to 14.8 percent at the end of 1996. Over the same period, the share of real estate in the portfolios of the finance companies went up from 9.1 percent to 24.3 percent (cited in Renaud, Zhang, and Koeberle 1998).

These figures actually underestimate the role of property in the Thai financial system. The majority of Thai bank loans were based on collateral with property as the asset of choice. With rapidly rising prices, even to non-property companies, the property placed as collateral could be used to raise more loans, whose proceeds could in turn be used to purchase yet more property, fueling asset price rises even further. Rising interest rates associated with attempts to defend the baht, combined with restrictions on lending, sent the property markets into a downward spiral. When the inevitable currency devaluation came, unhedged foreign currency borrowers went bankrupt, further destabilizing the system.

seen in Malaysia, for example. One of the things that has characterized financial breakdowns such as the one in Asia in the late 1990s has been reliance on short-term international borrowing, which can be cut off rapidly if there is a loss of confidence in the country in question. Foreign investors want a chance to get out fast (which is not possible if they all try to do so at once). Because mortgages are potentially good collateral—at least where foreclosure can be enforced—and can be expected to be a way of getting more long-term foreign money, they can decrease the dependence on hot money.

Because of its multiple interfaces with the broader economy and financial sector, housing finance (more broadly, real estate finance) plays a significant lever role, either positively or negatively. Under some circumstances aggravated by the adoption of an improper model, housing finance can be a major contributor to macroeconomic instability in both developed and emerging markets. For example, both the United Kingdom and United States mortgage markets were substantially liberalized during the 1980s and suffered significant stress on their housing finance systems, housing markets, and broader economies by the end of the decade. In the former case, an exogenous event turned a boom into a bust—in the United Kingdom, short-term interest rates increased from 7 percent to 15 percent in conjunction with the decision to bring the pound into the European exchange-rate mechanism. The shock resulted in a record level of arrears and repossessions, a sharp decline in lending, and a decline in nominal house prices. In the United States, the long-delayed resolution of the savings and loan (S&L) crisis coincided with an economic downturn—the real damage had been done during the preceding decade because of lax oversight and aggressive lending by bankrupt thrifts. Recent concerns relate to the impact of any potential burst of the larger and riskier subprime markets.

Mortgage Finance and the Distribution of Risk

Another core issue is the nature of the mortgage instrument promoted by the system and the way the political system deals with its implications. Miles (2004) discusses the U.K. system, which is bank-based with almost exclusive use of variable rate mortgages linked to short-term deposit rates. This system places a lot of interest-rate risk on borrowers who are not always able to hedge it. In the long run, this situation may lower the housing demand relative to what it could be with a wider range of instrument choice, or expose households to the sorts of macroeconomic risks that could wipe out their housing equity. In many emerging economies, long-term fixed-rate mortgages (FRMs)

Box 1.2. Mexican Past Crises and the Role of Housing Finance

In Mexico, there have been several episodes of currency devaluation leading to sharp increases in inflation and interest rates. In the early 1980s, Mexican banks were required to make fixed-rate loans at administered rates. A sharp spike in inflation and interest rates because of the 1982 devaluation left the banking system undercapitalized and led to nationalization. In 1995, the cycle repeated. There was a sharp spike in inflation and interest rates because of devaluation leading to cessation of bank lending, eventual sale of most banks to foreign competitors, and a burden to the economy in the form of bailout subsidies to banks and consumers. The downturn in the economy precipitated a banking crisis in which the share of nonperforming assets grew to over 40 percent. Individual residential mortgages comprised a large portion of the delinquent portfolio, and were a major focus of government intervention. Banks had 30 percent of portfolios in housing loans, mostly price-level adjusted. In 1995, when the government began aiding banks to restructure loans, half of the total funds available—an amount over $7 billion—were directed to restructuring mortgage credits. Government aid to the mortgage sector grew to nearly $18 billion by the end of 1996. Since this experience, the Mexican housing finance system has been restructured. It has been expanding rapidly and soundly thanks to better macro conditions, private market competition, new funding and risk management tools, and more efficient housing-policy authorities.

remain a relative luxury good, and floating or indexed loans still prevail, exposing households to interest-rate risk and banks to credit risk.

Another perspective was discussed by Laidler (1974), who argues that in a system where everyone's housing costs are tied to short-term rates it is more difficult to control inflation. This is because controlling inflation will require, from time to time, increases in interest rates that can be politically difficult to realize if they raise mortgage rates and the cost of housing for most homeowners. Hence, a benefit of a more bond- or capital-market-oriented system (whether done via banks or secondary-market facilities) is that it will allow borrowers to take less interest-rate risk, placing it in capital markets where it is easier to handle, and making the political costs of effective monetary policy less costly and more likely to be realized.[11] The fiscal costs of an under-developed or poorly designed housing finance system can be significant, as evidenced by the bailout of insolvent housing lenders and many borrowers in Argentina, Brazil, and Mexico.

House Prices, Housing Finance, and Economic Activity

There has recently been a great deal of interest in the evolution of house prices and their economic effects. Most OECD countries have experienced a substantial run-up in real house prices in recent years. An important question is whether these house-price booms will inevitably be followed by a house-price bust with reverse effects on consumption and output. An International Monetary Fund (IMF) analysis of asset-price booms and busts in the postwar period suggests a significant likelihood of a reversal.[12]

Their analysis found that housing-price busts on average occurred about once every 20 years, lasted about four years, and involved price declines of about 30 percent. While only about one-quarter of equity-price booms were followed by busts, about 40 percent of housing-price booms ended in busts. Both types of busts were highly synchronized across countries.

Both equity- and housing-price busts were associated with output losses (relative to the simple extrapolation of the pre-bust growth rate), reflecting declines in the growth rates of all the main components of private final domestic demand: consumption, investment in machinery and equipment, and investment in construction. The output loss associated with the typical housing-price bust (about 8 percent of GDP) was twice as large as that associated with a typical equity-price bust (about 4 percent of GDP). Output started to recover about nine quarters after the start of either an equity- or a housing-price bust.

Bank-based financial systems tended to suffer larger output losses than capital market-based financial systems during housing-price busts, while capital market-based systems tended to suffer larger output losses than bank-

---

11. The recent experience with the U.S. subprime market suggests that the dispersal of risk in the capital markets led to imprudent lending, leaving many borrowers with excessive interest-rate risk.

12. IMF 2004, Chapter 2.

Table 1.1. **Real Estate and Banking Crises—Selected Cases**

Financial crisis/stress	Consequences	Contributory factors
1973–75 U.K. secondary banks. Speculative development boom, largely in London offices.	Rash of failures and weakness among secondary banks. Bailout by group of clearing banks at a total cost of GBP 1.2 billion, equivalent to half their shareholder's equity, or 1.5% of GDP.	Preceding planning restrictions on supply. Extreme credit boom. Financial intermediaries.
1984–91 U.S. savings and loans. Speculative development boom in Southwest.	1,400 savings and loans. 1,300 banks failed. Cleanup costs estimated at US$180 billion, 3.2% of GDP.	Inexperienced lenders through deregulation of savings and loans. Moral hazard through deposit insurance.
1987–93 Norway. Bank crisis.	State took control of three largest banks with 85% of banking system assets. Recapitalization costs estimated at 5–8% of GDP.	Combined oil boom and problem real estate loans.
1991 Swedish banks. Lending boom for domestic and overseas investment/development.	Two of six major banks, 22% of banking system assets, insolvent. Three further banks in difficulty. Nonperforming real estate in special vehicles. State recapitalization costs estimated at 4–6% of GDP.	Deregulation of domestic and international investment. Credit boom. Financial intermediaries.
1991–94 Finland savings bank crises.	State took control of three banks accounting for 31% of bank deposits. Nonperforming real estate in special vehicles. Recapitalization costs estimated at 11–15% of GDP.	As in Sweden.
1990s–ongoing Japan. Systemic banking crisis.	Nonperforming loans estimated at up to 25% of GDP. Bank nationalizations, closures, mergers. Cleanup costs by late 1990s around 12% of GDP. Liquidation of intermediaries (Jusen) at a cost of US$6.3 billion.	Long preceding land-price boom. Special real estate financial intermediaries (Jusen). Moral hazard through state support for large banks.
Mid-1990s France. Bank crisis.	Stress bordering on insolvency in several major banks. Range of government-support measures; final costs estimated at the equivalent of 1% of GDP.	Unreliable valuations. Bank exposure to real estate through shareholdings in development and construction subsidiaries.
1997–2000 Asian crisis. Malaysia, Thailand, Korea... Systemic banking crises linking asset price and real estate bubbles with foreign capital flows.	Malaysia: two banks insolvent, nonperforming loans 25–35% of banking system assets. Thailand: State intervention in 70 finance companies and six banks. Nonperforming loans 46% of total loans. Net losses equivalent to 42% of GDP. Korea: Two banks nationalized, five closed, seven under special supervision. Nonperforming loans 30–40% of total. Fiscal costs estimated at 34% of GDP.	Long preceding land-price booms. Extreme credit booms and deregulation of international capital flows. Financial intermediaries (especially Thailand).

Sources: Barth, Caprio and Levine 2001; author's calculations.

based systems during equity-price busts. This is consistent with the high exposure of banks to real estate lending, and the importance of equities in household assets in capital market-based systems.

As shown in table 1.1, crises have resulted in major reductions in GDP and damage to banking systems.

While house-price volatility is an important factor in macroeconomic instability, the experience of the last 20 years has not been lost on regulators or innovators. Information systems, monitoring capabilities, and understanding are much better today in most countries. In addition, a forward market in housing prices is being established, following the work of Robert Shiller, which would, if it develops, allow homeowners to hedge the risks of house-price declines.

The volatility of house prices and the potential for a boom-bust is higher if the housing supply is severely constrained by land access and urban regulation problems, which drive housing prices up to unaffordable levels (see Glaeser and Gyourko 2003 for the United States and Malpezzi and Mayo 1997 for a number of developing countries). Creating a more elastic supply of housing can reduce the probability of adverse real estate cycles and sharp run-ups in house prices. In addition, the potential for destabilization is higher in less mature financial systems (for example, Russia, Ukraine). Under tight supply conditions, the expansion of housing finance—often through middle- and higher-income groups—may even worsen the overall housing affordability problem instead of providing the expected remedies.

Lessons for Emerging Markets

The first and perhaps the clearest lesson is that the performance of the macro economy, the legal system, and housing market regulations are inextricably linked to the development of housing finance. A stable, growing economy will encourage the growth of the housing finance system through lower inflation, lower interest rates, and lower systemic risk. In this evolutionary perspective, beyond a certain level of per capita income, housing finance will emerge with household demand for it; that is, as long as the macro, legal, and housing-market regulation environments are conducive to its emergence. In such cases, a virtuous circle can emerge as growth if the financial system promotes overall economic growth, and this higher growth, in turn, will encourage both further financial-sector and housing-finance development.

An important corollary of this first lesson is that housing finance does not work in unstable, volatile economies. Instability inevitability leads to less credit availability, less formal housing built, affordability problems for housing consumers, and greater risk for all concerned. In a word, macroeconomic instability creates a negative circle where less housing finance leads to less residential investment and slower growth in the economy. Attempting to break the vicious circle by promoting housing finance will almost certainly fail. Macroeconomic stability and a strong legal environment have to be present for housing finance to develop.

Macroeconomic stability and legal clarity alone are not enough though. Indeed, the evidence of the past decade suggests that housing finance policy is of fundamental importance in determining the resilience and vibrancy of the sector. After years of stagnation, across many countries, a thriving and buoyant supply of housing finance has emerged with remarkable speed. This sudden development is more than just the unintended consequence of improvements in the macroeconomic and legal environments. The world financial system, as Calomaris described it, is entering a new, liberalized financial paradigm at a time when liquid banks actively develop retail activities. In this regime, policy will no longer systematically deny households access to credit through direct or indirect restrictions. In the places where these restrictions are reduced, housing finance systems can and have emerged very rapidly.

Thus, the second lesson is that in the many countries with nascent supplies of housing finance, the development of coherent, sustained efforts to develop a more transparent, competitive supply of housing finance, be it bank-based or bond-based, is likely to have high economic and social returns. A strong housing finance system cannot only contribute to a broader, more resilient financial sector, it can also promote housing development, particularly of informal settlements, and improve labor mobility and the construction industry. In so doing, it can contribute to growth and stability in the economy. The growth and increased availability of mortgage credit can also be influential in creating better-planned urban environments with lower congestion, improved services, and less crowding. These positive effects of system development, however, will only come about with an appropriate policy framework. Indeed, in the wrong policy environment, unfettered private-housing finance development can be a causal factor in macro instability. The use of the wrong instrument, excessively risky lending, and unsustainable, badly targeted subsidies can lead to the collapse of housing finance institutions and markets, with large costs both to government (bailouts) and the economy (lost productivity, lower growth).

Hence, the third lesson is the need for a strong but nimble and delimited public role in sector development. Without a clear and focused public role, it is all too easy for financial liberalization and development of the housing finance system to be incomplete, with consequent adverse effects on the housing market and economy. Of course, greater competition leads to lower interest rate spreads, greater product variety, and more affordability. Further, the increased ability to borrow against housing wealth can increase consumption and investment, producing economic growth. On the other hand if the newly supplied credit carries implicit interest rate subsidies, or is financed through the taxation system together with the use of regulatory directives, as continues to be the case in many countries, it can lead to very costly financial sector problems. Similarly, the international experience has demonstrated that caution is warranted whenever there is rapid growth in lending of any sort. For mortgage lending, a concern with rapid growth may be even more pronounced, as mortgage borrowing typically involves a moderate-income family financing its largest purchase ever in a transaction with a financially sophisticated lender. Once again, experience has shown that in such environments consumer information and protection are necessary. Hence, while the private sector must be the chief risk bearer in any sustainable system, a strong and transparent public role is essential.

The final lesson relates to the importance of making sure that expanded access to finance does not simply finance sharp asset price increases. Recent years have witnessed extremely large and, as of yet, not well-understood house price increases in many countries (as seen in some Russian or Ukrainian major cities, for example). While talk of housing bubbles may be premature, it is certainly a valid concern when house prices increase as rapidly as they have in so many major cities both in developed and developing countries. While the full dimensions of this process are not yet understood, one important aspect of the phenomenon is clear: the important role that housing market conditions play in whether increases in demand are accommodated by increases in housing supply or housing prices. On this score, the evidence is unambiguous. Without a responsive housing delivery mechanism, including both new housing and the existing stock, improving access to housing finance will largely fuel price increases. Thus, the lesson is that attempts to improve access to housing finance must be deeply cognizant of underlying housing market conditions and policies.

CHAPTER 2

Structure and Evolution of Housing Finance Systems

Michael Lea

A characteristic feature of a housing investment is its relative size and long investment horizon, requiring large amounts of long-term finance. The aim of a housing finance system is to provide these funds to the producers and purchasers of housing, both rental and owner-occupied.[1] This simple description has spawned a broad array of institutional arrangements, ranging from contractual savings schemes; to depository institutions specializing in mortgage finance; to the issuance, sale, and trading of mortgage bonds and securities. All of these arrangements have been created with the same purpose in mind, to mobilize and channel funds from savers to borrowers in an effective way.

In an economy without a well-developed formal financial system, housing is either *self-financed* (that is, by equity accrued through many years of prior savings or through incremental construction; in most countries the majority of real estate transactions remain financed by cash) or *directly financed* between individuals (such arrangements are often referred to as informal finance). Direct finance can be provided by friends, relatives, small sav-

---

1. For comparative reviews of housing finance development, see Boleat 1985 and Diamond and Lea 1992. This taxonomy was originally developed by Boleat and expanded in Lea and Bernstein 2001.

ings and lending clubs (for example, *consórcios* in Brazil), or housing cooperatives or landlords (for example, the *chonsei* system in Korea). Although often the only alternative for households seeking to better their housing circumstances, informal arrangements are often inefficient and costly because the requirements of savers and borrowers are different, information is not equally shared, it is difficult to achieve scale, and lending is hampered by limited funding and risk-management capacities. Dependence on direct finance results in cities that are built as they are financed, with a considerable and visible proportion of self-construction and slum proliferation.

An alternative to direct finance are installment sales contracts, where developers finance purchase through deferred payments. This type of finance is seen in most emerging economies (for example, Egypt, Brazil, and Turkey). While more scalable than direct finance, it is also quite inefficient, as it ties up developer capital, making it more difficult to start new projects. Developers may also finance projects through presales, with or without mortgages. This can be quite problematic for buyers as they may bear both completion and quality of construction risk. This type of finance has been plagued with problems in some countries (China, Turkey, Russia, and Ukraine).

A sign of financial-sector development is the funding of housing by formal financial institutions. These institutions can be private-sector entities, which can be shareholder-owned or mutual organizations, or government-sponsored or -owned institutions (for example, state housing banks). Historically, a characteristic of many housing finance systems was the existence of a special circuit in which particular types of lenders enjoyed preferential financing, often operating apart from the broader financial markets (Diamond and Lea 1993). As economies develop and financial systems are liberalized, provision of housing finance often moves away from extensive reliance on special circuits toward integration of housing finance into the broader financial markets.

Mortgage Lending Models

Building Societies/Savings & Loans

In many countries, the traditional and still predominant mechanism for formal financial-sector finance of housing is the retail depository institution.

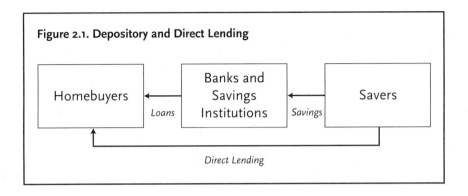

Figure 2.1. Depository and Direct Lending

Homebuyers ← *Loans* ← Banks and Savings Institutions ← *Savings* ← Savers

Direct Lending

In this system, an institution gathers savings from households and enterprises and makes loans to homebuyers (figure 2.1). By taking in savings from non-homebuyers, depository institutions can access a much larger pool of funds than through dedicated savings, including a stable mass of core deposits at a relatively cheap funding cost. There are several types of deposit-taking institutions, including commercial banks that offer a complete range of banking services, savings banks that deal largely with the household sector, and specialist housing-finance institutions (building societies or savings and loan associations) that focus their lending primarily on housing. A key feature of a depository system is that the institution originates, services, and funds the loan. Funding is primarily through retail deposits, but these institutions may also issue bonds and mortgage securities. Another important feature is the short-term, variable rate nature of the funding, compared to the longer-term housing loans.

Specialist-deposit-funded institutions have traditionally dominated the provision of housing finance in Anglo-Saxon countries (for example, Australia, Canada, South Africa, and United States) as well as in Commonwealth countries. The initial model for housing finance was the terminating building societies founded in England in 1775, later introduced in the United States in the 19th century (Mason 2004). The early building societies were formed to mobilize savings of lower- and middle-income households for the sole purpose of home construction. Members would agree to contribute regularly to the society, build houses together, and allocate houses by lottery until each member was housed. Once the defined group of members was provided housing and had repaid the loans, surplus assets, if any, would be distributed among members and the society would be terminated. Credit risk was lowered by the shared information about the groups' members. Variants can still be found in many lower-income countries particularly when commercial banks are absent from the market.

During the mid-19th century, societies developed into permanent institutions, attracting funds not just from borrowers but also from other savers, and lending for purchase of existing houses as well as for building new ones. This development loosened the bond that had previously existed between savers and borrowers. The permanent form had the advantage, however, of widening the investor base and offering a stable and relatively risk-free form of saving, greatly increasing the supply of funds for housing. Increased scale facilitated the hiring of permanent management.

Building societies are mutual institutions owned by their investors and borrowers. Savers purchased "shares" in the society that allowed them to participate in the surplus, if any, that existed after all of the group had received and repaid their loans. In this sense, members were risk takers, as their return depended on the performance of the institution and was not guaranteed. In later versions, savers received periodic dividends. As the permanent society developed, shares became interest-bearing deposits that could be withdrawn at par upon reasonable notice.

Through most of the 20th century, the building society/savings and loan (S&L) model dominated housing finance in the English-speaking world. These institutions were the cornerstone of a special circuit for housing finance supported by regulation (for example, in the United Kingdom, banks had high reserve requirements on housing loans as a form of credit control; in the United States, S&Ls had funding and tax advantages vis-à-vis commercial banks). Starting in the 1980s, this model began to lose influence and market share to commercial banks. The main drivers of change were deregulation (removing preferences and constraints, allowing broader asset and liability powers), demutualization, and institution failure (United States).[2] The failure of many U.S. S&Ls was a result of their inability to manage the market risks of providing long-term fixed-rate loans vs. shorter-term variable rate liabilities. Regulatory failure, initially by requiring fixed-rate lending and later

---

2. The reasons for demutualization included diversification of assets and funding sources, the desire to raise new equity capital, and the possibility of large payouts for members and management.

through regulatory and capital forbearance, contributed to the collapse. The remaining institutions have evolved into broader-based depository institutions but retained their focus on housing finance (offering variable rate mortgages). The mutual, specialized housing-finance model continues to exist in the United Kingdom, where the remaining societies compete on benefits provided to members in the form of lower mortgage rates and higher savings rates in lieu of dividends paid to shareholders. Today, however, building societies account for less than 25 percent of the U.K. mortgage market and S&Ls a smaller share of the U.S. market.

In many emerging economies, where variants of this model were introduced (for example, S&Ls in Latin America; building societies in Nigeria, Kenya, or Malaysia), these deposit-based specialized institutions either gradually lost ground against other models (for example, banks and mortgage companies in Malaysia) or were wiped out by losses related to excessive risks during phases of macro instability (hyperinflation, asset-liability mismatches, deposit runs, and so forth, particularly in Latin America). Nevertheless, there are advantages to the building society model for lower-income countries. The group nature and informational advantages of mutual organizations provide an advantage over other lenders in credit-risk management, an attribute shared with other mutual organizations such as credit cooperatives and credit unions (for example, Paraguay, Mali) and housing micro-lenders (for example, Peru or Bolivia, as discussed in a later chapter). While a marginal source of funding in developed markets today, mutual housing-finance specialists may still have a role to play in lower-income emerging markets with weak or government-run commercial banking systems. The danger (as evident from developed markets) is providing government support that creates a special circuit that delays the inevitable entry of commercial banks or non-depository lenders.

Commercial Banks

Commercial banks historically did not have a major involvement in housing finance. Their traditional purposes of financing business and providing means of payment lead them to a commercial, not a consumer, orientation. Prior to financial liberalization, this tendency was often supported by regulation that constrained banks from offering mortgage finance. Banks have concerns about the risks of providing long-term loans as well, if much of their funding comes from short-term deposits that can be withdrawn on demand. In many countries, regulators concerned about the volatility of real estate markets have also further constrained bank presence, although confusion has often existed between riskier construction loans to developers and safer individual mortgage loans.

Financial liberalization in developed countries has changed the role of banks in the mortgage market.[3] Central banks provide liquidity and deposit insurance, discouraging runs and reducing the concern over liquidity.[4] In stable economies, a proportion of core deposits can be safely used for long-term finance. Banks are turning to retail clients across the world in part because of a loss of their business lending to the capital markets. Long-term mortgage loans are attractive to banks that hope to cross-sell other services and develop long-term customer relationships. In most countries, banks have substantial brand, distribution, and funding advantages over other lenders, and have emerged as market leaders. Banks can be portfolio lenders, offering ARMs to reduce interest-rate risk; providers of short-term construction and warehousing loans; and sellers of loans in the secondary market.

Despite the growing attractiveness of mortgage lending for banks, there are many lower-income countries where banks still refuse to enter the market. Their ambivalence may reflect deep-seated concerns about the ability to manage risk, particularly credit risk in markets with weak legal foundations for collateralized lending, the relatively high cost of making smaller loans, and potential political risk over raising rates and enforcing liens. While improving the infrastructure and environment for mortgage lending is the long-run solution for obtaining bank entry, in the short to medium term,

---

3. Savings banks are major mortgage lenders in several European countries (France, Germany, Spain). They are often owned by state or municipal governments and can benefit from government backing. Cooperative banks have significant market share in Germany and the Netherlands. They operate as mutual organizations. Such institutions are not housing-finance specialists.

4. The ability of central banks to provide sufficient liquidity to keep banks lending is being tested in the credit crunch that started in 2007. Banks' concern over the quality of their portfolios has severely impacted the interbank and swap markets. The reluctance on the part of banks to lend to each other has been reflected in lower volumes and higher rates on interbank loans (for example, London Interbank Offered Rate). Central banks in Canada, Europe, and the United States have injected liquidity into the system and set up a term auction facility that will make loans available to banks at a non-penalty rate backed by a broader range of collateral than open market operations.

most lending may be done by specialized lenders. If well-run in a stable environment, the specialists may show that mortgage lending can be a safe and profitable business. This has been the case in Mexico, where successful Sociedad Financiera de Objeto Limitado (SOFOL) lending has led the banks to reenter the market.

Contract Saving Schemes

Contract savings institutions can be viewed as specialized depository institution circuits. Contract savings are major components of the housing finance systems of Austria, France, and Germany. They have been developed in Central and Eastern Europe (Slovakia, Czech Republic, and Hungary) as well as in a few French-speaking African countries (for example, Cameroon). They generate funds through loan-linked savings contracts, generally at a below-market fixed rate of interest. There are two variants to the system, the so-called closed system in which specialized institutions make loans funded by the contractual savings attracted from potential home buyers (for example, the Bausparkassen in Austria and Germany), and open systems in which banks offer the loans funded by the contractual savings held within their overall deposit base (for example, l'Epargne Logement in France). Contract savings are generally supported by government through savings bonuses and favorable tax treatment.[5] In France and Germany, the contract savings system provides supplementary credit (that is, second mortgages), while in Austria it provides primary mortgages. In the Czech Republic and Hungary, the system has generated considerable savings aided by significant savings subsidies, but produced comparatively few and small housing loans (mostly for renovation purposes). Unsubsidized contract savings programs have been introduced in India (unsuccessfully) and more recently in China, with limited success.[6] This model, its impacts, and limits are discussed in chapter 9.

---

5. Recently, France has reduced its support of the *epargne logement* system and Germany has eliminated the savings bonus.
6. A number of cities in China have housing provident funds (HPFs), primarily for state employees. While they have accumulated significant funds, their housing lending performance has been modest and a number of funds have been plagued with fraud. HPF loans account for approximately 20 percent of total Chinese housing finance lending.

Specialist Mortgage Banks

An alternative to depository institution lenders are mortgage banks (figure 2.2). In such systems, specialized institutions (mortgage banks) originate and service portfolios of mortgage loans that are funded by securities they issue. The securities (mortgage, or covered, bonds) are general obligations of the mortgage bank and are typically purchased by institutions with long-term sources of funds (for example, pension funds and insurance companies). The mortgage bank system dates back to the late 1700s and has been extensively used in continental Europe (particularly in Germany and Scandinavia) (EMF 2001). Mortgage banks offer both residential and commercial mortgages. A major feature of mortgage banking systems is the predominance of long-term, fixed-rate mortgages that are match-funded with corporate debt. The bonds are considered very high quality as a result of conservative underwriting, strong regulation, priority rights of investors in the event of bankruptcy, and transparent operations (mortgage, or covered, bonds are described in more detail in chapter 12).

Mortgage banks are transparent, efficient producers of mortgage assets; however, as with other specialist systems in developed countries, mortgage banks are in decline. Their reach is limited by their specialization, as their funding source constrains their product selection (that is, the need to produce standardized assets in high volume to achieve liquidity and low fixed

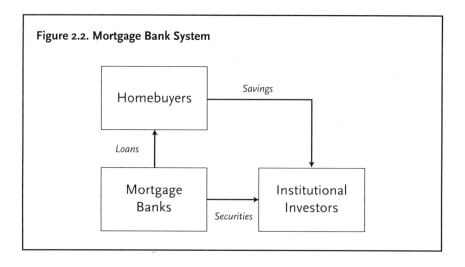

Figure 2.2. Mortgage Bank System

Homebuyers

Savings

Loans

Mortgage Banks

Securities

Institutional Investors

cost of funding) and their inability to provide other types of financial services (although they do function as brokers of other financial services). The
efficient funding mechanism of covered bonds has been extended to commercial banks in most countries (Chile, both Western and Eastern Europe,
and the United States). Also, many mortgage banks have been purchased
by commercial banks. In Germany and, more recently, Denmark, mortgage
banks have lost their monopoly on covered bond issuance. Thus, they are
likely to be folded into the general operations of their commercial bank parents over time.

Combining Different Systems

Figure 2.3 shows the market shares of different lenders in major developed
markets. Commercial and savings banks have more than a 70 percent market
share in all countries except Germany. Non-depositories (mortgage banks or

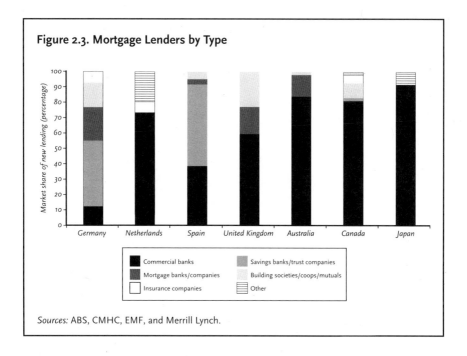

Figure 2.3. Mortgage Lenders by Type

Sources: ABS, CMHC, EMF, and Merrill Lynch.

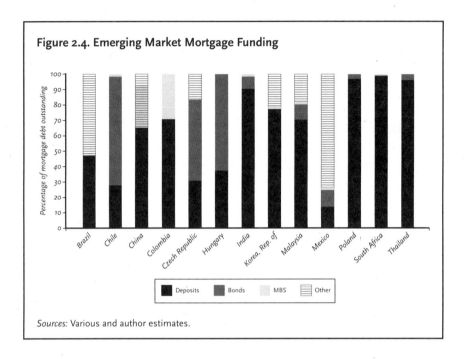

Figure 2.4. Emerging Market Mortgage Funding

Sources: Various and author estimates.

mortgage companies) have significant market share in Australia, Germany and the United Kingdom.[7]

Figure 2.4 shows the market shares of different types of lenders in a number of major emerging markets. In most countries, commercial banks and savings institutions dominate the provision of housing finance. Two notable exceptions are Brazil and Mexico, which have large housing provident fund (HPF) special circuits. These circuits are described in a later chapter. China and Korea also have sizeable special circuits. Note that figure 2.4 refers to funding share rather than lending share.

---

7. Note that the United States does not keep figures on lending by institution type. Most of the top 25 lenders that had a 87 percent market share in 2006 were commercial banks but all major lenders in the United States source mortgages through multiple channels including loans purchased from correspondents. The largest mortgage companies have acquired bank charters to add retail deposits to their financing options.

Secondary Mortgage Markets

Another approach that has gained popularity in developed and emerging markets is a secondary mortgage market (figure 2.5). A secondary market involves the sale of mortgage loans or mortgage securities backed by specific pools of mortgages. As such, it involves the transfer of the risks and owner-ship of mortgage loans to a third party. The loans are originated by a variety of primary lenders, including banks and specialized mortgage companies. Although portfolio lenders occasionally securitize pools of seasoned loans, a hallmark of secondary market-based systems is the widespread securitiza-tion of newly originated loans. They may be sold to specialized institutions called conduits or through special purpose vehicles (SPVs). These entities raise funds through issuance of securities backed (or collateralized) by the loans. The majority of residential mortgage loans in the United States are funded through the secondary market. Mortgage security issuance, while on

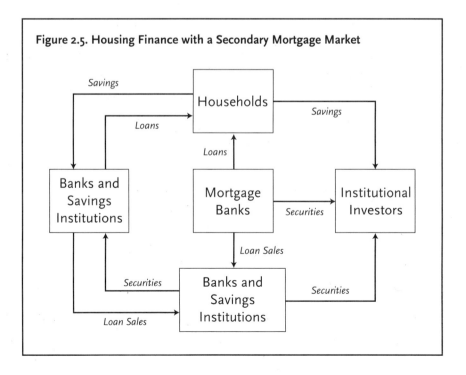

Figure 2.5. Housing Finance with a Secondary Mortgage Market

the rise, represents a small fraction of funding for emerging markets (for more detail, see the mortgage securities chapter).

Mortgage or housing finance companies are specialized non-depository institutions that obtain funds either through sale of loans or special circuit funding. In the United States, mortgage companies developed with the secondary market. They pioneered the unbundling of mortgage functions (below) as specialists in origination and servicing. During the 1980s and 1990s, independent mortgage companies were the largest lender class in the United States. More recently, many U.S. mortgage companies have been absorbed by the commercial banking system. Specialized mortgage companies were an important component of the recent subprime lending boom in the United States, but a number failed in the collapse of the market in late 2006 and 2007. The existence of secondary markets facilitates the easy entry (and exit) of such lenders.[8]

Introducing New Lending Models: Mexico and India

In Mexico, the Sociedades Financieras de Objeto Limitado (SOFOLs) were created to provide mortgage finance after the collapse and withdrawal of commercial banks. They focus on the low- to moderate-income sector and initially obtained their funds from the Central Bank and World Bank. The SOFOLs showed that lending to low- to moderate-income households can be profitable with manageable credit risk. In recent years, the SOFOLs have issued mortgage securities and moved more upmarket. As of 2006, a majority of their funds were coming from the capital markets. At the same time, the commercial banks have reentered the market and have purchased several SOFOLs.

Until recently, the Housing Finance Companies (HFCs) were the major providers of housing finance in India. The Housing Development Finance Corporation (HDFC), a private-public partnership, was the first specialized housing lender in India. It initially received funding from its investors

---

8. A major cause of failure was the inability to obtain short-term funding for their inventory (loans held for sale) and loans subject to repurchase. Mortgage companies obtained such funds through warehouse lines of credit with commercial banks and through issuance of commercial paper. The commercial paper market dried up in fall 2007, and banks refused to extend or roll over the warehouse lines because of concerns about the quality of the loans pledged as collateral.

Box 2.1. SOFOLs—Mexican Mortgage Companies

The SOFOLs (Sociedad Financiera de Objecto Limitado) were born in 1993 as a result of the North American Free Trade Agreement, with a limited scope. They were created just before Mexico entered the worst economic crisis in its history, which devastated the banking industry, resulting in their withdrawal from the mortgage market. Along with two housing pension programs described later, the SOFOLs have been the major mortgage lenders in Mexico until recently. In 2006, they provided over $5 billion in mortgage funding, representing 24% of the market. In the previous years, they had a much higher market share, but it was reduced by the sale of the largest SOFOL, Hipotecaria Nacional (National Mortgage), to the largest bank, BBVA Bancomer, in 2005). SOFOLs are specialized financial institutions that grant mortgage (both construction and permanent loans), consumer, automotive, agricultural, and other kind of loans (that is, working capital). For the past few years, they have successfully competed with commercial banks that have returned to the market. They serve the middle and lower market with more than 50 percent of clients with incomes below eight minimum wages. They specialize in the origination and servicing of loans and have low default rates (less than 3.5 percent). Initially funded through a state-owned liquidity facility (passing on refinancing loans from the public sector and the World Bank), 70 percent of funds now come from the financial markets, including 38 percent from mortgage-backed security issuances in the bond markets (domestic and international).

and through the issuance of bonds. Subsequently, HDFC and other HFCs were funded by the National Housing Bank, which was created as a regulator and liquidity facility for the sector. HDFC showed that housing finance is profitable even in a market where foreclosure and repossession are nearly impossible. The HFCs thrived during the time that state banks were not allowed to provide housing finance. Financial sector liberalization has led to strong entry by banks, which now have a dominant market share (HDFC has formed its own bank). HFC market share has fallen from 61 percent in 2001–2 to 34 percent in 2004–5. Inevitably, all but the largest HFCs are likely to be absorbed by banks.

Box 2.2. HDFC—Creating a Market

The Housing Development Finance Corporation (HDFC) was incorporated in 1977 with the primary objective of promoting home ownership by providing long-term finance to households for their housing needs in India. At that time, there was very little housing finance provided in the country as the state-owned banking sector was prohibited from lending and only government lending programs existed. HDFC was promoted as a private-sector institution with an initial share capital of Rs. 100 million. HDFC was primarily funded wholesale in its first decade, with loans from international donors. HDFC launched a retail deposit program in 1991 and created a bank subsidiary in 1995. HDFC was declared India's best-managed company by *Asia Money* in 1995. It has promoted private-sector housing-finance companies in Bangladesh (Delta Brac) and Sri Lanka. HDFC was a pioneer in instruments (first ARM in 1999), securitization (2000), Internet loan approval (2001), and business process outsourcing (2001) in India and is an acknowledged leader in corporate governance and financial institution efficiency. As of 2005, HDFC had about $3.1 billion in mortgage loans outstanding, representing a 28 percent market share.

Unbundling of Mortgage Value Chain

A major emerging characteristic of mortgage markets is functional separation (or unbundling) in which specialists perform the various functions underlying a mortgage loan (Jacobides 2001).

As shown in figure 2.6, in the bundled model of mortgage lending a financial institution performs the major functions of origination, servicing, funding, and portfolio risk management. These intermediaries may utilize the services of third-party vendors, such as mortgage insurers, appraisers, and credit agencies. A single firm, however, accomplishes the primary functions. The portfolio lender originates a mortgage to a home buyer, services it, and performs the pipeline risk management and portfolio management functions, including funding. Portfolio lenders may be specialized institutions such as savings and loans, building societies, or European-style mortgage banks, or general-purpose depository institutions (commercial banks, savings banks).

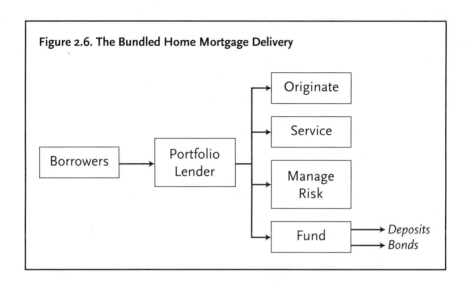

Figure 2.6. The Bundled Home Mortgage Delivery

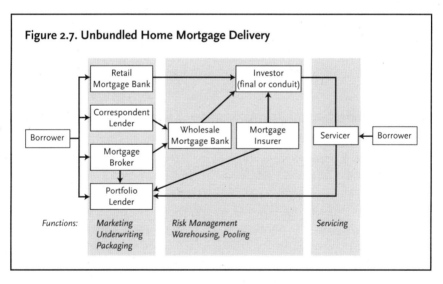

Figure 2.7. Unbundled Home Mortgage Delivery

Figure 2.7 shows the unbundled mortgage delivery system. In this system, the functions of origination, servicing, risk management, and funding are unbundled and provided by different specialized entities.

For example, mortgage origination is no longer confined to retail branches of financial institutions, although they remain important distribution chan-

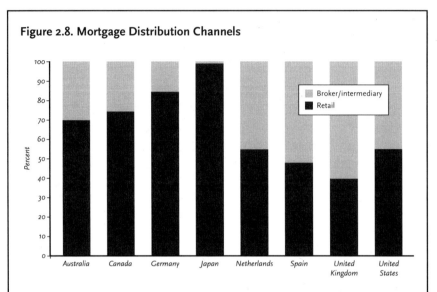

Figure 2.8. Mortgage Distribution Channels

Sources: Mercer, Oliver, Wyman 2003 (Germany, Netherlands, Spain); MBA 2006 (United States); Realty Times 2004 (Canada); Market Intelligence Strategy Center 2005 (Australia); Building Societies Association 2005 (United Kingdom). U.S. percentage assumes correspondent split 50:50 between retail and broker/intermediary.

nels. Mortgage intermediaries (introducers, brokers) are increasingly impor-tant in developed markets (figure 2.8). These entities may be specialists in mortgage origination or originate mortgages in conjunction with other activities such as real estate brokerage, providing financial advisory services, or building homes. Mortgage brokers are becoming a more important distri-bution channel in the new EU member countries (more than 50 percent of new originations in the Czech Republic and Poland) and recently in India. They remain underdeveloped in most emerging economies, but should take more importance as mortgage markets grow in size and competitiveness. Correspondent lenders close loans in their own name (but underwritten to the specifications of the ultimate investor) and immediately sell them to larger, wholesale lenders that can get better execution upon sale in the sec-ondary market. The Internet is rising in importance in mortgage lending, but primarily as an adjunct to existing distribution channels. "Pure" Internet origination has not yet proven itself as a stand-alone channel, as it depends on other channels for fulfillment.

The institution that originates the loan may or may not be the one that services it. In recent years, mortgage servicing has become much more consolidated in the United States, with the top 10 servicers administering over 70 (2007) percent of the market. Various aspects of servicing, such as arrears management, have become even more specialized, as the importance of this function has risen with the advent of the subprime mortgage market in developed markets such as Australia, the United Kingdom, and the United States. Outsourcing of administrative and information technology (IT) functions for both origination and servicing, whether by commercial banks or specialist lenders, is also becoming more commonplace, but there again mostly in developed markets rather than emerging ones.

In the unbundled system, there are a wide variety of investors in housing loans, ranging from depositories to mutual funds. Investors provide funds to the housing market by funding whole loans or investing in mortgage bonds or mortgage-backed securities. In the global market, they may be either domestic or foreign. Credit risk management is often specialized as well, provided by third parties such as mortgage insurance or bond insurance companies (public or private) for the benefit of investors.

Three major factors driving unbundling are competition, technology, and the development of mortgage securities. Housing finance is becoming a more competitive business on a daily basis, creating spread compression and incentives to cut cost. Administrative activities such as servicing lend themselves to automation and scale economies that can be achieved through consolidation and outsourcing. Improved and more timely access to information facilitates monitoring of agent behavior, reducing both cost and risk associated with unbundling.

The subprime debacle of 2007 exposed a fundamental flaw in the disaggregate model of mortgage lending. With the rise of the secondary market and sale of loans, most players in the market became fee driven. Loan brokers receive fees to originate loans. Lenders receive fees to sell ("gains on sale") and service loans. Investment banks and rating agencies receive fees to create, rate, and sell securities. Each of these players is more volume oriented than quality oriented. This unbundling creates agency problems resulting from a divergence in incentives between the agents to the transaction and the ultimate risk takers (investors). While brokers, mortgage companies and investment banks will continue to play an important role in the market, the secondary market share will shrink substantially and new models of compensation and risk management will need to be developed.

Yet, in most emerging economies, fees and margins of the lenders—net of assessed or perceived costs and risks—remain too large to create incentives for unbundling and outsourcing. In addition, many banks remain culturally reluctant to transfer to any third party any information of commercial and financial value about their loans and clients. Therefore, unbundling remains limited to a few functions such as housing appraisal, and in fewer cases, mortgage origination and, to some extent, mortgage default insurance (more as a credit-risk management tool than as actual unbundling). A higher scale of competitiveness would be needed to create the incentives to realize the net gains of unbundling. Secondary market development is a necessary major catalyst for unbundling, as it creates incentives for specialized origination and servicing as well as third-party credit enhancement.

State-owned Lenders

In many countries, government-supported or -controlled institutions have a prominent role in the provision of housing finance. The largest housing finance institutions in the United States, the Federal National Mortgage Association (Fannie Mae) and Federal Home Loan Mortgage Corporation (Freddie Mac), are government-sponsored enterprises operating in the secondary mortgage markets, with —until the 2008 rescue by the federal government—private shareholders but a government charter and both funding and tax advantages. Until recently, the largest housing finance institution in Japan was the Government Housing Loan Corporation, a government entity.[9] There is an emerging privatization trend, with former government-supported lending institutions in Argentina, Australia, France, Korea, and Spain being partially or totally sold to the private sector. The nature of state intervention has taken different forms (for example, support to securitization conduits or to mortgage insurance products, smarter subsidies, preferential

---

9. The Government Housing Loan Corporation has been converted from an originator and matched funder of mortgages to a secondary market institution that both guarantees securities issues by private lenders and purchases closed loans, and issues mortgage-backed securities. It has been renamed the Japan Housing Finance Agency.

regulatory treatment of mortgage loans) but the trend has been away from state-owned institutions, notably state housing banks, because of their poor performance as inefficient lenders, failure to meet housing policy objectives, and crowding out of private market participants (chapter 10).

Conclusions

The use of one or more of these systems depends on the stage of development of a country's markets as well as government policies. Housing finance usually emerges as a retail activity. Wholesale funds mobilization develops if the banking system is constrained from supplying sufficient mortgage credit to meet demand or if capital market sources of funding are more cost effective. The issuance of mortgage securities, however, is premised on the existence of several conditions, including a supportive legal and regulatory framework, sizeable and standardized primary mortgage markets, and well-developed bond markets. Specialized lenders can create efficiencies; however, they need an external funding source such as a government lending window or secondary market. Experience suggests that specialized lenders can thrive in a market for a period as long as their funding can incorporate bond markets and be competitive with retail (deposit) sources. Their viability will ultimately depend on the willingness of investors to buy mortgage-backed securities and provide short-term funding, which in turn depends on their confidence in the credit quality of the underlying assets. Eventually, however, banks are likely to take the dominant market share reflecting their inherent distribution, brand, and funding advantages (including central bank support).

CHAPTER 3

Mortgage Instruments

Michael Lea

A wide variety of mortgage instrument designs have been created to meet the varying needs of borrowers and lenders. In general, there is no one ideal mortgage instrument for a market, although as explained below there are clearly instruments that are not appropriate for some markets or types of lenders and borrowers. A robust mortgage market will have a variety of instruments that can be tailored to the varying needs of borrowers and lenders.

What are the desirable attributes of a mortgage instrument from a borrower's and a lender's perspective? A borrower is interested in the affordability of the loan, both at inception and over its life. The lender is interested in getting an acceptable risk-adjusted rate of return over the life of the loan. This presents a conundrum—often an attempt to improve the attractiveness of the loan for the borrower or lender creates a problem for the other party. For example, an interest-rate cap on an adjustable-rate mortgage (ARM) reduces the potential payment shock and default risk for borrowers but can reduce the yield of the loan for lenders.

Fixed-Rate Mortgages

Perhaps the most important parameter in mortgage-instrument design is the determination of the periodic interest rate. The critical factor is the level of inflation in the economy. Inflation creates problems for housing finance as it increases the level of interest rates (to compensate for expected future price increases) and their variability. As shown in figure 3.1, the appropriate class of instruments for a market will depend on the inflationary environment (both the level and the volatility of prices and interest rates).

Fixed-rate mortgages (FRMs) are most suitable for low to moderate and stable inflation and interest-rate environments. In such environments, the premiums for expected inflation and its variability are relatively low and stable. In higher and more volatile inflation environments, FRMs become either prohibitively expensive or too risky for lenders to offer. There are some notable examples of spectacular failures for lenders offering FRMs in high-inflation environments. In the early 1980s, Mexican banks were required to use FRMs at rates set by the government. An inflation spike following currency devaluation bankrupted the banks and led to their nationalization.

Long-term FRMs present formidable risk-management challenges for lenders, which is why they can be safely offered only in countries with devel-

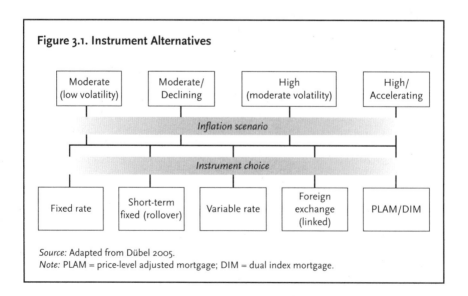

Figure 3.1. Instrument Alternatives

Source: Adapted from Dübel 2005.
Note: PLAM = price-level adjusted mortgage; DIM = dual index mortgage.

oped capital markets. There are two sources of risk for lenders—interest-rate risk arising from a mismatch between the durations of lender assets and liabilities and prepayment risk arising from the interest-rate sensitivity of borrower repayment.[1] Interest-rate risk led to the bankruptcy of a majority of the savings and loan (S&L) industry in the United States in the 1980s. It is very difficult to manage in the absence of developed capital markets and investors with long-term liabilities (for example, pension and insurance companies). As such, these products are a luxury good unaffordable in most emerging markets.

In most countries offering long-term FRMs, borrowers are charged a prepayment penalty for the option to repay their loan early; however, a prepayment penalty limits the term over which the rate can be fixed—typically from 5 years (for example, Canada, Netherlands) up to 10 years (Germany). The magnitude and term over which a prepayment penalty can be charged is a matter of controversy. For example, in France the penalty is limited to 3 percent of the outstanding balance, which lenders claim does not adequately compensate them for the risk. In Germany, the lender can charge a yield-maintenance prepayment penalty—but the term over which the penalty can be applied is 10 years (for a 25–30 year amortization period). There has been considerable debate in Germany over whether borrowers can prepay when they move and how the penalty is calculated (for example, whether lender profits are an acceptable component in the penalty). Significantly, there are only two countries that have long-term FRMs with unlimited prepayment options for borrowers—Denmark and the United States. In those countries, almost all of the FRMs are financed in the capital markets, where sophisticated investors can price and manage the prepayment risk. The cost of the option is embedded in the interest rate and can vary substantially over time, as shown in figure 3.2.

In Canada and a number of European countries, the dominant instrument is a rollover or short-term FRM. The rate of these instruments is initially fixed and adjusts periodically (for example, every one to five years) with a longer amortization period. The borrower is subject to a prepayment penalty for repayment during the fixed-rate term, but can typically make partial prepayments without

---

1. For example, if interest rates fall, borrowers will refinance their loans, shortening the maturity and exposing the lender to reinvestment risk. If rates rise, borrowers may keep their loans longer, creating extension risk for lenders.

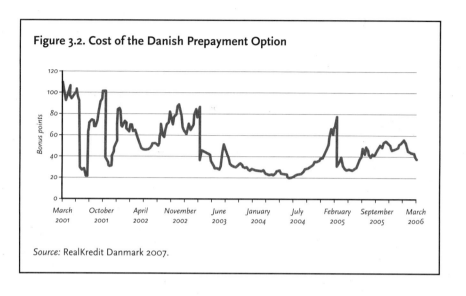

Figure 3.2. Cost of the Danish Prepayment Option

Source: RealKredit Danmark 2007.

penalty. These instruments work well in markets where lenders can issue matching term debt or use swap markets to lengthen their liability maturities. As such, they may be useful in more mature emerging markets where lenders have access to medium-term funds. Borrowers benefit from a fixed rate during a limited period, and can typically choose the term over which their rate is fixed; however, they can be exposed to unlimited rate change at the end of their fixed-rate period, as the rate is market determined at adjustment.

Adjustable-Rate Mortgages

The most prevalent instrument class in the world is undoubtedly the adjustable- or variable-rate mortgage (ARM). These loans perform well in moderate inflation scenarios, as the rate can be adjusted to changes in inflation and real interest rates. Their popularity derives from two characteristics: depository lenders lessen their interest-rate risk by offering ARMs and borrowers improve initial affordability with ARMs because of the relatively low starting rate.[2] For borrowers it is somewhat of a gamble that their income will keep

---

2. Lenders seeking to originate ARMs often offer starting rates below the natural (for example, index + margin) rate to enhance initial affordability. These "teaser" rates can create payment problems for borrowers as the loans adjust to market.

pace with payment changes—this characteristic means that ARMs are not suitable for all borrowers (that is, borrowers with unstable or fixed incomes) or high-inflation economies. ARMs are well suited to moderately inflationary environments where interest rates, prices, and incomes move together with modest changes. They are more problematic in high-inflation environments characterized by large interest rate changes and sluggish income change.

The ability to change the interest rate makes ARMs appealing to lenders, as they allow lenders to better manage interest-rate risk (particularly for banks with short-term deposit funding). In turn, ARMs allow lenders to offer lower margins (reduced exposure to interest-rate risks) and extend their loan maturity (potential immediate and significant affordability gains).

Figure 3.3 shows the proportion of ARMs in developed markets.

There are two important ARM characteristics that deserve mention. First is the index used (if any) to determine rate adjustments. At one extreme there may be no index—the lender may adjust the rate at its discretion. This is

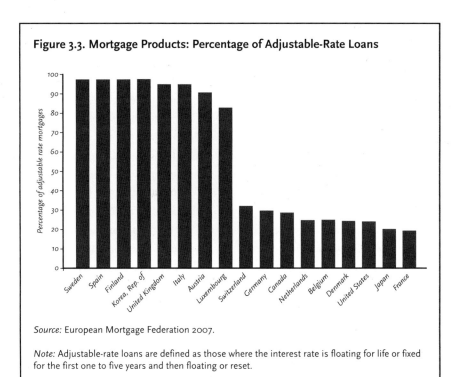

Figure 3.3. Mortgage Products: Percentage of Adjustable-Rate Loans

Source: European Mortgage Federation 2007.

Note: Adjustable-rate loans are defined as those where the interest rate is floating for life or fixed for the first one to five years and then floating or reset.

the standard instrument used in the United Kingdom and other countries that adopted the building society model. In most cases, the lender changes the rate according to changes in its cost of funds. This can be advantageous to borrowers if the lender primarily raises funds through retail deposits. These liabilities adjust less rapidly than money-market rates and shield borrowers somewhat from interest rate fluctuations; however, in less competitive or developed markets this instrument can create problems for borrowers if lenders abuse their privilege by manipulating rates.

In many countries, lenders are obliged to use a published index which is beyond their control and transparent to borrowers and the market. While these characteristics are useful to borrowers, they can create complexity for borrowers and may lead to greater payment volatility if the indices are more volatile than retail funds. Spain has the most developed regulations on ARM indices, allowing a mix of indices as determined by the Bank of Spain.[3] Amendments to the mortgage law in Turkey in 2007 allowed variable rate mortgages but required the use of indices as determined by the Central Bank.[4]

The other important characteristics of ARMs are caps on the periodic rate or payment increase and the maximum (minimum) rate for the life of the loan. Caps represent an important consumer safeguard, but they come at a cost, as they potentially reduce the return on the loan to the lender and the attractiveness of the product and are expensive to hedge—which is anyway not possible in most emerging markets due to a lack of derivative instruments. Caps are more common in countries that require indexation of ARMs (United States, Spain, France) and less common in countries with discretionary ARMs (Australia, United Kingdom). The recent mortgage law in Turkey requires a life-of-loan cap but leaves it to the lender to determine the parameters. In some countries (Malaysia), caps are limited to social housing loans.

ARMs have become more heterogeneous over time. In Australia and the United Kingdom, the most common instrument is the standard variable-rate mortgage (a reviewable instrument), which is often preceded by a one-to two-year initial fixed-rate period. In the United States, hybrid ARMs are common. In a hybrid ARM, the rate is fixed for one to five years, after which

---

3. See http://www.bde.es/tipos/tipos.htm as well as the legal database on the Bank of Spain Web site.
4. Capital Markets Board of Turkey, mortgage law amendments, March 2007 http://www.cmb. gov.tr/.

Box 3.1. The Limits of Adjustable-Rate Mortgages (ARMs)

Excessively risky ARMs are at the heart of the subprime crisis in the United States. As underwriting standards were relaxed beginning in 2004 (in anticipation of continued house-price inflation), lenders began offering loans with fixed rates for two to three years, after which the loan rate became adjustable (so-called 2/28 and 3/27 loans). The initial fixed rate was below market and the margin to which the loan adjusted was large, guaranteeing a payment shock upon adjustment. The loans were made with the assumption that they would be refinanced at the end of the fixed rate period. The combination of funding problems for non-prime lenders and falling house prices invalidated this assumption. Another potential problem loan is the pay-option ARM.* Many borrowers that take this loan are qualified and make their initial payments based on a deeply discounted rate (1 percent). The unpaid interest is capitalized and the loan negatively amortizes. Although this loan was typically provided to borrowers with a good credit history, the combination of high initial loan-to-value, negative amortization, and potential payment shock makes it exceedingly risky in a falling house-price environment. The differential experience of these instruments is shown in the figure below.

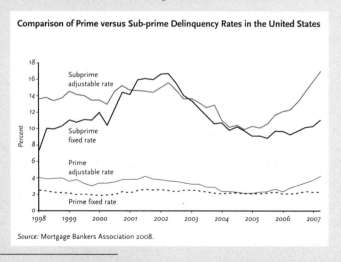

Comparison of Prime versus Sub-prime Delinquency Rates in the United States

Source: Mortgage Bankers Association 2008.

---

* A typical pay-option ARM gives the borrower four amortization choices: minimum (typically, the first month below market rate), interest only, 15- or 30-year amortizing). Most pay-option ARMs have a very low initial rate used to qualify the borrower. The rate adjusts after one month to one year, subject to a payment cap. These features generate negative amortization. The loans will recast to full amortization either at the end of five years or when a negative amortization cap is applied (110%–125% of the original balance), which can generate significant payment shock.

the loan becomes an indexed adjustable rate instrument. ARMs in Thailand can be of flexible term. The payment remains constant and the term adjusts with interest rates. A disadvantage of this instrument is the requirement for the initial term to be less than the maximum to allow flexibility to increase the term if rates rise.[5]

Indexed Mortgages

A final class of products is instruments designed for high and volatile inflation environments. These instruments attempt to reduce the impact of inflation on nominal interest rates to make loans initially more affordable. They also index payments to inflation or income in an attempt to make loans more affordable over time. The most popular are the price-level adjusted mortgage (PLAM) and the dual index mortgage (DIM).

The PLAM is an FRM in real terms—the rate is set at the beginning of the contract and fixed for the life of the loan, and principal balance and payment are adjusted periodically for changes in a price index. Typically, the balance

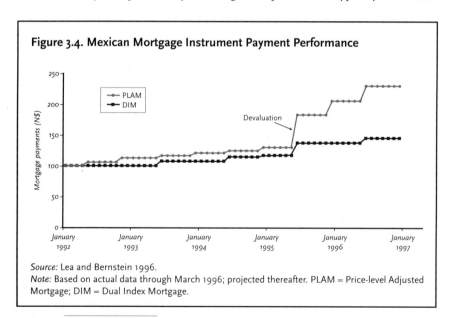

Figure 3.4. Mexican Mortgage Instrument Payment Performance

Source: Lea and Bernstein 1996.
Note: Based on actual data through March 1996; projected thereafter. PLAM = Price-level Adjusted Mortgage; DIM = Dual Index Mortgage.

---

5. The shorter initial term increases the initial monthly payment, reducing affordability.

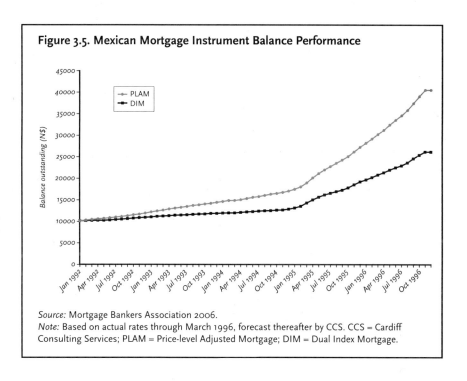

Figure 3.5. Mexican Mortgage Instrument Balance Performance

Source: Mortgage Bankers Association 2006.
Note: Based on actual rates through March 1996, forecast thereafter by CCS. CCS = Cardiff
Consulting Services; PLAM = Price-level Adjusted Mortgage; DIM = Dual Index Mortgage.

is adjusted frequently (monthly) and the payment less frequently (annually),
leading to negative amortization on the loans. PLAMs have been used successfully in Chile since the early 1980s. They are primarily financed through
the issuance of matching mortgage bonds purchased by institutional investors (particularly pension funds that find that the real rate bonds are a very
good match for the real rate pension liabilities). Chile has fortunately benefited from a stable and declining inflation environment since widespread
use of the instrument began.

The experience with PLAMs in other markets has not been as satisfactory. Commercial banks in Mexico were using PLAMs in the early 1990s.
The sharp devaluation of 1994 (the "Tequila crisis") led to a rapid increase
in inflation (from 10 percent to 50 percent and higher within a year). The
resulting payment shock was unbearable for borrowers and led to massive
defaults (over 50 percent of mortgages went into default). Figures 3.4 and 3.5
show the relative performance of PLAM and DIM mortgages before and after

---

Box 3.2. Colombia: Difficulties with Indexed Mortgages

Colombian savings and loans, the Corporaciones de Ahorro y Vivienda, had a relatively long and successful experience with PLAMs until the late 1990s. A sharp deterioration in the economy, however, along with a Supreme Court ruling that required a change in the index, led to high levels of default and a serious asset-liability mismatch for lenders. By the late 1990s, the Corporaciones de Ahorro y. Vivienda had developed a sizeable interest rate imbalance between their deposit liabilities that paid a nominal peso rate of interest and their mortgage loans that were indexed to the inflation rate through the Unidad de Poder Adquisitivo Constante (Constant Purchasing Power Unit of Exchange; UPAC) price index. The dramatic increase in deposit interest rates in 1998 led the government to modify the UPAC formula to incorporate both changes in interest rates and inflation in the determination of the value of the UPAC index applied to mortgage loans. Colombia's Constitutional Court subsequently ruled against the change in the indexation mechanism and instructed banks to restate the value of mortgage loans back to the time when the original change to the UPAC index was made, applying only the inflation index to the newly named Unidad de Valor Real (Real Value Unit; UVR) index. The downward adjustment to the value of the banks' mortgage loans that this caused further exacerbated loan portfolio problems that were already severe after debtor defaults resulted from rising indexed interest rates.

---

the devaluation (Lea and Bernstein 1996). While the DIM had more modest payment increases, the negative amortization was considerably greater.

The DIM attempts to address the affordability problem by indexing the payments to wages but allowing the accrual rate on the loan to vary with inflation or a nominal interest rate. Once again, the basic mortgage design dilemma arises—in an attempt to maintain affordability for the borrower over time, a new problem is created: if the wage and rate indices diverge for a period of time the loan may not amortize. This happened to several vintages of DIMs in Mexico during the 1990s because of the Tequila crisis and aggressive initial terms (although these loans performed better than the PLAMs).[6] DIMs were

---

6. A particular issue in Mexico is the use of the administratively determined minimum wage for payment indexing.

also used in Brazil. Another problem occurred there, however—the government manipulated the payment index for political reasons, bankrupting the mortgage finance system. DIMs were introduced in Poland with more conservative parameters but never achieved consumer acceptance because of their inherent complexity (Chiquier 1998).

DIMs create asset-liability management problems for borrowers and lenders. They can experience large negative amortization, which can result in negative equity and greater default risk if house prices are not rising as fast as the balance on the loan. Additionally, DIMs may have extended durations (the term can lengthen to accommodate the negative amortization, but typically up to a limit), potentially creating a positive remaining balance at final maturity. The Mexican government has attempted to deal with both of these problems. In the early years of DIM usage, the government underwrote the risk of a positive balance at maturity for (government-owned) lenders. More recently, the national mortgage bank (Sociedad Hipotecaria Federal; SHF) developed a novel scheme to reduce the funding risk of DIMs, allowing them to be financed through the issuance of price-level adjusted securities. SHF offers a wage-price swap for DIMs. The borrower pays an up-front premium of 60 basis points to a fund that balances the differences between the cash flows from a pool of DIM mortgages and those of price-level adjusted securities. If wages lag prices, the fund contributes additional cash to the security pool to make up the shortfall. If wages rise faster than prices, the fund balance increases, in effect providing a great insurance against future real-wage decreases.

Several lessons can be drawn in examining the experience with high inflation mortgages. First, although they can ameliorate the impact of inflation on mortgage payments, improving affordability and reducing the risk of default, they can only do so within a range of inflationary outcomes. Severe shocks like those seen in Colombia and Mexico will overwhelm the instrument, leading to adverse results. Second, there must be a matched funding source for the instruments. Lenders without a matching liability will not be able to manage the cash-flow risk they generate. Finally, these instruments are very complex, presenting challenges to both lenders and borrowers. It is likely that many borrowers with these loans do not really understand their dynamics—past experience has suggested the lender's staff may not understand them as well.

Another indexed instrument gaining popularity in relatively high interest rate environments are loans indexed by foreign exchange (FX). These loans adjust balances and payments to changes in the exchange rate or are denominated in foreign currency. FX-indexed loans have been especially popular in transition economies (over 50 percent of loans in Poland, Romania). These loans carry great risks for borrowers and lenders. A sharp devaluation can lead to a payment shock for borrowers whose incomes are in the domestic currency. Similarly, a devaluation can lead to significant losses for unhedged lenders. The potential for this occurrence was demonstrated in Turkey, with a 24 percent devaluation of the Turkish lira in 2006. Fortunately, there were relatively few Euro-denominated mortgages in Turkey at the time.

Several central banks, including Poland and Romania, have attempted to get banks to reduce their FX lending through imposition of higher reserve or capital requirements on FX-indexed loans (see chapter 8 on consumer protection, which deals with this subject in greater depth).

Interest-Only Mortgages

Another key characteristic of mortgage design is the amortization formula. The standard mortgage instrument is a level-payment, fully amortizing loan.[7] This rather rigid design calls for equal monthly payments over the life of the loan.[8] The dominance of the level payment loan has been dictated by the servicing systems available to lenders and the desire to keep borrowers on a steady payment schedule. This design, however, is not suitable for borrowers with uneven incomes or who are suffering from a temporary income shortfall.

In recent years, there has been a rise in interest-only mortgages in the United Kingdom, the United States, and several other developed markets. A

---

7. There are variants to this design, including the constant amortization mortgage, which has a level principal payment and declining total payment over time, and the graduated payment mortgage, which has a rising payment over the first few years (and resultant negative amortization) before leveling out at a constant payment higher than a standard mortgage loan for the remaining life. The constant amortization mortgage has the disadvantage of higher initial monthly payment, reducing affordability. The graduated payment mortgage enhances affordability at the beginning of the loan—with the disadvantages of possible payment shock, negative amortization potentially deflating borrower equity, and longer duration.
8. For ARMs, the payment is recalculated at the new rate upon adjustment based on amortization of the loan in equal payments over the remaining term.

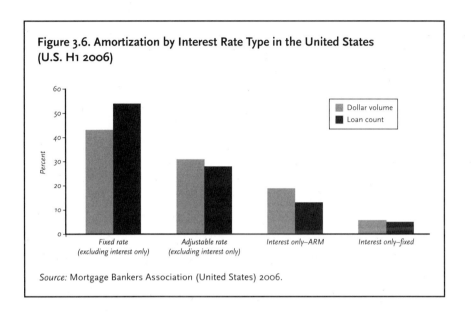

Figure 3.6. Amortization by Interest Rate Type in the United States (U.S. H1 2006)

Source: Mortgage Bankers Association (United States) 2006.

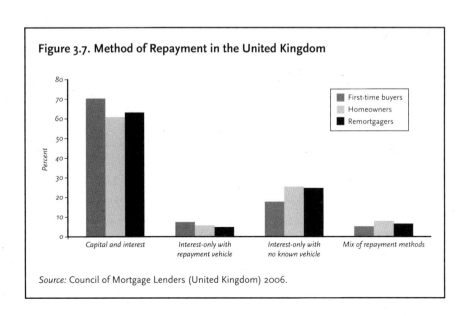

Figure 3.7. Method of Repayment in the United Kingdom

Source: Council of Mortgage Lenders (United Kingdom) 2006.

primary motivation has been to enhance affordability. The structures differ (figures 3.6 and 3.7). In the United States, the loans are interest only for a number of years (for example, five to ten), after which they revert to amortizing (with concomitant increase in payments to reflect amortization over the remaining term). The loans can be fixed or variable rate. In the United Kingdom, interest-only mortgages are variable rate, but the majority do not have an identified repayment vehicle (perhaps a legacy of the endowment mortgage, which was an interest-only loan with a companion insurance policy designed to repay the principal upon maturity—but which often did not during the 1990s).

In recent years, the flexible mortgage has been introduced in a number of developed countries. The flexible mortgage allows borrowers to take payment holidays (typically limited) without penalty. This feature is attractive to borrowers with uneven income (for example, teachers and commissioned salespersons, or those subject to short-term unemployment). More advanced versions (for example, the pay-option ARM) in the United States allow borrowers to choose from a menu of payment options, including negative amortization, to accelerated amortization. While providing affordability benefits, flexible mortgages may carry more risk for borrowers and lenders. As they have not yet gone through an interest rate cycle, it is too early to judge their performance. Default rates on pay-option ARMs have been strongly increasing in the United States.

Reverse Mortgages

Another class of mortgage, the reverse-annuity mortgage or shared equity loan, is targeted at aging populations. These loans allow homeowners to consume some or all of their housing equity to support their retirement income needs. The borrower can take a lifetime annuity, term annuity, or lump-sum payment at funding and the lender gets a portion of the property value (or appreciation) upon sale or death. The amount of the payment depends on the equity in the home and whether the payments are for a fixed term or for the life of the borrower. In the United States, the borrower can remain in the home until they die, and the loans are insured by the government mortgage insurer (U.S. Federal Housing Administration [FHA]). Such loans are likely to gain in popularity as the population ages.

Lessons for Emerging Markets

The choice of mortgage instrument should be consistent with the macroeconomic environment. FRMs will not work for lenders in volatile macroeconomic environments. The risks are too great for lenders to manage and their mandated use will greatly restrict the flow of mortgage credit or lead to large losses for lenders. ARMs can work with moderate inflation, but the potential for payment shock is great in volatile environments. Indices increase transparency but also complexity. Interest rate and payment caps can reduce payment shock but at the cost of reduced expected yields for lenders, particularly if no hedging instruments are available. Loans have been designed for high-inflation environments with limited success. There is no free lunch—PLAMs, DIMs, and FX-linked mortgages carry many risks and will not substitute for the benefits of a low-inflation environment. With macroeconomic stability and financial deepening, a wider variety of instruments can be made available, including fixed-rate and non-constant amortization mortgages. Capital market funding, however, should be available before long-term FRMs are offered.

CHAPTER 4

Primary Mortgage Market Infrastructure

Sally Merrill

This chapter addresses the key functions needed to support an efficient primary mortgage market: property appraisal; mortgage-related insurance products, including catastrophic insurance against earthquake and flood; and assistance with credit risk assessment via credit bureau information. The successful development of these support functions and of a sound mortgage market is mutually supportive. For example, the increasing sophistication of the appraisal industry both responds to, and supports, a growing primary market. Similarly, the demand for property insurance is a function of a growing mortgage market that enables insurers to achieve diversification and scale economies and offer reasonably priced products. As these support functions help to measure and share the risks, they shape the evolution of primary mortgage markets (needed before developing secondary mortgage markets) and they facilitate the penetration of housing finance markets through lower-income groups.

Yet, these support functions do not represent absolute prerequisites for would-be candidate lenders, as demonstrated by the Housing Development Finance Corporation (HDFC)—pioneer and now leader of housing finance in India—which went forward without any of these supports in place (plus the critical lack of long-term funding, and of any enforceable foreclosure).

An effective appraisal process is arguably the most important of these functions. The accuracy of the valuation, through its impact on loan-to-value (LTV); the level of property insurance; and the validity of higher- or lower-risk weight assignments ultimately impacts credit risk, collateral risk, capital charges for banks, and improved affordability for the borrower. Building a credible appraisal industry, however, is demanding and takes time.

Credit bureau reports on borrower debt and loan repayment history are crucial inputs to determining credit risk through both the debt-to-income ratios and knowledge of past repayment behavior. Many emerging markets have trouble convincing leading market lenders and other suppliers of credit that information sharing is beneficial to all. Moreover, of course, newly established markets require time to develop credit histories and other information that ultimately offers the benefits of a full-service credit bureau.

Finally, mortgage-related insurance products are an important means of sharing collateral and credit risk and avoiding default and repossession. These include property insurance and mortgage life insurance, and, in a few countries, disaster insurance. Property insurance should clearly be mandatory, and fortunately, this is generally not a difficult insurance product to develop. Similarly, various approaches exist for mortgage life insurance products. In contrast, developing catastrophic risk insurance in countries prone to natural disasters such as hurricanes, floods, or earthquakes has proved to be a very daunting task, even in developed markets. A few higher-income emerging markets are paving the way, however. These products differ from mortgage default insurance (which shares credit risk with lenders [chapter 13]) developed in some emerging markets.

Worldwide trends, especially in appraisal, but also in credit information and disaster insurance, will assist emerging markets in developing effective support functions. These trends include the following:

- international efforts to standardize and improve appraisal methodology and certification of appraisers;

- development of more complete databases and IT platforms, leading to use of quantitative methods and modeling in both appraisal and credit scoring (many countries still lack any useful database on housing markets and prices);
- establishment of credit bureaus in many emerging and transition markets; and
- slow but steady progress in developing viable approaches to catastrophic risk insurance, combined with increased access to international reinsurance for emerging markets.

There has been worldwide movement toward standardization and conformity in appraisal methodology and appraiser qualifications. Also, although less widespread to date, credit scoring has become more prevalent with the use of consistent, quantitative estimates of credit risk. The reasons for this push are compelling. As funding of mortgage loans in both local and international capital markets becomes widespread, rating agencies and investors alike demand consistent underwriting information in valuing the portfolios. Similarly, as implementation of Basel II proceeds, lenders' capital requirements on residential mortgages will be influenced by obtaining the lower-risk weights on qualifying loans; this, in turn, demands consistency and conformity to accepted standards of valuation and underwriting.

Finally, although numerous emerging and transitioning nations are in the process of developing secondary markets based on mortgage-backed debt products offered in local or international capital markets, there is increasing realization that the primary market must exhibit effective standards before a secondary market can thrive. This implies sound and transparent approaches to controlling credit and collateral risk via good appraisal methodologies, credit information, and support from insurance products offered by appropriately capitalized and regulated insurers. In sum, a sound primary market and prudent underwriting depend on a solid infrastructure able to value and protect collateral and to determine the relative worthiness of would-be borrowers.

Appraisal

The Importance of Sound Appraisal

An accurate assessment of the value of residential real estate may be the most crucial support function in mortgage lending. First, without consistent and accurate appraisal to guide LTV decisions, lenders cannot achieve their desired distribution of risk and portfolio size. The level of LTV has been shown to be the single-most-important predictor of default, and thus the accuracy of the valuation is key to knowing "true" LTV levels. Without this assurance, "real" LTV levels in emerging markets are likely to be lower than what might be expected, because risk-averse lenders reduce the appraised value by a significant percentage (the so-called "haircut") or rely on their clients to pay a higher price than what is officially declared to the seller or developer. Second, capital market funding, especially if internationally accepted ratings are sought, will be much more difficult without acceptable appraisal practices among the underwriting standards. Finally, the valuation is again linked to collateral risk, as it may form the basis for the level of a homeowner's property insurance coverage.

In the last 15 years, appraisal quality and methodologies have received a great deal of attention in the United States and throughout Europe. A number of real estate crises have reemphasized the importance of competent appraisal practices: the U.S. savings and loan crisis of the 1980s, real estate asset bubbles in various OECD countries and the Asian collapse in the 1990s. As a result, the U.S. and European appraisal industries have developed more stringent standards for methodology, certification, and ethics, which are now contributing to improvements in appraisal practices worldwide.

The strong push to standardize appraisal has spread to numerous emerging markets. As noted, the "internationalization" of capital market funding of mortgage lending requires standardized and transparent underwriting criteria, especially if rating agencies are involved. In addition, under Basel II, regulators are looking to standardize the risk-weight treatment of various categories of mortgage lending, and receiving the lower recommended risk-weight assignment will require adequate valuation processes. Finally, the appraisal standardization effort joins a broader effort to standardize financial-sector functions, such as international accounting and regulation.

Developing an Appraisal Industry

A number of important elements are required in developing an effective, transparent, and professional appraisal industry. These include the following:

- adherence to internationally accepted norms of appraisal methodology;
- adequate accreditation standards and educational and professional training opportunities under which a group of appraisal professionals can emerge, and also participate, in ongoing educational opportunities;
- independence from parties to real estate transactions and acceptance of an accepted code of ethical conduct;
- appropriate fee structure
- appropriate levels of government regulation and development of a structure of taxes and fees in real estate transactions that support transparency and honesty; and
- a professional association of appraisers responsible for enforcing these requirements.

International Standardization of Appraisal Methodology

For the last two decades, appraisal methodologies and valuer qualifications have become more standardized and codified, providing an important benefit to development of appraisal competency in emerging markets. Several major groups have played important roles: the International Valuation Standards Committee (IVSC),[1] the Royal Institute of Chartered Surveyors, the U.S. Appraisal Institute, the U.S. Appraisal Foundation, and The European Group of Valuers Associations' development of the International Valuation Standards has been guided by three main principles:

---

1. An IVSC publication, *International Valuation Standards, Sixth Edition*, 2003 (International Valuation Standards Committee 2003), is an important international documentation of valuation concepts and valuation codes of conduct. The latest edition also contains a white paper, "Valuation in Emerging Markets," which is intended to assist valuers in emerging markets and guide development assistance efforts by national institutions, IFIs, and other donors.

- facilitating cross-border transactions in international property markets by promoting transparency in financial reporting and reliability of valuations performed to secure loans and mortgages;
- serving as a professional benchmark for valuers around the world; and
- providing standards of valuation and financial reporting that meet the needs of emerging markets and newly industrialized countries.

Market Value (MV) is the approach recognized by IVSC, the Appraisal Institute, the Royal Institute of Chartered Surveyors, and many other EU and OECD countries.[2] MV is the standard adopted by numerous emerging markets as their benchmark as they develop their appraisal industries. Market value is defined as the estimated amount for which a property should exchange on the date of valuation between a willing buyer and a willing seller in an arm's length transaction after proper marketing wherein the parties had each acted knowledgeably, prudently, and without compensation. MV includes the cost approach, sales comparison approach, and income capitalization approach. For residential real estate, the sales comparison approach forms the key basis of valuation, and secondarily the cost approach is a basis of valuation; for commercial real estate, in contrast, the income capitalization approach is paramount. Unlike larger and riskier loans to finance commercial property, single-family mortgage loans normally do not require any costly renewal of a detailed appraisal, as long as the portfolio performance is satisfactory.

The move to standardize appraisal within the EU has revealed a difference in the appraisal methodology used in Germany, Austria, and Hungary, among others, which rely on a concept called mortgage lending value (MLV) to appraise the collateral of the mortgage loans that back covered mortgage bonds. As defined by IVSC, MLV is a "value at risk" concept: the valuer makes a "prudent assessment of the future marketability of the property by taking into account the long-term sustainable aspects of the property, the normal and local market conditions, and the current use and alternative appropriate uses of the property."

---

2. For detailed information on the definition of market value, see IVSC and Appraisal Institute publications, available at www.appraisalinstitute.org, and the Royal Institute of Chartered Surveyors' "Red Book."

According to the German Pfandbrief Association, MLV is based on the following principles: assessment of future marketability, elimination of speculative elements, long-term sustainable use of the property, and considerations of the conditions of local real estate markets. Thus, MLV introduces into market value the notion of "smoothing" of market trends, rents, and yields, in order to eliminate some cyclical effects inherent to real estate markets, and to provide a more conservative estimate for the purpose of rating high-quality and long-term covered bonds. MLV is a more conservative concept than MV, as implicitly recognized by the Basel I Accords.[3]

Does this dual approach between MV and MLV matter for emerging economies? A country like Poland uses both methods, which simply mirrors the fact that mortgage lending is done by both universal banks (which use MV) and specialized German-style mortgage banks (which use MLV). As noted, pressures to define a single international standard are being driven by the global rise of mortgage-backed securities (residential mortgage-backed securities [RMBS] and covered bonds), and by the risk-based approach of Basel II, in which the LTV is of paramount importance. Most emerging nations have adopted the MV approach, which had emerged as the worldwide standard, probably because of its operational simplicity in countries where no historical data records are required for MLV. On the other hand, smoothing out some conjectural short-term fluctuations through collateral prices is a laudable purpose for assessing the quality of long-term mortgage securities. This point has gained visibility through the ongoing adverse cycle in the United States, where the market values of housing assets related to subprime loans are rapidly declining with adverse effects on the value of residential mortgage backed securities. Yet, parties other than appraisers may be better positioned to forecast real estate cycles and determine corrective discounts (MBS arrangers, rating agencies, or regulatory authorities).[4]

Both MV and MLV have valid advantages and disadvantages, and it is likely that countries that have historically used MLV will continue to do so, as least so far as it is a regulatory requirement for their covered bonds. The

---

3. For commercial loans, the preferential risk weight treatment (50 percent) is only accorded if the loan does not exceed 50 percent of MV or 60 percent of MLV.
4. The German regulatory authorities periodically revisit the minimum discount rates applied by appraisers.

MV-MLV duality matters less as long as it is clear to lenders and investors of mortgage-backed debt which approach is being used.

Appraiser Qualifications, Appraisal Associations, Independence, and Ethics

The key international appraisal organizations strongly emphasize the importance not only of establishing methodological standards, but also of ensuring more professional implementation and enforcement. The issues include establishment of self-regulating professional bodies, certification requirements, appraiser independence, disciplinary procedures, and professional indemnity insurance.

Issues of ethics and appraiser independence have received international attention. Both European (IVSC) and United States (Appraisal Institute) associations have published codes of conduct for appraisers. Appraiser independence from the control of both borrowers and lenders has been addressed worldwide, thus requiring the proper incentives for the appraiser to perform any unbiased valuation. In general, appraisals should be a credit administration function, most appropriately controlled by the credit risk or credit policy functions of the lender, not the credit production (loan officer) staff. Ordering and review of appraisals should be located away from the "hands, eyes, and control" of the loan staff. These principles are implemented as rules or at least as self-regulatory codes of conduct in several emerging markets (for example, Bank of Thailand appraisal rules for loan provisioning purposes). The increasing importance, however, of mortgage brokers, who are not subject to the same compliance rules as banks, continues to be a grey area.

While meeting the above-mentioned principle of independence, many lenders fear that the collateral value may be over-appreciated by external appraisers paid by borrowers, who may shop around to obtain the highest valuation. Therefore, even when contracting external certified appraisers, banks should keep sufficient in-home expertise to review the work of outside appraisers. They may also use statistical valuation models (see below) for pre- or post-quality control.

Quantitative Appraisal Models and Real Estate Data

Most emerging countries are confronted by a lack of reliable data on the evolution of housing prices and rents, thus affecting the quality of any professional appraisal, whatever the methodology or model. Beyond the data collected from or through official sources (registration offices, tax authorities, public housing finance institutions, and so forth), vital information must also be gathered from the market operators (appraisers, developers, realtors, banks, brokers, and so forth). In many emerging economies, market players are reluctant to share any information, although all parties would collectively gain from an effective real estate information center. Databases actively supported by market players (for example, Poland) perform better than those only supported by the public sector.

In countries where quality data can be gathered on a large scale, statistical models of valuation—automated valuation models (AVMs)—are increasingly utilized in developed economies, where real estate databases have become more widespread and accessible and have supported the development of complex AVMs and house price indices (HPIs). The United States, Denmark, Germany, Spain, and the United Kingdom are using these methodologies, and elsewhere in Europe AVMs are in the development phase.[5]

There are a number of approaches to AVMs: hedonic indices, repeat sales methods, and various hybrids of these. These models have a number of useful applications: mass valuation of real estate for tax purposes, valuation for development of HPIs, assessment of the error variances of conventional appraisals (quality control), loss mitigation analysis, and, as noted above, internal bank review and portfolio valuation. While the statistical aspects of the various models have advanced, the data quality and quantity for calibrating and testing them—across time, location, and property details—still determine their utility.

---

5. See Calhoun 2001; EMF 2000b; and Bates, Johnson, and Brzeski 1999.

The Challenges of Establishing an Appraisal Industry in Emerging Markets

The development of effective appraisal methodology in emerging markets faces numerous challenges and is inevitably a long-term process. Some of the many issues include the following:

- Emerging markets generally lack a sufficient number of adequately trained inspectors, especially those with all-important on-the-job experience. Appraisers are often engineers, trained in the cost replacement methodology, although estimation of MV for residential properties using the "comparables" MV methodology is the priority.
- There is no overview of the broader market and its trends on which to base a comparable estimation. Data are generally held by individual appraisers, realtors, and banks. Large databases, such as the Multiple Listing Service (MLS) in the United States, do not exist. Thus, even when appraisers are trained in the theory of market valuation, they are limited in their ability to put it into practice, especially effective utilization of the comparables methodology and the development of computer models. Commercial databases are unlikely to come into being until realtors, lenders, and appraisers recognize the benefits from cooperation and follow defined "rules of the road" for exclusivity and cost-sharing arrangements.
- Actual transaction prices may not be recorded in an effort to reduce the taxes and fees often levied on transactions; this renders the data less useful than would be the case if the true relationship between market price and the characteristics of the property could be studied and ultimately used to develop hedonic models.
- Appraisal associations must be established that create effective governance conventions, including rules for independence from lenders and buyers. A fee structure must be established that is "flat"; that is, does not represent a proportion of the valuation. The issue of independence from lenders, or from the banks' lending officers, or from developers—the official sale price of a newly built unit not always reflecting the actual market value—also needs more attention. Appraisal associations in most emerging countries have not managed

Box 4.1. Developing the Appraisal Industry

The Polish Association of Property Appraisers and the National Association of Romanian Valuers, the Romanian appraisers association, have both developed good appraisal industries in a limited time frame, having made good use of donor technical assistance and membership in international appraisal organizations. U.S. and British standards were used for licensing requirements, which include a college degree, specialized education, and on-the-job training. Poland's appraisers are trained in both the MV and MLV methodologies. In contrast, although the mortgage market is growing rapidly, there is no formal association of appraisers in India. India's premier housing lender, HDFC, handles the appraisal process as an in-house function. Over the years, an extensive centralized property database has been developed that can be tapped by HDFC's entire network of offices. In certain cases, independent appraisers are consulted, but it has been a conscious decision not to outsource this critical function.

yet to become credible self-regulatory bodies, capable of granting and revoking licenses, taking sanctions, providing training to their members, enforcing codes of conduct, and so forth.

- Appraiser fraud is an issue in both developed and developing countries. For example, "flipping" refers to the practice of buying a property at the market price, getting an appraiser to inflate the value, and reselling at the inflated price. While AVMs may be one approach to reducing such fraud, the requisite databases generally do not exist in emerging markets, as discussed. There is no easy fix to the problem. Requirements must be in place for minimum standards in training, experience, and adherence to international valuation standards, with offending appraisers subject to civil and criminal penalties. In addition, banks can use trusted, licensed appraisers to perform periodic spot checks.

As noted, one result of these valuation problems is the lender "haircut." Thus, a valuation, whether done by bank appraisal staff or an independent appraiser, is often arbitrarily reduced by a significant percentage (say, 15–30 percent) in order to compensate for unknown appraisal error. As a result, true LTVs are often lower than the stated value, which hinders both development of the MV approach and reduces affordability for many would-be buyers. Much can be gained, however, from the substantial international efforts noted above in standardizing methodologies and certification procedures.

Mortgage-Related Insurance Products

This section addresses three mortgage-related insurance products: property insurance, mortgage life insurance, and catastrophic insurance, which is most commonly utilized to assist against the devastation of earthquakes, floods, and hurricanes. Property insurance is now available in many emerging markets; it can generally be developed without significant delay as both mortgage markets and the insurance sector mature. Property insurance is usually the first insurance product to become a mandatory underwriting requirement for mortgage loans. Life insurance required for a mortgage loan can take two forms: a general life insurance policy or a life policy specifically geared to pay off the mortgage in case of the borrower's death or incapacitation; this latter is referred to as mortgage life insurance. This product, too, can generally be made available as a country's insurance sector matures. In contrast to these insurance products, disaster insurance is now available in only a handful of emerging markets. Structuring and funding disaster insurance is, in fact, a worldwide problem for developed and emerging markets alike, as it requires design of appropriate roles for government, more mature local commercial insurers, and international reinsurers, all in a complex context of ex ante funding strategies, risk modeling, and disaster mitigation planning.

Property Insurance

Property insurance is generally mandatory in developed markets, whether as a result of regulation, commercial practice, or both. For example, most bank regulators would cite mortgage lenders making loans without property insurance as an audit deficiency—that is, bad lending practice. Property insurers are generally multi-line insurers, offering other types of insurance such as car and commercial insurance; costs are reasonable, as a function of both scale and competition.

The most common, and most important, type of property insurance is for loss due to fire. Most lenders require minimum coverage amounting to the replacement cost of the structure, not including the value of the land. There are several types of policies, including fixed value and escalating value, the latter being adjusted with inflation or a construction-cost index. Lenders will insist that they are jointly named in the insurance contract or that their "interest" is noted. The initial amount of property insurance is highly dependent on the appraisal process.

Homeowner packages are also provided, insuring the contents of the homes against theft. Natural disasters such as tornadoes, lightning, and damage from internal water pipes may also be covered under some standard policies, as might structural damage under a home-builder warranty for new homes or resulting from termites, and so forth. Other types of protection, however, such as flood and earthquake, are "standard exceptions" in nearly all property insurance contracts, and are covered—if at all—in some type of disaster insurance, as discussed below.[6]

Whether formally regulated or not, property insurance is crucial in guarding against collateral risk. An increasing number of developing countries now require a generic homeowner's policy, particularly for fire insurance. The problem, however, is that market penetration is still very low, generally less than 5 percent of households, for example, in countries such as Turkey, Romania, and Mexico. In contrast, Colombia represents a "best practice" exception, with penetration of 30 percent for both general property and earthquake protection, as all mortgage lenders require such insurance. As a counterexample, however, property insurance is not required in the Philippines, which despite having a reasonably well-developed mortgage market, does not have adequate risk management for residential and commercial properties.

---

6. The EBRD *Mortgage Loan Minimum Standards Manual* indicates that both property insurance and mortgage life insurance should be regarded as a mandatory minimum standard; best practice would also include contents insurance (and mortgage default insurance, discussed in Chapter 13).

The problem is due, in part, to low income. Research has shown that the incidence of coverage increases as a country's income (per capita GDP) grows: there is a 1.3 percent increase in property insurance coverage for every 1 percent increase in GDP.[7] As noted in the introduction, the development of property insurance and the maturation of the mortgage market are mutually supportive. On one hand, mortgage markets require property insurance to reduce collateral risk, and on the other hand, a growing mortgage business provides the necessary incentives and scale for development of cost-effective homeowner property-protection packages. Higher insurance costs go hand in hand with limited scale and penetration, and low per capita income. As both the mortgage market and the insurance industry grow and become more sophisticated, competition, risk analyses, and increased scale will contribute to more efficient pricing. Regulators in emerging markets under a "best practice" approach should be encouraged to mandate property insurance as soon as possible.

A number of issues must be addressed in the course of making property insurance an integral part of lending, especially in the early phases of mortgage market development. These include the following:

- added expense for moderate-income borrowers, especially in the early phases of insurance industry development of the product;
- the adequacy of the appraisal function in providing an adequate measure of property value and of building standards and their enforcement in reducing risk;
- the adequacy of capitalization in the insurance industry and other regulatory parameters, such as solvency ratios, and appropriate insurance regulation (particular supervision of solvency, issue of "captive" insurers owned by lenders, and geographical dispersion).

Mortgage Life Insurance

Mortgage life insurance, a rapidly growing product line around the world, is typically life coverage equal to the outstanding mortgage loan balance at the time of death. The family or estate is thereby able to retain ownership

---

7. See the discussion in Gurenko and Lester 2004.

of the home without the responsibility of making the mortgage loan payment. Coverage is generally only for the primary borrower; joint coverage is available but not widely used. Although mortgage life insurance could be mandatory by law, it is generally simply dictated as commercial practice. When a voluntary program is in place, the premium rate is generally higher to allow the lender to earn a commission. Voluntary programs would usually have higher claims experience, since healthy people may be less likely to buy coverage.

Mortgage life insurance is available in a number of the more developed markets in Latin America, Asia, and Central and Eastern Europe. For example, Malaysia has had mortgage life insurance for about 10 years; although it is voluntary, more that half of the borrowers elect to buy it. Indonesian lenders also promote mortgage life insurance, with the premium included in the loan amount. Romania and Bulgaria provide other examples. A number of issues should be addressed in considering the merits of mortgage life insurance in emerging markets:

- Should the product be voluntary or mandatory?
- Are insurers sufficiently well capitalized and prudentially regulated?
- Are there supply constraints, such as appropriate actuarial tables? Availability of adequate medical exams?
- Should the policy cover limited or temporary disability as well (how to control)?

In the U.S. market, mortgage life insurance is a voluntary product. As noted above, however, the EBRD *Mortgage Loan Minimum Standards Manual* (2007) for emerging markets lists mortgage life as a minimum standard requirement. Clearly, mortgage life insurance needs adequately capitalized and regulated insurers, just as for property insurance. The issue of mandatory versus voluntary coverage is more difficult. Mortgage life insurance can be a useful additional tool in controlling credit risk, especially in newly expanding markets, but it does not substitute for other reforms needed to manage credit risks (effective foreclosure, credit bureaus, and so forth).

Catastrophic Insurance

Natural disasters, by their nature, are events with a low probability of occurrence and a high level of loss given an occurrence. Developed markets rely on the international reinsurance market to transfer and spread these risks.[8] Even in developed countries, however, private disaster insurance is not comprehensive. The potential losses can be so large or indeterminate that commercial insurance markets cannot provide sufficient coverage at acceptable prices. This has resulted in some countries supplementing the private market with public programs. Examples include France, New Zealand, the United States, Norway, and Taiwan. In addition, not all types of disasters are insured. While flood insurance is available (and mandatory in floodplain areas) in the United States, for example, earthquake and hurricane insurance may be very difficult to obtain, as risks are both high and geographically concentrated. Thus, given the limits of commercial programs, individual states have stepped in, with Florida providing hurricane insurance and California earthquake coverage (even so, only 10 percent of Californians have earthquake insurance). Finally, significant moral-hazard problems exist with earthquake and flood insurance, stemming from insuring buildings in areas expected (or known) to have higher probabilities of disaster, and this is likely to be an issue in emerging markets as well.

Catastrophic insurance coverage against natural disasters, most frequently against loss from earthquakes, flood, and hurricanes, is far less common than property insurance among developing nations. For example, whereas disaster insurance in countries such as the United States and France cover 40 to 100 percent of loss from some types of natural disasters, in developing markets less than 1 percent of losses are insured. Furthermore, emerging markets are far more vulnerable to disasters, for reasons stemming from both geography and limited financial and real estate sector development. While the absolute economic costs of natural disasters in developed countries are higher than in emerging markets, the relative cost of disasters is generally greater in developing markets, where infrastructure and buildings are less resilient. For example, the 1985 earthquake in El Salvador destroyed 27 percent of GDP and losses from flooding in Bangladesh have resulted in losses as high as 17

---

8. International reinsurers include Munich Re, Swiss Re, Lloyds, Berkshire Hathaway, and Axa Re.

percent of GDP.[9] The 2004 tsunami in the Indian Ocean has tragically under-scored the vulnerabilities in Asia.

A number of countries must deal with natural disasters relatively regu-larly, including Turkey, the Philippines, India, and Bangladesh. Yet, disaster coverage in emerging markets is limited by both low income and the rela-tively underdeveloped state of their insurance industries, which makes it dif-ficult to transfer risk to the international insurers. As a result, because risks (and thus costs) cannot be spread internationally, governments in emerging markets are unlikely to engage in ex ante risk management. They respond to natural disasters after the fact, relying on emergency funding and grants from donors and charitable organizations, although such Good Samaritan alternatives are not as effective as ex ante hazard-risk management.

Colombia, Turkey, and more recently Singapore provide best-practice examples of catastrophic earthquake insurance programs, while Romania, where earthquake risk is present but less serious, provides an example of insurers offering a variety of "package plans," including property insur-ance, mortgage life insurance (see box 4.2), and earthquake insurance. Other countries, such as Iran, are in the process of developing plans for disaster insurance programs, often with the assistance of the World Bank and other donors.

Emerging economies have much more work to do in developing disaster-coverage insurance products, in order to reduce long-term losses and recon-struction costs. In countries with high vulnerability to huge catastrophic events, there is a legitimate role for government to act as insurer of last resort. Care must be taken, however, to minimize the moral hazard inherent in government insurance. The cost for commercial insurers of keeping suf-ficient reserves ready and liquid would lead to huge sums in low-yield prod-ucts, the opportunity cost of which would be charged to their customers. In Turkey, disaster insurance is affordable because of adequate scale and because capital costs are reduced by the government's backup guarantee against catastrophe.

---

9. Gurenko and Lester 2004.

Box 4.2. Examples of Property and Disaster Insurance

Turkey. Turkey provides a good case study of both the positive effects of policy development and the problems initially caused by limited mortgage and insurance markets. In 1999, only 2 percent of households in Turkey had property insurance. The Turkish Catastrophe Insurance Pool, a risk-sharing arrangement among commercial insurers, the government, and the World Bank, was launched in 2000, following the devastating earthquake in the Marmara Sea in 1999. As of early 2006, penetration for earthquake insurance had risen to 18 percent—and over 13 million houses are covered—making Turkey second only to Colombia in terms of penetration.* Commercial insurers in Turkey write the earthquake policies but do not cover the risk; rather, most of the risk is passed on to international reinsurers, although Turkish insurers can provide additional coverage in excess of that offered by the pool.

During its development, the design of the Turkish Catastrophe Insurance Pool became a political issue: whether or not to make the insurance mandatory. The decision was taken to make coverage mandatory, but problems remain in enforcing this regulation. Turkey does not insure properties worth less than $5,000. Insurance is concentrated in Istanbul and Ankara, and the insurance markets in these cities are competitive. Penetration, however, varies widely— from 8 percent to 26 percent in different geographic areas. In addition, the renewal rate is only 33 percent, which the Turkish Catastrophe Insurance Pool intends to improve.

Colombia. Mortgage lenders in Colombia require both property and earthquake insurance; 30 percent of households are covered—a major exception to the low penetration in other emerging markets. In contrast with Turkey, Colombia's earthquake program is entirely commercial; policies are sold to reinsurers as in Turkey but there is no government disaster pool. The law requires that lenders contract with licensed insurance companies to cover assets.

(continued)

---

* Also, see Ozay 2006 (available at http://www.ceemortgagefinance.org/). Ferhan Ozay is Executive Vice President of Garanti Sigorta A.S., the insurance company that recently won the right to manage the Turkish Catastrophe Insurance Pool via competitive bidding.

Box 4.2. Examples of Property and Disaster Insurance *(continued)*

Overall risk in Colombia is covered via two types of protection. First, life coverage is included as part of the insurance that covers the mortgage debt. Life policies with coverage for death and permanent incapacity correspond in their value to the outstanding balance of the mortgage, which is periodically updated. Second, earthquake insurance is generally an annex to a fire insurance policy, corresponding in value to the "destructible" portion of the property, determined by the average cost of construction of similar structures in the area where the insured asset is located. At the discretion of the debtor, it is possible to take additional coverage, for example, for explosion, terrorism, water damage, and flood. In practice, insured households prefer to take complete coverage.

Structures are covered under fire and earthquake policies with no restriction unless their insured value exceeds the capacity of the reinsurance, which is automatically contracted (the coverage is automatic once the mortgage credit is authorized by the bank). The life insurance must comply with the terms of the reinsurance contract in terms of the maximum value insured, and considering the age, health condition, and occupation of the debtor (which also determine the premium).

Romania. Several Romanian insurers offer package deals covering property and disaster insurance. The property insurance includes fire and water damage coverage (package A); package B adds supplemental earthquake coverage, and package C adds storms, floods, landslides, riots, and vandalism. Property insurance is mandatory, but the others are not. Premiums are determined by how many packages are to be in effect, and by type of housing and construction.

Title Insurance

Title insurance is insurance against loss from defects in title to real property and from the invalidity or unenforceability of mortgage liens, after a title has been recorded. It is meant to protect an owner's or lender's financial interest in real property against loss due to title defects, liens, or other matters. It will defend against a lawsuit attacking the title as it is insured, or reimburse the insured for the actual loss incurred. Just as lenders require fire insurance to protect their investment, nearly all institutional lenders in the United States also require title insurance to protect their interest in the collateral of loans secured by real estate. The demand for title insurance has been mostly driven by the U.S. secondary-mortgage markets, as a requirement imposed by investors. As with mortgage insurance, the borrower pays the premium and the lender or investor receives the benefit in terms of cost and loss protection. The title insurance industry in the United States is quite profitable because of the accuracy of land registries in most jurisdictions and the widespread requirement for its use (even in cases of mortgage refinancing, new insurance may have to be contracted).

Although now available in many countries, it is principally a product developed in the United States mainly as the result of a comparative deficiency in U.S. land records laws. In most other developed economies, the land registration system sees the government determining in a conclusive way the title ownership and related encumbrances—any error made by the governmental office can lead to monetary compensation, but that aggrieved party usually cannot recover the property. By contrast, most states in the United States record documents without any official determining who owns the title or whether the instruments transferring it are valid, sparing the costs of legally skilled employees. But a third party must determine who owns the title by examining the indexes in the recorder's offices, scrutinizing the instruments to which they refer and making the determination of how they affect the title under applicable law. Title insurers perform these searches and make the determinations of who owns the title and to what interests it is subject. The insurance policies are fairly uniform and the insurers carry, at a minimum, the reserves required by insurance regulation to compensate their policyholders for their valid claims—notably important in large commercial real estate transactions. The policies also require the insurers to pay for the costs of defense of their insured in legal contests over what they have insured.

Title insurance has been introduced by U.S. companies in a number of emerging markets. Stewart Title offers insurance in 45 countries; however, their presence is often restricted to resort areas catering to foreign buyers. First American offers title policies in Asia, Europe, and Latin America.

In many emerging economies, title insurance is not a real prerequisite for developing residential mortgage markets, as lenders express confidence in the ability and performance of the individual attorneys they rely upon to examine title and mortgage documents prior to granting a mortgage loan. They can also rely on the conclusive determination by a government office that the recorded lien cannot be alienated. The product of title insurance may then be perceived as redundant or not worth its costs. A more serious threat sometimes comes from pre-registration issues with delays, costs, and uncertainties related to the transfer of title and granting of a mortgage lien, including the possible failure to register. Title insurance products cannot cope with that risk. The cases where a title is eligible to be registered but is subject to delay in establishing legal title and lien priority protection resulting from slow procedures for completing registration may correspond to an insurable risk, and gap insurance products may be developed during a transition phase until registration-process improvements bear fruits for lenders. Such was the case, for instance, in the late 1990s in Poland, at least in major urban centers such as Warsaw. In response, several private insurance firms began to offer a short-term "gap" insurance product to lenders whereby losses from borrower defaults that might occur during the registration delay period would be covered. The price of the product reportedly has dropped as a result of minimal losses and growing competition, and now costs about 60 basis points of the loan balance annually.

Credit Information Bureaus

The Importance of Credit Information in Mortgage Finance

Worldwide, credit information bureaus, which collect, maintain, and distribute data on borrower credit activities, are a crucial mainstay of underwriting for both consumer and small business loans. Known by a variety of names—for example, credit bureaus in the United States, credit referencing agencies in the United Kingdom, *centrale rischi* in Italy, or *Kreditschutzverband von 1870* (Austrian Credit Bureau) in Austria—credit bureaus are universal in developed economies and well integrated into the financial system as service bureaus for both lenders and borrowers. Increasingly, especially in the last decade, credit bureaus are now operating in many emerging and transition markets, and efforts are under way to develop them in many more. Thus, credit bureaus are now operating in many Latin American countries and in some of the higher-income countries of Asia, the Middle East, and Central and Eastern Europe.

Numerous types of lending depend on credit bureau information, including credit cards, small business loans, and personal loans. Solid credit information is especially important to risk management in mortgage lending. Credit bureau information addresses two of the "three Cs" of mortgage lending— *credit* and *capacity* (while appraisal, of course, upholds the third—*collateral*). Credit bureaus provide important insight into both a borrower's ability to pay, as evidenced by their past and current indebtedness, and willingness to pay, as evidenced by their debt repayment history. In addition, credit bureaus may be able to shed light on the source of down payment. Without the ability to determine whether the down payment has come not from own savings, but is rather a loan from another bank, lenders are at much greater risk than would otherwise be the case.

Credit Bureaus in Developed Markets

In many OECD countries, credit bureaus are sophisticated, automated, fast, and efficient. Three large international credit bureau companies—Trans-Union, Experian, and Equifax—are highly competitive and operate across numerous countries, including the United States and most of Europe. These companies have now also opened credit bureaus in several countries in Latin America, Asia, and the Middle East. In other countries, they have established partnerships and alliances; they may manage the credit information process, but do not own the credit bureau, or may be a joint owner or developer with other private entities or government agencies. These companies also compete for business with large financial-sector clients to serve as database managers and credit-scoring experts. Other credit bureaus also offer international services; Schutzgemeinschaft für Allgemeine Kreditsicherung (German Credit Protection Association; SCHUFA), the German credit registry system, for example, has a regional presence in assisting countries in Central and Eastern Europe (CEE).

Credit bureaus perform a variety of functions, generally serving as the main credit information sources in many countries, and are utilized by a large number of bank and non-bank lenders, as well as by households. They offer their clients credit reports, credit scores, credit-score modeling, and database management and interface, among other products. In the United States, there are also credit-score modeling experts who work with lenders, credit bureaus, and borrowers. Credit scores in the United States are often referred to as FICO scores, named after Fair, Isaac and Company, the company that pioneered the modeling process. FICO scores are fundamental to mortgage loan origination in the United States, and Fair, Isaac is expanding services abroad to emerging and developed markets, including Brazil and Germany, for example (Palla 2000).

The benefits of effective credit bureaus can be substantial. With regard to lenders, for example, one of the large international credit bureau companies claims that its credit information can decrease the proportion of bad loans in a lender's portfolio by 45 percent and credit card default by 40 percent.[10] Some banks are now basing servicing and delinquency strategies on credit scores.

Credit bureaus also offer borrowers and potential borrowers a wide variety of services. First and foremost, of course, persons can obtain (for a fee) their credit reports and credit scores. The bureaus also offer a variety of products to help the customer manage risk and get the best price for his or her credit, given his or her credit profile. Other services include "credit watch" and "score watch," a home valuation service for help in buying or selling, credit management services, a credit advice column, and information on the national distribution of credit scores.

Credit bureaus represent a critical part of a sound infrastructure for housing finance, but their usage should not be seen as a panacea or as a substitute for the many elements of a sound credit underwriting policy. For example, just before the crisis, the average credit score of successive generations of adjustable-rate subprime loans in the United States has been improving between 2005 and 2007, yet the resulting performance of these credit vintages as measured through non-performing loans has been worsening because of other prevailing risk factors like the decline of home prices.

---

10. From the presentation by Experian: "How a Credit Bureau Enhances the Credit Approval and Risk Management Process," by John Hadlow.

Credit Bureaus in Emerging Markets

Credit bureaus have now been established in many emerging markets: Peru, the Czech Republic, Thailand, India, Turkey, Poland, Croatia, Mexico, and El Salvador, to name just a few. Many other efforts are under way, for example, in Kazakhstan, Slovakia, Egypt, Russia, and Indonesia. Other markets have had, or still have, a limited form of credit information, usually managed by the central bank. The central bank, serving as the regulator of the banking sector, collects information on bad debts and defaults, which it will generally share with the banking sector. This activity, in fact, has been the precursor to credit bureau formation in many cases, and central banks have often become supporters or partners in credit bureau efforts. Generally, however, central bank databases have been viewed as inadequate to support effectively an expansion of lending, consumer, and small- and medium-scale enterprise lending, in particular. Although the central bank approach varies from country to country, the following limitations have been repeatedly cited:

- negative-only information, that is, data is gathered only when a loan fails;
- information only from banks, and not from the wide range of other lenders and credit providers, including non-bank financial institutions such as building societies and finance companies, microfinance lenders, utilities, and department stores; and
- data recorded for "large" loans only. The cutoff levels are generally larger than most mortgage and small- and medium-scale enterprise loans would be, so nothing is recorded when these loans failed.

Developing a full-service credit bureau is a long-term process in emerging markets. There are numerous barriers, including the structure of the banking system itself. Where there are a few dominant players, they often resist sharing information. As discussed in box 4.3, the Croatian Credit Bureau had to overcome reluctance by the banks with dominant market positions to join. In addition, there may be restrictive bank secrecy laws and problems establishing unique customer IDs. There is also the problem of cost: developing a bureau is not inexpensive, and potential members may not see that the risk-reduction benefits will ultimately out-

Box 4.3. Croatian Credit Bureau Development: HROK

The Croatian Registry of Credit Obligations (HROK) was championed by the Croatian Banks Association, which had to work diligently to overcome reluctance by banks with a major share of the market to become members. HROK, a private company owned by its member banks, was developed with assistance from TransUnion's internationally utilized systems, combined with European and CEE knowledge and support from CRIF, an international credit reporting service that operates International Institute for Risk, Security and Communication, the main Italian credit bureau. HROK will collect positive and negative data and will begin with banks and with information on numerous types of installment loans, credit cards, credit lines, and factoring; it will later expand to include other credit providers.

Source: Bohacek 2003.

weigh the cost. The Thai Credit Bureau has had to overcome barriers of both cost and lender reluctance.

The Indian credit bureau's history points to the importance of credit bureau information to mortgage lending. HDFC, India's groundbreaking mortgage lender, set up India's first credit information bureau in 2001 in partnership with State Bank of India (India's largest commercial bank), Trans-Union International, and Dun & Bradstreet. The Credit Information Bureau (India) Limited deals with both positive and negative information that is sold to its members. Currently, there are 87 credit grantors. Credit Information Bureau (India) Limited launched the operations of its consumer credit information bureau in April 2004. While the process of populating the database is still under way, the bureau will be useful for HDFC to tap into a larger customer base without compromising on credit quality.

Finally, credit bureau development in emerging markets has generally been taken one step at a time, often beginning only with banks and offering only basic information. Development plans, however, should (and generally do) contemplate expanding membership to multiple credit providers and providing additional and more sophisticated products addressing credit risk, so that a full-service structure is envisioned from the beginning.

What features would a comprehensive credit information service exhibit? This has been widely discussed in countries where credit bureaus have been under development. The issues include the following:

- *Coverage:* Will there be banks only or a wide sweep of lenders?
- *Reciprocity:* Are only those supplying data permitted to purchase data?
- *Ownership:* Will it be private or public or mixed?
- *Management and development:* Do it yourself or use an international company?
- *Data types:* Will both "negative" and "positive" information be covered?
- *Borrower types:* Will they be individuals, small businesses, and companies, with links between them?
- *Data format, standardization, and volume:* What scope is hoped for?
- *Bank secrecy rules and borrower ID issues:* Do they limit scope and operations?
- *Updating and accuracy:* How frequently are the data updated?
- *Consumer protection:* Are legal safeguards in place to enable correcting errors?
- *Modeling:* Will credit scoring ultimately be addressed?
- *Competition and efficiency:* Is the bureau a monopoly and expected to remain one?

Placed against these issues, credit information bureaus, and especially newly formed ones in emerging markets, face ongoing challenges. Comments gleaned from recent experiences in emerging markets (including Poland, Croatia, and Thailand) include the following:

Membership

Information should be collected from all banks, especially the major lenders, and ultimately include all alternative lenders: non-bank financial institutions, retail stores, finance and leasing companies, micro-lenders, utilities, and so forth. Reciprocity is a cardinal principle: only those providing data are permitted to purchase it, and they must have a legitimate purpose in requesting information. Staged development is important: begin with basic products, and then expand into value-added services such as scoring and antifraud. Should participation by lenders be obligatory, and if so, which lenders?

Ownership

Whether a credit bureau should be state-owned or private (a mix of the two), and the extent to which it is user owned, has been one of the most widely debated issues in emerging markets. Although there is no hard-and-fast rule, the majority of credit bureau experts and users worldwide opt in favor of full or majority private ownership. As with the financial sector overall, best practice is often not for the government to provide prudent regulation and a legal framework, but for the private sector to own and manage the credit bureau. Nearly all credit bureaus in the developed world are privately owned (with the notable exceptions of France and China).

Management and Development

Should a country try "do-it-yourself," or buy a black box? The issue is difficult: reinventing the wheel can be as costly in the long run as engaging a seasoned international firm. Another cardinal principle is economic justification. To be successful, the cost of establishing the credit bureau must be justified in terms of reduced risk and improved efficiency. Ongoing management poses similar issues, and emerging markets exhibit a wide range of solutions. As noted, the international credit bureau companies have affiliates in many countries where they do not own the bureaus, and most countries seek their help; they may be under contract to assist in development, and may or may not conduct ongoing management.

Data

Both negative and positive data should be collected—for example, all loan and credit types and amounts, and payment histories. Without this collection, lenders cannot compute capacity to pay and willingness to pay, or consider various "warning signs," such as obtaining many new credit cards. Other data may include public data, such as bankruptcies, pledges of real estate, and existing databases such as those from the central banks. Development of credit scoring capability, or providing banks with the information to do so, will go hand in hand with increased sophistication of the data and the data standardization process.

Consumer Protection

Consumer protection is an important issue that should be an integral part of any credit bureau development, including regulatory oversight, privacy protection, legitimate use criteria, and error corrections. Misinformation and mistakes have proved to be serious issues in the use of credit bureau information, as individuals and others may be wrongly denied loans or offered less advantageous terms than deserved. Individuals should have the right to access their data, to correct mistakes, to know the reason for rejection, and to know who has requested their information; the information must also be secure to fight against identity fraud. This is, however, an often-overlooked area in emerging markets. Credit bureau design should incorporate technological and organizational security and confidentiality. In Croatia, for example, the credit bureau has a control committee that includes both Central Bank and user representatives.[11]

In sum, credit bureaus have the potential to offer significant benefits to lenders, borrowers, and the government. For banks, costs should be reduced through both improved efficiency and reduced losses. Benefits to borrowers include easier access to financing, help in preventing over-indebtedness, and lower rates; bank spreads should fall (at least in a competitive lending environment). Regulators and the economy should benefit from more prudent lending, improved supervision potential, facilitated risk classification, and a reduced moral hazard of good borrowers "paying" for bad borrowers.

---

11. Bohacek 2003.

CHAPTER 5

Enforcement of Mortgage Rights

Loïc Chiquier, Olivier Hassler, and Stephen Butler *

"Mortgage" is a legal device by which a debtor pledges his residence to secure his obligation to the creditor that provides the loan to construct or acquire it. The mortgage is typically a public, registered agreement, and its creation is subject to certain legal formalities. The mortgage pledge is typically an accessory to the credit (it exists only so long as the debt remains unpaid). It is a non-possessory pledge, meaning that despite its existence, the debtor retains legal title to the residence. He or she is entitled to use and occupy the residence until he or she fails to perform his or her obligation, at which time the creditor has a preferred right to evict the debtor, sell the property, and recapture its investment.

The development of mortgage markets depends to a significant extent on how effective the procedures of mortgage enforcement are. In theory, the mortgage device should respond to everyone's interests. It provides the creditor with a preferred position over valuable collateral with long-term market value, while at the same time leaving the title and use of the home with the debtor and closely regulating all enforcement procedures. In practice, in

---

* See Butler 2003 for the report on which this chapter draws.

Table 5.1. Enforcing Mortgage Collateral

Country	Time (months) *
14 EU countries (except for Italy)	4–36 (most countries: less than one year)
Italy	60–84
Mexico	9–30 (average 20 months)
Colombia	28–48
Namibia	6–18
Thailand	12–60
United States	8.4 (average)

Sources: European Mortgage Federation 2002; Moody's Investors Services 2002; Department of Housing and Urban Development 2006; Cardenas 2003; and Calhoun 2005.
* From commencement of mortgage enforcement proceedings to execution of sale for typical cases, notwithstanding the additional time needed to distribute the sale proceeds.

many emerging economies, there is still a strong perception that these rights remain unbalanced in favor of the debtor to the detriment of the creditor, whereas developed markets have reached a better equilibrium through long experience.

This perception of a bias against creditors' rights is valid even though in practice today, lenders use mortgage foreclosure only as a last-resort tool of debt recovery, and consumers in most emerging markets, partly for cultural reasons, would rather prepay their mortgage debt than risk losing their homes and the social stigma of repossession.

Long delays, uncertainties, and, in some cases, a judicial bias against creditors' rights, weaken the collateral value versus the debt, discourage creditors from making more and larger housing loans, or make them seek alternatives to the mortgage that provide less legal protection to debtors. Part of the problem is the reluctance of policy makers and courts to evict citizens from their homes, which may be culturally offensive and politically unpopular. Even though there are few cases of mortgage execution in most emerging economies, efficient execution procedures may be needed to avoid the perception by citizens that repayment has no consequences and convince creditors that they are protected, thereby facilitating the access of housing finance to many more households. As noted by Van Order,[1] "strong foreclosure laws have been absolutely essential to the development of the U.S. secondary

---

1. See Van Order 2003.

market; if you want people to have good housing, you have to be able to take it away from them."

As awareness improves, there are an increasing number of countries implementing reforms to strengthen the effectiveness of their mortgage collateral system. Countries may be assigned to groups according to the amount of time needed to execute a mortgage: (i) the very expedient systems (less than a year, where most developed economies are found), (ii) the rather expedient systems (between one and two years, where many countries that undertook reforms may be found), and (iii) the ineffective systems (still more than two years in many emerging economies).

Does Mortgage Collateral Matter?

Shorter periods for execution and greater certainty in realization of collateral rights can reduce costs and risks, such as lost interest and principal losses from deterioration in the collateral value. Higher resale proceeds should benefit both the creditor and debtor. There is a growing body of empirical evidence that shows that an efficient system of mortgage collateral increases the welfare of society, as lenders make housing loans more accessible (to lower- or informal-income households, and through higher LTV ratios), and credit rates may reflect a lower risk premium, although this effect is not always observed through lower spreads.

The deterrence effect of an effective mortgage-enforcement system also improves the credit culture, as people are more likely to honor their debt obligations if there are significant consequences. On the other hand, banks are hesitant to engage in housing lending if the law says, as it did in Russia for many years following the collapse of the Soviet Union, that a defaulting borrower must be provided with substitute housing or kept as the creditor's tenant under a lease of indefinite term at a state-determined rent.

The expansion of housing lending is also discouraged by any lengthy and cumbersome delays in execution imposed by the courts, which encourage delaying tactics by defaulting debtors and their attorneys. Under such circumstances, the lenders must require significant down payment (that is, lower LTVs) from the borrowers in order to protect themselves. Even once a

Box 5.1. The Crisis of Mortgage Markets in Colombia

Mortgages markets had expanded between 1993 and 1997 through indexed loans mostly made by specialized savings and loan institutions. These credits were indexed on the UPAC (Unidad de Poder Adquisitivo Constante), whose definition has changed from an initial inflation index to a short-term market index. These products were revealed to be complex and hazardous, escalating debt balances and installments,

When market rates rose in 1998, a major portfolio crisis (24 percent nonperforming loans [NPLs] by 2002) aggravated by serious asset-liability mismatch issues was created. The Constitutional Court required the government to convert the portfolio into fixed real rates, which triggered a broader reform of the housing finance system and fiscally costly restructuring efforts (4.5 percent of the GDP). Many lessons may be drawn from this crisis, including the slowness of the judiciary system (delays of more than three years) in processing an impressive number of enforcements requested by mortgage lenders through courts (128,000 cases by mid-2002). Most lenders denounced the bias of courts against debtors, but an aggravating factor against the lenders was the high degree of hazard associated with their loans, coupled with the absence of any adequate credit information system.

court has issued a judgment, the executing officer may find further barriers to the actual sale of the property.

In Thailand, the judicial foreclosure process should take about one year, but cases through courts can take as long as five years because of complex court procedures that permit mortgagors to use legal loopholes to prolong their cases (although simplification has been recently gained through a more expeditious process of court hearings). In Colombia, courts were flooded by thousands of mortgage execution cases, with the process taking between two and four years. In many African countries (Nigeria, Cameroon), several years are needed to complete a forced property sale.

If mortgage enforcement is uncertain, financial regulatory authorities may be reluctant to grant banks regulatory incentives to hold mortgage loans or mortgage securities. An unsupportive legal regime for creditors could also affect the price and marketability of mortgage securities (such as covered bonds or mortgage-backed securities) and make housing finance less afford-able. It could also prevent attractive products such as mortgage default insur-ance from expanding, with adverse impacts again on the accessibility of the housing finance system.

Differences between Legal Systems

The key principles of a modern mortgage system existed in the Roman law, including:

- real property pledged without delivery of possession to the creditor;
- the "accessorial" nature of the mortgage right;
- the right of the creditor to sell pledged property to satisfy the unpaid obligation;
- the right of the debtor to excess proceeds of sale;
- the ranking principle of "first in time, first in right," and other prin-ciples to establish ranking among competing creditors;
- the pledge of present and future rights, as well as corporeal and incor-poreal property; and
- the continuation of the mortgage lien on real estate regardless of transfer of the ownership right.

These features remain the foundation of any mortgage law today, in both common and civil laws countries. Differences that are more important are observed on the cultural attitudes toward credit and indebtedness than on the substantive legal issues. Some minor differences found today include the following:

- In civil law countries, the notary can play a significant role in mort-gage transactions, including creation of the mortgage and enforce-ment through notarial writs of execution without court proceeding. In common law countries, various actors perform these roles, including licensed attorneys and courts.
- In civil law systems, the registration of the mortgage may have "con-stitutive effect" (the registration is necessary to give its legal effect);

however, in most civil law jurisdictions, this condition is required to make the act effective only against third parties.

- Some civil law jurisdictions do not permit a present pledge of property to be acquired by the pledgor in the future, challenging the validity of a mortgage executed prior to registration of the property right.
- In some civil law jurisdictions, a mortgage cannot be made for undefined debts that may arise in the future; however, debts may be defined with precision by formula or otherwise; for example, mortgages securing loans with adjustable interest rates or increasing principal balances may be created.
- Common law and some civil law jurisdictions consider a lease of real property to be a hybrid right that entails some characteristics of both real and personal rights; however, some civil law jurisdictions do not apply the mortgage concept to leases of real property.
- There may be an emphasis among civil law jurisdictions on public auction sale of mortgaged property. Delivery of possession of property to a creditor and alternative methods of sale, including negotiated or brokered sale, is more likely to be found in common law jurisdictions and civil law jurisdictions that have modernized their laws in recent years.

Even these perceived differences have many qualifications. Most systems differ in some respects at the margins, particularly in the procedural rules governing enforcement of mortgage rights. Some research suggests a distinct difference between civil code systems within the French tradition, and common law or civil systems within the Germanic tradition, reflected in long delays to complete mortgage enforcement in the former systems. These long delays are variously attributed to inadequate creditors' rights under laws of bankruptcy, the accumulation of small procedural delays, the slowness and inefficiency of court procedures, and lack of judicial regard for creditors' rights generally.

The importance of an effective system for registering property rights and transactions is critical. The issue of inadequate or inefficient title registration is well known and complex (different systems of property rights; different registration systems; complex technological, administrative, budgetary, and human resources issues; rapid expansion of illegal construction and informal housing settlements, and so forth), and beyond the scope of this inquiry. It should be stressed, however, that in many countries (for example, Egypt), the lack of an efficient and reliable title registration system has been so far the main barrier to greater mortgage lending activity, as registration of real property rights affects secured housing finance at practically every step.[2] Some key concerns with registration systems that have arisen in many emerging markets include the following:

- *Costs of notary certification and registration* (notably if based on the loan amount, leading to extraordinary costs to register and transfer the liens—6–12 percent in different states in India—which also makes mortgage securitization infeasible).
- *Speed of registration.* In most emerging markets, lenders will not release loan proceeds until the mortgage right has actually been registered, and in some cases until the right of the mortgagor to the property title has been registered first.[3]
- *Maintenance of priorities.* Particularly where registration is delayed, the law should provide meticulous procedures for maintaining ranking priorities.
- *Cheap and quick access to title information.* Creditors need to have cheap and efficient access to data on property ownership and encumbrances. In most EU countries, the registration system is electronic even if not always centralized.
- *Mortgage of future acquired property.* In some jurisdictions a mortgage cannot be registered until the debtor's title to the property is itself registered, greatly complicating transactions. In some places, lenders are forced to enter into a tripartite agreement with the buyer and seller of the property. The solution consists in assuring that future acquired property may be the subject of a mortgage, and allowing

---

2. The most important and essential uses of the registration system in mortgage lending are checking that the debtor owns the property and has the right to pledge it, identifying third-party rights to the property, and establishing the creditor's mortgage priority over other creditors.

3. The Russian mortgage law has made it possible for a mortgage to be established by including in the sale contract a provision that the residence is subject to a mortgage in a specified amount in favor of a specified lender, essentially creating a mortgage containing the standard provisions of the mortgage law that becomes effective simultaneously with registration of the contract of sale.

simultaneous registration of a property sale and a purchase money mortgage, simple remedies that a surprising number of emerging markets have not implemented.

- *Incomplete construction.* Some legal systems do not recognize incomplete construction as real property, which cannot then be registered, and therefore a construction loan mortgage cannot be registered until completion. In some cases, the creditor may register a mortgage against the land right and take a separate pledge of the building materials, or ask for a third-party guarantee.

- *Clear provisions on indemnification for registration errors.* Assurances that creditors will be indemnified for errors of the registry can enhance confidence in the registration system and mortgage lending.

Forms of Mortgage and Mortgage Documentation

Alternative Security Devices

In most of the developed world, the *conventional mortgage* is the prevalent legal device in housing finance. Until relatively recently, foreclosure enforcement would require intervention of a court; however, court intervention can be avoided through mortgage by deed (sometimes known as equitable mortgage), lease-purchase contracts, and installment sales contracts. All of these devices leave the property title with the creditor, and enforcement does not entail termination of a property right but enforcement of a simple contract.

The *mortgage by deed* is perhaps the oldest form of mortgage, and entails delivery of a deed—or legal title—to the creditor, subject to the creditor's contractual obligation to return the title when the debt is paid. It is still in use in some emerging markets, but rarely in developed markets. It has a modern equivalent in some U.S. states in the so-called "deed of trust," under which legal title to the property is held by independent trustees having a power to sell the property in the event the borrower fails to meet his obligation, but that device is essentially regulated as a mortgage. An equivalent device— the "*alineacao fiduciaro*" or *trust deed* by default translation—has existed in Brazil since 2001 and has proved to be a much more effective collateral device than the conventional mortgage lien.

Under a *lease-purchase contract*, the property title also remains with the creditor, as the property is leased to the debtor under an agreement, which credits his or her lease payments toward the price of the home and obligates the creditor to convey title upon full payment of the price. This system has developed in Brazil, Russia, Thailand, and Chile, notably for lower-income households that cannot gather the required down payment for a mortgage loan. It is also common through Islamic finance systems (*ijara* contracts). In Russia, it was the main form of housing finance under earlier anti-creditor mortgage laws, but abuses were reported by lenders recapturing the property value in excess of the debt amount and denying lessee or purchasers their accumulated equity.

The similar *installment sale contract*, a device used mostly by housing developers, is an executory contract under which the developer holds legal title, but grants to the purchaser a right of immediate possession of the home and to delivery of the title upon completion after a series of installment payments. This device has been observed on a large scale in most emerging countries such as Brazil or Turkey, where mortgage markets have not been developed through banks, as developers need to commercialize their production.

With each of these alternative devices, the creditor owns the title and avoids the pitfalls of ambiguous collateral laws, delayed foreclosure proceedings, unsympathetic courts, and debtor bankruptcy. The creditor possesses the property as well as any related incomes, without the need for a court judgment. But what makes these devices effective for the creditor reflects their weaknesses from the consumer perspective, as the debtor frequently is deprived of rights to redeem his property or to fully recapture his equity investment, or is burdened with the challenge of taking legal action against the seller in an environment where it is difficult for low-income households to get access to courts and legal assistance. These devices can be regulated to provide debtors with essential protections, but they usually represent a second best to improving the mortgage laws themselves.[4]

---

4. In the United States, most courts would rule that mortgage alternative devices should be treated as mortgages and be subject to the all of the substantive and procedural rules of mortgages.

The Land Charge

An alternative to the mortgage—used in Germany, Sweden, Austria, and several other EU countries—is the land charge. This is not an accessory to a particular obligation, but has an independent existence without regard to whether a debt exists. The land charge is typically registered against the property by the owner and remains in effect until terminated by him or her. Designation of the amount of the charge and the secured party is left to ancillary contracts between the owner and the creditor. The security is easily transferred from creditor to creditor without registration of termination or assignment of the charge (easier refinancing). Moreover, once registered, the land charge maintains its priority regardless of substitution of creditors.

The Mortgage Certificate

Another device is the "mortgage note" or "mortgage certificate," which is essentially a financial instrument transferable by endorsement of the present holder without the need for registration of an assignment of the mortgage in the land register. The mortgage certificate is issued based on a loan agreement and registered mortgage (or a pool of them in practice). The device permits the unregistered current holder of the obligation to prove his or her right to the security under the registered mortgage by establishing a chain of endorsements from the registered holder. This is not characterized as a listed security, but is simply a convenient tool to transfer mortgage loans to mobilize long-term funding (for example, Chilean "mutuos endorsables") for banks and mortgage lending companies to sell their mortgage loans to institutional investors such as insurance companies, which cannot by law originate them). The transfer of the mortgage certificate avoids the time and cost of preparation of legal documents, notary certification, and registration of transfer.

Mortgage Documentation

The conventional mortgage typically entails two legal documents: the loan agreement, or evidence of indebtedness, and the mortgage, though there are quite a few jurisdictions that use a single document incorporating both the loan and mortgage obligations.[5] The use of separate or not agreements is mostly a matter of tradition and convenience.

The standardization of loan documents and ease of transferability are both extremely important in systems that rely on secondary mortgage markets. From the consumer perspective, reducing the legal and registration costs of transactions, as well as providing simple and understandable legal documents, are also important objectives.

Secondary Mortgage Markets

Secondary mortgage markets access capital markets through mortgage bonds or mortgage securities, which are typically collateralized by large pools of individual loans and the mortgages by which the loans are secured. The legal terms of transfer of mortgages can have critical effects on the funding costs, including not only the preparation of legal documentation and registration fees, but also the task of registering assignment documents in each local registry office in which one of the large number of loans securing a mortgage bond or security is registered. The costs and inconvenience of registering transfer documents has induced some secondary market systems to forego registration, assuming certain legal risks in doing so, or to expedite the transfer from a simple list of assigned loans, or reduce the registration fees for transferring purposes. Systems like land charges (for example, Germany) and mortgage certificates can be very beneficial.

Other approaches to lower transaction costs include *central registries*, which track changes in the beneficial ownership of the loans while leaving the registered ownership unchanged, as in Sweden. Similarly, the U.S. Mortgage Electronic Registration System registers a single entity as the nominal legal holder of the mortgage, and this registration remains constant in the local legal registry throughout the term of the loan while actual beneficial ownership is recorded in a centralized database and updated as transfers are made. The Securitization and Reconstruction of Financial Assets and

---

5. Other jurisdictions, such as the United States, may use three separate agreements, depending on the transaction: the loan agreement, promissory note, and mortgage (promissory note is related to legal issues concerning transferability of financial obligations).

Enforcement of Security Interest Ordinance (2002) of India also authorizes a national "central registry" in which mortgage loans may be registered and assigned in bulk to facilitate securitization.

Procedural Issues in Mortgage Enforcement

The devil is in the details as far as procedures for mortgage enforcement are concerned. Mortgage laws differ significantly with respect to the rules of enforcement. Several distinct phases should be considered, each of which may have its own requirements and time constraints: notice of default, period of cure, demand for repayment (acceleration), issuance of the writ, appeal, notice and publication of sale, sale, eviction, and the distribution of proceeds.

Depending upon how each of these phases is addressed by law, time and expense may begin to accumulate, and evasive delaying tactics may be facilitated. There is no simple solution, but each step in the process must be scrutinized to determine whether it adds value, or whether it can be usefully eliminated or improved. If some incremental improvement can be made in each step, the overall reduction in time and costs can perhaps be significant.

What may initially appear as a relative detail may become a formidable barrier. For example, as observed in Tanzania and Uganda, the spousal consent required by law to be obtained by the lender often became a loophole permitting some debtors to get court injunctions against enforcement of their mortgage loans by invoking the existence of an undisclosed spouse— not a difficult feat in countries that recognize polygamy and informal marriages and lack accurate civil records.

Some laws authorize the execution of the mortgage to proceed without court supervision through a "private power of sale" granted to the creditor over the pledged property. When private sale is not permitted, judicial enforcement of mortgage collateral through order of execution typically remains mandatory, and the sale may be supervised by a state official in charge of the execution of judgments. Depending on procedures and appeal options, the court proceedings may be a mere formality or a main cause of delays.

Box 5.2. Judicial Enforcement of Mortgages in West Africa

The countries that belong to the West African Economic and Monetary Union and Communauté Économique et Monétaire de l'Afrique Centrale (Central African Economic and Monetary Community) zones in West Africa are part of the Organisation pour l'Harmonisation en Afrique du Droit des Affaires (Organization for the Harmonization of Business Laws in Africa) Uniform Treaties of 1997 and 1998 (on Securities, Debt Collection, and Execution Measures). These acts established a common basis for the enforcement of a mortgaged property, which must proceed only through the courts. The process is exposed to the ineffectiveness of court system, and plagued by many broader problems. The OHADA Treatise on securities and their enforcement is under way.

The system permits unregistered hidden liens. Enforcement procedures, inspired by a dated system in France, are complex and long. The debtors can pursue delaying tactics (demand conciliation, or object to the process, the date, and conditions of sale by motions and pleadings). The procedures of public auction suffer from a lack of active secondary housing markets. In the case of willful obstruction, delays can easily extend to five years. Yet, although this foreclosure process is difficult and unpredictable, it is an improvement over the old laws, and mortgages work better than other available forms of security. Mortgage is used beyond housing finance, sometimes by banks with the motivation of benefiting from some advantages that the prudential frameworks provide for this type of secured lending. Beyond enforcement, as in so many other emerging markets, another issue is to get registered property titles that can be mortgaged (not only in rural areas where customary rights prevail, but in main cities as well) because of inadequate land use rules and institutional or operational weaknesses that affect the registration offices.

Box 5.3. Judicial Enforcement in Mexico

Federal countries like Mexico show how enforcement procedures may vary. Foreclosure and resale had been costly and difficult for lenders until different states began to improve their civil proceedings. According to a 2002 Moody's report, the timing for enforcing a mortgage would vary between nine and 30 months across Mexico's 32 states (and even longer in a few states, like Chihuahua). Other delays occurred in final eviction, according to the attitude of the courts and the accessibility to public bailiffs. The report stressed differences displayed by the courts in terms of impartiality between debtors and creditors, professional use of their discretionary powers, and capacity to avoid backlogs. Because of these differences, most lenders have been avoiding mortgage lending in some states. Improvements to the legal framework were passed through a legislative package in 2003, which is anticipated to eventually reduce the average expected time to foreclose to less than two years. Nevertheless, the process to register or transfer property remains expensive in many states.

Non-judicial Enforcement

In most countries that permit a private right of sale, the debtor has the right to bring the case before a court to assert defenses against the claim or protest defects in the proceedings. The creditor—or an agent such as a trustee or a notary—may, however, take possession of the property and may be permitted to advertise and sell the property using its own means and methods, subject to some regulations regarding the organization and terms of the sale. In a number of civil law countries, the equivalent of the private power of sale is the writ of execution issued by a notary public, who serves an intermediary to verify the debt and supervise the actual execution sale, including the giving of required notices to the debtor and other interested parties.

Court proceedings are typically recommended by those who believe that courts would better protect the debtor, through, among other things, assuring clear and timely notices to the interested parties and adequate advertising of auction sales, reasonable sale prices, and so forth. Some unspoken premises of proponents of private right of sale regimes have been that banks act

Box 5.4. Non-judicial Enforcement of Mortgage Rights in Croatia

The judicial enforcement of a conventional mortgage can take up to three to five years because of backlogs in the courts. There is, however, a mortgage-by-trust deed device (Fiduciary Transfer of Title, or FTT) that is enforceable out of court by registration of a notary act certifying the occurrence of a default sufficient to terminate the debtor's property interest. The registration of the notarial act is necessary to vest absolute title in the creditor. Then, the creditor can sell the property without court supervision, subject to the usual rules of public sale applicable to any other mortgage sale. At the start, in practice some courts were permitting this form of non-judicial foreclosure, while others were not (based on some ambiguities in the law, the Zagreb land court would not allow registration of the notarial act of execution, referring the case instead to the municipal court). This reaction is not unusual in countries in which power of sale is new, and registrars can be among the main barriers to implementation as they refuse to register titles arising from a creditor's power of sale. Most of the housing portfolio remains secured by third-party personal guarantee loans.

responsibly in making loans and enforcing mortgage rights, that they are non-predatory and lack incentives to exploit the ignorance of borrowers, and that there are few good defenses to enforcement of a mortgage. The recent (2008–2009) events in the U.S. "sub-prime" mortgage market challenge some of those premises insofar as many borrowers may allege that they were duped into taking loans that they did not understand and could not afford by bank agents who had a financial interest in making loans without regard to the borrower's ability to repay. Whether these allegations ultimately are proven true or affect a significant portion of the troubled loans still remains to be seen, but if so this crisis may be an object lesson that the fair use of private rights of sale may depend on underlying mortgage lending practices.

Several countries that take the judicial approach to mortgage enforcement under their civil legal systems have managed to improve their proceedings by providing explicit and detailed guidance on each step of the process, limiting delays and possibilities of abusive appeals, eliminating arbitrary decisions, imposing financial sanctions against delaying tactics (for example, most states in Mexico since the 2002 and 2003 reforms; Namibia; Egypt, through its 2001 Mortgage Law; and soon Turkey, through its revised mortgage law), and creating courts specializing in debt recovery with better-trained judges. For example, Rwanda reactivated in 2004 a fast-track foreclosure procedure (voie parée) with severe time limits on appeals once a judge has agreed to foreclose, and established specialized chambers within the three busiest courts of the country.

Nevertheless, the numerous drawbacks of the judicial approach continue to be stressed by creditors, including long case backlogs, extensive delays based on frivolous motions and continuances of proceedings, and cases of courts displaying a bias toward the interests of debtors. The principle of equitable treatment of individual borrowers is laudable, but may produce adverse effects when courts are incapable of handling the cases expediently, and judges are granted a discretionary power to assess the appropriateness of the proceedings and to grant relief to mortgagors based on extralegal considerations of social justice.

Box 5.5. Non-judicial Enforcement of Mortgage Rights in Sri Lanka

In Sri Lanka, most of the legal system is based on the principles of English common law for commercial matters, but areas of law such as mortgaged property remain under the influence of the Roman-Dutch law. The Mortgage Act and Debt Recovery Act were modified in 1990 so that commercial banks (compared to only a few state banks before) were given the "parate" execution power, to foreclose and sell the property through auction without recourse to courts (after a board decision and press publications). These rights were extended to properties provided by third parties and to syndicated lenders. New questions have related to the extension of "parate" for a securitization special purpose vehicle (SPV). The timing of enforcement has been reduced to five months, but appeals can be processed through courts, resulting in longer delays. The debate is over whether banks have abused these rights, notably in small- and medium-scale enterprise lending (unduly accelerating the liquidation) or used it only as a last-resort solution. The government has been trying to suppress the "parate" for loans below 5 million rupees, which would be a severe blow to housing finance.

Box 5.6. Time in Foreclosure in Power of Sale and Judicial Procedure States in the United States

The United States may serve as a valid laboratory to test the hypothesis that non-judicial enforcement is more efficient than judicial ones, as non-judicial procedures are still not permitted in 20 states. The table below tends to confirm the theory.

Average time in foreclosure in the United States		
System	Number of jurisdictions	Months in foreclosure*
Power of sale	31**	5.1
Judicial enforcement	20***	9

Source: Federal Home Loan Mortgage Corporation 1993.
* Average time to actual sale of the property, without the statutory period for redemption of the property.
** AL, AK, AZ, AR, CA, CO, DC, GA, HI, ID, MA, MI, MN, MS, MO, MT, NC, NH, NV, OK, OR, RI, SD, TN, TX, VA, WA, WV, WI, WY
*** CT, DE, FL, IL, IN, IA, KS, KY, LA, MA, MD, ND, NE, NJ, NM, NY, OH, PA, SC, UT, VT

Box 5.7. Non-judicial Enforcement of Mortgage Rights in India

Different types of mortgage exist in India: (i) the traditional mortgage that is enforceable only through a court decision; (ii) the "legal mortgage" by registered deed, which can include a non-judicial power of sale; and (iii) the "equitable mortgage" by an unregistered deposit of the debtor's certificate of title with the creditor.

Through the Securitization and Reconstruction of Financial Assets and Enforcement of Security Interest Act of 2002, India extended the right of non-judicial enforcement to all forms of security interests and mortgages, provided that the secured creditor is in possession of the original mortgage deed. The act requires notice to the debtor demanding full repayment of the debt, and a 60-day waiting period, in which the debtor may redeem his property. If the debtor fails to meet this obligation, the creditor may possess the property, manage it directly or through an agent, or lease or sell it. Proceeds are held by the creditor in trust and

continued

Box 5.7. Non-judicial Enforcement of Mortgage Rights in India *(continued)*

applied first to the costs of the enforcement action, then to the debt, and finally
to other creditors. This power of sale is available only to the financial institutions
or their agents for their secured lending, and can be used only if the amount
due exceeds 20 percent of the principal amount and interest thereon (to avoid
abuses by lenders of this fast-track debt-recovery mechanism without debt
mitigation efforts). The debtor has 45 days to lodge an appeal with the Debts
Recovery Tribunal, but should then post a bond with the tribunal of 75 percent of
the creditor's claim (dissuasive against delaying tactics) unless a lower amount
is set by the tribunal. A successful appeal to the Debt Recovery Tribunal can
result in return of the property to the debtor and payment of costs and damages.

Four years later, lenders agree that this way is more effective and speed-
ier—under six months—than the traditional way, at least for the small residential mortgage loans, and that creditors may no longer hide behind a slow-
paced judiciary.

Box 5.8. Reforms of Mortgage Rights in Pakistan

In Pakistan, nonperforming assets have been plaguing the banking system,
notably because of an inefficient judicial system for recovering defaulting loans
(encumbered courts). The Financial Institutions Ordinance of 2001 created a
new foreclosure mechanism for the financial institutions to bypass judicial proceedings for mortgage claims. New rules aim to avoid delaying tactics often used
by debtors:

- a defendant debtor may mount a defense only with the permission of
  the court and only on the basis of substantive questions of law or fact;
- if court proceedings last for more than 90 days, the defendant can be
  required to furnish a security to indemnify the creditor;
- appeals of judgments must be made within 30 days and decided
  within 90 days, and execution will not be suspended unless the debtor
  repays; and

(continued)

Box 5.8. Reforms of Mortgage Rights in Pakistan *(continued)*

- if the court determines that objections to the sale are raised for the purpose of delay, it can charge the debtor with a penalty of up to 20 percent of the sale property price (symmetric penalty to the lender if the objections prove to be sustained).

The ordinance enables lenders to directly repossess and sell the property without court intervention, provided that several conditions are met (early notices, sales through public auction, or solicitation of tenders in which the lender may also participate). The police may be called to assist if the borrower does not evacuate. The ordinance specifies the few cases when the court will intervene (if no mortgage existed, or was paid in full, or if the debtor deposits the full amount of the debt as a security).

Some early decisions overrode the initial reluctance of registrars to validate such non-judicial forced sales. Problems come from cases where an ongoing tenancy contract deposits a security in the full amount of the debt. Courts have also been sensitive to debtors' contestation on grounds of insufficient prices of the forced sales. The recommendation made by the Mortgage Finance Advisory Committee has been to insert the notion of "reserve price" in the law, verifiable by independent valuers.

The best choice may depend on the circumstances in each country. For example, in some low-income countries, the judicial system may be plagued by many problems that cannot be solved quickly by mere changes to the laws: limited budgetary resources, excessive backlogs and delays, insufficiently trained and paid staff, and corruption. In such cases, improvements to the laws may be ineffective and out-of-court proceedings may be the only feasible alternative.

In some cases, the enforcement of mortgage collateral appears as more cost efficient, with private powers of sale, and such proceedings can also be designed to adequately protect the interests of debtors. The cases presented in Croatia, India, Sri Lanka, and the United States tend to confirm these views (also, Brazil since 2001, or Ethiopia since 1998). Yet, as noted earlier, significant improvements have also been implemented in judicial proceedings, and some countries, including Sri Lanka and Pakistan, have been facing issues with their attempts to develop non-judicial enforcement mechanisms.

Negotiated versus Auction Sale

Many judicially supervised enforcement procedures require public auction sale. There is a perception that public sale is a transparent procedure that provides greater assurance of obtaining a market price for the property, and allows interested third parties, such as guarantors and junior creditors, to participate and protect their interests.

As the success of the auction sale depends on the level of participation, evidence in developed markets suggests that participation is mostly limited to interested parties and professional property speculators. Auction prices rarely exceed the established starting price, or the amount of the debtor's obligations. In some places, such sales are also viewed as culturally offensive and the auctioned property tainted, lowering the auction value. In many small communities, it may be unacceptable for residents to bid on a neighbor's property, and newcomers may not be welcome in the place of a displaced and publicly humiliated neighbor. Negotiated sale through the intermediation of property brokers may result in higher prices and may be carried with the cooperation of the defaulting mortgagor, allowing him or her to avoid public attention. It should be stressed that the conditions of negotiated sale also can and should be regulated to assure protection of the borrower's interests.[6]

Responsibility for Sale

Laws differ in assigning responsibility for conducting execution sales: by the creditor itself; licensed firms engaged by the creditor; or the court, notaries, and court executives (bailiffs or clerks). Each alternative offers both benefits and problems. Court-supervised auction or sale procedures risk entanglement in court schedules and case backlogs. Even use of notaries and court

---

6. Detailed notices to the debtor and other third parties, preferential purchase rights and rights of first refusal to interested third parties, pricing based on independent appraisal, full accounting, and penalty for sale below reasonable market value.

officers can lead to delays. In some cases, a centralized executive office, often related to the Ministry of Justice, may be charged with the execution of all judgments and attachments, but these offices can be understaffed and underfunded, and become themselves a roadblock to efficient execution. Placing the responsibility on the creditor or professionals hired by the creditor creates the economic incentives to accelerate proceedings, but may create conflicts of interest that require adequate regulation.

Auction Sale Prices

Prices for sale of mortgaged property may be set by legal formula, or may be established by the auction. Forced sales may be inefficient as pricing mechanisms. Starting prices may be unrealistic. A creditor may bid only the amount of its debt, which could be far below the actual value of the property, and property speculators may bid only slightly more than the debt amount. Some mortgage laws require that the starting price for auction be set as a reasonable proportion of independently appraised market value (for example, Egypt 2001 Mortgage Law), and approved by the court or other public official. If this price is not reached, a second auction may be held at which the starting price is reduced, but not below a minimum. If all auctions fail, the creditor may be obligated to take possession of the property at a price established by legal formula.

Automatic reduction of starting prices for second auctions recognizes the inefficiencies of the auction mechanism, and that the creditor needs some surplus in the property to assure payment of costs and expenses of the enforcement procedure, including the costs of property improvement and maintenance. It creates, however, a disincentive to bid at auction sale, particularly for the creditor, since the only penalty for failing to bid at the auction procedure is perhaps a delay of some period in realization of the collateral.

Creditor's Right to Acquire the Mortgaged Property

In most systems, the creditor has the right to acquire the mortgaged property, either directly from the debtor or as a participant in the forced sale. Direct acquisition is a negotiated transaction between the creditor and debtor that results in delivery of title to the creditor in exchange for release of the debt (an efficient alternative to execution when the property value is close or below the debt amount) and results in a waiver of any further claims against the debtor. As a variant, the creditor may also assist the debtor in selling his or her property to a third-party purchaser.[7]

Direct acquisition or assisted sale can have substantial benefits for both sides, by avoiding public exposure, reducing the time and costs for realization of the mortgage collateral, and relieving the debtor of liability for any shortfall. The sale of the property under market conditions is likely to produce a higher price than a forced auction sale, to the benefit of both sides. This is usually permitted by direct negotiation and an arm's-length contract, although abusive transactions should be avoided (for example, by requiring that the debtor be fully informed about the terms of the transaction and have the right to reject it).

Creditors are also typically permitted to participate in a public sale, and their bids are automatically credited with the amount of the debtor's outstanding obligation. In the absence of a starting price, the creditor's bid will equal only the amount of the obligation, and subordinate creditors will bid the sum of their own and all senior obligations. Permitting creditors to participate in sales is sensible, as they may be the only motivated bidder, and creditor participation has no apparent prejudicial effect. This form of acquisition should be distinguished from the arm's-length negotiation described above, which takes place prior to and outside of the forced sale.

Notice, Cure, Rights of Redemption, and Stays of Execution

Most systems of mortgage finance require that prior to enforcement of a mortgage, a demand must be made on the debtor to cure his or her default, and a reasonable period be provided to him or her to do so. This procedure is often set by law as a prerequisite to demanding repayment of the entire

---

7. Some evidence suggests that assisted sale has become the predominant form of execution in the United States. How the recent collapse of housing markets and the explosion of foreclosures has affected that dynamic is not known.

mortgage loan (acceleration of maturity). The time between default and commencing enforcement procedures typically varies from 30 to 120 days. Notice requirements and periods for cure are good practices to be followed by lenders. Interest and other charges should continue to accrue during the cure period, and cure of the default requires payment of all amounts due to the lender at the time, including costs and penalties.

Once the time provided to cure default has been exceeded and the creditor has commenced proceedings, the debtor may still cure his or her default at any time up to actual sale of the property, but in this case only by repaying the entire loan balance and any costs, including attorneys' fees and court costs, incurred by the creditor. A rationale for limiting the debtor's right to reinstate the loan after repayment has been demanded is essentially to prevent a repeated and costly cycle of consecutive defaults and cures.

Some laws, particularly in the United States, provide mandatory rights of redemption even after the completion of the execution sale. During this period, the purchaser at the auction sale is prevented from taking possession of the property while the debtor is given additional time to raise funds to redeem his or her property. This redemption period can range from several months to up to one year. The practice of providing long post execution redemption periods has been criticized for increasing creditor's costs and, therefore, interest rates, threatening deterioration of the property, and decreasing interest in auction sales of property, but as with most issues surrounding enforcement, hard empirical data is scant.

Similar in effect to statutory periods of redemption, some laws or legal systems (for example, Tanzania, Russia) place it within the discretion of the court to grant a stay of execution, so that justice may be done with least harm to both parties if the ultimate remedy is delayed for some period. For example, this step might be taken if the debtor has a realistic chance of overcoming a transitory setback for health or employment reasons. Where such discretion is exercised, interest on the debt continues to accrue, and the debtor remains liable for any other damages caused to the creditor for delay. In systems where there is a bias against the rights of creditors, this type of discretion can lead to unjustified additional delays and should be limited, for example, to cases where the debtor can demonstrate reasonable chances of financial rehabilitation.

The same type of delay can be obtained by exercise of the court's discretion to grant delays and continuations in the proceedings, for one or another (sometimes) dubious reason, such as the unavailability of the debtor's attorney. The frequent rescheduling of proceedings at the discretion of the court can add substantial time to the enforcement proceeding. Abuse of this sort of procedural device should be addressed by law.

Bankruptcy and Other Preferences

In places where modern personal bankruptcy law exists, the filing of a bankruptcy may result in a suspension of proceedings to execute a mortgage against the debtor's property. The main questions are whether the duration of the delay and the mortgage residence is automatically included in the bankruptcy estate.

Many modern bankruptcy laws avoid making bankruptcy a "back door" to depriving the creditor of its right to security. Bankruptcy, however, may subordinate the mortgage lender's rights (from resale proceeds) to other interests like the cost of all legal proceedings and execution of judgments, or unpaid taxes and social debts (health, pension, alimony, and so forth) to employees and family. A good bankruptcy law would include provisions that preserve the mortgage creditor's priority over unsecured creditors by, for example, specifically excluding a mortgaged property from the bankruptcy estate.

Appeals

Frivolous appeals of judgments to higher courts can significantly delay execution on mortgage collateral. One key issue is whether an execution sale may proceed pending appeal, or whether it is delayed until the appeals are completed (years of delays may accompany a suspension). If execution sale is permitted to proceed pending appeal, the rights of the purchaser of the property must be protected by, for example, assuring reimbursement for his costs and reasonable investments in the property.

Various approaches to control abusive appeals today include the following:

- Assure that the elements of the case for collection of the debt and execution of mortgage are simple and clearly defined in the law, and the grounds of appeal limited. This has been the case in Chile through the 1997 Banking Act, where the enforcement of a mortgage must go through a court, but where a defaulting debtor has only 10 days to comply with a payment request through the court before this latter starts the enforcement (usual publication and public auction rules). Debtor's defenses for a five-day period is limited to only a few narrowly defined cases (debt repaid, prescription, action non-applicable to this defendant) grounded by written evidence and credible foundation. An appeal would also not suspend the forced sale procedure.
- Leave the decision to suspend execution pending completion of appeal to the discretion of the court, which should be in the best position to judge whether appeals are unfounded (but if the judiciary system is known to have a strong pro-debtor inclination, it may be necessary to prohibit narrowly defining the grounds for suspension of execution pending appeal).
- Require the debtor to post a bond or other financial undertaking that indemnifies the creditor for any losses that may be incurred during the appeal period, and to make the debtor liable for court costs and attorneys' fees in case his or her appeal is rejected, as implemented as part of broader reforms of the mortgage enforcement in India or Pakistan. The same approach is also reflected in the new mortgage law of Turkey, where execution can be delayed for two to three years by increasing the undertaking that an appealing borrower should deposit from 15 percent to 40 percent of the unpaid debt.

Eviction

Obtaining a judgment or writ of execution is sometimes only a first step, and the actual possession of a vacant property may be another matter. The inability of the creditor to obtain possession of the property in a timely manner may delay execution, increase costs, and perhaps threaten property deterioration. In jurisdictions in which courts or notaries must issue a writ of execution, the writ should include an enforceable order for possession and eviction. Where execution sale is the responsibility of a state or court entity, that entity should be responsible for delivering vacant possession of the property at the time of sale. In cases of non-judicial enforcement, eviction and possession should be carried out at the request of the creditor prior to or contemporaneously with the sale. The least desirable procedure is to place the burden of obtaining possession on the purchaser through a separate court action following the sale. The last resort of public force should remain a feasible option, however unpopular, that any government should be ready to provide, but obtaining assistance of public officials can be difficult in many countries.

Distributions

The last step in the process is the distribution of the proceeds of sale, and this can be a complex procedure. Performance can differ among countries, ranging from practically immediate in some places to up to a year in others. Much may depend upon factors such as whether the order of distribution is subject to approval, by a court or equivalent body, or whether the determination of priorities among competing creditors and other third parties is integrated into the early preparation of the execution sale. For example, in some systems requiring judicial proceedings, the order of distribution must be submitted with the request for judgment, leaving the burden of due diligence on the creditor, who has the greatest incentive to perform it quickly and efficiently. In contrast, where sales proceeds are collected and distributed by court executive agencies, there is often no incentive to accelerate distribution, and sometimes there is incentive to delay distribution if revenues can be earned from the interest rate float on execution proceeds in their accounts.

Alternatives to Mortgage Enforcement

While all systems seek to avoid dispossession or minimize its impact in some ways, the fact remains that a creditor may not be able to recapture its investment without either depriving the debtor of possession or shifting the loan obligation to some other party.

Forbearance

The formal processes for enforcement of a mortgage against a residence are perceived by many experts to be costly and inefficient, and depending on the relationship of the loan amount to the property value (LTV ratio) and the performance of the housing market, may often result in a loss to the creditor. This is true in jurisdictions such as the United States, where LTV ratios are relatively high, as such loans leave the creditor with minimal surplus to protect against declines in housing prices, delays in enforcement, and other potential losses incurred in the mortgage enforcement process. In such cases, attempts at forbearance and active debt mitigation, including payment deferrals and loan restructuring, may be less costly than a rush to enforcement of collateral rights. Losses may be less likely in countries where loan amounts are lower relative to property values.

In the United Kingdom, the search for alternative debt mitigation solutions before foreclosure is treated as a mandatory responsibility of the lender, which is a fair and symmetric treatment, notably as LTVs are high and foreclosure proceedings effective.

Forbearance can take many forms, including extension of maturities, lowered interest rates, and deferral and capitalization of interest payments. Whether forbearance is less costly than realization of collateral rights is an economic calculation that would have to be made in each system, and which may vary over time depending upon the mortgage lending practices, barriers to enforcement, and the dynamics of the housing market.

At another level, however, forbearance, or at least the attempt to find a solution short of enforcement of the mortgage, is viewed in some jurisdictions as a necessary element of fairness and the procedural protections afforded to debtors who are acting in good faith. In the United States and the United Kingdom, for example, the obligation to attempt solutions short of mortgage enforcement is deeply embedded in the practices of the industry, and enforced indirectly by major institutions such as the secondary market agencies, the government's own mortgage insurance program, or the industry association. In no developed market, however, is there currently a legal requirement to forbear or to modify the terms of a loan, and ultimately the terms of any forbearance remain the discretion of the creditor. Even under the current

(2008–2009) foreclosure crisis conditions in the United States, government approaches to forbearance entail financial incentives to lenders—including subsidies covering portions of reduced interest payments and lump sum cash payments to creditors for entering into and completing restructuring discussions with borrowers—rather than enforced forbearance.

Alternatives to Mortgage Collateral

Not all housing lending is mortgage based or microfinance based. There are alternatives to mortgage collateral and eviction as its last-resort consequence. In some societies, other tangible or intangible assets may be attached to the housing loan in an effort either to recover the credit or to discourage default. These approaches may avoid harsh results by shifting the risk and burden of default to other parties that may be more willing to seek accommodation with the debtor. Yet, international experience shows that the impact of these alternative techniques is valuable, but may not be sufficient to substitute for an effective mortgage system in order for a sound housing-finance system to scale up and become accessible.

For example, in most of the formerly socialist societies, all employment was under the control of the state. Thus, garnishment of wages was a direct and effective form of collateral for housing loans; given legal restrictions on foreclosure and eviction, garnishment was in fact relied upon. In other countries, this system remains quite effective for lenders toward public and private employees, at least until the employee loses or changes his or her job. Wage garnishment may be associated with payroll deduction in order to repay the loan, and should be seen as complementing the main mortgage system.

Personal guarantees from related parties represent another form of alternative to mortgage enforcement. They have been extensively used in countries such as India or Croatia, often as a second-best alternative to ineffective systems of mortgage enforcements rather than by a lender's preference. They can be provided by one or more family members, or even by employers. The theory is that the creditor will be compensated by guarantors, who will then have the burden of working out an accommodation with the debtor. The existence of personal guarantors may also be viewed as an incentive for the debtor to repay the loan and avoid opportunistic or strategic defaults.

Box 5.9. France: Guarantees as a Substitute for Mortgages

Another way to use a guarantee as a mortgage substitute is the French *prêt immo-bilier cautionné*, a housing loan guarantee that takes the place of a conventional mortgage. The main issuer of the guarantee is a well-rated financial institution—Credit Logement—which is capitalized by most mortgage lenders and operates independently with certain privileges. This system arose in response to the high costs of creating, registering, and enforcing conventional mortgage liens. Borrowers are charged guarantee fees and annual servicing fees, a portion of which may be returned to the borrower if the loan is repaid on time. The guarantor takes assignment of troubled loans from the insured creditors, and must then decide on the subsequent course of action with respect to the loans, including the possibility of registering and executing ex post a mortgage lien.

In societies such as India, where nonpayment of debt is considered a social embarrassment, communication between the borrower and the guarantors may be as effective as a court threat in producing repayment. This is especially true for loans made by small-scale mutual or cooperative organizations. Of course, personal guarantees only shift risk of default, sometimes onto someone who is no better able to bear it than the debtor, and may have to rely on the volatile evolution of the guarantor's incomes through the many years of the housing loan rather than the more stable value of real collateral. (In most legal systems, the personal guarantors, after honoring their obligations, have the right to execution of the mortgaged property.) In some countries, such as Croatia, the system may have reached its limit when lenders cannot find enough creditworthy guarantors free of debt or other guarantees.

Another remedy may come from a *mortgage default insurance program* (see chapter 13). Such insurers step into the shoes of the insured private creditor and may apply alternative debt-mitigation techniques to debtors. Again, this does not eliminate the risk but shifts the burden to all borrowers and taxpayers (if the fund is public), with the arguably beneficial effect of spreading risk broadly over a wider population.

Box 5.10. Housing Lending in Indonesia

The Indonesian State Savings Bank implemented a "community mortgage loan," which is used by low-income persons working in the informal sector to obtain land and construct housing. This credit is granted not to individuals, but to entire communities, which must first contribute cash or other value, including land, to a restricted fund to evidence discipline and willingness to save. In addition, the borrowers and community members must each make an additional contribution over and above normal loan payments to create a reserve fund against the possibility that certain members of the community may default. If there is no default, the reserve fund remains with the community. Recent reports suggest that this form of community lending has met with limited success.

For example, the U.S. Federal Housing Administration (FHA) for many years has operated a large program of mortgage insurance for low- and moderate-income persons. In most respects, the program operated as any other private sector insurer, and mortgages were frequently enforced against borrowers. Under pressure from stakeholder groups, the agency implemented a program whereby debtors, under threat of forced sale, could petition to have the FHA pay off the creditor and take ownership of the loan for providing forbearance relief to debtors who experienced financial setbacks but had a realistic possibility of financial rehabilitation. Research has suggested that this program has been costly and unsuccessful in ultimately preventing loss of the home.

Common Property Mortgage

Another hybrid approach is to *mortgage a common property* for a loan that is the joint obligation of the property owners. An example would be a mortgage loan made to finance construction of a building owned by a cooperative legal entity, in which each cooperative member holds a legal interest, as well as a personal right to occupy a specific home or space. The individual members benefit from the mortgage loan, but do not pledge individual property as security and may not be personally liable to the creditor for the loan. The individual's obligation to repay the loan is governed by the terms of membership in the entity. If an individual member fails to meet his or her obligations, the creditor continues to receive payment and avoids the need for enforcement of collateral rights. The risk, however, is shifted again to persons who must make their own arrangements with the defaulting party.

Depending upon the size and basis of the cooperative relationship, they may be more willing to seek accommodation than would a private creditor, and at the same time, individual members have greater incentive to meet their obligations. There may be a breaking point, however, and the cooperative mortgage may perhaps subject all members to greater risks than some of them would bear if they had taken their own mortgage loan.

Conventional mortgage techniques applied to commonly owned lands (particularly to lands held by customary property rights) are often less effective than other housing finance techniques such as microfinance and incremental housing development, as it is unlikely that creditors would be willing, or able, to execute on commonly owned and customary lands, and even more unlikely that they would be able to find purchasers for homes and lands that are traditionally occupied by relatives.

Minimizing Enforcement Actions

The most effective way of avoiding mortgage enforcement is to make loans only to good credit risks—that is, credit rationing based on *sound loan underwriting* criteria—and professional servicing, including preventive and active debt mitigation. Unfortunately, this is easier said than done in some emerging economies where credit information systems are underdeveloped, and lenders are dependent on the debtor's own representations (see other chapters of this book).

Another critical and related aspect of mortgage enforcement is *consumer information and education of mortgage borrowers* (see chapter 6), including complete disclosure of the costs of the mortgage loan, and the rights, obligations, and risks of the borrower. Borrowers should be provided with all pertinent information to determine whether they are willing or able to assume the burdens. This is critical, as housing may be the most important investment of the household's life. Some jurisdictions legally require complete disclosure to consumers of the costs, terms, and potential consequences of mortgage borrowing in a simple, transparent, and comparative manner. Good models are available in the EU (the European Standardized Information Sheet is used by most lenders on a voluntary basis). The more complex rules on mortgage-loan disclosure practices in the United States (Truth in Lending Act, Federal Reserve Regulation Z) have been the object of intense debate on their limited impact, notably for subprime mortgage markets.

125-57

EU
USA, selected
Countries

D14 R21
G21 R31 D18
E43 O16

Chapter 6

Consumer Information and Protection

Hans-Joachim Dübel with contributions from Simon Walley

Protecting the consumer of housing finance products has become an increasingly important and debated subject in both developed and emerging markets. One of the special characteristics of housing finance urging intervention is the creation of large financial exposures for the consumer and a burden for him or her to make sizeable payments over extended periods, coupled with the risk of losing his or her primary residence posted as collateral. In addition to this "credit" dimension, housing finance contracts also contain many financial options for the consumer (for example, early repayment) and the lender (for example, assignment or sale of the loan, rate adjustment), whose values are extremely sensitive to a changing market environment and whose outcomes may impose additional risk on the consumer. For these reasons, the "why" of consumer protection is rarely debated today.

The specific goals and approaches of consumer protection are more contentious, however, because of inherent conflicts with other developmental goals. This is already noticeable in the traditional definition of the goal of consumer protection, because it ensures a "fair deal" for consumers while allowing lenders to reach a sufficient return on their invested capital. Seen from a broader financial-sector development perspective, consumer protection often means solving conflicts between market efficiency on the one hand, and market stability and social protection on the other. For instance, the right of a consumer to repay a fixed-rate loan unconditionally conflicts with the goal to offer the lowest-cost fixed-rate loan, because of reinvestment risk for the lender. On the other hand, the ability to afford by young households through credit products with low initial payments may conflict with stability goals when the same product entails a possible future payment shock. It is clear that finding the optimum here is a difficult task.

Considering the varying stages of housing finance development, there can also be no one-size-fits-all strategy of consumer protection. Roles and characteristics of the agents—lenders, developers, courts, local governments—that have to implement any set of rules change, and new agents (for example, brokers) appear. With this environment, the cost-benefit balance of individual rules changes, as do their implementation requirements and the availability of supportive social and economic policies. Finally, there is the risk that rules accumulate without regular review and cutbacks, leading to overregulation or inconsistent regulation.

This section starts by briefly referring to the different interpretations of the consumer that lead to different perspectives of the role of consumer protection, followed by a more precise economic definition of the objectives of consumer protection. The third subsection discusses the canon of the most common consumer protection rules in more detail: a frequently used classification follows the typical loan life cycle and distinguishes between consumer information rules, enabling transparency of loan offers and possibly advice to assist his or her choice, and "material" consumer protection rules governing limits to products and lender covenants, as well as the foreclosure process. The section then proceeds by discussing the costs of consumer protection, including the role of different delivery mechanisms, which can range from financial literacy programs over industry self-regulatory mechanisms to full legislative coverage. It is then asked whether consumer protection must not be seen as a luxury good for emerging markets, and if not, what options there are for economizing the discussed costs. The section ends with conclusions.

Defining the Consumer

Developed Markets

Modern consumer protection law in developed markets is based on two competing concepts of the consumer. The first is where the consumer is considered broadly rational and able to make informed decisions and choices in their own interest based on the information available to them. In this school of thought, it is deemed sufficient to protect the consumer by ensuring adequacy of information and antidiscrimination.[1] The second approach is much more recent and contends that some negative contract outcomes, especially if related to the most vulnerable in society, matter for society as a whole. Even if full transparency exists and contracts are negotiated fairly, the weight of negative individual outcomes may justify the costs of intervention into contractual freedom.[2]

The tendency has been for Anglo-Saxon countries to adhere to the former, and for continental European and socialist countries to adhere to the latter concept. The fault lines, however, generally go through individual societies, where they traditionally fuel debate between consumer and lender groups and liberal and conservative political camps. Intervention into contractual freedom—so-called "material" consumer protection—as a result has remained hotly contested. The consensus area is consumer information and empowerment in contract negotiations, which is seen as a necessary, although not sufficient, element of consumer law by both schools.

Emerging Markets

From a historical perspective, the transfer of law from Western and socialist country sources to emerging markets has led to a certain level of diffusion of these competing concepts worldwide.[3] For example, recipient countries

---

1. The Utilitarian school of thought has roots in the Age of Enlightenment and can be traced to Bentham (1789), who also wrote one of the first critiques of usury laws.
2. See Rawls 1971. Antecedents go back to the Greeks (Aristotle), the Christian canonic interest prohibition, and Marx.
3. This economic school was developed inter alia at the World Bank. See LaPorta, Lopez de Silanes, Shleifer, and Vishay 1998, and Djankov, La Porta, Lopez de Silanes, and Shleifer 2002

of Western law in Latin America, the Commonwealth, and parts of Asia can be shown to have adopted creditor- or borrower-friendly contract laws and judicial processes, depending on the origin of law.[4]

In addition, there has been increasing transfer of law between emerging markets. A prominent example is Islamic finance rules, which combine the religious and social perspectives of the consumer in their respective societies, justifying significant intervention into contractual freedom, including into the admissibility of charging interest. Formal Islamic finance rules, in their various forms today, span the entire Islamic world and, through the introduction of Islamic finance products for immigrants, have started to influence consumer-lender relations in Western Europe.

A specific problem of many emerging markets is the multiplicity of various layers of law implemented over time—for instance, today's set of consumer protection rules in Egypt are an amalgam of Western (French, British), Ottoman, socialist, and Islamic rules. Many countries struggle to create their own legal "identity" from their complicated legacy.

Consumer Protection Objectives

Two key objectives can be distinguished for an effective framework that consumer protection should aim to achieve.

The first is *improved efficiency* of the mortgage market, especially by addressing the market failures that lead to reduced levels of competition, high costs of loans, or the exclusion of consumers. The most important failures arise from information asymmetries between lenders and consumers; the heterogeneity of consumers with respect to their financial education, gender, race, and other factors; and transaction-cost asymmetries, which limit the ability of consumers to react to lender action; for example, to an interest rate increase.

The second goal is *market stability* and *social protection*: stability in the sense of avoiding over-indebtedness of borrowers, with its consequences

---

for key papers.

4. Djankov, La Porta, Lopez de Silanes, and Shleifer (2002) show, for example, that Latin American courts in their French law tradition have been more protective of rental tenants than their Asian and African counterparts, which were inspired by English law, but less so than courts in former socialist countries.

for the solvency of lenders and systemic risk for the financial sector. Social protection is relevant in the sense of mitigating individual hardship caused by mortgage market outcomes; for example, a personal insolvency or the loss of the most important pension asset of the consumer, his or her personal home, and, more broadly, the consumer's vulnerability to market shocks.

Information Asymmetry between Lenders and Consumers

The mortgage market is a "textbook case for market failure caused by information asymmetry. One party is in the market continuously, the other very infrequently—sometimes only once or twice in a lifetime."5 Market failure due to information asymmetry has been a consensus intervention ground, and mandating disclosure from lenders to consumers a consensus intervention type.[6]

In mortgage finance, for example, the true costs of credit, the character of interest rate adjustment mechanisms, or loan termination conditions may be hidden from the consumer prior to loan closure. The Truth in Lending Act of 1968 in the United States, as a reaction to this, focuses on such disclosures. Roman law countries address the issue in their civil codes and special laws; for example, on disclosure of credit costs and terms.

Information asymmetries are even more pronounced in emerging markets, given that access to information is more constrained—for example, through a greater "digital divide"—and competition may be less active because smaller markets and lenders may have shorter histories. A frequent asymmetry arises if contracts are very complex because of the risk environment; for example, indexed products with ballooning debts that respond to inflation risk and may lead to residual debts for the consumer (see discussion below on Mexico and Brazil).

---

5. Guttentag 2002.
6. Credit market failures resulting from information asymmetry has been a key topic of economic research of the past 25 years. For an overview, see Stiglitz 2000.

Consumer Heterogeneity

Transparency standards do not overcome deficiencies adherent to the consumer's identity that disable him or her from overseeing the implications of closing a contract, limit the rationality of his or her market behavior, or render him or her a more likely a victim of abusive practices. Research in the United States shows that factors such as culture, education, and access to information matter in this regard, and that these factors are regionally concentrated.[7] To the extent that lenders systematically exploit these asymmetries, market failure may be the result. For example, so-called "predatory" lending practices to vulnerable groups may lead to predictably high default rates, ultimately leading to market breakdown because of spiraling costs. The current "subprime" lending default crisis has led to a breakdown for parts of the U.S. mortgage market, especially lending to minorities.

The main approaches to addressing consumer heterogeneity are to force lenders to disregard elements of the identity of the consumer upon underwriting (antidiscrimination), to penalize detrimental advice given by lenders and brokers to consumers under conflict of interest, and to enhance consumer education levels. The United States, which is characterized by both a very deep mortgage market and a great variety of consumers, has the most developed regulations in that regard.

Yet, abusive practices in the subprime market show how large the regulatory gaps still are.[8] Anti-discrimination and conflict-of-interest rules are starting to take hold in Europe, but so far not systematically.[9] Emerging markets still usually lack such standards. Consumers tend to be less educated in financial affairs, although in high-inflation environments, depending on individual education levels, the reverse has also been true.[10]

7. For example, Deng, Pavlov, and Yang (2004) find that borrowers from affluent western Los Angeles both refinance and move quicker than predicted by standard estimation techniques, while those in less affluent areas tend to stay longer than expected with their properties and loans.
8. A typical abusive practice in the U.S. subprime market has been to refinance fixed-rate loans into adjustable-rate loans with low initial "teaser" rates. In subprime, those teaser rates end after one to two years, resulting in a massive payment shock for borrowers as rates adjust to the fully indexed and fully amortizing level. Such refinancings were targeted at financially non-astute borrowers. The United States is now discussing a "suitability" standard in order to eliminate such and other practices.
9. Low, Dübel, and Sebag-Montefiore 2003.
10. For example, Argentinean consumers, hardened by decades of high inflation, are famous for their astuteness in financial management. The country has several daily newspapers dealing

Transaction Cost Asymmetries during the Going Concern

Material consumer protection in mortgage finance largely deals with assigning rights to consumers or limiting lender rights in order to reduce the impact of transactions cost asymmetries. Examples are price discrimination against consumers with seasoned contracts (for example, if loan rates can be unilaterally adjusted by the lender), rights to assign the loan to another lender that might impair the value for the consumer, and high charges or legal mechanisms that lenders may use to block early repayments. The reverse problem may arise, however, when contract law assigns consumer options that exploit lender transactions costs; for example, a consumer right of transferring the mortgage to another property, caps to indemnities on prepayments leading to a loss for the matched-funded lender, or options to delay foreclosure in case of default.

Because of the important cost effects of material consumer protection, approaches in practice have varied greatly. In the United States, the states enforced strong material consumer protection rules until the early 1980s, when federal deregulation overruled them.[11] In the EU, because of the large national differences in contract law the commission until today has not been able to expand the ambit of the Consumer Credit Directive of 1987 to mortgage lending (see box 6.1).[12] Material consumer-protection issues in the area of mortgage finance are also becoming increasingly prevalent because of the surge of consumer-protection legislation in emerging economies in the past decade.

Vulnerability of the Consumer to Market Risks

Mortgage lending overcomes the information asymmetry of a lender about the solvency of a consumer through collateralization, and is therefore an inexpensive form of consumer credit. The downside for the consumer is the cost of pledging the collateral; in the extreme case, the loss of his or her primary residence and most important pension asset. High externality costs

---

exclusively with investment and personal finance issues.
11. Saunders and Cohen 2004.
12. Dübel, Lea, and Welter 1997.

Box 6.1. "High" and "Low" Levels of Consumer Protection—The Clash of Approaches in Europe

Within the EU, there is considerable diversity of consumer protection regulation in mortgage lending. Among the larger nations, France has traditionally regulated material consumer protection issues more in-depth and in favor of the consumer than Germany and the United Kingdom. The Consumer Credit Directive of 1987 gave the starting signal for the creation of EU–wide minimum standards, to be eventually imposed on mortgage finance. From the beginning, it was subject to strong controversy:

First, even a low common minimum was not easy to find, because of strong historic differences in mortgage market practices. The most prominent examples were annual percentage rate (APR), early repayment, and rescission. A common APR definition was found to be problematic even for a majority of European products, in particular the dominating variable-rate products. German lenders objected to a universal prepayment option for fixed-rate mortgages in order to legally protect their matched-funding mechanism, Pfandbrief. Danish lenders refused to accept a rescission period because their regulation would not allow them to take pipeline risk.

Secondly, the proposed EU approach of minimum harmonization left room for countries with "higher" levels of national consumer protection to adopt stricter regulations. This meant that national regulators could use, and in fact do use, consumer protection as a trade barrier against foreign entry. For example, France, which limits prepayment penalties, could block German or British mortgage products coming with higher prepayment penalties. Germany, which effectively bans indexed products, could block most Spanish or Portuguese products.

The lesson from the European debate is that idiosyncratic market practices require considerable attention in law formulation and tend to lower the regulatory minimum unless they converge through competitive forces. Regional mortgage markets are also almost impossible to create without a strong political unifying force. Maximum harmonization could be a solution—that is, a positive-definition consumer law imposing deregulation on some members. The United States has historically followed such an approach by enforcing product standardization through the secondary mortgage market and federally regulating state law—so far with mixed results (see box 6.4).

for society may be the result if economic shocks—for instance, large house-price cycles or interest rate increases—force many consumers simultaneously into default. In developed markets, public housing and pension safety nets provide such defaulting consumers with a minimum of tenure and old-age retirement income security. In emerging markets, where shocks also tend to be more frequent and severe, absent sufficient safety nets, defaulting consumers are often left on their own.

Material consumer-protection standards, primarily concerned with the going concern, usually assign the costs of such cyclical or catastrophic risk to lenders, consumers, or government in an unsystematic fashion. Even in the United States, with well-developed foreclosure laws and strict practices, foreclosure prevention that might lead to loss minimization for both consumer and lender is still nascent. This is also typical for many Commonwealth countries. In France, by contrast, foreclosure prevention is the focus of an elaborate piece of consumer protection legislation, the *Loi Neiertz*. In Latin American markets, which experienced large interest-rate and house-price shocks, the lack of foreclosure prevention, inexperienced regulators combined with insufficient housing and pension safety nets has induced courts to intervene systematically on behalf of consumers, often resulting in significant losses for lenders. Where foreclosure was easily possible, in contrast, excessive forced sales rather than foreclosure prevention have worsened house-price declines (for example, in parts of Mexico during the Tequila crisis).

Protecting the Consumer through the Loan Life Cycle

Before Borrowing

DISCLOSURE

The U.S. Truth in Lending Act requires lenders to disclose to consumers for closed-end loans, among other things, the finance charge, the annual percentage rate (APR), the amount financed, and the total of all payments. Enhanced disclosure is required in other laws for "federally related mortgage loans"[13] and subprime mortgage loans with very high interest rates.[14] Disclosures in the United States have been criticized as cumulative and confusing, overreaching the information-absorption capacity of the consumer.[15] The European Union Home Loan Code, adopted in 2002, remedies some of the information overload by mandating a single information sheet for consumers; however, national regulations in Europe often go into much greater detail and cause similar problems as in the United States.

In emerging markets, unfair marketing is still a widespread problem, as lenders in most jurisdictions are not forced to disclose loan costs systematically. Recent regulations have started to address the issue. Box 6.7 reports the Mexican example.

Accurate loan disclosure is a sine qua non in mortgage finance. In particular, in countries where financial literacy is still not widespread, information given should be simple and understandable, and if possible it should be explained by independent parties to consumers (for example, consumer groups).

ANNUAL PERCENTAGE RATE OF CHARGE

The APR is central to the concept of disclosure. Box 6.2 discusses the conceptual problems of capturing different mortgage products in a single APR computation, which is impractical. Comparing APRs makes sense only for products with comparable terms and options content.[16] Choosing the right APR ambit is also pivotal: the U.S. Federal Reserve, which implements the Truth in Lending Act, requires interest, fees, points, and private mortgage insurance (if required by the lender) to be included in the APR. Title insurance, document preparation, appraisal fees, and other mandatory fees, how-

---

13. Real Estate Settlement Procedure Act. Most middle-income and practically all low-income mortgage loans in the United States are guaranteed by the federal government agencies or government-sponsored enterprises.
14. Home Ownership and Equity Protection Act; see discussion in box 6.5.
15. Guttentag (2002) and U.S. HUD and Treasury (2000) criticize the dual responsibility of Federal Reserve System (Truth in Lending Act, Home Ownership and Equity Protection Act) and HUD (Real Estate Settlement Procedure Act).
16. Guttentag (2002) proposes to compute APRs over multiple terms or over loan terms as specified by the borrower.

Box 6.2. Defining the Annual Percentage Rate of Charge

The APR is defined as the internal rate of return of future payment streams from consumers to lenders. Such a computation assumes a constant duration of the loan and invariability of loan terms over time. Unfortunately, since mortgages are pre-payable and often priced at variable rates or rates reset periodically, both assumptions are violated as a rule, rather than an exception.

Consider a standard variable rate loan with a two-year initial period of low fixed rates ("teaser" rates). This is the most frequent loan product in the United Kingdom, and gaining in popularity in the United States ("hybrid" ARM). For such a product, taking the APR over the fixed-rate period is misleading—it is known in advance that rates will not remain constant. Even the concept of an "initial" APR—comparing the teaser rates only—is misleading, since the lender can "claw back" any discount by overcharging in the variable rate loan phase. In contrast, so-called "tracker" ARMs following an interest rate index with constant contractual spreads can be compared with relative ease.

As a second example, compare the typical U.S. product, a 30-year pre-payable fixed-rate loan, with the typical German product, a 10-year non-pre-payable loan. Since U.S. borrowers frequently exercise the prepayment option, the effective duration of a U.S. loan is between four and seven years, after which a new loan is closed. In effect, the German loan has therefore a longer duration than the U.S. loan; closing costs will be amortized over longer periods, which leads to distorted APR results.

The conclusion is that APR comparisons in mortgage finance only make sense if the option characteristics of mortgage contracts—both on lender and borrower side—are taken into consideration.

ever, are excluded. In France, all third-party costs required by the lender need to be included in the APR.[17]

Despite the problems, an appropriately formulated APR may capture the main features of mortgage loans, which is essential to secure fair competi-

---

17. Guttentag (2002) suggests adopting broad definitions of all mandatory fees. Dübel, Lea, and Welter (1997) propose for Europe to operate with both broad (all mandatory fees) and narrow (lender costs) definitions.

tion. It is therefore central to mortgage market development. In emerging markets, slow amortization patterns are very popular in order to overcome initial affordability constraints. This invites abuse through high fee incomes spread over the life of the loan. Without an APR, very long-term loans thus appear cheap on rates, although they are in reality expensive.

CONSUMER LITERACY AND COUNSELING

According to U.S. government analysis,[18] financial illiteracy of consumers is at the core of consumer vulnerability to abusive lending practices. Some jurisdictions (for example, the United Kingdom) are therefore passing "responsible lending" rules forcing lenders to ask whether mortgage loans are suited for the consumer.

Lenders, however, face a conflict of interest when being explicitly mandated to perform counseling. The U.S. Housing and Urban Development Department (HUD) has therefore developed a Housing Counseling Assistance Program, under which brokers, housing agencies, charities, and consumer groups are certified and partially funded as counselors. Pre-borrowing counseling, in particular, is mandatory for loans to low-income borrowers that are eligible for Federal Housing Administration (FHA) public loan insurance. Similar certification initiatives exist in the broader market to secure absence of conflict of interest of brokers.[19]

Moreover, in many developed countries, an infrastructure of consumer groups provides counseling. Funding varies from public grants and endowments to consumer journal sales and service charges. Financial regulators or public consumer offices also provide online guides and references to counseling.[20] Consumer agencies, public commissions, and other bodies furthering literacy and counseling are quickly developing in emerging markets; for example, in Mexico (see box 6.7), Poland, or Korea.[21]

Prior to formulating regulations, it seems advisable to clearly analyze the conflict-of-interest situation. Tight lender regulations may be less produc-

---

18. U.S. HUD and Treasury 2000.
19. For example, the Upfront Mortgage Broker certification system.
20. For example, the British Financial Services Authority and the U.S. Federal Reserve System.
21. For a listing of agencies, see http://www.consumerworld.org.

tive than strategies to develop independent counseling agents, including an endowment with sufficient funding.

The Loan Offer and Closing

COOLING OFF

Regulations in developed markets generally allow for cooling-off periods of between three (United States) and 14 days (France, Germany), during which the consumer has the right to unwind the contract. The period is extended in cases where certain selling practices, for example, door-to-door, leave consumers little time to reflect on their decision. Cooling off may be a problem for mortgage lenders, if pipeline risk—the market risk taken by holding a closed, but not yet refinanced, loan—is high.

In emerging markets, a conflict may arise from a greater need for the consumer to reflect on his or her borrowing decision, especially if there is poor access to information and greater market risk for the lender. This would speak in favor of greater emphasis put on information and counseling, and curbing selling methods that rely on spontaneous decisions, such as door-to-door selling.

CIRCUMVENTION OF APR AND RISK OF OVER-INDEBTEDNESS THROUGH CROSS-SELLING

Cross-selling of mortgages with other finance products, most notably insurance, may lead to the circumvention of APR rules and conflict of interest of lenders between serving the consumer and adding income from a third source. The requirements for and length of mortgage insurance coverage is a highly contested issue in the United States. Kickbacks and referral fees to originators have been put under threat of criminal penalty by the Real Estate Settlement Procedure Act for "federally related mortgages." In countries that allow tax deductibility of both mortgage interest payments and insurance premia or contractual savings contributions, endowment mortgages paid down by life insurance or mutual funds are popular. If nonperforming, these instruments carry the risk of leaving consumers with residual debt.

Cross-selling poses a certain risk in fast-growing emerging markets that have weak or no APR frameworks and favor indebtedness through mortgage interest deductibility. Incentive structures should be set so as not to artificially favor indebtedness; for example, through leverage-neutral taxation. Broad APR definitions are needed to enable the consumer to capture the cost effects of cross-selling.

DISCRIMINATION AND PREDATORY LENDING

The U.S. Equal Credit Opportunity Act bars discrimination based on age, gender, marital status, race, color, religion, and national origin. In addition, U.S. federal agencies and government-sponsored enterprises are held to promote lending to underserved groups.[22] Similar policy instruments exist in the United Kingdom, but are still in their infancy in the rest of Europe. The "reverse redlining" problem lending to borrowers without regard to their ability to repay at exorbitant interest rates has been related to the deregulation of the U.S. mortgage market. Box 6.5 describes the ongoing struggle to find a balanced regulatory framework in this area.

In many emerging markets, regional and social heterogeneity is high, and so is lender redlining. Examples are multiethnic states (for example, South Africa and Iran) or states with high income inequality (for example, Brazil and India), or both. South Africa had passed antidiscrimination rules for mortgage lending in the early 1990s; however, real progress to greater downmarket penetration required the gradual emergence of new lender groups specializing in low-income lending.

Some emerging markets also operate public banks that distribute loans at highly favorable terms. Anecdotal evidence would suggest that this circumstance has favored requests for kickbacks by bank officials. Such situations can be resolved to the extent that the incentive for kickbacks, subsidies, is weakened, or penalties are increased. While there is no immediate predatory

---

22. These policies have not always been effective, as the recent almost-complete substitution of U.S. federally insured fixed-rate lending (FHA, variable annuity) through mostly adjustable-rate private-sector subprime lending demonstrates.

Box 6.3. Prepayment Indemnities—How Much is Too Much?

Fixed-rate lending may all but disappear (Spain) or become considerably more expensive (Denmark, United States) if prepayment indemnities are not practiced, capped at marginal levels, or even banned by consumer protection rules.

But even the most lender-friendly regulations (Germany) limit yield maintenance prepayment indemnities to a period of 10 years—a wholly arbitrary figure—to avoid very large amounts. Moreover, should the calculation of yield maintenance be allowed to include the lost future income of the lender from the loan, which, if not charged, without doubt would raise the costs of future lending? What should the policy be in "hardship" cases (for example, a forced move, divorce and so forth)? Finally, should the lender be required to disburse reinvestment gains that may arise if a borrower prepays during an interest rate rise?

The solution to some of these problems may be found in technology; for example, Danish non-callable mortgages can be prepaid through delivery of mortgage bonds, which means automatic disbursement of reinvestment gains and disregard of lost future lender income. In any case, solutions will require an informed economic judgment balancing the interest of lenders and consumers.

lending threat for emerging markets, excessive debt service burdens often arise with high levels of inflation, especially if inappropriate loan instruments are used.[23]

The Ongoing Concern

BACK-BOOK PRICE DISCRIMINATION

Overcharging of consumers in seasoned contracts is a frequent problem in markets characterized by unilateral reviewable and short-term FRMs. These products are still typical for most developed markets. There is evidence that seasoned borrowers of U.K. standard variable rate loans and German reset

---

23. For example, as a result of the so-called tilt effect of fixed-rate loans under high inflation, typical initial debt-to-income ratios in Iran by loan closing approach 50 percent.

fixed-rate mortgage loans are charged 50–150 basis points more than new borrowers upon rate adjustment.[24] Absent a fixed-rate market, contract terms are frequently unilaterally reviewable in emerging markets, especially in the Commonwealth countries that are dominated by the British thrift tradition, and in Arab countries.

Techniques to address price discrimination include the introduction of long-term fixed-rate mortgages (United States, Denmark), the specification of pricing benchmarks for short-term FRMs (Thailand, Canada), and mandatory linkage of adjustable or short-term fixed-rate contracts also to external benchmarks (France, Spain, Mexico). Benchmark provision for mortgage lending usually requires the active support of the Central Bank.

EARLY REPAYMENT

Consumers in developed markets enjoy a universal right of prepayment.[25] The value of that right, however, is frequently neutralized through indemnities in order to protect funding instruments. The United States liberalized the charging of indemnities in the 1980s; however, the purchasing practice of the federal agencies in the secondary mortgage market marginalized loans carrying them. In Europe, regulations vary between strict limits (France) and indemnities that allow the lender to recover his or her financial damage (Germany, Sweden). In some jurisdictions, court practice has eroded their amount (United Kingdom, Netherlands). Box 6.3 describes the problems of defining a consistent regulation.

Fixed-rate lending in emerging markets almost invariably carries legal ambiguity about early repayment, which raises the risk of lender reinvestment loss once inflation and interest rates fall and prepayments occur. Examples are Russia and Iran, where loan rates are fixed in local currency over the long maturities (15–20 years). Because of the potential scale of losses, lenders are tempted to block prepayments in such situations, which may force consumers to seek court arbitration.

---

24. See Low, Dübel, and Sebag-Montefiore 2003.
25. An exception is Germany, which allows legal exclusion of prepayments in cases when these are primarily motivated by financial considerations of the consumers.

It seems advisable for emerging markets to aim at a basic, yet funda-mentally complete, set of fixed-rate contracts with and without prepayment protections. In the latter case, the consumer would save the option premia while having to pay an indemnity at prepayment, for instance for loans with rates fixed up to about five years. The Danish mortgage market holds a good example for the coexistence of these products.

INTEREST RATE AND EXCHANGE RATE RISK

Mirroring the previous two issues, excessive debt service arising in interest-, inflation-index-, or exchange rate-linked mortgage contracts has been a sub-ject of interventions on behalf of consumers. Indexation schemes are fre-quently pegged to short-term market rates, which tend to be highly volatile. Exchange rate risk may render seemingly cheap fixed-rate loans that are denominated in foreign currencies highly expensive after a realization. Both issues are particular virulent in emerging markets. Recent court orders ruling in favor of consumers, when large interest-rate or exchange-rate shocks occurred, have been recorded, for example, in Colombia[26] and Argentina (see box 6.4).The conclusion from those cases would be to focus on pricing benchmarks that are good measures of long-term capital costs.[27] Foreign-exchange risk in mortgage contracts should ideally be avoided, unless pro-tective hedges or caps are available to the consumer or consumers receive incomes in foreign exchange.

Usury regulations are without doubt the oldest material consumer-protection instrument.[28] Usury rates are not determined a priori in most European legislations and the burden of determination of abusive practices is laid on the courts. Where rate formulations exist, they define a threshold as

26. In Colombia, the default crisis of the early 2000s was linked to a large real shock on interest rates. This triggered a judgment by the Constitutional Court that ruled that the variable mort-gage rate index used by the housing finance institutions (the UPAC), which was based on average nominal interest-rate levels, was invalid and that an inflation-based index should have been consistently used. This forced the government to refund borrowers for payments made in excess of the inflation-based index.
27. This would be measures of long-term interest or inflation rates, which can be derived from market signals. An example would be the Brazilian *Tasa Referencia* (or reference rate), a forward-rate measure of future interest rates.
28. The canonic prohibition of taking interest was lifted in Europe only in the 16th century. Until the 20th century, usury ceilings were mostly the only element of material consumer protection.

Box 6.4. Foreign Currency Mortgages—Low Rates, High Risk

Foreign currency mortgages are an important example of loan products with high future payment-shock potential for consumers, and, by implication, high default risk for the lender. The type of risk is analogous to price-level-adjusted contracts in local currency: foreign currency mortgages imply a periodic adjustment of the outstanding balance in line with the devaluation of the currency. Yet borrower salaries, which are usually paid in local currency, are unlikely to rise smoothly at the pace of devaluation, and in many emerging markets there is risk of shock devaluation as a result of economic or balance-of-payment crisis. To the devaluation risk is often added interest-rate risk in cases where rates in foreign currency have been chosen as adjustable in order to depress initial interest payment further.

Despite these risks, foreign currency mortgages have grown in popularity throughout the world, and particularly so in two regions:

- In Latin America, a large proportion of debt is traditionally dollarized as a result of the legacy of hyperinflation. There is considerable mismatch risk for banks, since loans are even more dollarized than deposits; Peru, for example, has around 70 percent of all its deposits and 75 percent of its loans in dollars, with over 90 percent of mortgage loans in dollars.

- Eastern Europe has also seen high levels of foreign currency lending, with loans being advanced in euros, Swiss francs, or Japanese yen. Although the interest rate differential has fallen in recent years, foreign currency loans remain popular. Poland, Hungary, and Ukraine have all seen high levels of foreign currency loans. In Estonia, foreign currency loans represent 88 percent of total lending.

- Particularly risky for lenders are large shock devaluations after long phases of fixed-exchange rate policies, which encourage indebtedness in foreign currency. In Argentina, as of 2001 the entire mortgage portfolio was denominated in U.S. dollars and financed with U.S. dollar debt. With the breakdown of the fixed-exchange rate policy and the devaluation of the peso—by 75 percent at one point—the

(continued)

Box 6.4. Foreign Currency Mortgages—Low Rates, High Risk *(continued)*

government in early 2002 decided to "pesify" all consumer debts, rather than allow an adjustment of the credit outstanding debt due by borrowers, as contractually agreed.*

Wary of high payment shocks for borrowers, regulators in Poland have responded by taking a stance against further growth in currency lending. A new regulation was put into force in July 2006 that includes a consumer education and awareness initiative. Consumers have to show that they are actively rejecting a domestic currency loan by signing a declaration to this effect. An information sheet with details of the risks of the products being purchased also must be given to the customer. The second strand in the supervisory response is to tighten the underwriting criteria by making banks review the client's creditworthiness based on the higher domestic-currency interest rate only. In addition, the capital requirements for foreign exchange (FX) lending are 20 percent higher, with further changes possibly in the pipeline.

---

* The forced pesification of liabilities (at a different rate) was only carried out, leading to the downgrade of dollar denominated MBS.

a multiple of or markup over the applicable mortgage rate (Germany, France, and Portugal). In Italy, the *average* market rate cannot be exceeded. In the United States, state usury regulations were dismantled by federal deregulation in the early 1980s, but in response to the tide of subprime lending at extremely high rates, are returning. In the United Kingdom, usury limits were repealed in 1818.[29]

Emerging markets feature the whole spectrum of usury regulations, from prohibition of interest in Islamic finance, to regulatory ceilings in French and German law descendents, to relative liberality in the Commonwealth countries. While predatory lending is less of a problem as long as even middle-class households often do not receive loans, there is potential for abusive charges once the markets deepen. Box 6.5 describes the difficulties in addressing this

---

29. Not coincidentally, an early fundamental critique of usury regulations was launched by a Briton, Bentham, as early as 1787.

Box 6.5. Consumer Protection in the United States and the Subprime Market

Consumer protection in the United States has traditionally been the role of the states. In a country with widespread federal interest-rate controls originating in the New Deal of the 1930s, state legislation gave rigidly formulated usury interest-rate ceilings a prominent role.

In January 1980, because of inflation, long-term U.S. Treasury rates exceeded 10 percent for the first time in history, and eventually reached 15 percent in 1981. The resulting mortgage rates of 15 percent, 20 percent, and more brought lenders into conflict with the usury laws. In a sweeping attack on state consumer-protection rules, the Reagan administration launched two federal acts (Depository Institutions Deregulation and Monetary Control Act, Alternative Mortgage Transaction Parity Act): the first overrode state usury ceilings and the second outlawed state material consumer-protection rules such as limits imposed on negative amortization clauses and prepayment penalties.

The deregulation of consumer protection enabled the development of the "subprime" mortgage market, a market that since the mid-1980s at the same time provided credit to high-credit-risk households and became the main playing field for abusive lending practices. According to the joint HUD and Treasury report of 2000, in 1999, the median spread over treasuries in the subprime market was 500 basis points, with 18 percent of borrowers paying a spread higher than 700 basis points. Not surprisingly, default incidence in the subprime market in 2001–2 was on average 15 times higher than in the prime market, with one in every 15 mortgages being in default (Saunders and Cohen 2004). Nevertheless, the market grew to an astounding 20 percent of new originations in 2006 (together with near-prime loans with limited documentation 35 percent of new originations). As of 2006–7, the subprime market spiraled into its second major default crisis within a decade, threatening the stability of the entire U.S. mortgage sector by adding to excess housing supply through a huge number of foreclosures.

Federal efforts in the 1990s had failed to seriously address the undesired consequences of the Reagan deregulations. The 1994, Home Ownership and Equity Protection Act had imposed heightened disclosure requirements just for

(continued)

Box 6.5. Consumer Protection in the United States and the Subprime Market
(*continued*)

extreme loan spreads over treasuries, which applied to only 0.7 percent of loans, and also did not end abusive pricing or contract clauses. The result is that by 2007—starting with North Carolina in 1999—the majority of U.S. states have started re-regulating mortgage lending. The subprime market crisis since 2007 has even raised the likelihood of a federal re-regulation of the sector.

problem in the United States. A particular problem is that loan volumes in emerging markets are often low, while origination and servicing causes high costs, which may push up cost-covering interest rates to very high levels.[30] It seems therefore not advisable to rigidly control interest rates. Alternatively, lenient ceilings could be adopted, allowing for derogations if lenders can demonstrate that their costs are higher.

RESIDUAL DEBT UPON MATURITY

In the interest of minimizing credit risk, mortgage loans should be repaid within their term—ideally before the consumer retires. We have seen above that even with standard products, this constraint is often not properly addressed. Lenders have a profit incentive to minimize amortization in order to retain a maximum base for charging interest. Loans with ballooning outstandings that are adequate in the presence of inflation often entail a heightened risk to generate residual debt. In the United States, such ballooning loans were liberalized in the 1980s. Several European countries, in turn, have put restrictions on such products.

Because of inflation risk, almost all Latin American markets use indexed products that—intentionally—lead to ballooning outstandings, but frequently—unintentionally—end in situations of residual debt at the time of loan maturity. Court rulings have often mandated government or lenders to cancel these debts. While the intended impact has been to protect retired

---

30. This issues is of particular importance for micro-credits, the transaction costs of which are necessarily high relative to the loan amounts.

Box 6.6. The Legacy of Brazil's Old Housing Finance System

Mortgage market development in Latin America has been constrained by a history of high inflation. High inflation carries the temptation to design products that may lead to large residual debts, especially when political intervention on behalf of borrowers comes into play. The main beneficiaries of such intervention have been members of the upper middle class.

From 1984 to 1993, Brazil, under the Sistema Financiera Habitacional (Housing Finance System) practiced dual-indexed mortgages (DIM), a product in which borrower payments and outstandings due to banks are adjusted to inflation by wage and price indices, respectively. Even in its plain vanilla form, the DIM product is subject to delicate stability issues, since too low initial payment rates may lead to failure of the loan to amortize.

In 1985, political pressure exercised by trade and professional groups in Brazil led to the application of several dozen different wage indices for the DIMs, each representing the wage trajectory of an individual profession. Mortgage payments moreover became systematically under-adjusted to inflation in a mixture of attempts to protect the affordability of borrowers in times of sluggish real income growth and distribution of political favors.

By the early 2000s, a typical Brazilian mortgage borrower of the 1980s—in general a high- or upper-middle-income household—had repaid only a fraction of his debt in real terms. Court interventions on behalf of these groups made sure that residual debt at maturity had to be cancelled by the lenders. To avoid lender insolvencies, a government fund—Fundo de Compensação de Variação Salarial (Wage Variation Compensation Fund)—was created, which by 2001 had produced a deficit corresponding to 4 percent of the Brazilian GDP. Fundo de Compensação de Variação Salarial is part of a larger legacy debt of the Sistema Financiera Habitacional that then totaled 10 percent of GDP and continues to rise.

consumers from losing their home, in many cases such intervention ended in distributing regressive benefits to consumers belonging to the upper middle class, who were given most of the real values of their houses for free. Box 6.6 discusses the Brazilian case, which is far from being isolated.

These experiences suggests that, as a rule, those loan instruments should be given priority that safely amortize within the contracted period even if this comes at the expense of slower market penetration. Moreover, lenders should be required to present the consumer binding amortization plans and, if amortization is contingent on external variables, clearly signal the possible risks.

The Back End: Default

AVOIDING FORECLOSURE AND PRE-FORECLOSURE

Avoiding foreclosure and pre-foreclosure is frequently in the interest of both lender and consumer, because of inefficiencies of the judicial foreclosure process. *Loi Neiertz* of 1989 was a formalized attempt to address archaic, but hard to change, judicial foreclosure practices in France: the law defines a formal mediation and counseling process between lender and consumer, in which government plays the role of the mediator. Approximately 90 percent of French default cases are thought to be resolved in such "amicable" solutions (solution amiable).

Even in Anglo-Saxon countries with relatively efficient foreclosure processes,[31] foreclosure avoidance is rising in relevance. During the 1989/90 default crisis, U.K. lenders adopted new strategies to stem the tide of repossessions. Independent arrears counselors were paid by the industry in order to do debt reschedulings and restructurings with over-indebted households. In the United States, after traumatic experiences in the industry downsizing wave of the early 1990s,[32] the public insurers FHA took the lead to develop regulations prescribing loss mitigation procedures, including mandatory debt counseling. Today, even secondary mortgage investors pay servicers premia to avoid foreclosure, for example, through freehanded sales and trading down to smaller houses.

Foreclosure avoidance is still not systematically developed in most emerging markets; however, some of the new consumer legislation has introduced a consumer right for loan restructuring (for example, Malaysia). Con-

---

31. See Butler 2003.
32. Moore (1989) describes foreclosure practices in Flint, Michigan, after the closure of a large car plant.

sidering the great inertia in undertaking court and bankruptcy reform, the introduction of a better-structured foreclosure process is a promising avenue in most jurisdictions for reducing credit losses for lenders while simultaneously protecting the consumer from residual debt.

FORECLOSURE

In Europe and the United States, consumers are protected by the need for the lender to obtain court orders and the right to retrieve any residual value of the house after a forced sale. Often, however, there is less protection against high arrears fees and legal charges that may eliminate any such residual value. More importantly, the auction process through courts is frequently illiquid, follows an antagonistic formalism, and leads to less predictable recovery values than freehanded or lender-supported sales.

Court formalism and inefficiency has unfortunately been a successful Western export product to emerging markets. Djankov et al. (2002) show that Latin American courts are leaders in legal formalism, taking up the French and Spanish traditions. They take significantly longer to evict rental tenants than do courts in African or Asian countries with English law tradition. Courts in former socialist countries are found to be the record holders, often asking lenders to provide substitute housing.

Clearly, inability to enforce efficiently through the courts—and parallel absence of meaningful pre-foreclosure arrangements—is a main reason behind the predominance of lease-purchase contracts in many emerging markets. In Brazil, approximately three-quarters of new housing transactions take place through lease-purchase; in Egypt, the share is approximately 90 percent. In lease-purchase schemes, the housing remains owned by the developer until the last installment. Consumer protection in this area has been notoriously weak.

On the other hand, courts in some countries remain extremely lender friendly or even biased toward the lender. In Iran, for instance, lenders can de facto repossess the house and are forced neither to sell any time soon nor redistribute any excess of the proceeds over the loan claim to the consumer.

In most emerging markets, the absence of a meaningful social housing system that could provide housing alternatives for defaulting borrowers is likely to instill some level of court bias in favor of defaulting homeowners.

This is the main economic point behind court delay in Poland, where a constitutional right of housing existed or continues to exist. The Polish government has responded with a program designed to provide emergency shelter for evicted households.

Foreclosure reform is likely to remain an obstinate problem anywhere, because of the power of legal traditions. Governments can create emergency housing solutions to give comfort to courts. Court reform itself should be high on the legal reform agenda. Specialized courts or tribunals (see below) may constitute alternative, more effective foreclosure mechanisms.

CONSUMER INSOLVENCY AND DISCHARGE

Dealing with residual debt after a foreclosure is the third element of consumer protection at the back end. A formal consumer insolvency law is now the standard in the United States and Europe. Solutions vary as to whether the lender is forced to choose between collateral and other consumer assets (United States) or can go for both (Germany). After the German reform of 1999, consumers in the EU are now generally discharged of their residual debt within three to seven years; however, residual income burdens and collaboration duties imposed on the consumers vary. In emerging markets, a flurry of general consumer protection legislation has been passed since 1995, which may be expected to create similar concepts of consumer insolvency.

In economic terms, residual debt discharge is a double-edged sword. On the one hand, it strengthens the collateralized nature of mortgage credit and avoids the "eternal debt tower" that treated consumers unfairly in many historic private law formulations. On the other hand, it provides additional incentives for consumers to see a mortgage default as an economic option whose exercise will come at the expense of the collective of performing borrowers, if house prices fall, for example. Lawmaking efforts in emerging markets should strike a middle ground to keep debt performance incentives for borrowers intact.

The Costs of Consumer Protection

Opportunity Costs of Regulation

There is little doubt that disclosure requirements, consumer education, and public certification and counseling measures yield high returns in a cost-benefit analysis. As the experiences presented above show, however, some degree of material consumer protection is needed, because significant abusive practices and risks for consumers prevail. Moreover, the benefits of internationalization and globalization for all consumers cannot be reaped without a level playing field of products across jurisdictions.

Whether that field should be wide or narrow is the subject of legitimate debate. Absolute protection of the consumer from abuse or risk is neither practical nor desirable. Material consumer-protection regulations may lead to the unintended disappearance of products or increases in the price of the mortgage for the consumer. In addition, the structure of the mortgage industry may become less competitive; for example, if lender growth strategies through product innovation become impossible to realize through excessive product standardization.

As in the analogy of durable consumer products, imposing greater consumer options in mortgage finance will increase product costs: for instance, in the case of the universal prepayment option on a 30-year loan, the rate increase is estimated in the range of 70–100 basis points.[33]

The exact costs, however, of reduced product choice and growth opportunities are hard to assess in quantitative terms. They depend moreover on the amount of substitution goods available; for example, curbing the subprime market through rate ceilings may efficiently induce more subprime borrowers to stay renters, if there is sufficiently elastic rental housing supply.

Moreover, costs are often contingent rather than current and explicit; for example, if consumers, because of restrictions imposed on fixed-rate mortgages, are encouraged to take up more adjustable-rate debt, the main cost factor is the increase in insolvency risk, which may or may not materialize in the future.

---

33. See Dübel and Lea 2000.

Consumer protection rules may also interact with banking regulations and public-mortgage-market intervention in a way that reduces
product choice and competition. Examples are the high-LTV and subprime mortgage markets, where lenders are bound by increased transparency, counseling, and usury pricing rules while banking regulators
curb risk taking. Where, however, does a valid market end and where
do abusive or excessively risky practices start? The experience of the
U.S. subprime market suggests that the seesaw of deregulation and re-
regulation may produce more pronounced distortions than a consensus regulatory approach would have.

The task when formulating consumer protection rules is therefore to try
to identify, quantify, and strike a balance between these current, future, and
contingent costs of regulation and the benefits from reduced incidence of
abuse and risk for the consumer. Such a decision must be supported by sufficient microeconomic analysis of the mortgage market, which requires a
minimum of data dissemination and analytical capacity.

Alternative Implementation Forms, Costs

Does the form of regulation matter for its cost-benefit balance? Industry
self-regulation, for example, through codes of conduct or pre-commitment
approaches to certain policy goals, has been popular, in particular if agreement over a new law could not be obtained.[34] They may serve as a collective
bargaining mechanism to build consensus between stakeholders, first within
industry and consumer groups, then between industry and consumer groups,
and finally between both and government. They also introduce an element of
market testing, which is often missing in cases of government fiat.[35]

In practice, voluntary agreements seem to end invariably in formal regulation, because they tend to treat disputed areas by negligence rather than
enforced political compromise. In the United Kingdom, the voluntary Mortgage Code, a lender Code of Conduct of 1997, has been replaced by compulsory Financial Service Authority (FSA) rules. The EU Home Loan Code

34. Dübel, Lea, and Welter 1997 proposed such a code of conduct to overcome the gridlock over
the transposition of the Consumer Credit Directive in the EU.
35. See Guttentag 2004.

covers only partial aspects of consumer information and required seven years of negotiation between industry and consumer groups. It is widely held to fall far behind the consumer protection agenda and will likely make room in due course for an enlarged Consumer Credit Directive.

Enforcement Costs

Whatever the scope and form of regulation, consumer protection needs a clear enforcement structure. Regulations must be developed, revised, and enforced, ideally by a single public body with a clearly defined mandate (see box 6.7 on the Mexican case).[36] Institutions providing consumer information, education, and counseling must be funded; they can be established by government itself (housing agencies, local or state housing offices), consumer groups, charities, or independent brokers and debt counselors. To settle conflicts in the going concern or an early stage of foreclosure, special tribunals or extrajudicial mechanisms, such as third-party arbitration and ombudsmen, have proved valuable.[37]

Court reform itself may add to efficiency if foreclosure cannot be avoided. A clear coordination between different agents in increasingly disintermediated financial systems is also important. Credit investors should provide incentives to servicers aimed at facilitating debt restructuring and rescheduling, and where private responsibility for settlement ends and the public safety net starts should be clearly established.

---

36. Guttentag 2002 notes the conflicts between Federal Reserve and HUD in the United States. Germany has started a consumer protection ministry that may rival the consumer protection role of the federal financial regulator, Bundesanstalt für Finanzdienstleistungsaufsicht (Federal Financial Supervisory Authority; BAFIN). France uses a single agency for the housing and housing finance sectors, L'Agence Nationale pour Information sur le Logement (National Agency for Housing Information).
37. Examples for tribunals are the Malysian Tribunal for Consumer Complaints, the Indian system of national and state commissions and district fora for consumer affairs, and the French system of *Tribunal d'Instance* dealing with over-indebtedness. Portugal has an independent national arbitration center for consumer credit. Independent ombudsmen originated in Nordic countries and have been successful in the British and German banking and insurance industries.

Is Consumer Protection a Luxury Good for Emerging Markets?

Emerging Markets Are Part of the Global Consumer Protection Trend

Consumers International, a global representation of consumer groups and agencies worldwide, reports that consumer protection laws have been passed since 1995 in many emerging markets, mostly in the form of general consumer protection acts. This follows the 1985 passage of UN Guidelines for Consumer Protection. Edwards (2003) indicates that progress is greatest in Latin America, where all countries except Guatemala, Cuba, the Dominican Republic, and Bolivia have passed laws. South and East Asian countries (for example, Indonesia and Malaysia, both in 1999) did likewise, while less developed South and Central Asian countries are lagging behind. In Africa, South Africa—through the excellent National Credit Act of 2005—and some other countries such as the Seychelles and Botswana have consumer protection laws, and a number of others are preparing them. A 2000 report by the group summarizes policies and institutions in Central and Eastern Europe, which are being transformed from their socialist predecessors, rather than recreated.

Appropriate Regulations May Support Financial Sector Development

The New Institutional Economics literature, developed among others at the World Bank, has stressed the importance of appropriate regulations for economic development. Applied to mortgage finance, the notion of appropriateness implies recognition of the specificity of an emerging market with regard to the lender, product, and risk environment.

The implication on expanding a housing finance system may be changes in weighting or priority; for example, between consumer information and material protection rules. For instance, improving information may be a priority in markets with fierce price competition on standard products, yet sees frequent acts of misstatements by some lenders to make the costs of credit appear less expensive. In contrast, material protection interventions may be a priority in markets featuring products with payment shocks (for example, foreign currency lending) that may increase over-indebtedness risk.

Ideally, the latter situation should be avoided altogether, and mortgage products should be initially kept simple and at low risk in the interest of all parties. In this situation, the regulatory focus will be on the front and back ends of the loan life cycle.

- Concerning loan closing, emerging markets should require, in parallel, sufficient loan disclosure and minimum contract content. They should support consumer education and assistance efforts. The simplest means of disclosure should be adopted, for example, self-explanatory, single-page term sheets and the mandatory quotation of the APR for the main product classes. Consumer groups will typically provide pre-closing education and assistance on loan offers against minimal, but ideally systematic, public financial support. Such measures will also improve the competition environment and be welcomed by most lenders.
- Functioning pre-foreclosure, foreclosure, and consumer insolvency regimes, as well as a safety net for defaulting consumers, are also central.[38] Courts (foreclosure, eviction) and local governments (rehousing the evicted) must be enabled to fulfill essential support functions. The servicing departments of lenders, however, should also receive training by, for example, public agencies to help avoid foreclosures that may produce lower recovery ratios than workouts and other pre-foreclosure techniques in many situations. For instance, during the Tequila crisis of 1994 in Mexico, a rush by lenders to foreclose lead to a spiraling price decline that maximized losses.
- An ombudsman, created by an industry group or with the regulator, can improve consumer-lender communications and avoid many court cases.

---

38. Without a social safety net in the form of alternative, lower-cost housing available for defaulting homeowners, it is likely that even the most balanced set of foreclosure regulations will meet resistance from courts. This is one of several areas where broader housing policies and consumer protection rules need synchronization.

Box 6.7. A New Consumer Protection Framework for Mexico

The Federal Law on Transparency and Promotion of Competition in the Guaranteed Credit Market of 2002 introduced minimum consumer protection standards for mortgage finance in Mexico.

In the fields of disclosure and transparency, the law defines a total cost of credit concept, a disclosure standard for contract terms, a binding loan offer period of 20 days, and appraisal standards and authorization of appraisers, as well as minimum contents of contracts. The federal housing finance agency, SHF, is mandated to provide monthly comparative loan-offer information to consumers.

As expected, in an economy with a history of high inflation, material consumer protection concentrates on setting rules for interest rate adjustment. Variable rate contracts are permitted if they follow a public reference rate. Spreads over the reference rate may vary only within contractually determined limits. Prepayment of fixed-rate loans is not generally cost free, but the Central Bank and Federal State Secretary for Economy may jointly determine prepayment conditions and penalties to be then paid. Prepayment charges for variable rate loans, however, are limited to 1 percent. There are no usury ceilings for interest rates.

While it is too early for a proper evaluation, the current framework can be expected to provide for simplification and greater efficiency of borrower-lender relations in a market historically plagued by frequent court and political interventions. At the same time, there seems to be room for consolidating the supervisory structures that the law created in combination with other consumer protection legislation. Currently, the federal consumer protection agency, Profeco; SHF; the Central Bank; the Commission Bancaria (Banking Commission); and the Federal State Secretary Ministry for Economy share responsibilities for detail formulation and enforcement of consumer protection regulations in mortgage finance.

There are situations where developing more complex products or products with potential payment shocks is unavoidable, for example, in the presence of inflation risk. Even with full disclosure and guidance, many consumers will not understand these products. Central banks or regulators here can support appropriate product regulations, for example, through providing appropriate base indices for rate adjustment and establishing simple pricing and re-pricing rules. Public agencies can provide lenders with caps or swaps (foreign currency, interest rates, negative amortization) to protect against the downside risks of such products, which should not fall on consumers.

The Mexican example reported in box 6.7 seems to be a good reflection of these specificities. It strengthens the front end—information and disclosure— and structures the going concern only as far as the main risks—inflation risk— are concerned. It should be noted that the federal housing finance agency SHF offers swaps to lenders in order to shield both borrowers and lenders from certain price risks of the dominant mortgage product used in Mexico.

Understood as a means of structuring the relationship between lenders, consumers, and government without introducing excessive legal formalism, consumer protection is not a luxury good for emerging mortgage markets, but rather an integral part of the overall financial sector infrastructure. It is self-evident that emerging market countries should use their chance to avoid the mistakes of many developed markets, which have found themselves in repeating deregulation and re-regulation cycles following changes in political colors and, often, overregulation.

Conclusions

Both consumer information and material protection rules are a necessity in an industry characterized by information asymmetries, consumer heterogeneity, transactions costs, and complex products carrying multiple options. It is the degree of standardization of lender covenants and products, not the fact that some standardization must occur in the interest of the weakest consumers, that is a worthwhile subject of debate.

These economic points have been blurred in the understandable thrust to deregulate an overregulated mortgage industry in developed markets of the 1980s and the subsequent polarized policy debate. Much of that debate can be traced to the traumatic experiences of high inflation and is increasingly obsolete. Today, the practical difficulties in determining an appropriate level of consumer protection should have priority. These arise because of the idiosyncrasies of mortgage lending, especially funding and risk management mechanisms.

The trend in emerging markets has been to quickly develop their consumer protection frameworks. For them, in the mortgage sector, in particular, the front end—consumer information and education—and the back end—foreclosure, eviction, and insolvency, should be the central focus of a strategy to develop adequate regulations. Appropriate regulations and institutions should be created that ease the burden of courts and reduce the widespread political risks. This also requires an economic support strategy; for example, supporting institution building of courts, local governments, consumer groups, or, more radically, alternatives to homeownership for those completely unable to borrow safely. An initial limitation to simple, low-risk mortgage products that require less legal structure and impose less regulation costs will be in the interest of all parties, lenders, consumers, and government.

Chapter 7

Construction Finance in Emerging Economies

Loïc Chiquier

Construction finance refers to the funding of land development and building construction. As such, it is an essential—even if often overlooked—part of any effective national housing finance system. New housing in most emerging economies is typically provided through informal construction (slum development or just nonconforming housing), owner-built individual housing, and developer-built housing.

As the pressure of urbanization and the failure to eradicate slums drive the formidable challenge of providing modern affordable housing in emerging economies, so does the role of professional developers capable of delivering such housing increases. Planned developments allow for the inclusion of infrastructure, such as access roads, water, sewerage, and power as part of the initial construction process. This is as opposed to the prevailing production model of incremental building or slum proliferation, where the provision of ex post infrastructure to the informal neighborhoods is all the more expensive. This positive evolution has been observed in countries such as Mexico or Thailand.

Construction finance is vital for financing any housing supply system capable of meeting the challenges of increased demand for formal housing in emerging economies. Developers can be associated with different forms of construction finance, each of which can play an important role: developer equity, buyer deposits (including presales), developer finance to buyers (installment sales), construction loans provided by financial intermediaries to developers, and, more recently, bond markets through the securitization of construction loans.

The supply side remains severely constrained because of difficulties in leveraging sufficient debt and in accessing land and construction permits within reasonable time frames and budgets. As a result, housing prices keep rising to ever-less-affordable levels. Without debt leverage, developers invest more of their own capital into projects, thus reducing the size and number of overall projects. This also pushes developers to orient their production toward higher-income households more likely to pay cash or to be creditworthy for the developers own installment sales program.

Construction finance can also refer to self-construction by individuals, which is the predominant form of finance for lower-income groups in many emerging economies. Financial institutions have great difficulty in administering loans to self-constructed units because of their small scale and because of difficulties in securing collateral prior to completion. Lenders also subject themselves to considerable construction risk through rising costs or delays, which may affect the loan repayment.

Construction finance therefore helps to increase the supply of units for occupation, boosting the level of home ownership, and improving the quality and efficiency of projects, notably for affordable housing.

In many emerging markets, financial institutions limit their credit exposure to developers for legitimate reasons, which include a significantly higher exposure to credit risk. Developers are often vulnerable, thinly capitalized, and sometimes even relatively unprofessional in conducting their construction activities or the other critical aspects of project management (notably legal, administrative, financial, and commercial). This situation is then reflected in high lending spreads (typically between 5 percent and 10 percent in many emerging economies), and limited levels of banking exposure to the construction sector (as observed in Poland or Thailand).

Inhospitable regulatory environments for developers in many emerging markets hold back productivity growth that would come about through larger-scale affordable units. Costly and lengthy red tape is associated with acquiring land, developing zoning rules, registering and transferring titles, and obtaining utility and construction permits. According to De Soto 2000, the procedures in Egypt to gain access to desert land for construction purposes and to register these property rights takes between six and 14 years (77 steps through 31 entities). Developers also have to cope with market-unfriendly tax and labor laws, which creates an uneven playing field when contrasted with the informal sector. The productivity of emerging market developers may also be held back by inefficient organization of functions and tasks, difficulties in obtaining standardized building materials, and the heavy reliance on cheap labor as opposed to modern building equipment and machinery. The construction sector is also often subject to a lack of competition and entry barriers. The low productivity in the construction sector tends to also affect the construction materials industry. This industry is characterized by small, informal suppliers who survive by avoiding taxes, evading safety standards, and paying only a fraction of their energy bills, while larger-scale suppliers look for protection from competition through import tariffs and licensing restrictions.

Another common symptom of a stagnating sector is the high concentration of loans made by banks to a small number of developers. Only a limited number of developers are able to meet the prudent underwriting lending standards set by banks that would include criteria on financial strength, ownership of the land under development, and a solidly established reputation as a developer, which is critical for presales. This financial concentration often limits the competitiveness of the real estate sector and the affordability of new housing, notably toward smaller projects that may very well fit the local market realities, land supply constraints, and market demand.

Many countries require reforms in real estate development financing in the following areas: (a) more effective equity and debt instruments for developers, (b) more security for the households making advance payments (in some cases for the entire amount of the project) and carrying most of the construction risk, and (c) more households pre-qualified for mortgage loans. The main constraints observed on the supply of housing are access to titled land and access to construction finance. Issues about land use and urban regulations are not developed further in this chapter, which will focus on the financing side of property development, covering difficulties in obtaining finance and innovations taking place to overcome these obstacles.

Real Estate Development Process and Risks

There are many complex risks related with every phase of development projects, notably related to the often hazardous regulatory process (land infrastructure and construction permits), the construction phase (possible delays and additional costs), and the commercialization (sales) policy.

Real estate developers span a spectrum of operating models, from individuals to partnerships to small and large corporations. They may specialize in land acquisition and development, ultimately selling the improved land to a builder, or they may take the project through to completion. They need funds to obtain land, obtain the necessary permits and authorizations, provide or have the local government provide basic infrastructure, construct the building(s), and sell them. This process is typically lengthy, meaning that the developer has funds tied up in the project for an extended period. The length of the development period is a key risk factor, as it exposes the developer to possible cost increases and additional technical delays. By definition, the developer is also exposed to market risks, as the initial assumptions made on the demand for a given product and price may have been wrongly estimated. Developers are exposed to real estate price cyclicality, which is difficult to forecast without reliable information systems on housing markets and prices.

In the absence of permits and infrastructure, the land value is limited, which is why the land acquisition phase is mainly financed through developer equity. An incomplete structure is also worth relatively little, and value can be lost quickly if construction is slowed or stopped. During construction, value depends largely on the capability of the developer to see the project through to completion. It is also critical to isolate developer risk from the project risk, which is a challenge in some countries where developers are used to commingling cash and proceeds from various projects. For example, in France, there is now an obligation to create a special company for each project. All these aspects differentiate construction-project finance from a more standardized underwriting policy for retail mortgage lending.

The initial step in the process is land acquisition. Larger developers may acquire significant amounts of land in advance of development (land banking), but more frequently, it is a specific parcel (which can accommodate one or several buildings). In most emerging economies, acquiring land and financing land infrastructure remains the toughest and most enduring challenge, and represents a formidable disincentive against the development of formal affordable housing units. In developed markets, developers may use options contracts to tie up the land while conducting market research and obtaining permits. The option gives the holder the right, but not the obligation, to purchase the land for a stated price within a specified period of time. Options reduce the risk and the time frame over which developer equity is committed; however, such options are rarely observed in emerging economies.

An inhospitable regulatory environment for real estate development in terms of authorizations and permits (administrative red tape, but also corruption of local authorities and agencies) adds costs and risk to development and in many cases can preclude formal finance. In many African countries, a lack of land and property security (for example, provisory or conditional titles, which cannot be recognized by the financial intermediaries) inhibits formal development.

The main other legal difficulty for the developer lies in transferring titles to buyers. Many countries do not permit any early transfer before the physical completion of the building. Such provisions aim to avoid having households become owners of illegally built units, but adversely affect the project funding, as clients cannot obtain mortgage financing during the construction phase. Better solutions could impose some third-party monitoring of the construction process and protection of the advances paid by the clients to the developer.

In countries where developers are exposed to adverse laws and regulations, creative financial instruments for mitigating risks, as presented below, will be of limited use.

Financing by Buyers

In many emerging and transition countries (for example, China, Poland, Russia, Turkey, Egypt, Brazil and so forth) a large portion of developments are funded by consumers through advance deposits or presales.[1] The deposits

---

1. Many variants exist to capture these advances; for example, through "share financing" schemes (individuals paying a portion in advance for apartments under construction of a given project) or purchase of "targeted bonds" issued by the developer for a similar purpose.

may be for a portion of the price or the entire amount. Presales with deposits help lenders to verify the strength of demand for a project, but in most developed markets, this advance is small, more to demonstrate the commitment of the consumer than to finance the developer. In less developed markets, it is a major source of finance, either in lieu of formal finance or in addition to it. Developers may prefer pre-sale finance, as it lessens the risk (the sales price is determined in advance) and cost (avoids construction period interest; developers may also earn income on unused portions of deposits). In sum, a certain level of pre-sale should be part any sound credit underwriting policy of banks to demonstrate the commercial and financial viability of the project, but this should not become the main or sole source of construction finance, as it would transfer an excessive level of construction risks to buyers.

Indeed, presale finance can be very risky for the consumer. As seen in several countries (Russia, Ukraine) problems occur when there is no construction lending but large advances paid by consumers, and the developer fails to deliver the expected housing product (quality, time, price), leaving households to take the whole risk and face dire legal straits in trying to recover their advances. Consumers, especially those that earn low or moderate incomes, frequently commit all of their savings to make a down payment. Should the project or developer fail, individual consumers rarely have the resources to pursue a case in court to recover their deposits, which is unlikely when the developer is bankrupt or has left insufficient assets. If the unit that is delivered does not meet promised standards, a consumer who pre-purchased with a mortgage has little recourse except to default on the mortgage and pass the problem on to his or her lender (the main cause of the few nonperforming mortgage loans in China). In particular, consumers are usually ill equipped to judge progress or quality of construction of a large development project. Several scandals of this nature have been made public (for example, Ukraine, 2005).

Improved procedures are needed to better secure the buyer's rights to the unbuilt property. This could include making better use of the advances paid during construction to create an individual property title before the completion of the project. An ideal confidence builder for all the parties may be performance bonds or an insurance policy contracted by the developer from worthy third parties. Both these methods would provide greater security by enabling a new contractor to be brought in quickly to complete the project if the original contractor should fail. These systems have worked well in developed economies, but not yet in emerging economies, as the whole profession of developers must also gain in experience and professionalism, which in turn will allow private markets to rate their performance and better manage this construction risk.

A payment and performance bond is a financial tool used to guarantee completion of construction in the event of a developer or contractor default. A performance bond guarantees that a commercial construction contract is upheld as agreed between contracting parties. The payment bond guarantees the payment of materials and labor by the contractor to all subcontractors and material suppliers. Construction lenders are the parties most likely to require a payment and performance bond in order to reduce construction risk. The cost of the bond is borne by the borrower or developer. Such bonds are issued by surety companies, a special kind of insurance company. The surety company determines if the developer or contractor is bondable by looking at its financial statements and performance record, but will also scrutinize the project whose completion is under guarantee.

In Brazil, the legislature introduced in 2001 a legal instrument to distinguish and preserve the equity of the households from the equity of the developer, should the latter become insolvent. The developed real estate assets (*patrimônio de afetação*) are legally separated—and registered as such—from the overall equity of the developer. A supervision commission, including household representatives, is responsible for verifying the development process. In case of a developer's bankruptcy, purchasers may finish the building; however, they would also be jointly liable for taxes and labor obligations of the affected assets, thus creating possible complications.

In Algeria, a mutual guarantee fund "Fonds de Garantie & de Caution Mutuelle de la Promotion Immobilière"—sponsored by the state—covers the advances made by clients to developers. The 1993 law on real estate development included a framework for the sale of housing units before the construction is completed and the possibility for the developer to require advance payments from clients. The developer is required to cover the advance payments against its insolvency through a guarantee fund. The Fonds de Garantie & de Caution Mutuelle de la Promotion Immobilière was established for that purpose in 1997 and became operational in 2000. The decision to grant the guarantee and the setting of the premium is made by the fund's committee, which the developer or related parties are forbidden from participating in. The main criteria examined by the fund are land ownership, building permits, and the legally defined format of the sale agreements, but the fund does not perform any actual screening of the developers or of their projects. The fund usually takes the property being developed as collateral. Developers pay membership fees and a risk-based premium of between 1 percent and 2 percent for each project (key criteria: self-finance of the developer, amount of advance payments, history and status of the developer, and quality of the collateral). The fund also helps households by checking the consistency between expenditures and construction progress, and developers who use the advance payments instead of freezing buyers' deposits in escrow accounts. At the end of 2004 (after five years of operations), 800 programs were insured ($500 million). The fund now has a database on developers' performance, critical to build any accessible rating system of developers. The fund has developed no real certification function yet,[2] but has the potential to become a self-regulatory body capable of becoming a quality label. If well implemented, such a solution may be appropriate for protecting the advances of households, but it should be stressed that this guarantee would not secure the available financing needed to finish the construction process in the event of a developer's failure.[3] The risk is all the greater given that the lien on the partially built property is of little use if its market value is less than overall costs.

A more secure system—and therefore costly in terms of charged premiums—would also cover this risk (the fact that the housing units may not be delivered at the right time, at the expected price or quality) through private insurance products or performance bonds.

Nevertheless, the protection of the consumer can go too far, as shown in Turkey. Banks do not like to lend to most developers, viewing them as risky and undercapitalized. Thus, they make loans to consumers who pre-purchase the house. Problems in the timing and quality of construction led the Turkish Consumer Protection Agency to require that banks retain full liability for poor quality or untimely delivery for a period of five years for the full purchase price of the property. This excessive protection is an inhibitor to bank

---

2. The fund has rejected no applications, in an environment of acute housing shortages and many public developers.
3. Buyers can request a judicial injunction to complete construction by any means at the expense of the defaulting developer, but if insolvency is the reason behind the default, it is likely that this remedy remains theoretical.

lending.[4] A new law passed in March 2007 reduced this liability to the first year of the loan.

Financing by Banks

The developer and the bank should share the vast majority of the project risk, as these institutions have the resources and expertise to manage it. In many countries, construction lending is a widespread and profitable business for banks. The banks employ engineers and architects to judge project progress and quality, thus mitigating risk. They can underwrite the developer to ensure that it has the requisite experience and resources to complete the project. The bank can use progress payments combined with periodic reviews by experts to manage the project risk. Construction lending is riskier than permanent finance—thus the ability to charge an appropriate interest rate reflecting risk is important to the market.[5] The interest rate, as well as the degree of leverage allowed by the bank will depend on the risk of the project, market trends, and the strength and reputation of the developer.

The typical construction loan process is illustrated in figure 7.1. The developer acquires the land, and the bank finances the construction and sometimes part of the land infrastructure, typically a short-term (six- to 24-month, depending on the size of the project) progress-payment loan, which is repaid from sales of individual houses or units. The same or different lender may provide mortgages to finance purchase.

There are a number of obstacles in obtaining bank construction finance, however:

- The weakness of developers in many countries, characterized by limited own equity (in order to scale up debt and large-scale projects), poor accounting practices, and a lack of financial transparency (for

---

4. Many, though not all, developers are part of conglomerate groups, including banks, in part motivating the connection. The law, however, applies to any bank loan, even if provided by a lender unaffiliated with the developer.
5. In some markets, lenders have offered reduced interest rates in return for a share in the sales price. This reduces the construction cost for the developer and aligns incentives between the bank and the developer; however, it increases the risk for the lender and may be prohibited by regulators.

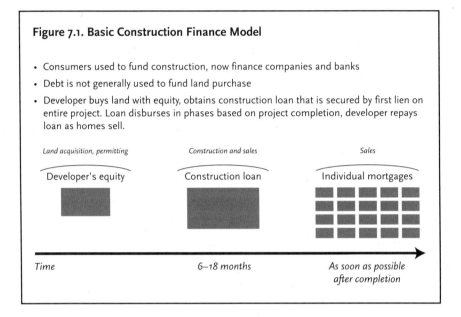

Figure 7.1. Basic Construction Finance Model

- Consumers used to fund construction, now finance companies and banks
- Debt is not generally used to fund land purchase
- Developer buys land with equity, obtains construction loan that is secured by first lien on entire project. Loan disburses in phases based on project completion, developer repays loan as homes sell.

Land acquisition, permitting   *Construction and sales*   *Sales*

Developer's equity   Construction loan   Individual mortgages

Time   *6–18 months*   *As soon as possible after completion*

example, in many emerging economies very few developers are listed on stock exchanges) and, sometimes, unethical business practices. Regulators may require minimum developer equity for bank lending; for example, the People's Bank of China (PBoC) has recently taken several measures to cool off construction finance by mandating that banks require at least 35 percent of own equity from the developer. Paradoxically, this has increased the amount of presale financing as developers attempt to minimize their equity investment.

- A lack of expertise within the lending institutions. Lenders need in-depth knowledge of local real estate markets (prices, demand drivers, and so forth), the realities of the sequenced development process, and the capabilities and capacities of developers, and also must be experts in project management. This line of business is appropriate for banks, but growing it safely requires specific skills and legal techniques. Due diligence must be conducted on development and construction firms to verify their track records, ensure their integrity, and evaluate their capacity to manage the construction and sales processes. Ongoing supervision must be conducted on each project to ensure financial integrity, proper delivery and quality, progress in completing distinct stages of the project linked to loan disbursements, and so forth. Sometimes, banks enter this specific lending without adequate capacities.

While there are no shortcuts in proper risk management, there are techniques that banks can use to mitigate risk. One example is to ring fence-project assets financed by the construction loan from the rest of the assets of the developer (see Brazil example). Isolation helps to ensure that, should the developer have difficulty completing the project, the bank as first lien holder will be able to transfer its management to another developer to finish the project. Isolating the project also helps to distinguish buyers' cash deposits from other cash the developer manages, and so may increase the likelihood of returning the deposits should the project not move forward. Ring fencing can be done by segregating the land and structures in a special-purpose, limited liability company that is legally off the developer's balance sheet. Thus, in the event of developer bankruptcy, the project can be transferred to another developer to complete.

Alternative solutions are constantly being developed, although they are often far from perfect. Besides the models described for Brazil and Algeria, here are a few more remedies recently introduced in various countries, most combining public reforms and market forces:

In Ukraine, housing construction funds have been recently introduced to regulate the construction period process. Prudential regulations are applied to the management companies of the funds, including capital and reserves requirements for developers expressed as a significant portion of the collected advances.[6] In case of a difficulty, the fund manager can change the developer. In practice, the developers sponsor management companies, so the system remains limited by a lack of independence. At least financial risks are better shared between the developer and households, and a regulatory body (as a new function assigned to the non-bank financial regulator) exercises on- and off-site oversight functions to ascertain that collected funds are used as appropriate. At this stage, this system has not been stress tested. Their use remains recent, limited, and not mandatory. It may play a more effective marketing role among developers as a quality label, and is similar to escrow

---

6. A total of 20 percent for the capital and 10 percent for the operational reserves.

in which part of the advances are held in reserve until various completion milestones are hit.

In Pakistan, the financial authorities have contemplated the project of imposing external rating for construction lending. Two rating agencies have developed a methodology to assess the relative capacity of the developer to deliver as per specified terms and quality, as well as the transfer of the ownership in time, but the project has not been enacted yet. This proposal aimed at enhancing standards among developers and helping investors assess their risks, but rating agencies cannot substitute for the lender's responsibility to originate a sound portfolio of construction loans. The other technical hesitation related to whether the developer or the development project should be rated. The alternative road now contemplated consists of first developing an overall legal and regulatory framework for the development industry.

Funding from Capital Markets

In Mexico, market mechanisms have been introduced to improve the process. Developers do not ask for large advances from clients—notably among lower-income groups—but seek construction bridging loans from SOFOLs (specialized housing finance lenders), and get repaid by the sales proceed upon completion of the homes when their clients take out long-term mortgage finance. The government entity Fondo de Operacion y Financiamiento Bancario a la Vivienda (Operating Fund and the Housing Bank Funding; [FOVI])/SHF was the main source of funds for construction loans made by SOFOLs, but it has now stopped in order to refocus its activities to support long-term mortgage markets. As a result, a large proportion of these bridging loans have been securitized (about $1.4 billion by early 2006). The structuring of these securities is relatively complex and tailored to the specifics of these bridging loan receivables, cash flows, and risks. Bridging loans are originated, disbursed, and serviced by SOFOLs according to specific conditions, including a complete feasibility study, a detailed schedule of disbursements according to the supervised progress of the project, individualized units sold through mortgages through the construction period, preventive servicing procedures and specific workout-phase procedures for development projects likely to default, and so forth. These securities can also enjoy a partial guarantee by the public SHF. This securitization helped to leverage resources and expand the scope of affordable housing projects, without exercising excessive pressure on the households or the lenders. This mechanism also helped to enhance transparency, safety, and standardization among different construction projects.[7]

In the United States, bank financing leaves the lender confronted with a significant risk if the developer defaults. Bank financing has therefore gradually made way for commercial mortgage-backed securities, which pool such loans and sell them off as securities to institutional investors. As the risk is then spread, credit rates may be lower. There has been a more recent trend, however, of more construction loans back on the balance sheet of banks, as bond markets tend not to offer the same level of operational flexibility that a bank may provide to a developer.

Financing of Buyers

Developers are a natural distribution channel for residential mortgage credit, as they want to sell houses as soon as possible to repay their own debt and redeploy capital in other profitable projects. The developer has an incentive to minimize costs and maximize the speed of the mortgage origination process, but has no exposure to the quality of the resulting credit. But in some emerging economies where mortgage lending is hardly accessible, in order to sell their units some developers have no choice but to provide credits to their clients; for example, through sale installments or even loans when the law permits. The developer usually retains the property title until the last installment or the sale contract, or may offer a leaseback contract.

Variants can be found in many countries, including Egypt, Brazil, Ivory Coast, Russia, Georgia, or India, as a telling sign of an underdeveloped mortgage finance system. The price and level of installments are adjusted to reflect an equivalent fixed rate of return, which is often high and not disclosed—as other credit features are—in a transparent and comparable way. The term of

---

7. Developers are selected according to their recognized professionalism. Projects must comply with several criteria: maximum 65 percent LTV for construction projects—lower LTV for land infrastructure—limited to large cities, good commercialization strategy, trust accounts where sale proceeds are paid, clients eligible for future mortgage loans, possibility of out-of-court property recovery to transfer the project if necessary to another developer, etc.

these loans is usually between three and seven years. The credit affordability is limited, although better than with no credit at all. The performance of these loans is usually good,[8] as the developer keeps control of the property title and can replace a delinquent client. Some of these housing credit receivables have been securitized in Brazil. Buyers have certain risks—in the event of a developer's failure, they may not be able to obtain title or receive credit for their payments. This happened in Russia.

Other cases of abused households refer to immediate evictions processed by developers after one single declared late monthly installment, without refunding the buyer with the interests as part of prior installments (which implies a huge penalty in inflationary times).

Although most developers would prefer actual mortgage loans to be extended by banks to finance their clients, when this is not possible, they must require larger equity advances from their clients (commercially and financially unattractive); delay repaying their own suppliers, sub-contractors, and land sellers (including the state, as in Egypt); or raise additional equity to facilitate customer purchase. Many developers do not have sufficient treasury capacities to offer such advances, as the economic nature of their activities require them to roll over their equity and profits as rapidly as possible into new land and development operations. The need to provide such credits also represents a barrier against competitiveness for smaller and new developers. When real estate markets face an adverse cycle, developers also find it difficult to keep providing long-term lending, thus further depressing housing markets.

The servicing of these loans may be delegated to agents or even to mandated banks. A professional lender is normally better equipped than a developer in loan underwriting and servicing standards, risk management, and cross-sale of other services. Lenders are typically subject to guidelines related to risk concentration, consumer information, and providing servicing-performance incentives, and have developed procedures in case of construction delays. In the event of significant inflation, installments should be indexed. In Brazil, the law limits the credit rates of such loans at an index (Consumer

---

8. The pool performance reported by some developers in Brazil (for example, Rossi) would be superior to the mortgage portfolios held by banks. In Egypt, only 2 percent of such loans are estimated to be non-performing. Some of these developers are said to be quite flexible when a loan needs to be restructured.

Price Index) plus 12 percent as a capped real rate. This yield is considered to be quite attractive compared to other market benchmarks. Unlike mortgage loans, such installment-sale loans extended by developers are not supervised by the Central Bank. Some of the developers have started to either securitize them or sell them directly to interested banks (usually with a discount, but the all-in price is still more attractive than through securitization).

A more advanced step for developers consists of capitalizing some profes-sional and regulated mortgage lending institutions such as Mexican SOFOLs that would provide mortgage loans to households. Another funding step consists of mobilizing capital markets through the securitization of these loans, as in Brazil and Mexico. An apparent obstacle comes from the lack of credit standards and financial supervision, but it may be overcome by sea-soned and performing loans and the use of professional servicers and secu-ritization conduits.

Other Regulatory Aspects

Bank regulators typically set restrictions on construction lending in terms of allowable LTV ratios, appraisal norms for the underlying collateral, and portions of the project that are allowed to finance. For example, in the United States, banks are restricted to 65 percent LTV for raw land, 75 percent LTV for land development or finished lots, 80 percent of multifamily residential construction, and 85 percent for one- to four-family residential construc-tion. In addition, unlike residential mortgage loans, construction loans do not usually have the benefit of any lower-risk weighting for capital adequacy purposes, because of their inherent higher exposure to real estate cycles and credit risks.

In some countries, banks are not allowed to provide land loans, while in others the ratio of land to total loans is restricted (for example, to a portion of the bank's equity reflecting the riskier nature of the lending). Lenders also have to have a clearly defined and documented lending process for real estate, including origination policies and methods, target markets, appraisal guide-lines, and staff qualifications.

G21 G32
G21 G28
R31 L51
016

USA
Thailand
Mexico
Poland
Spain
Colombia

CHAPTER 8

Risk Management and Regulation

W. Britt Gwinner and Michael Lea

All lending involves a variety of risks that must be allocated, managed, and priced, but the 10- to 30-year maturities and the legal aspects of mortgage lending pose unique risks. Risk taking by lenders and investors should be regulated and supervised—by both regulatory authorities and market participants. The principal risks associated with financial intermediation are well known: credit, market, liquidity, foreign currency, operations (or business), and political. Mortgage value depends on a host of factors, including house prices, interest rates, and the legal environment for enforcing the mortgage lien. Mortgage lenders establish risk measures and methods for mitigating risk that reflect these characteristics. In many cases, measures appropriate for mortgage lenders differ from risk measures and tolerances for shorter-term and unsecured lending.

In addition to product-specific issues, real estate lending can be a source of systemic risk, as banking and real estate crises are frequently correlated. The fact that inappropriate lending, pricing, and risk management can create problems for the broader financial system and macro economy presents special challenges for regulators.

By definition, emerging markets suffer from a lack of public, detailed financial information, and they lack liquidity in both the financial and real estate markets. The lack of information and liquidity, along with the cyclical nature of the property markets, can lead lenders and regulators to restrict the flow of credit to housing, to the detriment of the market and economy—in particular, to moderate- and lower-income borrowers. Yet effective risk management techniques and enlightened regulatory policies can create a climate for safe lending.

In this chapter, we review the major risks present in mortgage lending, review how they are managed in an emerging-markets context, and highlight the way regulations shape the market. We end the chapter with a concise summary of the factors that led to the subprime crisis in the United States as a case study in risk management and regulatory issues.

The Risks of Housing Finance

Like all lending, housing finance is exposed to a number of risks. These risks can be classified into seven categories:

1. *Credit risk:* the risk that the money will not be returned, with whatever interest or other charges are due, in a timely manner;
2. *Liquidity risk:* the risk that the money will be needed before it is due;
3. *Market risk:* the risk that changes in market conditions will alter the scheduled cash flows (real or nominal) among the parties involved in intermediation. This includes interest rate risk, prepayment risk, inflation risk, and exchange rate risk;
4. *Agency risk:* the risk that a divergence of interests will cause an intermediary to behave in a manner other than that expected;
5. *Operations or business risk:* the risk that the organization, controls, information systems and technologies are inadequate for safeguarding the institution;
6. *Systemic risk:* the risk that a crisis at one institution or in one part of the system will spread to the rest of the system;
7. *Political risk:* the risk that the legal and political framework within which the lending takes place will change.

The ability to manage and price these risks is a major determinant of the availability and cost of housing finance, as well as the provision of credit for affordable housing. The ability to do so in turn depends on the soundness of the economic, primary market, and regulatory infrastructure. The two most important prerequisites for managing risk in housing lending are macroeconomic stability and an effective legal framework for property ownership and mortgage lending.

Macroeconomic stability is very important for several reasons. First, it has a major effect on the demand for mortgages. High rates of inflation and nominal interest rates are typical features of many emerging economies. These features have the effect of reducing mortgage affordability. A volatile economy also affects the supply of funds and the characteristics of mortgages offered by lenders. In a volatile environment, lenders are concerned about liquidity risk and reluctant to offer long-term loans. This may lead them to not offer mortgages or only offer short maturity loans that in turn are less affordable for consumers. Lenders and investors may prefer short-term assets, in part because of the difficulties of forecasting inflation and interest rates and thus the cash flows of their portfolios. FRMs create substantial cash-flow risk for lenders in volatile environments.[1] Variable rate mortgages are riskier for borrowers in a volatile environment, as interest rate change causes payment shock. In turn, this increases the credit risk of mortgage lending (for example, Colombia, Mexico from the early 1990s).

The distinguishing characteristic of mortgage finance is the use of the mortgage lien to secure the loan. As a result, credit risk depends on (1) the borrower's ability to pay the loan from income or other resources; (2) the risk that, in case of default, the collateral sale price will be less than the outstanding balance on the loan plus costs of foreclosure; and (3) the risk that the collateral cannot be seized in a reasonably rapid manner.

The inability to foreclose and repossess the collateral in the event of default is a major source of risk in many emerging markets.[2] The time and expense in foreclosure deter lending, particularly for lower-income households, and raise the cost of borrowing. Extensive research shows that banks provide a greater supply of larger mortgages at lower rates of interest in regions and countries

1. See chapter 3 on mortgage instruments.
2. See chapter 5 on legal issues.

that have shorter and more dependable foreclosure processes (Pence 2006; Jappelli, Pagano, and Bianco 2002; Clauretie and Herzog 1990).

Many of the same factors that restrain the growth of mortgage finance also create challenges for regulators: legislatures may not fund regulators at adequate levels, and courts may not support regulatory actions. Difficulties in enforcing the mortgage pledge increase the cost of resolving failed institutions when public authorities are forced to take them over. Special foreclosure powers for public authorities may reduce the cost of resolving crises, but in the long run serve to enforce market distortions.[3]

In many developing countries, issues related to land title remain a major barrier to housing finance. An accurate and comprehensive land registration system is a necessary condition for effective property rights. The lack of an effective title registration system is a major barrier to the development of markets in used housing, which are often more affordable than new construction. It is also a barrier to lending, as borrowers that cannot establish clear title to their property cannot pledge it as collateral for a loan.

Credit Risk

The two primary measures of credit risk are 1) probability of default and 2) loss given default. Probability of default measures the likelihood that the borrower will fail to make payments over the life of the loan. Loss given default measures the net cost that the lender will suffer in the event of default and foreclosure. Loss given default is termed as a loss because lenders usually lose when they have to foreclose and sell a property. Losses from foreclosures arise primarily when house prices overall have declined, but they may also stem from the costs of maintaining the house if it remains vacant for a period after foreclosure, and from the legal fees and other costs of foreclosure.

Mortgage lenders underwrite credit risk in three broad areas: 1) the ability and willingness of the borrower to repay the loan; 2) the value of the collateral relative to the loan amount; and 3) the lender's ability to efficiently

---

3. For example, Colombia created a company to dispose of the assets of failed banks in the wake of the 1998 crisis. This company, Central de Inversiones S.A., was given legal powers to foreclose and evict borrowers that reduced its cost, but did nothing to create confidence on the part of private-sector lenders that lacked such special powers and so faced much longer average recovery periods and costs.

enforce the mortgage lien in case of default. Each of these is assessed at the time the loan is originated, and periodically throughout the life of the loan.

Lenders gauge the borrower's ability to pay by comparing monthly debt payments to income, and by assessing the presence of liquid reserves, savings, and investments. The most common measure for ability to pay is the ratio of the monthly debt service or the mortgage payment to monthly income, also known as the effort ratio. The debt service-to-income ratio is calculated by dividing total monthly debt (including mortgage loan payment, monthly installment payments, and minimum payments on all revolving debt) by gross monthly income. The higher the ratio, the greater the stress that debt payment places on the household.

In the past, average acceptable debt service-to-income ratios ranged between 25 and 35 percent. In recent years, there has been an upward drift in maximum (and average) ratios. This reflects the generally benign conditions associated with relative macro stability in many countries. It also reflects the frequent underreporting of income in emerging economies. Thus, in Egypt lenders are by law permitted to lend up to 40 percent for normal loans and 25 percent for social housing loans. The same maximum applies in Thailand (despite the fact there was a major market downturn in the mid-1990s); however, in Indonesia and Argentina, two countries with recent bouts of instability, the maximums are only 30 percent, and in Romania the maximum is 35 percent. Lenders may vary permissible debt sevice-to-income ratios to take into account compensating factors, such as the presence of liquid reserves after closing of the purchase transaction, low LTV, or the presence of mortgage insurance.

Lenders generally assess willingness to pay by collecting information on the borrower's historical record of payment of other debts, such as consumer loans and auto loans. Increasingly, the technology of credit scoring is spreading as a way to collect a range of information to predict the performance of a given borrower and express in a single number their willingness to pay the mortgage.[4] Credit scores reflect the borrower's payment history on all debt over a given period of history. Although credit scoring has been introduced in some emerging markets (Brazil, Mexico) a lack of data (particularly through a complete cycle), and the unwillingness of many lenders

---

4. See chapter 4.

to share proprietary performance data, limits its usefulness as an underwriting tool.

The amount of equity the borrower has in the property is a major factor underlying willingness to pay. Thus, one of the simplest means to manage mortgage credit risk is to set a maximum acceptable LTV. The less certain lenders are regarding future house-price trends or the legal support for enforcing the mortgage lien, the less likely that high-LTV lending will emerge. In emerging markets, with limited experience in lending, relatively volatile property markets, and less certain legal environments, regulators tend to establish a ceiling on LTV. In Korea, the limit is 60 percent for nonspeculative and 40 percent for speculative areas. In China and Russia, the limit is currently 70 percent; in Romania, 75 percent; whereas in Egypt and Mexico it is 90 percent. There is a 100 percent limit in Thailand and no maximum LTV in Poland. In other countries, limits are imposed by covered bond legislation (Hungary, 70 percent; Chile, 75 percent).

Mortgage lenders set thresholds for the credit risk of loans that they will originate based on their risk tolerance as lenders and on the financial return that is available in their market if they bear different levels of credit risk. To estimate probability of default and loss given default at origination, lenders require information on the property, primarily an appraisal of its market value and information on the borrower, such as the amount and stability of monthly income, other assets the borrower may hold, the source of the down payment, and the borrower's credit history.

The lack of credit information is a significant barrier in most emerging markets, as borrowers often do not have a credit history or ability to prove their income. Many emerging-market borrowers are employed in the informal sector, so their income is often more volatile and difficult to substantiate. Still other borrowers systematically underreport income to avoid taxes. Lenders have begun using nonstandard ways to underwrite or qualify borrowers. The experience of Thailand (box 8.1) is instructive.

Credit risk management takes place through servicing as well as the original underwriting of a loan. Effective servicing involves more than payment collection but also active monitoring of repayment performance and corrective actions once delinquency begins.

Lenders can reduce the credit risk of mortgage lending by securing the repayment stream; for example, through payroll deduction (as does Mex-

Box 8.1. Innovative Underwriting in Thailand

The Government Housing Bank (GHB) of Thailand has developed a number of innovative ways to underwrite loans to lower-income households (Khan 2004). These include the following:

- Hire purchase prior to mortgage: House purchasers lease for three to five years, after which they can become mortgagors upon record of regular monthly installment payments;
- Regular payment incentives: borrowers that save regularly prior to obtaining a mortgage benefit from a lower interest rate.

GHB spearheaded the creation of a credit bureau to share the credit histories of their 700,000 borrowers, 90 percent of which are low to moderate income (loans below $25,000).

ico's Institute of the National Housing Fund for Workers, known by its Spanish acronym INFONAVIT), or direct debits of borrower's current bank accounts (as do South African banks). Collections are a challenge for borrowers with informal incomes. Mexico's SOFOLs place repayment offices in the developments they finance to allow the borrowers to repay the loans in cash near their homes (boxes 2.1 and 8.2). This is more effective than asking them to come into a lending or bank branch, which may be inconvenient or time consuming, and works in a country in which the mail services are not reliable.

Lending to lower-income households generally involves greater risks for lenders than higher-income loans. The income of poorer households is less stable and more difficult to document. Such households typically have short or negative credit histories and fewer resources to withstand shocks. In addition, the transaction costs of making housing loans—particularly smaller, affordable loans—often make them unattractive for lenders. Relatively small loans to low- or moderate-income households require more work (that is, higher transaction costs) and usually result in less revenue than larger loans to middle- and upper-income households.

Box 8.2. Proactive Servicing in Mexico

Since 1996, the SOFOLs have been providing mortgage loans to low- and moderate-income households (incomes two to eight times minimum wage) in Mexico. As of mid-2004, they had an outstanding portfolio of approximately $4.5 billion (Babatz 2006). Their delinquency rates are below 2.5 percent. They have pioneered innovative underwriting and servicing techniques for the affordable housing market in Mexico, including point-of-sale servicing and use of nontraditional measures such as rent and utility payments for informal borrower credit histories. Without subsidies, SOFOLs serve households earning between the median income and the 75th percentile, where banks traditionally served households earning more than the 75th percentile.

In Mexico, SOFOLs arose after the banking crisis of the mid-1990s to provide affordable housing finance. They have been highly successful in managing the risks and costs of servicing this market.

Other Risks

Liquidity Risk

Liquidity risk refers to the risk that money will be needed before it is due. A lender faced with short-term and unstable sources of funds (for example, sight deposits, short-term bank loans) may not make mortgages because of the risk that it cannot meet its cash outflow needs. Assets that cannot be pledged as collateral for short-term borrowing also increase liquidity risk.

Liquidity risk is not unique to housing finance but is rather a broader financial sector stability issue. In modern financial markets, central banks provide the ultimate backstop for liquidity. In addition, deposit insurance reduces the likelihood of massive withdrawals from depository institutions; however, the long-term nature of mortgages creates greater liquidity risk than other types of lending. This is frequently cited as a reason why banks will not provide housing finance in emerging markets. Lenders manage liquidity risk through funding diversification and planning.

Liquidity risk is subject to regulatory constraints such as ratios of long-term assets to long-term liabilities or liquid-to-total assets. Such regulations can be deleterious to the mortgage market, however. The West African Economic and Monetary Union sets a minimum of 70 percent for the ratio of long-term assets to long-term liabilities and does not include core deposits in its long-term liability definition. In countries with no bond markets and little long-term finance, the inability to provide long-term mortgage loans out of core deposits effectively precludes lending.

One way for government to improve the liquidity of mortgage assets is to accept mortgage securities as collateral at the discount window—a solution massively used by the central banks of countries affected by the subprime crisis to maintain some liquidity in the mortgage backed securities market.[5] Nevertheless, independent central banks may not wish to provide specific sector support or may be uncomfortable with the credit quality of the securities. Government can take a limited and targeted role in reducing liquidity risk for primary lenders by backing a liquidity facility.[6]

Liquidity risk is especially apparent for non-depository lenders, as shown in the current U.S. subprime mortgage crisis. Many such lenders funded their inventory held for sale with commercial paper or warehouse loans from banks. When investors became nervous about the credit risk of the lender and collateral, the lenders found themselves without access to short-term funding, leading to forced asset sales into a depressed market and bankruptcy.

Market Risk

Market risk stems from uncertainty with respect to expected inflation, actual inflation, real interest rates, and exchange rates. Lending for a longer term, as for housing, greatly increases these risks. The macroeconomic environment and the characteristics of the mortgage instrument are the principal determinants of cash flow risk. For example, a low-cost prepayment option may be a desirable feature of the mortgage instrument for the consumer, but it significantly increases the cash-flow risk to the lender. Environments that

---

5. Central banks widened for this purpose normal eligibility criteria of MBS to their rediscount window.
6. See chapter 15 on mortgage securities.

are more volatile generate greater risk, which reduces the affordability and availability of funds. FX-denominated mortgages may have attractive rates at a particular point in time but exchange-rate fluctuation can lead to significant cash-flow risk for mismatched lenders and borrowers. In Mexico, the government has created an innovative risk management program to cushion the risk of macroeconomic shock for borrowers and investors.

There are a wide range of metrics and methods to understand and mitigate market risk by both lenders and investors. Well-run institutions employ a range of tools to understand their market-risk position and manage risk within the tolerances set by management and the board.

Managers of deposit-funded lenders have to trade off stability of net income with stability or growth in the estimated market value of equity. Net income measures the periodic income available as a result of the lender's operations. Changes in the market value of equity reflect the value that management creates for shareholders. While it is management's primary task to maximize the value of shareholder's equity, that overall goal has to be bal-

---

Box 8.3. Managing Market Risk

Since 1999 in Mexico, mortgages have been originated with a market-risk hedge that is intended to cope with extraordinary or permanent decreases in real minimum wages. This swap allows borrowers to make payments that are linked to the minimum wage index while the loan principal is indexed to consumer price inflation, protecting lenders (Babatz 2006). The swap is implemented under the administration of Sociedad Hipotecaria Federal (SHF), a government-owned mortgage development bank. The borrower and the government share the cost of the swap. The former pays a 71-basis-point fee that, in conjunction with a credit line backed by the government, creates a fund intended to meet a temporary lack of payment flows to securities issued by the lender. The fund is arranged to be able to support a 25 percent deterioration in real wages over a 30-year period. If the fall is higher (lower) the SHF would incur losses (gains). The swap allows borrowers, particularly lower-income borrowers, to have a loan with payments better matched to their incomes, while lenders get payments that more closely conform to investor requirements.

Box 8.4. Polish Foreign Exchange Lending Requirements

Polish authorities have been concerned about the rising proportion of FX-denominated loans among their residential mortgages—62 percent by the end of 2005. This trend resulted from the low nominal rate of Swiss franc mortgages relative to zloty-denominated loans. While the Swiss franc loans are initially more affordable, borrowers earning zlotys are exposed to FX fluctuations, which can create greater credit risk. A ban was considered but abandoned as market unfriendly. The Commission for Banking Supervision instead issued recommendations in 2006 related to mortgage lending, including for FX-denominated loans. Banks are expected to adjust their underwriting policy (notably through a lower LTV), and assess the creditworthiness of clients by assuming the higher credit rate of a Polish Zloty New (PLN) loan, and a loan principal augmented by 20 percent to simulate the impact of a devaluation. Banks are expected to periodically assess the quality of their mortgage portfolio, and particularly exposed banks are expected to conduct periodic stress tests assuming a devaluation of 30 percent persisting for 12 months. The stress test results are reported to the National Bank of Poland. Banks must also improve their credit information to clients in a comprehensible way. They should first offer PLN loans, obtain from the client a written consent of being aware of the FX risk, and simulate loan repayments in a negative devaluation case (rate as of PLN credit loan, and a principal higher by 20 percent).

anced with the need to maintain relatively stable net income and the capacity to pay dividends.

The financial terms of a mortgage loan (that is, fixed or floating rate, constant or price-level-adjusting principal) allocate market risk between borrowers, lenders, and, in many markets, investors. FRMs place market risk in the hands of the lender, and require matched funding and protection from prepayment risk. Floating rate and inflation indexed loans place at least some market risk in the hands of the borrower, and require attention to payment shock (treated above under credit risk), and to any mismatch between the nature and timing of the indices to which the loans and the liabilities that fund them are linked (basis risk). Economies that have less liquid fixed-income markets may have difficulty in establishing a reliable index for floating rate mortgages.

An increasing source of market risk in Central and Eastern European countries arises from the heavy use of mortgages denominated in or indexed to foreign currencies. In Poland, 62 percent of the outstanding loans were FX linked at the end of 2005, with even higher percentages of 80 percent in Ukraine and 82 percent in Romania. The regulators in these countries have expressed concern about the borrower credit risk associated with currency devaluation, as well as the lender market risk stemming from unhedged positions. The National Bank of Romania has adopted a basic capital adequacy ratio of 6 percent for mortgage loans, instead of the 4 percent rate applied in most European countries under Basel I. As part of the effort to encourage lending in local currency, the National Bank of Romania raised the basic capital required for FX-denominated assets to 130 percent of the basic ratio. Additionally, banks are restricted to an absolute lending ceiling for FX loans of 300 percent of their capital. The National Bank of Poland has recently adopted tough disclosure and risk management guidelines for FX lending (box 8.4).

Agency Risk

Agency risk occurs when there is a separation in the functions of lending. Agency risk occurs at the primary-market level, where lenders may depend on brokers to market and process loans and appraisers to value the collateral. In secondary markets, investors depend on third-party originators and servicers to underwrite, collect, and remit payments. It is also a major concern in government guarantee programs, as the government is exposed to a moral hazard (use of guarantees leading to more risky behavior). The presence of agency risk increases the cost of lending and securitization. Lenders and investors manage agency risk with contract terms, quality controls, and technology. Nevertheless, this risk materialized at various levels of the lending chain in the United States, from unscrupulous bankers and appraisers to moral hazard in securitized portfolios, and was a driver fo the subprime crisis.

Operational Risk

Operational risk is a broad, catch-all topic, including risk of loss from incomplete documentation, automated system failures, data entry errors, rogue traders, and computer security breaches. The transaction intensity of the mortgage business makes mortgage lenders particularly subject to operational risk. The documents that establish the mortgage lien are usually long and complex. The long term to maturity of mortgages increases the likelihood of error. Mortgage originators need effective controls, systems, and business processes to manage the credit underwriting process and all of the associated paperwork. Mortgage servicers need robust automated systems and controls to efficiently process the monthly payments on the thousands of relatively small, long-term loans that they make. Banks that issue mortgage bonds or mortgage-backed securities need robust and sophisticated systems to administer the monthly cash flows to investors for maturities of 10 years or more.

While it may seem obvious that mortgage lenders should employ effective operational systems and internal controls, the lack of such systems has magnified losses in most mortgage-related financial crises. In credit booms, lenders have often loosened control of processing legal requirements in the press to compete for loan volume. This was the case in Mexico, Indonesia, Thailand, and Colombia in the 1990s, and in the United States in the 1980s and in the recent subprime lending boom. In the wake of each of these crises, it was found that many banks lacked the basic documentation to enforce mortgage liens.

Operational risk can become more important as the mortgage value chain is "unbundled" through securitization. As separate participants specialize in elements of the process (for example, origination, servicing, securitization), there are more actors involved and additional chances for operational error, as control over separate steps moves from one organization to another. Traditional bank regulators may not have authority or responsibility for regulating servicers. In the United States, Europe, and Mexico, the industry has come to rely at least in part on rating-agency evaluations of the capacity of servicers. In Colombia, the mortgage securitization firm Titularizadora Colombiana sets the industry standards for servicer capability, and rates the separate servicers as a way of indicating the firms eligible for servicing loans it will purchase.

Systemic Credit Risk

Systemic credit risk can arise if there is a sudden and sharp decline in property values. The decline may be local in nature (for example, a large firm leaves the area or goes bankrupt) or national (for example, because of a large, unanticipated change in the inflation rate). A market failure may exist if lenders cannot diversify mortgage credit risk. For example, U.S. S&L associations were forced by regulation to operate on a narrowly defined geographic basis until the 1980s, and were exposed to significant concentration risk (for example, the oil-producing states in the Southwest). Mortgage insurance can diversify risk and increase the supply of mortgage credit.[7]

Real estate prices move in cycles, sometimes with tremendous volatility, which creates risk for lenders and for the stability of financial systems.[8] Volatile real estate prices make it difficult to value the collateral underlying the mortgage, and to assess the credit risk of mortgage portfolios. During Colombia's real estate bubble of the 1990s, residential real estate prices rose 28 percent between 1992 and 1994, and then fell 30 percent between 1994 and 1999.[9] Because of this and other factors, including rising unemployment and the structure of the inflation index of the loans, defaults rose to a third of the system-wide mortgage portfolio, and the resulting collapse of several specialized mortgage banks lay at the core of the financial system crisis. Similar stories can be told for real estate lending in Japan in the 1980s, in the oil-patch states of the United States in the 1980s, in the East Asian crisis of the 1990s, and in the rise and decline of subprime lending in the United States.

The subprime crisis demonstrates how real estate bubbles can be propagated across the global financial system. A real estate bubble created in part by loose monetary policy in the United States was intensified by a mortgage bubble that became a mortgage and real estate bust affecting all types of lenders in the United States and abroad.

---

7. See chapter 13.
8. Wheaton 1999.
9. Cardenas and Badel 2003.

Research shows that real estate bubbles may result from co-movement with the overall economy, from policy choices such as changes to tax law, or from myopia on the part of economic actors.[10] Policy makers in both developed and emerging markets make policy choices that produce or deflate price bubbles.[11] It can be argued, however, that myopia is worse in emerging markets, where information is scarcer and markets are less efficient. Real estate markets in developed economies generally enjoy greater price transparency, more efficient markets for urban land, and better market infrastructure, including efficient property and lien registry systems, lower transaction costs, stronger legal frameworks for ownership and contract enforcement, and more sophisticated financial systems. These features can mute the effects of a bubble and provide for a more rapid adjustment to a collapse in prices.

Political Risk

The political risks of mortgage lending relate to events that reduce earnings from mortgage lending because of political intervention in the selection of borrowers, the rate adjustment process, the mortgage terms and conditions, or the foreclosure and eviction process. For example, the Colombian Supreme Court invalidated the index used on mortgage contracts in the middle of a severe economic downturn, leading to substantial losses for mortgage lenders. A new government in Nicaragua forgave the mortgage loans of the state housing bank upon assuming power in 1979, only to have the bank attempt to reinstate the loans at a later date when the financial implications of this action became clear (Mathey 1990).

The Role and Tools of Regulation

Effective regulation can foster the creation of more stable and resilient lenders and financial markets. These can support the extension of housing finance, contributing to economic growth and individual welfare. The long history of

---

10. Wheaton 1999.
11. See for example, DiPasquale and Wheaton (1992) on the effect of tax code changes in the United States on real estate prices during the 1980s.

Box 8.5. Keystone Bank

On September 1, 1999, the U.S. Office of the Comptroller of the Currency closed the First National Bank of Keystone, saying investigators were unable to account for some $515 million of the $1.1 billion assets recorded on the books of the 85-year-old bank. The bank had long been the economic mainstay of Keystone, a small town in a depressed coal-mining region of West Virginia. It soon became clear, however, that bank officer fraud, risky bank strategies, and poor oversight had turned Keystone's only financial institution into one of the costliest failures for the Federal Deposit Insurance Corporation since the Great Depression. Losses to the Federal Deposit Insurance Corporation (which compensates depositors for insured deposits when a bank fails) rose from that early estimate of $515 million to estimates in spring 2002 of $780–$820 million.

Keystone's failure at the height of the late 1990s economic boom sent shock waves through the regulatory and banking community. It concentrated attention on bank exposure to subprime loans and securitization risks, and on the need for regulatory bodies to act decisively when they suspect that management might be obstructing regulatory scrutiny.

Keystone's business centered on providing high LTV home equity loans, including home improvement and debt consolidation loans. It was feted as one of the most profitable small banks in the country and in 1999 it reported assets of $1.1 billion. Beginning in 1993, the small-town bank began to purchase ever-larger volumes of low-quality loans from third parties to repackage into asset-backed securities that could be sold to investors in the financial markets. By 1999, it had processed some $2.6 billion of loans in nearly 20 major deals. On the liability side of its balance sheet, it took advantage of the emerging wholesale deposit market to an unusual degree. This market allowed banks to collect deposits in chunks of millions of dollars from brokers, as opposed to the traditional route of gaining new funds by attracting larger numbers of individual, local depositors.

Concern about its rapid growth led the U.S. Office of the Comptroller of the Currency in 1997 to transfer responsibility for reviewing Keystone to a unit that focused on problem banks, and in 1998 the bank was banned from accepting any further brokered deposits. In July 1999, examiners discovered by means of direct

(continued)

Box 8.5. Keystone Bank *(continued)*

verification with the bank's loan servicers that $515 million in loans carried on the bank's books were not owned by the bank. On September 1, 1999, regulators closed the bank. Investigators found that loans recorded on the bank's books had been sold and the value of certain residual interest grossly inflated. Bank officers engaged in extensive fraud, siphoning off loan payments to personal accounts.

At an industry level, the collapse revealed the level of losses that can be incurred when a small bank begins to take advantage of innovations in banking and financial markets such as wholesale brokerages and securitization. Some commentators blamed the authorities for not closing the bank sooner, citing a lack of cooperation between regulatory agencies, particularly the Federal Deposit Insurance Corporation and the U.S. Office of the Comptroller of the Currency. For its part, the U.S. Office of the Comptroller of the Currency said that the case had helped to alert it to the risks in subprime lending and the complexities of asset securitization and residual valuations.

Source: Sunguard Bankware Erisk 2002.

financial bubbles and panics shows that financial market participants have not always been willing to hold adequate capital, to disclose fully the risks they engage in, or to manage risk effectively. The challenge for authorities is to balance the faster economic growth that can follow from lighter regulation against the costs that may result from the failure of lenders. In general, regulation should provide positive incentives for a variety of competitive institutions to deliver financial services to those who demand them. On specific technical issues, such as financial reporting, disclosure of risk, and appropriate levels of risk-based capital, authorities can look to international standards for guidance.

Research shows that incentives for prudent banking through transparency and market discipline are more effective than regulations based primarily on rules and checklists.[12] Emerging market financial-disclosure rules are often below international standards for best practice, security trading

---

12. Barth, Caprio, and Levine 2001 and 2006.

tends to be infrequent and illiquid, and audit rules are often weak. In such an environment, regulators can contribute significantly to economic growth by improving disclosure regimes and by instilling greater market discipline.

Effective supervisors in any market depend on a variety of tools, including risk-based examinations, off-site monitoring using reports, statistics, analytical models, monitoring of housing and financial markets, and dialogue with management. As financial institutions in sophisticated markets have engaged in increasingly complex businesses, some of the largest and most costly bank failures have resulted from a lack of understanding of risk on the part of management, investors, and regulators (box 8.5). As a result, in all markets, it is essential that regulators examine financial institutions, verify the accuracy of their disclosures, assess their financial health, assess the quality of their financial risk management, and monitor the effectiveness of external auditors and credit rating agencies.

International Standards for Reporting and Capital

Globalization of financial markets has brought with it the promulgation of international standards for safety and soundness regulation and for financial disclosures that seek to better address the risks of new technologies. The Basel Committee on Banking Supervision of the Bank for International Settlements (BIS) has set standards for bank safety and soundness regulation (the Basel Core Principles)[13] and for risk-based capital requirements (the Basel I and Basel II accords).[14] The International Accounting Standards Board has promulgated International Accounting Standards (IAS). All of these efforts have involved extensive consultations between regulatory and other authorities in developed countries, and to a lesser extent, emerging markets.

Although its terms and shortcomings pose challenges, more than 50 emerging markets are moving to adopt Basel II, albeit on country-specific schedules that are slower than that established for internationally active banks from G-10 countries.[15] The weakness of financial regulation in many emerging markets is a source of ongoing concern. Financial regulators in

---

13. Basel Committee on Banking Supervision 1997. See http://www.bis.org.
14. For the source documents describing the Basel accords, see the BIS Web site, www.bis.org.
15. Fratzscher 2004.

many emerging markets have yet to implement many of the central tenets of the Basel Core Principles, potentially leading to material weaknesses in the implementation of Basel II. Some aspects of Basel II are inappropriate for emerging markets that lack well-developed capital markets. Basel II fails to directly address market risk in the banking book, an omission that is particularly important for the regulation of mortgage lenders. There is a risk that implementing Basel II in the absence of an adequate infrastructure would lead to results that would at best be misleading, and at worst could lead to regulatory arbitrage and a material misunderstanding of the risks that banks face.

Finance companies, mortgage bankers, and securitization companies often fall outside of the purview of prudential bank regulation because they are not thought to affect the integrity of the payments system, and because they do not capture deposits. So long as they are supposed not to pose a systemic risk to the financial system, it has been widely considered in most countries that non-depository lenders should enjoy lighter regulation. This consensus was challenged in the case of Thailand, where bank lending to lightly regulated finance companies help precipitate the 1997 crisis. The approach has been challenged again in the subprime crisis, where the vast majority of the riskier subprime lending was carried out by lightly regulated subsidiaries of depository institutions or effectively unregulated non-bank lenders. The issue is to determine whether the greater economic growth that may result from lighter regulation outweighs the risks to the system that may result from institutional failure or from having unregulated entities create assets that are traded in the broader system.[16] The subprime crisis has changes the terms of this trade-off (see the last section of this chapter).

Provisions

A provision is a reserve that the lender establishes against expected losses on its portfolio of residential mortgage loans. As part of managing risk, banks should regularly review the quality of their loan portfolios. The supervisor

---

16. Carmichael and Pomerleano 2002, 190.

should assess the bank's ability to identify, classify, monitor, and address loans with credit quality problems in a timely manner.

Supervisors generally set provision requirements for lending institutions, and the content of these regulations varies widely among countries. Where data is available and loans are standardized enough to calculate expected loss, lenders should base the *general provision* on the estimated expected losses of the portfolio. For instance, in Canada, the United States, Hong Kong, and Mexico, for portfolios of homogenous loans, such as residential mortgages of a given cohort, interest rate, and loan maturity, the general reserve reflects the statistically expected lifetime loss on the portfolio.[17] Thus, the general reserve will be equal to the average default and loss rates experienced for loans of the type that make up the portfolio. Distinct from the general provision, *specific provisions* represent likely losses on individually identified loans, and are created as loans actually default, generally as a growing percentage of the outstanding balance as time in default passes.

IAS 39, "Financial Instruments: Recognition and Measurement," determines provisioning requirements for loans held on balance sheet. From an accounting perspective, a loan should be fully provisioned (that is, 100 percent) once the lender believes it will not be able to collect. In practice, the definitions and thresholds for provisioning vary widely among countries. Provisions can be used to manipulate earnings. In good times, since provisions are tax deductible, banks have an incentive to excessively provision in order to reduce taxes and reserve income for later periods. In a time of crisis, lenders may preserve earnings by failing to provision against rising defaults, postponing the harm to profits and shareholders' dividends. Alternatively, provisions have been a source of regulatory forbearance in times of crisis. As defaults grow during a crisis, regulators may allow lenders to postpone the recognition of loss, as they did during the S&L crisis in the United States during the 1980s.

Provisions are a matter of judgment informed by available information. Supervisors should develop regulations for general and specific provisions that reflect the best estimate of the quality of the loan. In mortgage lending, it is possible to generate such estimates in markets that have an adequate data history. Where data is inadequate, supervisors should prescribe provisioning

---

17. Laurin and Majnoni 2003 and Poveda 2000.

> ### Box 8.6. Spain's Statistical Provision
>
> One of the historical shortcomings of loan provisions has been their pro-cyclicality. Banks have a tendency to reduce provisioning levels as time passes from a credit crisis. In the event of a new shock, they are forced to quickly raise provisions to compensate for rising defaults. In an attempt to counter this pro-cyclicality, since 1999, Spain has imposed what they call a statistical provision that is designed to be countercyclical by using statistical expectations of loss to determine the provision. Provisioning is based on (statistically) expected losses. When loan specific provisions are low, a "dynamic" component is added to them and accrues. When the need for specific provisioning exceeds expected losses and statistical provisions, the previously accumulated surpluses are used to cover the gap.
>
> In the Spanish system, Banks may estimate risk using a standard methodology provided by the Bank of Spain, or they may use their own estimates of expected risk, given demanding requirements for the data and quality of their models, including the requirement that data cover at least one full credit cycle. In the standard methodology, residential mortgages are considered to be low-risk assets, and carry a 0.1 percent coefficient for the purposes of the statistical provision, versus 0 percent for risk-free assets, and 1 percent for consumer loans.

rules that reflect what is known of local performance, and of performance in other countries with similar characteristics but better data.

For instance, Argentine banks are required to hold a 1 percent provision against all current loans, with escalating percentages as delinquencies advance. The required provision for delinquent or doubtful collateralized loans is roughly that of uncollateralized loans at each stage. Therefore, a collateralized loan that suffers from "inadequate compliance" requires a 3 percent provision, while an uncollateralized loan in a similar condition requires a 5 percent provision. Interest accruals for loans in excess of 90 days of delinquency must be completely provisioned against. Loans considered unrecoverable must be completely provisioned, whether collateralized or not. Mortgage loans in default may benefit from a provision of less than

100 percent if the bank obtains a letter from a lawyer attesting to the value of the collateral.[18]

In terms of international standards, the Basel Committee has issued a consultative paper that provides principles that are in line with IAS 39.[19] Neither the consultative paper nor IAS 39, however, provide uniform loan classification techniques, nor a standard procedure to assess loan risk.[20] Thus, regulators have to balance prudential considerations against somewhat vague accounting requirements.

Capital Requirements for Primary Lenders

Capital is the reserve held against any kind of unexpected or extreme financial risk. The capital requirement should reflect risk—it should change as the risk level of the institution changes, and so reward better risk management. Capital should represent a bright line for the regulator and for the regulated. Capital requirements should provide a signal to the markets of the risk that the institution bears.

Over the past 20 years, many lenders and regulators have revolutionized their approach to managing capital, moving from a static, historic approach to one that is risk-based and forward-looking. Large, internationally active banks have moved the farthest, adopting sophisticated, quantitative approaches to risk management and capital allocation.

Mortgage lenders in the United States and Europe have led the development of quantitative models for credit and interest rate risk, involving options-based approaches to address issues particular to mortgage lending. Mortgages present specific credit-risk issues for managing capital: dependence on local real estate market dynamics; dependence on the appraised value of the collateral; and dependence on the ability to execute the mortgage pledge in case of default. The long term to maturity of mortgages can add volatility to the value of capital.

It is management's responsibility to measure, monitor, and mitigate risk in its business. Minimum capital requirements exist as reserves against

---

18. Banco Central de la República 2005.
19. Basel 1998.
20. Laurin and Majnoni 2003, 2.

extreme events. They are created under the assumption that management does its job correctly. Supervisors can use examinations and disclosures to prove that management is sound, and when they reveal problem circumstances, supervisors can take action, such as requiring additional capital. Each lender's management and board should have a plan for managing capital in terms of the risk appetite and risk profile of the institution. Supervisors should review the adequacy of the bank's risk assessment and the capital requirement that follows. There should be active dialogue between the lender and supervisor on the risks the lender takes and the means that it employs to mitigate those risks.

Basel II Capital Standards and Mortgage Lending

Basel I created a preference for mortgage lending, according a 50 percent risk weight for low LTV loans. This was done under the assumption that mortgage lending was demonstrably safer than other forms of lending. This has not always been the case, particularly in emerging markets.

Many issues particular to mortgage lending are addressed in the Basel II standards.[21] Several are not, including geographic diversification and the market risk of mortgages held in the banking book. Basel II capital standards that are directly relevant to mortgage lending address: the credit risk of loans held in the banking book, credit enhancements, and investments in mortgage-backed securities.

In applying Basel II capital standards, the lender and supervisors may choose between two broad levels of sophistication. The choice depends on the technical capabilities of the lender, the complexity of their business, and the capacities of the supervisor:

- The standardized approach is an extension of Basel I with additional risk categories that allow for selected refinement of the risk sensitivity of capital requirements. It is likely to be the approach of choice for less sophisticated banks, and for emerging markets that

---

21. The chapter focuses on the applicability of Basel II to mortgage lending in emerging markets. It does not address many of the equally important challenges that face emerging market implementation of Basel II in other asset classes.

Box 8.7. Colombia Crisis

By contrast, to some developed economies, the regulatory authorities in emerging
economies may have reasons to consider that residential mortgage markets
should not be treated as a low-risk class of assets, if the legal framework is
inhospitable to lenders and if the macroeconomic environment is instable. This
concern is acute after experiencing a brutal crisis often preceded by a long period
of good performance. Most Latin American countries went through such an
ordeal with significant fiscal impacts in order to bail out borrowers or lenders
(Brazil, Colombia, Mexico, Argentina, Uruguay, and so forth). The recent crisis
of the mortgage sector in Colombia (1997–2002) was severe, as shown below.
It was caused by a macro crisis (GDP contraction, higher market rates, unemployment, fall in housing prices) and by a legal and regulatory instability (long
foreclosure delays, but also legal changes to the whole portfolio, which was made
of hazardous indexed loans). The portfolio quality has recovered since (less than 5
percent nonperforming loans [NPLs]) thanks to debt restructuring programs and
to the securitization of NPL mortgage portfolios.

Mortgage Loans 90 Days Delinquency Rate

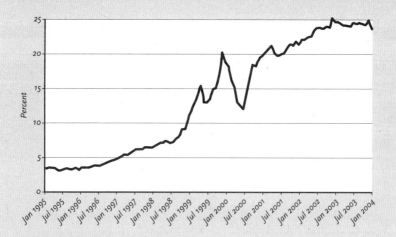

Source: Titularizadora Colombiana, March 2006.

move to Basel II. The most important issue for mortgage lenders under the standardized approach is the risk weight for mortgages retained in the banking book. For large internationally active banks, this will fall from 50 percent under Basel I to 35 percent under the Basel II standardized approach in the case of residential mortgages. Also important for mortgage finance, the standardized approach allows for the use of external credit-rating agency ratings of credit enhancers (such as mortgage default insurers), and of asset-backed securities, including MBSs. Use of credit rating agencies presents challenges for emerging markets, which often have no such firms, or lack the practical ability to enforce standards for credit ratings.

- The internal-ratings-based (IRB) approach permits banks to hold capital according to their own estimates of risk parameters such as the probability of default and the expected loss given default of their credit portfolios. In efficient mortgage markets, where mortgage lending represents the safest business lines of many banks, the IRB approach will result in a dramatic lowering of risk weights, to as little as 10 percent.[22] IRB requires sophisticated technology and technical staff on the part of both lenders and supervisors. Lenders must demonstrate that their models and the procedures for using them are well developed and robust, and their data adequate to assess risk. In general, Basel II requires at least five years of detailed data history for a given asset class to establish default and loss statistics. This is inadequate for mortgage lending, given the long cycles of real estate prices. Supervisory agencies need budget to employ, train, and retain staff with the capacity to evaluate the lenders' models and methods.

The reduced risk weight for mortgages in the banking book recognizes the high value of the mortgage pledge in countries with liquid real estate markets, well-defined valuation rules, and efficient contract enforcement. In well-developed mortgage markets, foreclosure may take as little as three months. In emerging markets, however, foreclosure generally takes years, and expected losses rise quickly with the length of time required to foreclose.

---

22. The risk weight for residential real estate has a 10 percent floor that will be imposed for at least the transition period to adoption of Basel II, defined as the first three years of effectiveness of the accord. (Basel 2004, paragraph 266, page 58).

As a result, the Basel committee notes that the 35 percent weight should be applied only when valuation criteria establish the security of the collateral, and where the default experience of mortgages justifies the lower weight. Otherwise, supervisors should require a higher risk weight.

Unless they can demonstrate lower risk, emerging market regulators should not adopt a 35 percent risk weight for mortgages. Few emerging market regulators have the resources to supervise the IRB approach to capital standards, and none of these will adopt it within the time frame of wealthy countries. For example, Russia and Colombia will continue to require a 100 percent risk weight as they move to adopt Basel II according to their own schedules. Thailand, on the other hand, is applying a 35 percent risk weight for loans below 3 million baht, despite the fact that the regulators are not adopting any other part of Basel II.

Basel II also asks regulators to determine capital requirements for operational risk. Operational risk is measured in terms of the likelihood of processing errors and associated expected losses, and the likelihood of incidents such as undesired access to proprietary systems by computer hackers. There is, however, a scarcity of data on operational risk in every market, be it well developed or not, and the methodology for developing assessments of operational risk is immature. Given the lack of data and research for G-10 internationally active banks, it is likely to be some time before extensive quantification of operational risk is available in emerging markets.

Capital Requirements—Supervisory Standards

Basel II calls on regulators to evaluate the quality and accuracy of each bank's risk assessment, risk management, and internal controls. Pillar 2 places responsibility on banks to improve their risk management practices. Supervisors are responsible for judging the efforts of banks to assess and mitigate risk. Supervisors are to intervene where necessary, including by requiring additional capital. The Basel committee expects regulators to use Pillar 2 to determine the regulatory and capital treatment of risks that are not explicitly included in the capital adequacy requirements of Pillar 1. Three of these risks are particularly important for mortgage lenders:

Credit Concentration Risk

Basel II is silent on the topic of geographic diversification, an important omission with respect to mortgage markets. Real estate values are driven by local economic and regulatory factors, so geographic diversification plays an important role in mitigating credit risk in mortgage lending. One estimate showed that the economic capital required for a portfolio of regionally concentrated loans to highly rated borrowers in the United States would be two-and-a-half times that of a diversified portfolio to similarly rated borrowers (Calem and LaCour-Little 2004). This is intuitive for countries with large, economically diverse territories such as the United States or China. Even in small countries, however, house-price levels and trends can vary dramatically between the centers of major cities and the surrounding countryside. For instance, in Armenia, the price per square meter for housing in the center of the capital is more than three times that of the country's second city. Further, Armenia is a good example of another emerging-economy phenomenon, where rapid residential real estate price increases in the most economically active region of the country are driven by speculation more than by the need for shelter.[23]

Supervisors should gather and publish data on house price trends in local and national markets. They can use this data to estimate default and loss rates, and so gauge the risk of regionally concentrated loan portfolios. Supervisors may also simulate stresses to lender portfolios using historically based worst-case scenarios. In concentrated markets, and particularly where there is a risk of speculative bubbles, regulators should be wary of overexposure to a single region or location, and should raise capital requirements for riskier portfolios. Supervisors should encourage mortgage lenders to diversify their portfolios.

Market and Liquidity Risk

Portfolios of 15- or 20-year mortgages require similar term funding. While floating rate mortgages may reduce interest rate risk, they still present

23. Like many emerging economies, Armenia lacks viable individual savings vehicles aside from real estate. Banks pay less than the inflation rate on deposits, there is no public market for equity or debt securities, and there is no private pension system.

liquidity risk. Banking supervisors generally use ratios to monitor liquidity risk as described above. Some, however, have adopted more involved stress test requirements. While Basel II does not include standards for market risk in the loan portfolio, many countries require lenders to apply industry best practice for asset liability management, and some impose capital requirements for the lending portfolio. In 2002, India's National Housing Bank, promulgated guidelines for asset-liability management at India's specialized housing lenders, which are known as housing finance companies (HFCs). HFCs are permitted to take deposits and make residential mortgage loans. The National Housing Bank guidelines reflect the specific risks of longer-term mortgage lending funded by short-term deposits. The rules include guidance for the development of financial indicators of risk and management information systems to monitor term mismatch and liquidity on the balance sheet. At the time they were promulgated, they were flexible in that they recognized the lack of management and automated systems at many HFCs. The guidelines envisioned an evolution from simple techniques such as categorizing cash flows by maturity buckets or bands, to calculating duration of equity and risk-adjusted return on capital. Importantly, they also address the governance aspects of market risk management, calling for HFCs to establish risk committees for both management and boards of directors.

Argentina's standard is demanding in that it expects all banks to be able to estimate value at risk for every asset class in both domestic and foreign currency. At the same time, it necessarily requires a number of assumptions about the structure of the balance sheet. Risk capital for interest rate risk of non-quoted assets such as loans is based on the estimated maximum expected loss of the value of the net asset position at a 99 percent confidence interval over a three-month time horizon. Capital requirements for net asset positions are defined in terms of assumptions about which liabilities fund which assets. The Argentine regulation allows banks with strong capital, assets, management, earnings, and liquidity (CAMEL) ratings to recognize that a large part of their deposit base is effectively permanent, even if contractually short term in nature. These banks are permitted to assign up to 50 percent of short-term deposits to fund long-term fixed rate assets. Adjustable rate loans that have a rate linked to an external index are considered to have a maturity equal to the reset frequency of the index. For adjustable rate loans with administrative variation, where the bank has the contractual ability to vary the rate, 40 percent are considered to be fixed rate, reflecting the experience in most countries that, in case of crisis, banks are not able to raise the rate on such loans as quickly and as high as market conditions might dictate. This inability to adjust rates in time of crisis reflects the heightened credit risk that results from such moves, as well as political pressure to keep rates stable.[24]

Mortgage Loan Design

In many markets, lenders have employed loan design techniques to reduce the initial payments required on a mortgage, and so make it possible for the borrower to initially afford the payment. These may include "teaser" interest rates that start out lower than market, but escalate with time, or "negative amortization" features that trade off a lower initial payment with a growing principal amount. Such loan designs may lead to higher defaults if house prices fall or interest rates rise unexpectedly. A proliferation of exotic loan designs contributed to the high default rates in the Colombian crisis and led to a reaction by the Supreme Court to ban the designs and allow only fixed-rate lending (real and peso). Likewise, after the devaluation shock and banking crisis in Turkey in 2001 all indexed and variable rate loans were outlawed. The mortgage law passed in 2007 allows these instruments but requires life-of-loan caps and detailed disclosure to borrowers.

Supervisors should require lenders to provide stress test results for all portfolios of loans, and they should pay particular attention to the assumptions and results for complex product designs.

Other Regulator Actions

Regulators can encourage or require other actions to strengthen the mortgage lending systems of individual countries. Such actions can be particularly important to reduce the probability and severity of housing cycles.

---

24. Banco Central de la República 2005.

Real Estate Market Information

One step is to actively foster the development and publication of accurate, detailed information on real estate prices and transactions. In any market, speculative price bubbles are hard to spot until after the fact; however, the task of detection is made more difficult if there is a lack of consistent information on the prices themselves, and on the factors that lead to changes in real estate prices. Regulators in many markets track the performance of real estate markets. Central banks and regulators in China, the United Kingdom, and many other countries monitor real estate markets. Thailand (GHB) set up a Real Estate Information Center in 2004 to provide real-time price and transaction data—in part to help policy makers spot bubbles that preceded the Asian financial crisis of 1997. SHF is doing the same in Mexico. The U.K. Financial Services Authority (FSA) discusses the impact that a possible fall in house prices would have on consumer wealth and expenditures, on the health of lenders, and on the economy as a whole in its risk outlook for U.K. financial markets (FSA 2006).

Management and Reporting Standards

Regulators should produce management standards and reporting requirements for lenders, and include adherence to these standards as part of examination criteria. Lenders should be able to articulate a coherent and reasonable strategy for lending to a given real estate market and their means for mitigating risk in that market. Riskier products should have limits in terms of total assets or total capital. Examiners should review plans for credit risk, market risk, and operational risk, and compare performance of lender portfolios and of management against the plans.

Examples of such rules in the United States include three interagency regulations:

- On real estate lending, U.S. regulators require that each lender establish and maintain written policies that establish appropriate limits and standards for real estate lending, and that these be reviewed by the board of directors at least annually. These standards must establish portfolio diversification standards, prudent underwriting standards, and loan administrations standards. The regulation requires lenders to monitor conditions in real estate markets where they operate. [25]

- On lending for residential real estate construction, regulations require that lenders demonstrate understanding of and expertise regarding real estate construction lending. The rules set LTV requirements for construction loans, and for the use of appraised values in establishing LTVs. For instance, the value used for a construction loan must take into account not only the assumed price of the final units to be sold, but the remaining costs that would be incurred to complete the project and market the units.[26]

- Guidelines were recently proposed for offering nontraditional mortgage products such as interest-only loans. These set requirements for the underwriting of riskier adjustable rate loans, such as those that have built-in rate increases. They also would impose additional reporting requirements to the regulator for lenders that offer such products.[27] These guidelines proved to be of little effectiveness, and have been replaced by more forceful prescriptions since 2007 (see the section on the subprime crisis).

Taking Corrective Actions

In markets that are very rapidly rising, regulators may be compelled to take action to reduce speculation. Such actions could include raising capital requirements for real estate loans, lowering the permitted LTV level for mortgages, requiring lower payment-to-income ratios for new loans, or imposing taxes on sales of properties held for less than some threshold period considered longer than the time horizon of a short-term speculator. Such actions, however, could intensify real estate cycles if timed wrong.

In some markets, such as Shanghai, anecdotal information indicated that in 2004 and 2005, speculative investment surged with many buyers who were

---

25. Federal Reserve 1998.
26. Appendix C to Part 208 of the Code of Federal Regulations (CFR)—Interagency Guidelines for Real Estate Lending Policies.
27. Federal Reserve 2005.

holding properties for less than a month or two. The Chinese government undertook a number of short-term responses, such as lowering required LTVs for loans in Shanghai and imposing taxes on owners that held properties for less than five years. While these measures appear to have had an effect in slowing down price increases, they had a negative effect on the mobility of middle-class households via the five-year minimum hold to avoid tax. In considering such measures, it could be possible to limit transactions to the upper end of the market, where price speculation is likely to be greater since valuations are already higher, by definition.

The U.S. regulators face a challenge with the weakness in the subprime mortgage market. Underwriting was clearly relaxed and inappropriate loan products sold to borrowers in this market segment. There is active discussion of tightening underwriting guidelines and determining product "suitability" (See Consumer Protection, chapter 6), but regulators must be careful in promulgating these rules, as a sudden contraction in credit availability will exacerbate the foreclosure problem.

Financial Reporting and Disclosures by Primary Lenders

Accurate and thorough financial reporting contributes to market discipline and efficiency. Accounting standards provide detailed rules for reporting balance sheet values and periodic income and expense. Pillar 3 of Basel II provides standards for information disclosure that help investors and regulators to better understand the risks carried in a lender's portfolio. In addition, lenders should disclose indicators of the level of market risk that they incur in funding long maturity mortgages.

Developed market mortgage lenders should face little challenge in complying with IAS standards for loan accounting or with Pillar 3 core quantitative and qualitative disclosure requirements for credit risk and market risk. In many emerging countries, however, more detailed disclosures for credit and market risk will have to await the development of improved systems and management methods.

In most emerging markets, the move to regulation based on market discipline is constrained by the lack of a supporting infrastructure of financial reporting practices. Many emerging markets have not yet adopted IAS or clear rules for audit practice and auditor independence. Most emerging market regulators lack the budgets to hire enough technically qualified staff at salaries that are competitive with the private sector. As a result, they are often unable to supervise rapidly innovating business processes in detail. For example, neither Colombia nor Russia has fully implemented IAS, and regulators in each face substantial challenges in enforcing existing standards.

In an efficient market, investors penalize lenders that fail to comply with disclosure standards. In less efficient markets, regulators and auditors have a greater role in promoting and enforcing disclosure standards. Beyond reporting of operational risk parameters, the difficulties with Pillar 3 in emerging markets are likely to lie in obtaining legal authority to require financial disclosures, and in obtaining regulatory resources to enforce such standards. Further, markets will have to develop more depth to accurately value assets such as mortgage servicing rights.

Regulation of Secondary Mortgage Institutions

As discussed in the mortgage securities chapter (see chapter 12), secondary market institutions have been created in a number of emerging markets. These include both liquidity facilities and mortgage securitization companies. Many of the former have been created with extensive involvement of the Central Bank, which directly or indirectly supervises their activities (for example, Egypt, Jordan, India, Malaysia, Trinidad). In Mexico, the liquidity facility is subject to prudential regulation by the unified banking and securities regulator. Sound prudential regulation of liquidity facilities is in keeping with their principal function of supplying liquidity and capital market access to mortgage lenders. Their security issuance is regulated and supervised by domestic security regulators and local rating agencies.

Case Study: The U.S. Subprime Crisis

The United States' crisis in subprime mortgage lending revealed a number of failings in industry risk management and regulation. Emphasizing the importance of good risk management and regulation, the subprime crisis has disrupted international financial markets to an extent exceeding all expectations. Even though riskier subprime ARMs made up no more than 8 percent of all U.S. mortgages in 2006 (MBA 2007), the ripple effect of the unexpected rise in subprime defaults has already led to the failure of several U.S. non-bank lenders, a well-regarded U.K. lender, and a German Landesbank. Uncertainty about the exposure of highly rated European and U.S. banks to subprime defaults revealed fundamental weaknesses in international credit markets, and created an international credit crunch.

The Property Boom and Loose Credit Underwriting

The recent real estate boom and the decline in long-term interest rates were important contributors to the rise of subprime lending. National average property prices rose 86 percent between 1996 and 2006 (Shiller 2007). While all mortgage lending grew rapidly with rising house prices, subprime lending came of age in this most recent boom. Subprime originations rose from 9 percent of total mortgage lending in 2001 to 20 percent in 2006. Property speculation grew as the boom persisted. Lenders came to rely more on the rising value of collateral to secure the loan than the borrower's ability to repay from income. The quality of loans deteriorated and underwriting criteria were relaxed (Demyanyk and Van Hemert 2007). In 2006, 38 percent of subprime loans had a combined LTV of 100 percent or more. Half of all subprime loans had low or no documentation of borrower income or assets. As property prices began to decline between 2005 and 2007, many of the more highly leveraged borrowers found themselves in negative equity, with the value of the debt exceeding the value of the house, making it impossible to refinance these loans. Speculative borrowers with negative equity are much more likely to default than other borrowers. By the third quarter of 2007, serious delinquencies (90 or more days delinquent or in foreclosure) for subprime loans rose to 11.38 percent from 6.78 percent in 2006 (and about 18 percent for ARM subprime loans) By comparison, serious delinquencies on prime conventional mortgages rose to 1.31 percent from 0.79 percent in the same period a year earlier (MBA 2007).

Reduced Reliance on Credit Enhancements

Loosened underwriting contributed to decreased use of mortgage insurance (MI). MI provides an important third-party review of underwriting quality, and a credit enhancement that facilitates securitization. Lenders encouraged low- and moderate-income borrowers to take out more profitable subprime ARMs instead of FHA or privately insured FRMs by offering faster disbursement and reduced documentation requirements. Until 2006, federal tax rules favored 100 percent "piggyback" financing with a combination of an 80 LTV first lien and a 20 percent second lien piggyback mortgage at a higher rate of interest. The market share for loans originated with MI fell from 26 percent in 1997 to 11.5 percent in 2006.

Risky Loan Design

The design of many subprime loans exacerbates the effects of declining house prices and rising interest rates, leading to increased defaults. Riskier designs include ARMs with complex features, interest-only mortgages, and more complex designs. For instance, to make loans initially more affordable, many subprime ARMs featured low interest rates for a relatively short period of two or three years ("teaser" rates) that subsequently adjusted sharply higher. These loans were termed 2/28 or 3/27 because the initial fixed-rate period could be two or three years, but the loan amortized over 30 years. Other loans, known as "option ARMs," enabled borrowers to pay a variable amount each month, allowing for minimal or no amortization and capitalizing any unpaid interest into the principal outstanding. Even option ARMs, however, eventually require the borrower to adhere to a minimum payment schedule. So long as house prices were rising quickly, borrowers could wait two or three years and then use property appreciation and their recent payment history to refinance out of risky loans. Once house prices began to fall, however, many highly leveraged borrowers found themselves unable to either refinance or to make the new, higher payments. At the end of September 2007, serious delinquencies for subprime ARMs reached 15.63 percent, 4.25 percent higher than the serious delinquency rate for all subprime loans (MBA 2007).

Lack of Consumer Information

The poor credit quality of subprime loans is exacerbated by poor levels of consumer information. U.S. laws require detailed disclosure at the time of purchase or refinance, but in a format that is difficult to understand with many details extraneous to their understanding the risk of the loan (Guttentag 2002, 2004). This is a particular concern when lending to households with limited levels of financial education. Some subprime lenders have engaged in aggressive marketing and predatory lending behaviors (FTC 2007). This is symptomatic of the fee-based compensation system and a breakdown in the historic incentives for solid underwriting in the securitization market.

Breakdowns in the Behavior of Participants in the Securitization Value Chain

The subprime crisis revealed weaknesses in the incentive structure of the securitization model. Historically, the incentive to maximize volume and reduce costs by loosening underwriting standards has been countered outside of the subprime market by the need to maintain a good reputation with servicers and securitizers, and contractual requirements to buy back loans that default too early. The reputation incentive was attenuated by cost and market pressures. There has been strong demand for high-yield securities with little attention paid to due diligence by investors. Rating-agency default models have not adequately reflected default risk, and the expectation of rising house prices reduced lender concerns about possible defaults. The difficulty of enforcing contractual loan repurchase requirements became clear in the early part of 2007, as early payment defaults rose, and many non-bank lenders were driven into bankruptcy by demands that they take back the defaulting loans. Thinly staffed servicers lack the capacity to handle a large volume of loss mitigation efforts, and so move quickly to foreclosure, further depressing housing markets.

The Influence of Trends in International Capital Markets

Capital market trends contributed to the growth in subprime lending, the loosening of underwriting standards, and to the subsequent international liquidity crisis. First, since the financial crises of 1998, there has been an accumulation of liquidity on the part of international investors. As inflation, sovereign risk spreads, and nominal interest rates fell in most countries after 2000, investors have increasingly struggled to find opportunities to earn returns greater than inflation. Securities backed by subprime mortgages offered such an opportunity, given the high nominal interest rates paid by the underlying collateral and the high credit ratings conferred by product structuring and third-party credit enhancements, such as by monoline credit insurers. Between 2001 and 2006, the portion of subprime originations that were securitized rose from 46 percent to 75 percent (Ashcraft and Schuermann 2007). Unable to evaluate rating agency models and unable or unwilling to model increasingly complex structures, international investors relied on credit rating agency analysis instead of their own research. Rating agency models of subprime loan performance, however, did not take into account the declining underwriting standards, house price declines, or interest rate increases that became evident in 2007. As subprime defaults rose above rating agency expectations, the performance of lower-rated subprime securities deteriorated.

Reduced Transparency Resulting from Complex Security Structures and Incomplete Information on Exposures

The subprime crisis was worsened by the complexity of subprime securitizations, the fact that they are not traded on exchanges, and a lack of clarity as to which investors are exposed to potential losses. Many subprime transactions involved successively packaging subordinated bonds to create highly rated securities, which are in greatest demand. Subordinate bonds from several deals were often packaged and structured to create a highly rated bond. In the absence of exchange-based market makers, it becomes difficult to obtain quotes when there is uncertainty about the value of the underlying collateral. In addition, privately placed securities are not subject to specific disclosure rules. Furthermore, comprehensive data does not exist on the holdings of subprime-backed securities by hedge funds or other special investment vehicles. Nor is there public data on the exposure of major banks to these funds. As performance of subprime collateral worsened, it became difficult to price subprime-backed bonds, to trace the potential performance of structures, or to assess the effect on investors. As a result, many market participants stopped transacting as they waited for the picture to clear. The lack of disclosures and due diligence was made worse when banks created leveraged investment funds known as structured investment vehicles that issued short-term debt against higher-yield, long-maturity subprime securities.

Regulatory Failures in the United States Contributed to the Growth of Risky Subprime Lending Practices

There are multiple national and state regulators involved in mortgage lending, all of which were slow to address the well-publicized risks of relaxed subprime credit underwriting. Many non-bank U.S. lenders are not subject to prudential regulation. In all, 30 percent of subprime loans were made by lightly regulated subsidiaries of banks and 50 percent were made by independent mortgage companies that are not subject to prudential regulation (Gramlich 2007). While several federal regulatory guidance notes were issued on subprime lending, they did not apply to the unregulated non-depository lenders. Beyond the issue of unregulated lenders, prudential regulators and legislators have been reluctant to impose suitability requirements on mortgage lenders.

The Risks of Subprime Practices and Those of Lending to Moderate- and Low-income Households Should Not Be Confused

It is important to note that problems with low-income subprime mortgage borrowers resulted primarily from failures by lenders and investors, and not from low borrower income. FHA loans to households with income levels similar to lower-income subprime borrowers have not defaulted in unusually large numbers during the past two years. The success of microfinance in emerging markets has demonstrated that low-income households can manage debt, and that lending to low-income households can be profitable.

The Subprime Crisis Was Avoidable

Many U.S. policy makers raised issues about the boom in subprime lending for a number of years prior to 2007. The crisis resulted from a disregard of basic credit precepts, such as the need for robust loan underwriting standards, the need for financial transparency, and the risks of excessive leverage. Developing-country policy makers can avoid these mistakes by ensuring that lenders follow long-established rules for credit management and consumer protection, and that capital market access is provided with a variety of tools in the context of reasonable standards for transparency.

Selected
countries

R21 G21
R31   O16
D14   N20
P34

CHAPTER 9

Contractual Savings for Housing

Hans-Joachim Dübel

This chapter explores the use of contractual saving schemes for housing (CSH) as a way to finance housing. CSH has been historically a central mechanism of raising capital for housing finance. With the broader use of capital markets in developed financial markets today, it has become primarily a complementary financing tool to bank-financed mortgage loans. Yet, CSH have enjoyed renewed growth in recent years, as the product has been exported to Eastern European countries, as well as farther afield, such as to China or India. CSH schemes are also popular in the Middle East and North Africa and parts of Latin America.

The concept is simple, relying on the potential borrower to save money over a number of years, thus building up some equity, while at the same time demonstrating their reliability and capacity to repay a debt. Once the saving period is over, a loan will be advanced to the saver, which will typically be equal or represent some low multiple of the amount already saved. Both loan and accumulated equity are jointly disbursed. In the most widely encountered variant, interest rates for savings are fixed below the market rate; the incentive to follow through on the scheme is provided by the promise of a similarly below-market, fixed-rate loan.

The simplicity of the product, however, comes with risks in terms of liquidity and interest rates, both for the financial institution and the saver or borrower. In many countries subsidies have been attached to CSHs in order to address these risks, and the net impact on housing finance systems has not always been positive. It is therefore advisable to study the benefits, risks, minimum institutional requirements, and subsidy dependency of the system carefully before implementing it.

The section starts by describing the features of today's CSHs, followed by a brief overview of their historical development.[1] It then discusses the main benefits and risks of CSH schemes, their suitability for housing-finance-system development purposes, the minimum institutional requirements for lenders, and questions of subsidization. The section ends by drawing conclusions for emerging markets.

Key Features of a Contractual Savings Scheme for Housing

General Character

CSHs link the savings efforts of an individual to a collective fund with the entitlement to receive a loan from this fund at a future date. CSHs, in their simplest form, therefore, make funding from other sources unnecessary. Since CSH does not require a developed market for savings capital, it is one of the oldest and simplest collective funding mechanisms in housing finance.

Basic Structure of a CSH Contract

In a CSH contract, the individual agrees with the lender to receive a loan in the future after the successful completion of a savings phase. At this point, accumulated savings and loan amount are disbursed together toward a housing finance purpose.

---

1. For an earlier analysis of the French and German systems, see Lea and Renaud 1993.

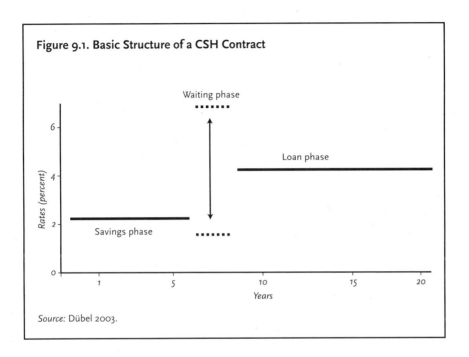

Figure 9.1. Basic Structure of a CSH Contract

Source: Dübel 2003.

The typical CSH contract life has three phases: the savings phase, a waiting phase between the dates of formal loan eligibility and actual loan allocation, and the loan phase. CSH contracts are long term, as mortgage loans; they will be closed over 10 and 20 years, and longer. The savings phase typically takes between one-fourth and one-third of the contract maturity; for example, five years followed by a loan amortizing over 10 years. The length of the waiting phase in a CSH contract may vary, depending on the availability of funds from the saver collective or the capital market. Figure 9.1 shows the basic structure.

Open and Closed CSH Schemes

Open CSH schemes use capital market funds for loan allocation, if a short-fall in liquidity from a lack of new savers arises. In this way, a waiting phase can be excluded or minimized; however, because capital market funds are mixed with collective funds, it is impossible to guarantee a fixed-loan interest

Table 9.1. Main Differences between Open and Closed CSH Schemes

Product feature	Open CSH (l'Épargne Logement)	Closed CSH (Bausparen)
Rate determination	Variable deposit and loan rates	Fixed deposit and loan rates
Deposit interest rate	Competitive after-tax yield	Below market after-tax yield
Loan interest rate	Deposit rate plus fixed servicing fee	Deposit rate plus fixed spread, rate usually below market
Loan volume	Loan interest paid cannot exceed 2.5 times deposit interest received	Loan-to-savings multiple of 1–1.5 times accumulated savings
Waiting phase	None	Lender cannot waive waiting phase, minimized through special reserve

Source: Dübel 2003.

rate in advance. Open schemes therefore generally carry variable deposit and lending rates. Their main value lies in providing a savings product and a simplified access to a loan, that is, a credit option. An example of an open scheme is the French Épargne-logement (table 9.1).

Closed CSH schemes, in contrast, rely solely on the resources provided by the saver collective. Apart from loan amortizations, new liquidity is derived exclusively from the deposits made by new saver generations. This entirely intergenerational financing structure enables closed CSH to offer fixed-interest rates on both the savings and loans sides. Still, some interest rate risk emerges in closed schemes through the risk of liquidity gaps that is traditionally managed by letting contracts ripe for allocation wait for loan disbursement until liquidity is reestablished (figure 9.1). The waiting phase, however, can be minimized through proper liquidity management techniques, and in advanced systems today is very short. Essentially, thus, the closed CSH contract with its fixed-rate loan promise adds an interest rate option product to the savings- and credit-option products of the open form. An example for a closed CSH system is the German Bausparen (table 9.1).

As will be shown further below, closed schemes have frequently run into liquidity problems, especially when operating in high-inflation environments. Therefore, semi-open schemes have evolved that combine aspects of open schemes—for example, inflation indexation—with aspects of closed schemes—fixed real deposit and lending rates.

Financing Function of CSH

CSH schemes are designed to provide long-term funds for housing; however, because they rely either mostly (open schemes) or exclusively (closed schemes) on collective resources, the financing function of an individual savings contract is economically limited relative to the scale of a larger housing finance investment, for example, a new house.

For example, taken together, the disbursements for new lending in closed-schemes can by definition not exceed the sum of new savings and loan amortizations in any given period. Unless there are many savers who decide to not take up a loan (good brothers), this limits the loan amounts that can be promised to an individual saver in relation to his or her savings. A typical closed CSH contract will thus fund loan volumes only moderately greater than savings amounts (see below). Open CSH schemes can provide higher multiples, albeit only at variable interest rates.

Because of the limited financing amounts per contract, CSH loans from closed schemes need to be co-financed by other loans in the case of larger investments. This may require the subordination of CSH loans to mortgage loans. In the German Bausparen system shown in table 9.1, for example, CSH loans are typically second mortgages to a first mortgage loan from a mortgage or savings bank.

CSH and Other Housing Finance Products

The following discussion is focused on regulated, permanent, voluntary, closed, and bank-managed CSH schemes. At this point, reference to other housing finance products is useful.

While CSH schemes originated in the mutual building society movement (figure 9.2), almost all present-day building societies operate with open funding mechanisms, using deposits and partly issuing securities. Building societies have generally abandoned the direct link between prior savings and loan eligibility.

CSH-type mechanisms are also applied by many public-housing finance schemes in emerging markets that collect contributions from salaried employees against promising to make loans to them. The link between prior savings and loan entitlements in such schemes, however, is usually weak. Moreover, mandatory contributions create a completely different incentive structure for savers.

As a collective mechanism doing lending based on the prior creation of a payment history, CSH schemes contain strong elements of microfinance. Because of the binding loan promise they make, however, institutions that manage CSH schemes are typically more tightly regulated than microfinance lenders. Their closest analogs are insurance companies, which also manage collective funds earmarked to specific payouts.

As a source of second-tier debt and evidence of repayment commitment, CSHs compete with a number of access products to mortgage finance, most notably, mortgage products addressing insufficient equity (for example, piggyback second mortgages) and mortgage loan insurance.

Historical Development of CSH Schemes

Developed Mortgage Markets

CSH schemes and their managing institutions grew out of the Anglo-Saxon building society movement of the late 18th and early 19th century. The first such society was created in Britain (Birmingham) in 1775; the United States followed in 1831 (Frankford, Pennsylvania). All British colonies adopted them until the 1850s. In 1869, German sponsors made the first attempts to found building societies (Breslau); however, it took until 1924 until the first society was successfully launched (Heilbronn).

Given the nascent stage of capital markets, until the 1920s, building societies anywhere were operating under contract savings principles: obtaining a 10-year mortgage loan from a U.S. S&L association in the 1920s, for example, required a contractual savings period of typically five years.[2]

It is instructive to compare further developments in the United States and Germany. In the United States, the S&L system was fundamentally changed in the 1930s, when the federal government had to address a national mortgage market crisis. A 1934 act introduced federal insurance for fixed-rate loans

---

2. See Vittas 1995.

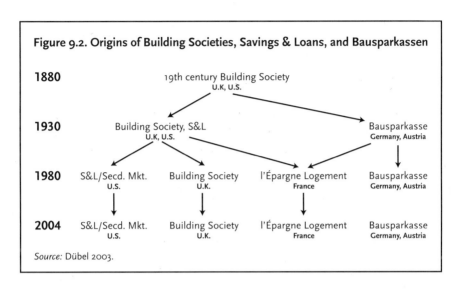

Figure 9.2. Origins of Building Societies, Savings & Loans, and Bausparkassen

Source: Dübel 2003.

with up to 20 years maturity and LTV ratios up to 80 percent. Moreover, deposits invested into an S&L became explicitly insured, which facilitated the attraction of deposits made by savers not interested in receiving a loan.[3] Taken together, these steps considerably weakened the mutual character of the S&Ls, eliminated the need to prior collection of savings from prospective borrowers. The U.S. system further changed in the aftermath of the 1980s S&L industry collapse which saw the transfer of much the financing function to the semi-public institutions Fannie Mae and Freddie Mac as well as a swift development of the securitization and insurance markets allowing for lower borrower equity. In the United Kingdom, many building societies converted to a bank charter in the 1980s and 1990s after the building societies lost their preferences as housing finance providers.

Germany in the 1930s moved in the opposite direction. Regulations for Bausparkassen were passed in 1934 that defined a closed (that is, exclusively collectively funded) system producing fixed-rate loans—on a pure private basis without government intervention. In 1938, government regulation designated Bausparen to the role of second mortgage provision. Also, after the war, the German housing finance system remained mainly private and split between first and second mortgage lenders; mortgage securitization

---

3. See Colton 2002.

and insurance developed only recently. Austria in 1939 adopted the German regulations, but after World War II, with government intervention in the form of large-volume preferential second mortgage lending, assigned to Bausparen the role of first mortgage lending.[4] France initially created the l'Epargne Logement scheme as a closed scheme with fixed rates in 1965, but modified it in 1970 due to high inflation to combine elements of British building societies (variable interest rates, open funding) and German Bausparkassen (fixed spreads between the variable lending and savings rates, public savings premiums).[5]

CSH in Emerging Markets

CSH schemes have developed spontaneously in many economies with developing financial systems, or financial systems in distress. An example is the Mexican Autofinanciamentos of the 1980s that responded to insufficient capital supply for housing finance.[6] The origin of the German Bauspar system in the 1920s is related to a dearth of capital market funds for housing during a period of high financial-sector stress.[7]

However, only few spontaneous schemes graduate into permanence. The CSHs that are currently in existence in emerging markets are typically derived from successful European schemes with a developed regulatory structure. Examples are Nicaraguan, Peruvian, Tunisian, and Moroccan schemes, which were designed along the lines of the French l'Epargne Logement, or the Bauspar schemes in the Czech Republic, Slovakia, Hungary, and Slovenia that follow the German or Austrian models. More recently, closed CSHs have been launched in India and the province of Tianjin, China with the support of German Bausparkassen. There are plans to introduce CSH in Russia.

Apart from mandatory schemes not covered in this section, public housing institutions have also ventured into CSH as a means to attract low-cost

---

4. In Austria, after World War II public loans became the main second-mortgage funding mechanism allowing Bauspar loans to be ranked first. In Germany, in contrast, savings banks and mortgage banks insisted on being secured by first mortgages, which led to the subordination of Bausparen.
5. See Lea and Renaud 1995 for a detailed comparison of the French and German schemes.
6. See Bernstein 1996.
7. See Berndt, Degner, Hamm, and Zehnder 1994.

Box 9.1. CSH—an Islamic Finance Product in Iran

Loan promises linked to deposit schemes are an everyday life feature in Iran and widely socially, religiously, and legally accepted.

Contract savings deposits, including for housing finance purposes, were officially recognized by the 1987 Law on Usury-Free Banking as *gharz-el hasaneh*, that is, deposits compatible with Islamic finance principles, which enjoy a preference in the bankruptcy code. The Law on Usury-Free Banking makes it impossible for banks to pay returns on deposits of a "predetermined figure," for example, fixed interest. In addition to lotteries and random "profit" allocations, loan promises are only one of three allocation mechanisms allowed to generate a return on deposits.

In addition to the only regulated CSH deposits offered by the public housing bank, Bank Maskan, it is estimated that there are hundreds of unregulated schemes in Iran offered by banks and savings cooperatives.

---

deposits. Several institutions in Asia, Latin America, and Africa run them, often with the intention of formalizing informal market practices that have widespread cultural support. An example detailed further in box 9.1 is the Iranian housing bank, which relies for most of its funding on CSH. In Islamic finance with its prohibition of interest, loan-linked deposits play a special role as one of the few admissible shariah-compliant deposit products.

Managing Risk under a CSH Scheme

Risk Profile of CSH Contracts

CSH contracts in the open form generate two and in the closed form three linked financial products, with the associated implications for lender risk profiles. All contracts combine a savings and a credit option product:

- *Savings product.* CSH savings deposits are legally daily callable by the saver, as ordinary bank demand deposits. However, the entitlement to receive a loan or a savings premium subsidy, which both enhance the deposit yield, will typically be linked to a minimum length of the savings phase. Moreover, lenders are often entitled to delay or even block savings withdrawals, especially if reserves are low.[8] This incentive structure turns a *de jure* short-term deposit into a de facto long-term deposit, mitigating liquidity and interest rate risk for lenders.[9]

- *Credit option product.* The saver is contractually entitled to a loan broadly proportional in size to his or her savings amount, with usually only unrestrictive additional underwriting. In properly regulated schemes, however, the lender can still turn down a prospective borrower or housing object in order to limit credit risk. In addition, CSH rarely uses price discrimination by credit risk: loan pricing will generally be identical for all savers. The reason is the strength of the creditworthiness signal that a successful savings effort over an extended period provides for the ability to service a loan.[10]

The main risk management advantage of open CSH schemes is minimal, or diversified, liquidity risk through the option to attract additional capital market funds. The main disadvantage is a higher vulnerability to credit risk, as interest rate risk is higher under variable rate contracts. Proponents of closed CSH systems argue therefore that the central value of the CSH, the isolation of a collective from interest rate volatility, is diluted, and that open schemes are effectively building societies. In the closed CSH system, in contrast, the interest rate volatility is minimized by providing the saver with an interest rate option product.

- *Interest rate option product.* Closed CSH systems fix both deposit interest rates and future loan interest rates upon contract signature. Since there is no obligation for the saver to borrow in the future, this is tantamount to acquiring an interest rate option, which the saver may or may not exercise, depending on the interest rate situation

---

8. For example, German lender Schwäbisch Hall reserves the right to delay payout of withdrawals for 6 months. Further delays are possible if aggregate withdrawal requests exceed 25 percent of the sum earmarked for loan allotment.
9. As a result, CSH deposits are usually classified as term deposits in banking statistics.
10. This is particularly important in the context of the current widespread introduction of risk-based capital requirements in mortgage finance through the Basel II banking regulations, which have brought along an increasing differentiation of pricing between different credit risks.

at the time when his or her investment need occurs. To finance the interest rate option, deposit interest-rate levels will usually be below market.

An indirect advantage of closed schemes is therefore a reduction in credit risk through greater interest-rate stability. The downside, to be explored in detail below, is that closed CSHs may be exposed to significantly higher liquidity risk compared to open CSHs, should their conditions become unattractive for new saver generations.

The subsequent discussion focuses on some key risk-management issues in closed CSH systems.

Demand Fluctuations

The saver will value the CSH contract by simultaneously determining the value of the loan interest-rate option embedded in the fixed-rate loan promise and any loss in savings income relative to the market rate that he or she may incur in the first period as a price for receiving the option.

In particular, the option to receive a future loan for a fixed interest rate will rise in value, if the saver expects interest rates to rise. Moreover, the more the value of the interest rate option rises, the higher the volatility of interest rates is. The CSH contract may in fact become extremely valuable as a protection against interest rate risk from the saver's perspective. This is a characteristic situation for countries with high levels of monetary instability or banking sector fragility, in which fixed-rate housing finance products are often not available at all.

In a macroeconomic stabilization scenario with declining interest rates and decreasing interest rate volatility, however, the reverse will be true: the option value and therefore the contract value and savings incentives may drop to very low levels. The contract value may even become negative if the opportunity costs of higher remunerated savings today exceed the value of the interest rate option.

Because of these interest rate dynamics, demand for new savings contracts with specified fixed terms will vary with the current interest rate environment as well as saver's perceptions of future interest rate trends. Figure 9.3

Figure 9.3. Closed System CSH Contract Demand and Capital Market Rates, Germany, 1973–2007

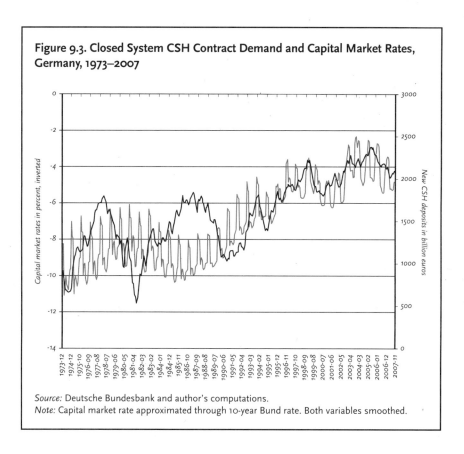

Source: Deutsche Bundesbank and author's computations.
Note: Capital market rate approximated through 10-year Bund rate. Both variables smoothed.

shows how in the past 20 years in Germany the inverse of capital market rates and demand for CSH loans closely correlated with each other—that is, when capital market rates declined the demand for CSH rose, and vice versa. Such fluctuations require liquidity management at the financial-institution level in the form of technical reserves ('bauspartechnische Sicherung') in order to avoid potentially long waiting periods.[11]

---

11. Distortions in the high inflation phase—a liquidity crisis in the 1980s had lead to long waiting periods—disrupt the correlation for earlier years. As a consequence of the events of the 1980s, a new technical reserve was introduced in Germany with the purpose to minimize waiting periods.

Inflation Risk

In an inflationary context, the low and fixed savings returns of closed CSHs—usually between 0 and 5 percent—lead to an erosion of the value of deposits and therefore inability to provide a sufficient house financing contribution. This problem can be addressed with two strategies: savings subsidies that lift deposit rates closer to market levels, or a conversion of the closed scheme into a semi-open scheme retaining only fixed real interest rates while using

Box 9.2. Prepayment Risk in the Austrian Market

Austria's Bauspar system traditionally operated with a relatively high 6 percent fixed loan rate (as opposed to about 4 percent in Germany). In 1999, Austrian mortgage rates dropped by for the first time in decades below 6 percent. The banks not only aggressively competed among themselves for greater market share; they also did so with Bausparkassen, with whom they had formal co-financing arrangements.

Since Bauspar loans were pre-payable—consistent with the logic of a closed savings system aimed at minimizing use of loanable funds—the Bausparkassen were hit by an unprecedented prepayment wave. As the returns on government bonds, the main alternative asset for Bausparkassen, had dropped already to 4 percent, the mismatched Kassen experienced severe spread compression and even some negative spreads.

The reaction was a change in the predominant loan product from a 6 percent fixed-rate loan to an adjustable-rate loan with a 6 percent interest cap; initially, even a wholly adjustable-rate system had been considered, but the government had refused to continue to pay savings premiums for a system without any interest-rate risk protection. The Bausparkassen started an institutional trans-formation, and with the change in the loan instrument opened their financing structure. At least one institution—S-Bausparkasse—today offers mortgage loans up to €300,000 (for a couple) without a contractual savings requirement, and acquires funding from both contract savings and capital market sources (including MBS).

inflation indices to adjust outstanding balances or nominal components of interest rates.

As an example of the former strategy, after introducing the scheme in 1992 the Czech Republic and Slovakia used savings subsidies that fully compensated for the difference between contract and market savings rates. The predictable result was high initial profits of the CSH institutions, who invested their excess liquidity while contracts had not yet become ripe for loan allocation at market interest rates into securities.[12]

The alternative to indexing CSH contracts on both the savings and loans sides at the time was practiced in Slovenia, where the National Housing Savings Scheme operates with fixed real S&L rates over a base rate that is published by the Central Bank. The resulting interest rate is variable, but still offers some risk protection through constant spreads.

Box 9.2 shows with the Austrian experience that the reverse problem, disinflation risk, also may be problematic for closed CSH systems. Since, for liquidity management reasons CSH loans are usually pre-payable, if contract rates are set too high, a drop in market rates to levels below the CSH lending rate may force the managing institution to reinvest large sums prepaid at low or negative spreads. In the aftermath of the crisis, Austrian Bausparen was moved from a fixed-rate to a variable-rate system with caps.

Contract Design Flaws

Even under stable macro conditions and absent demand fluctuations, closed CSH systems remain exposed to latent illiquidity risk through badly designed contracts. On this micro level, liquidity risk is a function of four factors, three of which are contractual: the minimum amount of savings required, the length of the minimum savings period relative to the loan term, and the loan-to-savings multiplier. The fourth factor is behavioral and needs to be estimated by the CSH lender: the number of "good brothers" (savers who do not take loans) relative to the totality of the saver collective.

The key contract design variable is the loan-to-savings multiplier, which in its simplest specification is the ratio of the value of the loan claimed divided

---

12. See Dübel 2003.

by savings accumulated at the point of calculation. An individual contract will be ready for loan allocation, if a certain threshold value of this multiplier, or equivalent "effort ratios" of the saver vis-à-vis the collective, has been reached.[13] Typical actuarial values for admissible loan-to-savings multipliers range between 1.2 and 1.5, depending among other things on the assumptions about the share of good brothers in the portfolio.

CSHs that violate actuarial contract design rules will generate extended waiting periods for savers willing to take up a loan, and possibly even lose credibility. Nevertheless, they can be frequently found in inflationary environments in emerging markets, especially in cases where no measures have been taken to preserve the real value of savings, as described before, and thus high loan-to-savings multipliers are conceded.

Box 9.3 describes the Iranian case, in which excessive loan-to-savings multipliers resulted in the illiquidity of the scheme run by the national housing bank.

Box 9.3. Illiquidity of the Iranian Housing Savings Scheme

The Iranian national housing bank, Bank Maskan, according to an analysis done by the author in 2004, managed a collective CSH fund with individual contract parameters as follows: length of minimum savings period relative to loan term: 1/30 (minimum length: six to 12 months, depending on loan amounts); loan-to-savings multiplier: 7-10 (maximum levels); 0% savings rate and 15% loan rates. The choice of short savings periods and large multipliers responds to the erosion of savings through inflation—between 15 and 20 percent in recent years—and in particular, house price inflation.

Based on the chosen calibration, however, and despite the high spread, the fund cannot reach a steady state-situation in which cash inflows equal outflows. As a result, the housing bank uses additional market-priced funds to fill the cash flow deficit. Since it cannot raise loan rates under its contract savings commitment, the housing bank's margin is squeezed by the higher marginal cost of non-collective funds.

(continued)

---

13. The threshold values vary by type of product; for example, in the German Bauspar system there are "fast" and "slow" saver products.

Box 9.3. Illiquidity of the Iranian Housing Savings Scheme *(continued)*

The liquidity gap arises even though the good brother ratio of the scheme stands at 65 percent. Many of these good brothers are reportedly willing loan takers, that is, potential bad brothers, but are rationed by the housing bank because of insufficient funds. This rationing occurs also through low maximum loan sizes (underadjustment to inflation) since legally the housing bank is not allowed to impose a waiting period after loan eligibility has been reached. As a result of unattractive conditions, the scheme faces the danger of losing credibility as a housing finance solution among the population.

Once created, resolving such situations is difficult: if the saver has a legal right to obtain a loan without waiting period,[14] significant bailout efforts that usually involve public subsidies may be needed. The equally problematic alternative is the ad hoc conversion of the closed scheme into an open scheme; that is, the funding of the loan claims with a mix of capital market funds and collective funds, which implies changing the interest rate conditions on existing contracts.

Misallocation of Excess Liquidity

The reverse problem, an excess liquidity with resulting problems in properly allocating funds to housing investment, may arise in the case of schemes that have attracted deposits too quickly, for example, because of high subsidies or deposit rate controls elsewhere in the financial system.

The problem is exacerbated if CSH loan investment conditions are handled too rigidly, or there is substantial scope for credit risk. In the Czech Republic, because of the exorbitant deposit growth rates pushed by large subsidies and initially restrictive investment conditions, it took 12 years after the inception of the system, until 2005, for the aggregate loan-to-deposit ratio of the system to surpass 30%. As a way to invest the excess funds, the institu-

---

14. In developed CSH systems, the managing institution is not allowed to promise immediate loan allocation after the eligibility threshold has been reached, in order to gain a degree of freedom of liquidity management.

tions acquired large bond portfolios, including mortgage bonds which helped to reduce general mortgage market interest rates to one of the lowest levels in Europe.[15] Since a massive cutback of subsidies in 2004, loan growth has surpassed deposit growth and in 2007 the loan-to-deposit ratio has reached 47%, still a low ratio for a S&L system. The share of CSH deposits actually invested in low-interest rate CSH loans remains at only 10%.

Box 9.4 describes another case of how in Tunisia a combination of deposit rate regulation elsewhere in the financial system and restrictive loan investment conditions in the 1970s led to similar problems of excess CSH deposit accumulation. The perceived inability to finance housing and the interest rate liberalization of 1983 triggered a withdrawal wave of savers that made a restructuring of the scheme unavoidable.

Box 9.4. Liquidity Fluctuations and Disconnect from the Housing Finance System in Tunisia

The Tunisian Caisse Nationale d'Epargne Logement was created in 1974 as a public lender that developed a closed CSH with fixed S&L rates to fund its operations. Contract parameters were sufficiently conservative (four-year minimum savings; loan multiplier of 2) to avoid illiquidity. As interest rate controls prevailed in Tunisia—real interest rates dropped from 3 percent in 1974 to minus 9 percent in 1983—and government subsidized the system, demand for CSH deposits became very dynamic.

Problems arose in the early 1980s, because the system had generated too few loans relative to its high liquidity levels: loan eligibility was limited to new construction, yet low loan-savings multipliers only allowed for small loans, and complementary first mortgage loans were unavailable or unaffordable to the target group of the system. A latent confidence crisis in the ability of the scheme to finance housing solutions became manifest in 1983–4, when the government removed interest rate controls and withdrawals of CSH deposits rose.

(continued)

15. According to computations by the Czech Academy of Social Sciences, mortgage bond to mid-swap spreads averaged -51bp throughout 2001–2004; spreads to government bonds averaged 17bp over the same period.

Box 9.4. Liquidity Fluctuations and Disconnect from the Housing Finance System in Tunisia *(continued)*

In 1986, Caisse Nationale d'Épargne Logement was transformed into a housing bank, Banque de l'Habitat. At that point, all lending rates were adjusted to market rates and tenors were lengthened. The closed CSH became replaced by a semi-open CSH, with S&L rates now determined through fixed spreads over the financial market index TMM. In the 1990s, private lenders also entered the market for CSHs, and Banque de l'Habitat became only one of their suppliers. Under the semi-open schemes, loan multipliers have doubled (from 2 to 4), raising the available financing volumes. Most lenders now also offer complementary mortgage loans.

Excess liquidity risk can be limited through reduced savings subsidies, removal of deposit rate distortions, and more flexible loan-eligibility criteria.

CSHs as a Policy Choice in Emerging Markets

The introduction of CSHs in emerging markets has been advocated based on three financial sector arguments:

- The lack of long-term funding instruments, hindering specifically the development of fixed-rate mortgage products;
- Problems of access to mortgage finance for young and low-income households because of high down-payment requirements and low credit-risk information availability - in that regard it is claimed that CSH can contribute to greater financial stability;
- As a means to generate loan supply in areas not covered by standard mortgage finance and characterized by low loan volumes and high servicing costs, especially modernization and small property-transaction loans.

A fourth, macroeconomic argument has been that CSHs contribute to a greater mobilization of savings for housing and therefore general economic development.

Careful analysis should be applied when determining whether these problems exist, what their magnitude is, and what alternative solutions exist that address them at minimal costs to society.

Mobilization of Savings

Although CSH clearly adds to the menu of term deposits and thus will stimulate savings, there is only weak evidence supporting the introduction of CSH, primarily from the savings mobilization perspective. The monetization of emerging economies depends primarily on macroeconomic stability and the soundness and distribution power of the banking system. Lack of access to bank deposits, or weakly managed banks, are serious problems in many

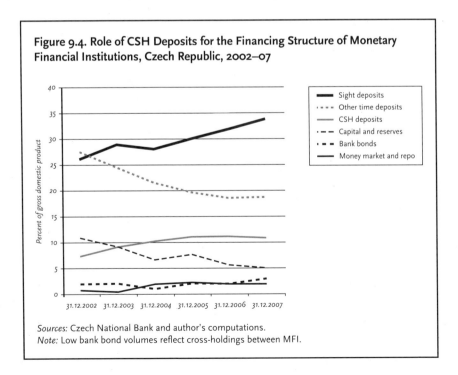

Figure 9.4. Role of CSH Deposits for the Financing Structure of Monetary Financial Institutions, Czech Republic, 2002–07

Sources: Czech National Bank and author's computations.
Note: Low bank bond volumes reflect cross-holdings between MFI.

emerging markets, but these problems should be overcome by a broad-based banking-sector development strategy. Shortly after CSH were introduced in the Czech Republic, a national banking crisis related to non-performing old debts assisted CSH deposit growth as CSH institutions were exclusively foreign. Later the entire banking system was sold to foreign owners, and consumers ceased to make a distinction. We have seen in the cases of Iran (box 9.3) and Tunisia (box 9.4) that regulations may limit the development of alternative deposit instruments, but here the appropriate answer should be deregulation. It has also been argued that CSHs specifically contribute to a larger overall savings ratio,[16] but such claims seem rather dubious if not tested against the alternatives of developing other contractual savings instruments, such as life insurance, pension funds, and mutual funds, or simply savings arising from paying down a mortgage loan. In contrast, a too aggressive strategy to introduce CSH may crowd out of other classes of deposits. Figure 9.4 demonstrates the inverse relation between CSH deposits and other time deposits in recent years in the Czech Republic, where high historic subsidy levels lead to CSH deposits absorbing up to 37 percent of time deposits in 2006.

Lack of Long-Term Funding

Similarly, the case for CSH as a long-term funding instrument necessary to support housing finance in emerging markets is weaker than it was historically for developed markets. As a class of deposits issued through retail banking mechanisms, CSH deposits are inexpensive to distribute, usually protected under existing deposit insurance mechanisms, and thus are relatively low cost and liquid. As organized mortgage securities markets and their institutional investors develop globally, however, these advantages fade. Where such institutional finance is available and stable, fixed-rate lending can be supplied on a truly matched-funded basis and thus will impose less interest rate risk for the lender than CSH deposit funding.[17] Absent loan mul-

---

16. See Börsch-Supan and Stahl 1991 for an analysis of the Bauspar system in Germany.
17. CSH deposits are a hybrid between term and demand deposits: they are formally callable daily, with the likelihood of exercise of the call option being blocked by the embedded incentives (loan promise, public savings premia). The lower these incentives, the higher the likelihood of exercise of the call option and the shorter the duration of CSH deposits.

tiplier restrictions, mortgage finance can also provide larger individual loan volumes than CSH.

The choice will depend on relative costs of and stability of access to bond finance versus CSH finance, which is determined by the macroeconomic risk situation, relative regulatory costs and relative public subsidies, and investor risk appetite, among other things. Figure 9.4 shows that as the CSH deposit funding share declines in the Czech Republic due do declining subsidies, the bank bond market catches up in financing function. For systems with higher bond market instability, however, CSH can be a useful additional long-term funding source. In Russia, for example, due to a repeated history of banking failures, mid-sized banks have great problems to tap the bond markets and seek for CSH as a diversification source for long-term funding. Similarly, there is potential in India and other cases, where bond market development has been slow.

Credit Risk Mitigation and Financial Stability

CSH has even more obvious advantages in an environment of high credit risks of mortgage lending, which in emerging markets is created by income uncertainty, high credit-information opacity, and high inflation-risk levels. High inflation levels, in particular house price inflation, may even jeopardize financial stability in developed markets.

In such environments, risk mitigation through the provision of sufficient equity is often superior to a pure risk management or transfer approach (for example, through a mortgage-loan insurance product enabling higher LTVs). There are two main mechanisms:

- *Reduced leverage:* CSH increase the equity buffer available for first mortgage lenders in case of a default—the equity portion contained in a CSH disbursement generally accumulates with other downpay-ments to a larger equity position. Higher equity of the borrower at stake helps to rationalize both housing purchase and loan under-writing decisions, especially with regard to controlling inflated house prices.

Box 9.5. CSH System Choice in Transition Countries in the 1990s

Over the past 15 years, most transition countries have developed housing finance institutions that are similar to Western European ones. The markets are dominated by universal banks, but include mortgage banks or universal banks issuing mortgage bonds and national housing funds. CSH choice has been highly controversial.

- The Czech Republic and Slovakia were the first countries to adopt a closed CSH system run by special bank Bausparkassen in 1992/3 . Both countries subsidized CSH initially very highly with the aim of deposit rates matching high market levels during the initial transition phase. This rendered the schemes very popular but also cannibalized the housing policy budgets.

- Against this backdrop, Poland cancelled a 1997 law proposal introducing Bausparkassen (Chiquier et al. 1998). A system managed through special accounts by universal banks similar to l'Epargne Logement, Kasy Mieszkaniowe, remained. Kasy Mieszkaniowe became illiquid and ceased to write new business by 2001. A key reason was the support through tax credits rather than premium grants, which discouraged its use as a mass scheme. Lithuania, for similar reasons as Poland, and with the smaller mortgage market, in 2002 decided against introducing Bausparkassen.

- Slovenia in 1999 introduced a housing savings scheme managed by the National Housing Fund with the goal of increasing competition between banks and bringing spreads down. The scheme is semi-open, operates with a loan-to-savings multiplier of 2, a transferable right to receive a housing loan from the bank and has thus brought high liquidity into the housing market. It is only moderately subsidized.

- Specialized CSH institutions also in the meantime exist in Hungary, Croatia, and Romania. The system is being discussed in a number of countries, including Russia and Armenia.

- *Signalling of creditworthiness through pre-savings:* Borrowers with low ability to pay are filtered out before they reach the loan stage, and vice versa borrowers discriminated by the market receive a chance to demonstrate their ability to pay.

There is little emerging market evidence available as yet to test those hypotheses. In the Slovenian case, a high loan-to-savings multiplier has been held to have lead to increasing house prices in the presence of inelastic land supply, which has prompted government to address the latter problem. In both the Czech and Slovakian cases to make CSH work in practice as a risk mitigant for first mortgage lending, legal problems still need to be overcome. The Austrian CSH crisis of 1999 (box 9.2) also suggests that the risk sharing between different lenders may be unstable for competition reasons.

Similar problems, however, are shared by competing instruments, such as mortgage insurance. Also, there appears to be support to the signaling argument for pre-savings. Czech lenders charge ca 50bp higher mortgage interest rates to borrowers without a CSH contract, due to higher credit risk. In developed markets, the recent U.S. mortgage market crisis can be seen as evidence to support both equity and signaling functions that CSH can deliver. It is less convincing, as has been argued, to cite German or Austrian house price stability as linked to the use of CSH, as both cases feature high rental housing shares in the total housing stops. This not only pre-empts a subprime market, but also early homeownership and allows for longer pre-savings periods.

The downside is that where access to credit is available accumulating large savings volumes may generate excessive costs for borrowers, due to foregone capital gains and extended rental tenure, which is why CSH got marginalized in historical perspective. Also, as shown with the German case the system itself is not shock-proof—especially under high and volatile inflation. Finally, the U.S. crisis suggests that in a system with a strong focus on providing second mortgages even small adjustments of the legally admissible LTVs may lead to far higher credit risk levels than historically incurred by the Bausparkassen.

Stimulation of Modernization and Small Transactions Lending Market

The case for CSH is strongest, when considering its use outside the "standard" mortgage finance market for new construction or purchases. CSH offers not only small-volume loans, its closeness to microfinance techniques means that frequently costly or unavailable mortgage registration can be avoided.[18] This means also that the system is self-targeting towards lower-income house-holds. The cases of Slovakia and India show that paramount importance of the distribution approach for such target groups: Slovakia's P.S.S. was able to distribute tens of thousands of small loans very fast, while BHW initially failed in the more challenging Indian environment. Even as financial sys-

---

Box 9.6. Attempts to Introduce CSH in India

The BHW Home Finance in India is a subsidiary German Beamtenheimstät-tenwerk (BHW) Bausparkasse, now part of Deutsche Postbank. The Easy Home Loan Deposit scheme was created in 2002 as a closed fixed-rate system, regu-lated as other fixed-rate deposit schemes applicable under the Indian mortgage company charter. The scheme entailed a savings phase at 5 % p.a. over 3 years and a loan phase at 7 % p.a. at 5 years. The loan-to-savings multiplier was limited to 1. The scheme was not specifically subsidized beyond the general tax prefer-ences for mortgage borrowers; in exchange for the absence of savings premia, contract conditions prohibited savings from being withdrawn prematurely.

The scheme was initially well received by consumers. In the Indian context char-acterized by high levels of informality, the target groups were lower-income and lower-middle-income households for whom the available funding could mean an option to buy low-cost housing or land; however, many of those households have no bank accounts and BHW over time ran into difficulties to organize distribution and collection. After a series of problems with collection agents, the scheme was discontinued by BHW in 2006 and accumulated savings were reimbursed. BHW as of 2008 plans launching a new scheme whose details have yet to be disclosed.

---

18. In the Czech Republic and Slovakia, for instance, between 2/3 and 4/5 of CSH loans are not collateralized by mortgages. Reconstruction and modernization loans make up for roughly half of the portfolio.

tems develop and access to bank accounts becomes universal, viable alternative small-loan offers from universal banks may not appear because of high
origination and servicing costs. CSH lenders can overcome this through specialization and a large numbers of loans. CSH also has advantages over unsecured consumer loans, whose rates charged are generally very high because
of higher credit risk.

Institutional Requirements for CSH Lenders

Regulation of CSH Schemes

Analogous to insurance schemes, CSHs come with significant control
problems since a managing institution, the "lender," derives its profit from
investing the resources on behalf of a saver collective. The saver collective
does not only need protection against credit risk, but also against a misuse of
funds saved below market rates for investment, generating market rates for
the lender. A similar problem arises between collectives at different times,
as CSHs have built-in incentives to prefer current over future saver generations that might be left without sufficient liquidity to receive loans. Since
CSH schemes are of the greatest value when interest rates are fixed, and their
funding instrument is callable, liquidity and asset-liability management risks
require greater detail regulation than in the case of a traditional building
society or mortgage bank, which are both matched funded. For these reasons, CSHs should be formally regulated.

At the core of CSH regulations should be the definition of balance sheet
and cash flow principles for the legally and technically separate fund owned
by the saver collective. The fund manager should be required at least to be a
regulated financial institution that is specially licensed for managing CSHs.
Especially in closed schemes, the licensing should require separate risk-
management capacity within the institution and a specific set of rules that
consider the mathematical limitations and risk profiles discussed above. Particularly important are proper contract design and in higher inflation contexts sufficient technical reserves for liquidity management. Regulators and
onsite and offsite supervisors should have staff specially trained for analyzing
and supervising CSHs.

Clearly, a system promising to offer non-mortgage and second mortgage loans needs also carefully defined underwriting criteria. Frequently encountered legal rights to a loan after the savings phase, let alone options to inherit such rights, are an impediment to sound underwriting. Incentives should be given to register mortgages wherever possible, for example, by addressing registration costs and legal issues. In addition to loan underwriting, liquidity investment criteria are central.

The existing approaches to regulation and supervision are not uniform. European CSHs are mostly enabled by special laws; however, with quite different solutions.[19] More worrisome, the recent schemes implemented in emerging markets seem to be more lightly regulated than their European counterparts (for example, India, proposal in Russia). This seems to be inadequate, given their risk content, especially if a fixed-rate loan promise is given in a volatile interest rate environment.

A more far-reaching institutional specialization of CSH lenders than licensing, that is, as specialist banks, has been criticized as leading to an undesirable fragmentation of the banking system in emerging markets.

In fact, universal banks offering CSH under licensing appears as the most efficient option for smaller financial systems. Peru, Nicaragua, and Slovenia have followed the French example in that regard.

The specialist bank solution has been adopted in Germany, Austria, the Czech Republic, Slovakia, and Hungary. The argument here has been for maximum risk-management quality and exclusive business focus. P.S.S. in Slovakia, for example, may be credited with having pioneered a new origination, servicing, and risk management infrastructure for the Slovakian housing finance market.[20]

A possible compromise model for emerging markets could be a building-society-type specialist bank offering CSH next to other housing finance products. An example is S-Bausparkasse in Austria. Its business model com-

19. The German banking act (Kreditwesengesetz), for example, goes as far as *outlawing all deposit-taking that is linked to a loan promise*; the exception being tightly regulated CSH deposits under the special bank system of Bausparkassen. This system is supervised by a specialized department of the supervisory authority. The French legislation does not require a special bank for operating CSHs. Regulation takes place under a special unit of the treasury that also oversees other contract savings, such as insurance and pension schemes.
20. It should be noted that most specialist banks offering CSH in the mentioned countries are subsidiaries under holding structures that offer the complete range of banking or contractual savings products.

Table 9.2. CSH Subsidies in Central and Eastern Europe Compared

	Germany	Russia	Hungary	Czech Republic		Slovakia	
Status	Current	Proposed	Current	1992–2003	Current	1992–1997	Current
Minimum savings period*	7 years	5 years	4 years	5 years	6 years	no constraints	6 years
New savings premium in percent	8.8	20.0	30.0	25.0	15.0	40.0	15.0
Maximum premium amount in US$	117	499	360	195	156	186	112
Optimum new savings amount in US$	1330	2496	1200	780	1040	465	745
Income limit in US$**	33280	None	None	None	None	None	None
Annual subsidy yield in percent***	2.44	7.52	13.83	9.23	4.75	n.a.	4.75

Source: Author's research.
Notes: * shorter minimum savings periods exist if consumers take out housing loans early, ** for singles, value doubles for couples, *** assumptions: income tax exempt savings yield at 20% marginal income tax; no income tax deductibility of savings; interest paid on accumulated subsidies; annual subsidy payment; no closing costs of CSH institution.

bines scale and flexibility on the product and funding side with a sufficient risk management and regulation framework for CSH.

Subsidies for CSHs

CSH Subsidies in Emerging Markets

The question of whether CSHs deserve special savings subsidies as part of the overall housing policy menu is very controversial. The high and diverse subsidies proposed and implemented in Central and Eastern Europe CSH have put heat under that debate.[21] They allowed CSH institutions to fund themselves very cheaply as the government picked up the difference between CSH deposit rates and market rates. Those subsidy yields reached levels between 5% and 14% in Central Europe, much higher than in Germany. Large returns

---

21. See Diamond 1999 for an attack on CSH subsidies in Central and Eastern Europe.

Box 9.7. CSH Subsidies in Hungary

The Hungarian housing finance system has been traditionally deeply subsidized; the HUF mortgage subsidy schemes introduced under the Szechenyi plan in 2000 and abolished in 2005 had offered interest rates as low as 3-5% with market rates well above 15%. In the same spirit and in addition following the Austrian CSH subsidy dogma to always match bank deposit rates, the Hungarian CSH system offers deep savings subsidies; an extremely short minimum savings period of only 4 years in combination with a high state premium of 30 percent of the annual savings amount as well as comprehensive tax exemptions enhance the 2% paid by the Bausparkasse by another 14% to even above market deposit rate levels. Given the higher Forint and house price inflation, also more relaxed maximum eligible savings amounts are chosen than in neighbouring countries.

Still, due to the deep HUF loan subsidies until 2005 followed by a surge in foreign currency loans (2007 > 80%, mostly Swiss Francs) and amnesia about the associated risks, the success of CSH so far is only moderate. The current estimated 250,000 outstanding contracts represent only a twentieth of the level of the Czech Republic, with a comparable population size. During 2007, however both new savings contract enrollment and fiscal expenditures considerably picked up. HUF 18.6 billion of premiums were paid in 2007, up from 14 billion in 2006, and the current financial market turmoil that reduces foreign currency loan supply and creates volatile HUF financing conditions is likely to further enhance demand.

Box 9.8. Planned CSH Law and Subsidies in Russia

During 2008, in Russia concrete plans were discussed to introduce a Bauspar system. Russia's banks suffer from considerable funding mismatches. A number of mid-sized banks challenging the market leader Sberbank, the national savings bank, has limited access to deposits and heavily relies on the volatile Eurobond and interbank markets. Apart from the operations of the agency for home mortgage lending (AHML), which are limited by fiscal constraints, there is no long-term refinancing market for mortgages. Long-term savings could be a welcome diversification instrument.

(continued)

Box 9.8. Planned CSH Law and Subsidies in Russia *(continued)*

The Russian law has been proposed by German Bausparkasse Schwäbisch Hall. The proposed regulations soften the German law in a number of points. Examples are lower requirements to use mortgage collateral for housing loans, a higher ratio of interim financing to total lending, and a lower level of technical reserves designated to minimize waiting periods. Also, with a maximum state premium level of RUR 14,000 p.a. (USD 560), a minimum savings period of only 5 years and a state premium ratio of 20% of savings, the subsidy program promises to become expensive. Compared to the Czech Republic, the maximum state premium p.a. planned for Russia is 3 times as high, compared to Germany 4-8 times (differentiation by marital status). Also, Germany and the Czech Republic now feature minimum savings periods of 7 and 6 years and state premium ratios of 8.8% and 15%, respectively.

on equity of CSH institutions were the result, especially in the setup phase where funds are exclusively invested at market rates.[22] For fiscal reasons, some countries had to cut back later; however such cutbacks have come with long delays (Czech Republic).

The subsidy debate highlights the lack of certainty of CSH institutions over the intrinsic value of their product. However, subsidies—at least of the scale given in Central and Eastern Europe—are not an essential feature for the successful introduction of CSHs. See box 9.6 for the Indian case, where the access-to-credit motivation proved sufficient to attract demand; the scheme failed for technical reasons. Nor do specific risk aspects of CSH require permanent subsidies (see discussion above). The same can be said about mortgage loan and insurance products, however, which are nevertheless frequently subsidized as they benefit mainly the politically powerful middle class. CSHs have therefore not been an exception in attracting sometimes large amounts of economically hard-to-justify subsidies.

---

22. See Dübel 2003 analyzing the case of the largest Slovakian CSH institution P.S.S.

Guiding Principles

CSH subsidies can be justified only as part of a consistent overall housing finance subsidy framework.

The first guiding principle here should be neutrality of user costs of capital for different instruments, considering all subsidy sources.[23] Neutrality should be observed in particular in the market for high LTV loans or equivalent insurance products, which is highly sensitive to the subsidy and public-guarantee structure.

Evaluation criteria of CSH subsidies should moreover consider the efficiency with which they are allocated, for example, by assessing the investment multiplier and substitution effects as compared to other housing finance instruments.

A central point here is to ensure a sufficiently high loan-to-deposit ratio: in the Czech Republic, CSH deposits became so strongly subsidized that the loan-to-deposit ratio stagnated until very recently at low levels and CSH effectively subsidized the broader mortgage sector. Starting from almost identical initial conditions, CSH had a more robust lending performance in Slovakia with close to 100% loan-to-deposit ratios since early after the system's inception. Alternatively, subsidies can be specifically tied to a loan takeout, a decision France took concerning l'Épargne Logement subsidies in 2003 and Germany implements from 2009 onwards.

Alternative forms of equity support for borrowers, such as grants or partial use of tax-preferred retirement savings accounts for downpayments, should also be considered. Finally, while CSH schemes are partly self-targeting through the small loan amounts they produce, income and other limits may considerably improve the targeting efficiency.

Conclusions for Emerging Markets

CSHs continue their existence despite the swift capital market development in housing finance. They conceptually fit into an early financial-sector devel-

---

23. Dübel 2003 compares mortgage-market subsidies in the Czech Republic and Slovakia and finds that the subsidy dependency of CSH loans is higher than of mortgage loans in the former case, and lower in the latter case.

opment context as an initial mortgage product and into a mature financial-sector development context as a product generating access to credit for young and low-income households as well as nonstandard housing finance loans.

The system offers a number of advantages, including its simplicity, a way to mobilize long-term liabilities, and, in the absence of credit scores or formal income, it can provide a lender with proof that the borrower is able to service a mortgage loan. The ability of the system to function within informal environments is particularly relevant for emerging markets. The commitment made during the savings phase and the deposit that is accumulated greatly reduce the credit risk of operating in environments without formal institutions providing credit scoring and credit histories. A final and important advantage of the system is that it can allow long-term fixed-rate loans to be offered, even in environments where long-term fixed-rate funding may be unavailable.

Despite some expansion to emerging markets the schemes have had difficulties in the presence of changing economic circumstances and macro instability. Falling interest rates in emerging markets in particular have meant that potential borrowers would have little incentive to start saving at below-market rates in a CSH system in order to lock in a future lending rate now. Falling rates, moreover, tend to interact with strong house price growth, which could mean that initially contracted loan amounts will be insufficient to buy a property and savers that have the option to borrow immediately rather than saving and borrowing later will forego capital gains.

The CSH mechanism is also heavily reliant on new savers coming onboard and providing liquidity for the continued disbursement of loans. In a stable inflation environment the system can work well attracting new savings, but inflation cycles may mean the system is exposed to corresponding demand fluctuations. A reacceleration of inflation in particular can result in loan rationing, which in a contractual scheme can damage confidence. Even in a benign inflation environment, contract design discipline is needed to avoid intergenerational snowball effects. CSH systems in emerging markets therefore need liquidity-stabilizing mechanisms such as a technical reserve fund and proper risk-management capacity.

A danger is, moreover, that policy makers in emerging markets take the savings disincentives in a falling interest rate environment, or the heavy reliance of the CSH on sufficient new savers in the steady state, as an excuse for introducing large and permanent savings subsidies. Such subsidies are not a necessary condition for the long-term success of a CSH. Experience has shown that, when inappropriately applied, especially during the introductory phase, fiscal costs can be substantial and the amounts of savings generated can no longer reasonably be channeled into loans and housing investment.

Policy makers looking to CSH as a tool for developing their housing finance systems should assure themselves that the appropriate regulatory framework is in place that is able to deal with the specific type of risks arising from CSH. Any excessive dependency of these schemes on regressive and costly subsidies should be avoided. Policy makers are advised to compare the advantages and shortcomings of this model with alternative housing finance systems within their respective countries and market environments, in order to manage credit risks, facilitate access to housing finance, and to mobilize long-term funding.

Selected countries

G21 R21

R31

L32 016

L33

CHAPTER 10

State Housing Banks

Olivier Hassler and Bertrand Renaud

At some stage of their financial development, many countries have established and used state-controlled banks to provide finance for housing. Although their overall performance has been quite disappointing, both in terms of financial performance and social impact, this model continues to attract the attention of policy makers, as observed for example in Africa, where more state-owned housing banks are being created or contemplated.

Housing has deep social implications and is part of any national shelter strategy. Hence, confronted with a market failure, the absence of provision of finance, or a deficient coverage of mortgage markets throughout the income distribution, governments are induced to choose an intervention method that may quickly yield results—or at least be seen as a visible sign of a political will. The temptation is then great to use the state housing bank model, which has kept resurfacing in many countries, although the model often does not offer an appropriate answer to the issues underlying the market failures. Like many other types of state-owned banks, housing banks often fail to achieve the balance between conducting efficient and viable banking operations, and pursuing their social housing goals.

The chapter is organized by first providing a short description of state housing banks (SHBs), then by delineating their rationales, and analyzing the reasons why many of them failed. Available safeguards and alternative options to achieve the same goals are then discussed. Finally, some strategies to make existing institutions evolved are discussed.

A Brief Overview of State Housing Banks

Definition and Classification

SHBs in this discussion are taken as public-sector financial institutions operating in the retail housing finance market. This definition excludes state-sponsored second-tier mortgage institutions, be they state-sponsored entities acting as liquidity facilities or securitization agencies, or vehicles channeling public resources toward primary lenders (Federal Mortgage Bank of Nigeria [FMBN], Gabon Compte de Refinancement de l'Habitat, Venezuela Banco Nacional de la Vivienda [National Housing Bank, Venezuela]). Provident funds that are retail housing lenders but are not banks (for instance, INFONAVIT in Mexico, PAG-IBIG in the Philippines, and Housing Trust in Jamaica are also excluded [see chapter 11, where housing provident funds are treated in greater depth]).

Because of the importance of funding in the business model, and the different kinds of issues that it raises, a simple typology of SHBs can be made according to their dominant source of funding.

1. Most of their funds are deposits, as in Chile (BancoEstado), Brazil (Caixa Economica), Algeria (Caisse Nationale d'Epargne et de Prévoyance [CNEP]), Tunisia (Banque de l'Habitat), Iran (Bank Maskan) or Thailand (GHB). These banks, which are typically savings banks, have a strong funding basis, and the ability to offer a wide range of banking products.

2. Specialized banks without any large-deposit collection capacity that raise funds on bond markets. This was the case with Banco Hipotecario Nacional in Argentina; Crédit Foncier in France, a quasi–SHB until 1999; and the Credit Immobilier et Hotelier in Morocco.

3. Banks that mostly use public finance sources such as mandatory savings or wage taxes, central bank facilities, or government grants and loans. Although rarer, this model exists or has been used, for instance, in Cameroon (Crédit Foncier du Cameroun), Pakistan, and Bangladesh (House Building Finance Corporation [HBFC]).

Types of State Housing Banks

There are many variants of SHBs driven by financial policies and shaped by the local environment and its evolution. For example, some SHBs date back to the post-World War II period prior to the macroeconomic reforms and financial liberalization that started in the 1980s. Since then charters, mandates, sources of funds, regulations, and operations have often changed for the SHBs.

In Latin America, state housing banks that combined apex functions (refinancing facilities), some regulatory powers, and direct lending were created in most countries in the late 1960s and early 1970s. Most have been closed during financial crises, but some survive in some of the smaller countries and financial markets of the Caribbean and Central America (Dominican Republic, Guatemala, or Nicaragua).

In Brazil, Caixa Economica Federal is a hybrid of a development bank and a retail commercial bank, including the functions of a SHB. It offers a large variety of services, and has become the largest mortgage lender after the takeover of the Banco Nacional de Habitaçao. Caixa, which has a large deposit base, and also channels most of the payroll tax funds earmarked for housing finance from the Fundo de Garantia do Tempo de Serviço (FGTS) provident fund, and fiscal transfers from the government.

In Central and Eastern Europe, state-owned savings banks have taken a large share of the mortgage lending market, but have also evolved into universal commercial banks exposed to increased competition from other mortgage lenders.

In economies where the commercial banking sector is small and the mortgage finance infrastructure is only partially in place, there is considerable interest in creating new SHBs. This is the case in Sub-Saharan Africa where

SHBs have been established or revitalized (examples: Ivory Coast, Congo, Mali, Senegal, Gabon, Namibia, and Rwanda).

In some countries, state entities combine retail housing-loan services with real estate developer functions. Examples can, or could, be found in Thailand, Indonesia, Algeria, Egypt, Rwanda, or Pakistan. This is a dangerous combination, notably when projects are driven by some political considerations, because of the lack of independent assessment of development market risks and the absence of a specific capital buffer that a prudent lender requires from developers.

The Rationale for Creating a State Housing Bank

The rationale for SHB is linked to the broader issue of state involvement in finance. In extreme cases, some SHB, for instance in Pakistan, Algeria, or Iran, reflect a legacy of specialized sector banks implementing a centrally planned economy policy. With economic liberalization, the debate has shifted toward how to best address the observed failures of market forces in responding to social or economic needs: (i) Should the state intervene through SHB to serve the population underserved by the private sector? or (ii) Should the state implement background reforms, adequate regulation, and proper incentives to favor the expansion of markets?

As set out in other chapters in this book, the government should play a role in supporting the development of housing finance systems. There are segments of the population that are underserved, or not covered at all by the market, and not only during the early phases of development. None of the successful mortgage finance systems in existence today have developed without some form of active support by the government. The practical question is whether, and under which conditions, an SHB has the ability to efficiently fill market gaps. Within this context, SHBs generally represent an attempt to provide an institutional answer to three kinds of actual and relevant issues:

- Provide a financial service that the market fails to offer. As a driver to jump-start the market ("the infant market argument"), the SHB is then seen as a pioneer and leader in housing lending, helping to improve the lending infrastructure and demonstrating the commercial feasibility of such lending among other financial institutions.

- Cater to the needs of segments of the population underserved by the commercial financial sector. Lending to lower- or informal-income groups, or to households who live in areas not served by bank networks, involves higher origination and servicing costs, higher risks, and fewer cross-selling opportunities. SHBs are perceived as a natural substitute to mainstream lenders, notably because their profitability goals may be lower than private lending institutions, and because of to the implicit state backing of their risk exposure.

- Provide a useful policy implementation tool, as SHBs are visible and easy to create. They can react to instructions given by governments. For instance, the Thai government selected housing as one of the drivers of the economic recovery from the 1997 crisis, by using GHB to channel below-market mortgage loans to stimulate construction and absorb an excess of unsold homes on the market. In France, Crédit Foncier, which had a quasi-monopoly on the main type of subsidized housing loans, was used to transmit the variations in the volumes of housing subsidies deemed necessary to enliven, or dampen, demand cycles.

The Model Failed in Many Countries

A striking feature when looking at the large number of SHBs created since the middle of the 20th century is the frequency of bailouts and rescue operations. This has been observed across different economies and institutions, such as Algeria (CNEP, 1997), Argentina (Banco Hipotecario Nacional, 1990–3), Brazil (Banco Nacional de Habitaçao, 1996, and Caxia Federal in 2001), Cameroon (Credit Foncier du Cameroun), Colombia (Banco Central Hipotecario, 1998), France (Credit Foncier de France, 1996–9), Indonesia (Bank Tabungan Negara, 1997), Ivory Coast (BHCI recapitalized twice), Pakistan (HBFC, 2001), Rwanda (Caisse Hypothécaire du Rwanda, 2003), Tanzania (1995), and Uruguay (Banco Hipotecario del Uruguay [BHU], 2002), among many others.

Box 10.1. The Fiscal Cost of Bailing Out State Housing Banks

Banco Hipotecario del Uruguay (BHU). Made vulnerable by a high delinquency rate (40 percent NPL in 2001) and considerable asset-liability mismatches, BHU collapsed during the Uruguayan financial crisis of 2002. Besides a restructuring plan that included a change of business model, the bank was recapitalized—for the third time since the mid-1960s. A first capital injection was carried out by the government in 2002, for about $730 million. At the end of 2004, the company's equity was still negative by an equivalent amount. BHU's lending activity was interrupted until 2006, which did not prevent its financial situation from worsening. Further recapitalization measures through the transfers of assets and liabilities were still ongoing in early 2006. The recapitalization needs could amount to $1.5 billion, or 93 percent of the loan portfolio outstanding in 2001.

Bank Tabungan Negara. This Indonesian SHB had been entrusted in 1974 with the distribution of subsidized housing loans. Bank Tabungan Negara had a monopoly on the subsidy scheme. Being funded by loans from the Central Bank at privileged conditions enabled it to extend much longer-term loans (20 years) than the private sector, and to win an 80 percent market share in volume despite charging a larger intermediation margin. The poor recovery performance— the delinquency rate went above 25 percent at the end of the 1980s—put Bank Tabungan Negara in a precarious financial situation. The bank managed to improve its risk management, achieving some improvement in this area, but at the same time sought to expand its business by diversifying it toward corporate lending. The lack of capacity in this area was evidenced by a high level of arrears: 100 percent of the corporate loans went into default during the 1997 Asian crisis. When Bank Tabungan Negara transferred its impaired loans to the agency in charge of restructuring the banking system, it incurred an overall loss exceeding $1 billion, more than 20 times the yearly budgeted amount of housing subsidies.

Crédit Foncier du Cameroun. This is a specialized institution that was established in 1977 by the government. Its loan portfolio, about $150 million * at the end of 2004, is mostly funded by a wage tax and marginally from savings deposits. In

(continued)

Box 10.1. The Fiscal Cost of Bailing Out State Housing Banks *(continued)*

the 1990s, CFC ran into deep difficulties caused by two main reasons: (i) very low recovery performances—80 percent of the portfolio was nonperforming—partly because of defaults by the government itself and other state-owned entities, and (ii) excessive operational costs. The company incurred large recurrent deficits, made an irregular and ill-conducted diversification attempt toward commercial banking, and went into deep organizational and financial distress, resulting in a sharp reduction of its activity. The regional Central Bank required several times that draconian measures be decided by the public shareholders. Restructuring plans were designed in 2003–4, and a de facto recapitalization took place by allocating the accumulated proceeds of the wage tax to the company's own funds, a non-budgetary support that can be estimated to have amounted to at least two thirds of the gross loan portfolio.

Sources: Moody's Investors Service Banking System 2004; Gandelman and Gandelman 2004; and Hoek-Smit and Diamond 2004.
* Gross figure

Some have been closed down; others have been recapitalized several times. The fiscal cost of the respective bailouts both through the SHB and their clients has been staggering, notably in comparison with the on-budget programs of social housing subsidies, suggesting a dramatic policy failure in these countries in the long run. For example, the last restructuring of the Caixa Econômica Federal (CEF) in Brazil in 2001 fiscally cost about $8 billion, or 25 budgetary years of the main federal program of social housing subsidies.

These failures evidence a higher degree of vulnerability than normal banks. This reflects structural weaknesses within the SHB model, related to a permissive attitude toward risk management and operational policy, and administrative- and rule-based culture (rather than risked based), amplified by some implicit state backing. The sensitivity to crisis is also caused by specialization, which may lead to an excessive exposure to real estate market downturns, amplified by hazardous diversification attempts in commercial real estate. This section analyzes more precisely the factors behind this structural fragility.

State Housing Bank Failings

Weak Corporate Governance

A first series of flaws can be found in the legal foundations of SHBs, which are often governed by a special legislative act in derogation of general corporate and banking status. These acts often lower the accountability and profitability requirements that private entities must meet because of the quasi-state-agency status of the bank. Related to this status are also restrictions in the business model, in particular over lending operations (types of loans, specified interest rates, business limitations, and so forth), which add some.

More important perhaps than majority ownership itself is the power of appointing the management and control over the bank's business policies through management. These powers most frequently belong to a financial authority. In many cases, management results from appointment of a senior official from the ministry of finance, central bank, or another state institution, rather than professional bankers, giving the institution a more administrative than financial culture. Moreover, the government exercises direct access to the management of the bank and the conduct of its business; for instance, in the setting of lending conditions. This organization goes hand in hand with often weaker oversight by the financial supervisors. State banks are often subject to less stringent prudential requirements than other banks, as well as reporting obligations. This, jointly with a prevailing administrative approach, facilitates weak accounting systems and internal controls. One of the telltale signs of major problems at a housing bank is when it does not produce reliable and timely reports on its financial position and on its subsidy programs.

Government control also makes the role of the board of directors often of little relevance as an outside evaluator of the bank's performance and its compliance with the public interest objectives that it is supposed to pursue, often characterized by quantitative housing-policy targets. Too much government intervention in the bank's management, as well as the board of directors' incomplete mandate, can lead to accountability deficiencies.

Seeking a balance between social goals and financial efficiency should be the core function of the management, but this often turns into a compromise between political interference and rent-seeking behavior. Opportunities for politically driven business interventions trade off against privileges exploited by the SHB to its own advantage, at the expense of the public good. This may result in some kind of implicit agreement by which the SHB bows to political pressures while the politicians allow the SHB to capture some public benefits. The linkage to government often gives the bank the ability to influence policy decisions. This would typically be to promote the interests of the SHB and may not coincide with the best interests of the wider population.

Lax Management of Credit Risk

The portfolio performance of SHBs is often poor, with a common NPL ratio of 20 to 30 percent in emerging economies. It has reached 70 percent or more in some cases. The intensity of NPL problems may even be hidden by poor accounting practices and misleading loan classifications.[1] Several reasons may explain this unfavorable outcome:

Because of the subsidization of loans and the application of administrative rules, risk-based lending may be partially replaced by "formula lending" that does not allow SHBs to differentiate among customers according to their credit risk.

In mortgage markets where private players are active, adverse selection takes place that is confined to "formula" lending, to the detriment of the SHB.

As a public policy tool, the government assigns the SHB goals based on new loan production rather than improving performance or pursuing politically unpopular measures such as recoveries from nonperforming loans.

Loan servicing in SHBs is often mediocre, because such lenders tend to be more lenient than commercial lenders, and borrowers are more inclined to be delinquent when borrowing from a state-owned bank. Moral hazard is significant in the model, and seems difficult to avoid.

---

1. For instance, the classification of nonperforming accounts takes place after a longer-than-normal arrears period, or is partial (interest only, or one loan only despite a larger exposure of the same debtor).

Assets/Liability Mismatches

One of the major policy motivations for setting up a SHB is to offer long-term loans, notably at a fixed rate (more attractive and secure for households). The private sector may not offer such loans if it cannot manage the liquidity and interest-rate risks. This may be because of an inherently unstable core deposit base, underdeveloped bond markets, or an absence of hedging tools. Providing long-term fixed-rate loans may be a reason to establish an SHB, but such an institutional move does not provide a remedy to the underlying issue: creating an institution does not create a source for long-term resources. This confusion often ends up transferring a significant amount of financial risks to the taxpayer. Some selected examples show how common this problem is:

In Japan, the Government Housing Loan Corporation was created in 1950 to finance the postwar reconstruction. Its funding was mainly public (special government program and grants). The Government Housing Loan Corporation loans to house purchasers would have a first 10-year period with a fixed rate below market and a 25-year period with a preset fixed interest rate.[2] As such conditions could not be matched by private markets, other lenders were crowded out in this spectrum of maturities (and focused on shorter-term loans).

In Iran, the Bank Maskan offers long-term loans up to 20 years at fixed rates funded mostly with savings-for-housing schemes where the minimum requested duration of the preliminary savings period varies between six months and 3.5 years and the ratio between accumulated savings and the amount customers are entitled to borrow can be as high as 7. There is no hedge for the long-term loans the bank commits itself to extend.

In Mali, the Banque de l'Habitat was established in 1995. Despite a short-term funding base (including savings-for-housing schemes of a maximum and minimum period of one year) and a lack of external matching resources (limited bond markets), it has been granting mortgage loans for up to 20 years. Its liquidity risk is large,[3] and interest risk worse, especially with con-tractual housing schemes, which set the level of rates in advance.

---

2. In 2002: 2.755 and 4 percent respectively.
3. Public entities have been directed to deposits funds with Banque de l'Habitat (Mali)—a far from stable solution.

The Banco Hipotecario de Uruguay (BHU) was created in 1912. BHU was the predominant provider of housing finance and had 80 percent of the market in 2002. BHU cumulated three types of asset-liability mismatches: (i) liquidity risk—20-year loans, while most of the funding was sight deposit; (ii) interest rate risk—loans were granted on a fixed-rate basis before switching to a variable rate regime; and (iii) currency risk: after 1980, U.S.-dollar-denominated deposits grew to a significant percentage of BHU's liabilities while loans remained mostly denominated in indexed local currency.

Many housing bank failures resulted from this type of imbalance, taking a heavy toll on the national resources as the mismatches worsened during a crisis and the subsequent rescue operations.

Misallocation of Subsidies and Rent-Seeking Policies

As part of their social lending mandate, SHBs are often the privileged and sometimes exclusive vehicles of rationed subsidies. That channeling may create various problems. The SHB that allocates the subsidized loans is in a position to exercise some discretion in the allocation of the assistance, even if it must comply with eligibility criteria. In some cases, this leads to fraud or corruption among the bank's staff. More commonly, part of the subsidies end up supporting the SHB itself. There is always a temptation to use a "free" resource to cover operational costs, which are often higher than normal and would be difficult to sustain in a commercial environment. The problem is aggravated when subsidies are incorporated in the funding of the SHB; for instance, through the provision of resources at below-market rates, as this lower funding cost results in an above-normal intermediation spread and is not entirely passed through to the borrowers.

In this case, economic inefficiency develops on top of the social misallocation of benefits.[4]

More indirect forms of support exist, such as government guarantees along with their impact on investors (lower risk weight, eligibility for liquidity ratios, or reserve requirements), but also implicit guarantees, tax relief, or

---

4. These flaws are amplified when government funding is carried out through Central Bank lending. Creating high-powered money to finance long-term investments is bound to eventually lead to escalating inflationary pressures.

other preferential features granted to the SHB, such as more effective foreclo-sure proceedings unavailable to other lenders. These indirect benefits seem less costly, as they do not appear in budget expenses, but (i) they make any social cost-benefit analysis of the SHB intervention difficult to measure, and (ii) they may prove difficult to remove when the market has developed.

SHB as Obstacles to the Growth of Housing Finance Markets?

Many of the design flaws presented above are interrelated. Poor governance is involved in a loose recovery policy and free purchase of financial hedges; that is, through transferring balance-sheet mismatches to the government. Capturing subsidies is an inducement not to observe strict discipline in managing risks. When all these shortcomings are present, SHB can have a negative effect on the development of the market and the extension of access to housing finance, if this privileged subsidy circuit excludes other players from the market, and if the privileges do not remedy the deficiencies of the infrastructure of credit markets, such as the dearth of long-term capital in the economy. To the contrary, SHB may introduce further market distor-tions by being able to offer products that no competitors can ever match. This impact goes beyond the moderate-income segments that SHBs are sup-posed to serve. Because of their low profitability and poor track records in managing credit risks, it is fairly common to see SHBs shift their actual com-mercial target upward in the income distribution and finally compete with mainstream lenders on their ground.

Available Safeguards and Alternative Options

Before creating an SHB, government should determine what type of market failures are constraining the development and deepening of the market. If the unwillingness of the commercial financial sector to promote housing finance is the result of structural deficiencies and not the existence of more profitable and easier lines of business, an SHB will not foster the development of the supply—and to the contrary may stunt it. This will also be true if the market impediment lies in macroeconomic conditions. There are examples where the strengthening of the market infrastructure and the improvement of the macroeconomic conditions were sufficient to jump-start the market. For instance, Estonia has built in a little more than a decade a housing finance system that reaches 25 percent of its 2005 GDP. In Pakistan, the improvement of the financial parameters and the liquidity of the banking sector triggered a surge in the supply of housing finance. Loans outstanding went from YSD 330 million at the end of 2003 to 900 million at the end of 2005. This was achieved without any involvement of the SHB, which was itself being overhauled.

If the government considers that an institution is the right answer because the problem is the absence of a "market maker" and of development engine, then its design should meet some critical conditions to ensure it efficiently fulfills its social and economic purposes.

Good Governance

The first condition for making an SHB work is to establish its operation on strong corporate governance principles and insulate it from short-term political interference. These principles include the clear definition of corporate goals, transparency of results, independence and accountability of the management with respect to the board of directors, clear and independent risk management organization, separation of ownership, and control functions.[5] One prerequisite is to submit the SHB to general corporate laws and, above all, to the standard oversight of the banking regulator.

Public-private partnerships can be a way to ensure the existence of checks and balances, by creating an inner pressure for corporate results and helping to insulate the SHB from political interference. This solution runs the risk of exacerbating the capture of subsidies or other benefits by the private sector.

---

5. For a detailed analysis, see OECD 2004 and BIS 2006. See also van Greuning, Hennie, and Bratanovic 2003.

Autonomy of Funding

Establishing an SHB without ensuring its ability to raise funds autonomously is a sure recipe for the failure of the model. Without a savings mobilization capacity, resulting from either the absence of a deposit network and/or to the underdevelopment of the capital market,[6] an SHB is entirely dependent on government support. Funding loans through budgetary resources opens the gate for abuses and market distortions as mentioned above. Moreover, it is an economically inefficient solution, since it results in stringently constraining lending volumes and subjects them to uncertainty and volatility. Private lenders are never on an equal footing. Most of the limited number of examples of SHBs that have evolved successfully are banks that are issuing mortgage-related securities, thereby pioneering at the same time the development of the capital market: BancoEstado in Chile, GHB in Thailand, Banco Hipotecario in Argentina, and Crédit Immobilier et Hotelier in Morocco (which opened the MBS market in 2003).

Alignment of Corporate Interest with Market Development

The challenge of SHBs comes from mixing financial objectives and social objectives. It is extremely difficult to keep a balance between the two series of incentives. Any organization that enjoys privileges and a rent situation will seek to maximize for itself the benefits stemming from these advantages—a risk that not only exists in the case of wholly state-owned banks, but also when private partners are associated with the structure.

That is why it is of utmost importance to separate subsidies from finance and not let them become a source of income for the bank. Also, it is critical, besides good governance rules, to design business plans that clearly include performance objectives, define indicators, make the renewal of special advantages conditional on the achievement of objectives, and ensure the transparency and the publicity of the actual achievements by the SHB.

---

6. An essential feature for a specialized, nonbank. An archetypical example of such an arrangement is Crédit Foncier de France, the inception of which in the mid-nineteenth century was backed by the simultaneous creation of mortgage bonds.

Examples of SHBs Meeting These Conditions

Success is defined by contributing to the overall market development and providing finance to underserved categories, while achieving self-sustainability both in terms of financial results and of funding. Very few SHBs are reported to have fulfilled these expectations.

In Asia, the GHB of Thailand has been operating on a commercial basis without being dependent on state subsidies and has managed to run its commercial activities in a professional and competitive manner. Its leadership in lower-income housing finance rather reflects its strategic position vis-à-vis other lenders, than any privilege. The bank has played an innovative role and was a price leader during the takeoff of the housing finance system during the 1980s and early 1990s.

In Chile, BancoEstado is an example of where the market differentiation between the SHB and other banks reflects different business strategies, not the existence of special privileges. Its case is reviewed as such below.

Box 10.2. The Case of BancoEstado (Chile)

BancoEstado—originally Banco del Estado de Chile—was created in 1953 through the merger of four state-owned S&L institutions. While historically mainly focused on lending for housing, it has recently engaged in strategic diversification and has become the third commercial bank of the country. The bank's customer profile evidences the emphasis on low- and middle-income groups; * it has a 25 percent market share of mortgage loans in terms of value, but over 70 percent in terms of numbers of loans. Yet, the recovery performance of the bank on these loans is high, with a three-month delinquency rate steadily below 1 percent (0.62 percent in 2007) and better than the average of the Chilean banking system. ** Its net return on assets is satisfactory (0.48 percent in 2004–5), albeit lower than the countrywide average of 1.27 percent.† The two key success factors are (1) BancoEstado has always been operated on commercial principles. Although the government appoints its board members, except one, its management is composed of professionals rather than political appointees or civil servants. The bank is subject

(continued)

Box 10.2. The Case of BancoEstado (Chile) *(continued)*

to normal banking regulation and supervision, including asset-liability management norms. Its shareholder, the state, imposes a strict profitability
requirement: the bank pays a corporate income tax at a higher rate (40 percent)
than private companies, and pays out 75 percent of its profits as dividends. The
bank is managed with full autonomy vis-à-vis its sole shareholder. It is prohibited
to lend to other state-owned entities. (2) BancoEstado has a large savings-
collection network resulting in attracting a large population of small savers (80
percent of the country's savings accounts, but the average amount of its accounts
is about one-third of other banks). Moreover, the active geographic extension
policy allowed the bank to be the only financial institution present in 65 percent of
the municipalities. Thanks to its customer base, and not because of some distribution privilege,‡ BancoEstado is the main channel for housing subsidies.

---

* Below the income threshold for bankability, it is the government that provides housing finance—until
2002 through mortgages directly extended by the Housing Ministry (with a very poor recovery rate); now
merely through subsidies.
** This quality is of utmost importance for the cost of funds in Chile, where a large portion of mortgages
are funded through bonds that are PT securities guaranteed by the loan originators and collateralized by
the loan's portfolios.
† Fitch Ratings 2006.
‡ Housing subsidies in Chile do not pass through the accounts of lenders, but benefit directly to
households, with a requirement of prior savings, and their allocation is neutral vis-à-vis the distribution
network.

Box 10.3. The Case of the Government Housing Bank (GHB) of Thailand

GHB was established in 1953 under specific legislation with a dual purpose:
housing finance and housing development. The latter activity was transferred
to another government body, the National Housing Authority, in 1973, when the
company experienced a crisis triggered by losses on its developer loans. The
GHB was recapitalized and assigned a new strategy. It became a commercially
run institution, which abides by good corporate governance rules, focuses on the
quality of its portfolio, and posts positive results ($109 million in 2005 for assets
totaling $13.3 billion). GHB developed a network of more than 120 branches,
which allowed it to mobilize funding through its deposit base. GHB succeeded in
combining the support to lower-income groups and the function of a driver

(continued)

Box 10.3. The Case of the Government Housing Bank (GHB) of Thailand *(continued)*

for the whole market development. It does provide loans at below-market conditions, by concentrating on providing lower-income borrowers with the benefits of the advantages its enjoys as an SHB: lower spread on bond issues, absence of dividend, and, for a long time, lesser capital requirements than other lenders. Also, GHB participates in some government-lead social housing and slum upgrading programs—targeting households that the financial system would not serve. At the same time, GHB plays a role as a market developer. Its activity has not prevented the overall growth of the supply of finance for housing, provided now by 17 other players. It played a countercyclical function during the 1997–2001 fall of the mortgage market: while lending by commercial bank dropped, GHB's activity level remained the same and its market share jumped from its traditional 29 percent range to over 35 percent. It is sponsoring market infrastructure developments through its involvement in the inception of a retail credit bureau, a real estate information center, and a mortgage insurance scheme. In mid-2006, the Housing Bank announced a $1 billion issue of MBSs, the largest securitization transaction ever in Asia except Japan.

Policy Alternatives

Market development can start spontaneously, but this is not the most common process. More often, there is a need for a driving force, or a "market maker," to spark the growth of the supply in an embryonic market. Besides establishing a SHB, a government may want to consider alternative routes to broaden access to housing finance. It must be stressed that whatever option is chosen, it cannot be successful if, in parallel, the basic obstacles that motivate the abstention of market players—mortgage lending infrastructure, stability of funding, macroeconomic conditions, and so forth—are not addressed.

Regulatory or Contractual Credit Orientation

In some countries, credit direction has been used to overcome market failures. In the United States, the Community Reinvestment Act of 1977[7] seeks to prevent "redlining" of underserved areas by imposing on banks minimum requirements to provide financial services—and, in the first place, offering bank accounts. India is another example of administrative direction, with the concept of "priority lending" requirements, including for the housing sector, which lending institutions must fulfill. In underdeveloped markets, this approach can be ineffective if the basic environment remains weak, in particular in terms of adequate funding and effective credit-risk management tools. In Nigeria, for instance, quotas for home lending—5–6 percent of total lending—had been prescribed in the early 1980s, but remained ineffective because of the shortcomings of the lending environment, and despite sanctions provided for by the Central Bank. The regulation was dropped in 1993.

A more fruitful approach, which can better take into account lenders' constraints, is to induce financial institutions to serve lower-income groups through contractual arrangements. This is the route chosen by South Africa, where the largest commercial banks signed in 2005 a memorandum of understanding with the government, in line with the broader 2003 Financial Sector Charter, in which they committed themselves to provide a certain volume of loans to the low-income market segment over four years. Participating banks adjusted their lending policy accordingly, developed new products,[8] and established new departments dedicated to affordable housing loans.[9]

Second-Tier Institutions

Instead of creating a primary market lender that may ultimately compete with or crowd out other lenders, a government may consider supporting a

7. Diamond 2002.
8. See FinMark Trust 2007, Rust 2007 and 2008.
9. It should be noted that this solution is not without its problems. Issues surrounding sharing of credit and market risk have meant that it is not fully implemented in South Africa's townships.

second-tier institution (liquidity facility or conduit as described in the capital markets chapter). There are two potential advantages: a second-tier institution may have a catalytic effect on the market by opening up new funding channels, and it may reduce barriers to lending by mitigating uncertainties or additional risks that block market development. This approach only works if the primary market is sufficiently developed and bond markets exist, however. Government ownership or backing (for example, through guarantees) of a second-tier institution can be a more efficient form of subsidy because it benefits the whole primary market instead of being reserved to a privileged circuit at the detriment of other players. There are therefore convincing examples of secondary market facilities that have actually played a catalytic role in the development of the housing finance market (see the related chapter in this book). Such an approach, however, does not address in itself all the concerns described above, in particular the shortcomings of mixing finance and subsidies and the risk of the institution capturing part of the state support. Care must be taken to calculate and budget the contingent liability of such support, for which the institution must be an agent with fiduciary obligations rather than a recipient that is in a position to pass only part of it on to the market.

Public-Private Partnerships

As an alternative to creating a specialized housing bank, a government may wish to stimulate mortgage lending through strategic investment in or initial support to housing finance companies. The advantage to this model could be the ability to combine private-sector managerial efficiency with government policy goals.

The main successful example is HDFC in India. HDFC, established at the end of 1977, was promoted by Industrial Credit and Investment Corporation of India (ICICI), the then state-owned development bank, and particularly by the personal involvement of its chairman. ICICI, however, only invested a small amount—5 percent of the total of seed capital in the new institution. The government also brought initial support by guaranteeing the company's long-term debt, and directed public-sector institutions, in particular, insurance companies, to finance HDFC. Moreover, a regulation was passed that made loans to specialized housing finance companies eligible for the priority lending obligations imposed on commercial banks. HDFC grew to become the main driver of the market development, acting as the promoter of other specialized institutions as well as the supporter of other housing-related services, while at the same time being a successful business. Key for this success was the actual, but limited, support by the government that did not conflict with a business model focused on recovery policy and resource mobilization.

Such a combination has been difficult to replicate elsewhere up to now. HDFC helped establish similar institutions in other countries, for instance, Bangladesh and Ghana. Despite the expertise and dynamism of these two institutions, the model has not been successful as in India because of unfavorable context—lack of efficient external funding and negative impact of an SHB in one case, macroeconomic instability in the other. This shows that an institutional model is itself not enough, but that structural and environment conditions conducive to housing finance are required in any case.

"Double Bottom Line"—Social and Commercial—Private-Sector Lenders

There is an increasing interest around the world in combining financial viability with social benefits in sectors such as housing that are at the crossroads of finance and social purposes. Instead of developing a proprietary instrument, government may want to foster the development of entities susceptible to bringing business-based solutions to the needs of households underserved by the mainstream financial sector. In many countries, there is an array of microfinance institutions or financial cooperatives that can, or could where a proper environment exists, develop housing finance products. This is the case in several African countries, for instance: Caisses Populaires du Burkina Faso, Nyesigiso cooperatives in Mali, Banques Populaires du Rwanda, and MUCODEC in Congo. In Paraguay, the quasi-sole providers of housing finance are credit unions or financial cooperatives. Given the often deep penetration of such networks in the income spectrum, they might be a more efficient use of public sponsorship than specialized state entities with a narrow scope.

Exit Strategies

For the countries where inefficient SHBs exist, there are few exit solutions besides winding them down. These alternatives are constrained by the bank's condition and the financial context in which it operates.[10]

Enable a "Corporatization Process" to Create a Commercially Run Institution

Ensure the SHB operates on commercial principles (profitability, as evidenced by tax and dividends-payment capacity, a condition for sustainability). This approach typically involves the removal of privileges and distortion factors to establish a level playing field for other lenders. In turn, this requires the separation of subsidies from finance by having two separate balance sheets: one for the social subsidy program of the state managed by the bank, preferably for a fee, the other being the commercial balance sheet of the bank meeting the reporting standards of any commercial bank.

The government must make sure that the housing bank falls under the direct regulation and supervision of the bank regulators. Also, the corporatization process typically involves bringing in a new set of experienced bank managers who will instill financial and administrative discipline.

Two recent experiences illustrate this strategy: Pakistan, with the transformation of the HBFC, and Algeria, with the turning around of the once-crippled CNEP.

HBFC, in Pakistan, established in 1952, was for a long time the sole provider of formal finance for housing. HBFC was an institution run by non-professional bankers. It relied mostly on Central Bank for its funding at below-market conditions. It did not target modest households as it should have, and had a very lax recovery policy. The government decided in the late 1990s to put HBFC back afloat, and to bring it up to acceptable efficiency standards with the view of eventually selling it to private investors. Shutting the institution down was seen as politically unfeasible since HBFC was at that time the only lender of any significance in the country. A recapitalization

---

10. A valuable perspective on state-owned banks can be found in Caprio, Fiechter, Litan, and Pomerleano 2004.

was carried out, mainly through Central Bank debt forgiveness. The granting of new credit facilities by the Central Bank was brought to a halt. Consequently, HBFC was obliged to considerably reduce its new lending activity and to focus on payment recoveries, which had become its only source of funding. A new management was appointed, chosen from among professional bankers. A deep modernization of internal procedures and information system was undertaken, and corrupted practices were fought. Currently, new demand-driven products are being designed, and the participation of private shareholders in the company's capital is being considered.

CNEP in Algeria is basically the Algerian savings bank, with more than 6 million accounts. It used to have the monopoly on real estate finance within a state-owned banking system, both for individuals and for public housing programs. The state massively used this savings channel for financing public developers. For many years, CNEP operations were largely driven by administrative and political criteria. Many loans were granted without clear property title, especially to public developers, to which land used to be allocated through simple administrative allotment letters. Moreover, CNEP's own development subsidiary was directed by public authorities to build programs that met low demand. Nonperforming loans ended up amounting to about 75 percent of the portfolio, including loans to the in-house developer.

In 1997, the government bailed out the institution plan at a time where a deregulation policy opened real estate finance to other players. The "Caisse" was recapitalized and turned into a commercial bank subject to Central Bank oversight—instead of being based on a specific law and regulated by the Ministry of Finance. Part of the impaired public-developer portfolio was exchanged for treasury bonds. In a new restructuring plan in 2000–1, the government bought unsold stocks of housing units for DA 13.7 billion (US$180 million) and sponsored the selling of 35,000 other units.

New management launched a forceful reorganization, focusing on the overhaul of the accounting system and on the recovery policy. The emphasis on recovery implied a fall in the production of new loans, but the recovery rate reached 85 percent on the pre-restructured portfolios, and 95 percent on the post-2000 production. Since 2004, CNEP has resumed more active lending.

Partial or Full Privatization

Bringing in market discipline and economic business strategies can be strongly buttressed if private partners, who will require profitable results and risk-based management, are brought in, while at the same time the shareholding government retains a say in the general strategy of the institution. The danger with partial privatization, however, is that private investors may be rent seekers who exploit privileges rather than pursue sound business or development strategies.[11] Therefore, seeking to establish a private-public partnership should rely on a true commercial franchise for which the government provides initial support, and should be accompanied by the dismantling of any market-distorting advantages.

Banco Hipotecario in Argentina[12] is an example of success in achieving the association of private shareholders who pursue a commercially oriented policy and a government with enough influence to guide the company toward market segments that are complementary of the mainstream banking sector. Banco Hipotecario Nacional was an SHB operating since the last years of the 19th century. In the 1980s, it was the main provider of mortgage loans in the country. Its funding sources were deposits from public sector entities and loans from the Central Bank.[13] Its performance was increasingly poor. Its customer base shifted upward in the income distribution. The bank incurred considerable mismatches between short-term liabilities and 25-year maturity assets that followed different indexation mechanisms. Because of the discrepancy between the loan balance appreciation and housing prices, as well as a lax recovery policy, the portfolio quality drastically deteriorated, ending with a 67 percent rate of nonperforming loans. These conditions resulted in a severe crisis, leading the Central Bank to intervene in 1987. Banco Hipotecario Nacional's deposits were transferred to Banco de la Nación, and it was prohibited from direct lending.

For a while, Banco Hipotecario Nacional became a wholesale lender extending loans through a network of correspondent banks. In 1991–3, it

---

11. The example of American government-sponsored enterprises shows that the benefit of government support can be diverted not only by the corporation's staff, but by its shareholders.
12. See Cristini and Moya 2004 and Gautier, Hassler, Freire, Goytia, Clichevski, Cristini, and Moya 2006.
13. This is the opposite of the company's original concept, which implied the issuance of mortgage bonds.

went through a deep restructuring. It contributed to the promotion of the market by providing funding to primary lenders. It developed original construction finance structures, set out underwriting standards for unsalaried borrowers, and entered into partnership with some provincial housing agencies in charge of low-income housing (Instituto Provinciales de Vivienda). In 1996, following a 1995 law that established a securitization framework, it pioneered the issuance of MBSs.

The next step was to partially privatize the company, a part of a more general policy promulgated in 1996. In all, 46 percent of the bank's capital—from then on, Banco Hipotecario SA (BHSA)—was sold to private investors in early 1999. Interestingly, despite retaining a majority of shares, the government handed over control of the board of directors to the latter, who appoint nine out of 13 directors. The privatization law authorized the bank to directly lend to primary borrowers again. In exchange for various obligations meant to support social policy goals,[14] the law kept the benefice of certain privileges,[15] but provided for a sunset clause, set in August 2007.

During this decade, housing finance surged in Argentina, with all the major banks offering the product. BHSA retained a leading position in the market.[16] The company's recovery performance and profitability strongly improved, and it became the first Latin American company to issue AAA mortgage securities in the United States. Yet, BHSA kept a special role in moderate- and middle-income market segments, resulting in particular from partnerships with local government assistance programs. The soundness of its operation was demonstrated by the way it overcome the 2001–2 crisis, despite being deeply affected by it. It was the first Argentinean entity to reschedule its external debt, and reopened the domestic securitization market in 2004. NPL ratio quickly fell below the 2001–2 crisis level.[17] The company's main challenge is to diversify its funding sources and expand its deposit base.

---

14. The main obligations are to allocate 10 percent of the construction loans to small cities, to maintain a fund allowing debt forgiveness to borrowers in distressed economic situations, and to ensure a balanced geographical distribution of loans.
15. Income tax relief on loans extended before 1997, right of selling and managing mortgage-linked insurance products, and special procedures for forced sales.
16. BHSA market share jumped to over 30 percent of new lending after the 2002 crisis, which brought mortgage lending to a halt for awhile. In terms of loans outstanding, its market share is about 20 percent.
17. A total of 7.3 percent of all loans at the end of 2005, and 5.9 percent in December 2006 (Fitch Ratings 2006).

Conversion of an SHB into a Second-Tier Refinance Institution

This option is rare because it is generally not realistic. The administrative culture that prevails in many housing banks is incompatible with that of a capital market organization; in addition, the operations and systems would need a total overhaul. Although the Argentine case experienced some success in becoming—temporarily—a second-tier financier, the example of Nigeria is more representative of the difficulties of such a conversion.

State Support to Private Sector

SHBs often are the sole, or at least the dominant, provider of housing finance (Brazil, Mali, Pakistan before 2003, and Uruguay). In this case, their operation cannot be stopped suddenly: market capacities have to be built up first or in parallel, for fear of depriving households of an already all-too-limited supply of financial services.

Several experiences can be mentioned as being very successful in avoiding an interruption in the finance supply, and in fostering the growth of alternate finance providers on a sound basis.

In Jordan, the government in 1973 created the Housing Bank for Trade and Finance, according to the classic, pre-liberalization-era housing bank model: a special law, a specialized activity, and implicit subsidies (tax exemption, reserve requirements). The bank—which was a public-private partnership— was conservatively run, with the objective of economic efficiency prevailing over political interferences. Its existence, however, was not favorable to the entry of new players in the market, and its actions did nothing to establish a source of long-term capital. Therefore, the Jordanian government decided to change its status in 1997. Its specific framework was removed, and it was authorized to become a full-fledged commercial bank. The Housing Bank for Trade and Finance diversified its activities, and progressively stopped lending for housing. In the meantime, a second-tier liquidity facility, the Jordan Mortgage Refinance Corporation (JMRC), was created with the purpose of raising capital from the nascent bond market and of lending this relatively long-term resources to any participating mortgage lender. As described in chapter 12,

Box 10.4. The Case of the Federal Mortgage Bank of Nigeria

At the end of the 1960s, in the context of National Development Plans, the government of Nigeria developed a policy of direct intervention in the housing sector, both as a provider of new units and of housing finance. The existing specialized lender, the Nigeria Building Society, was bought by the government, and, in 1977, converted into a new organization, the Federal Mortgage Bank of Nigeria (FMBN). Established on a specific legal basis, and wholly owned by the federal government, FMBN was entrusted with providing long-term housing credit, either as a retail or a wholesale lender. Its funding sources were the federal budget, the Central Bank, and the banking system, which was directed to allocate a minimum percentage of its lending to housing. The system proved ineffective. FMBN recovery performance was very low. The overall investments in housing dropped during this period.

At the end of the 1980s and early 1990s, the government switched to a liberalization policy, and sought to foster private-sector lenders, but within a specialized, subsidized circuit led and supervised by public institutions. Primary mortgage institutions (PMIs) were established within a framework for specialized companies, modeled on building societies. FMBN transferred its primary lending activity to a state-owned PMI, the Federal Mortgage Finance Limited, to become a second-tier refinancier and also the regulator and supervisor of the PMIs. * In 1992, the National Housing Fund (NHF), mainly funded by mandatory contributions from salaried employees, was created to provide funds at below-market conditions to the PMI system through FMBN. The new structure failed to have any catalytic effect on the supply of housing finance. The Federal Mortgage Finance Limited, which inherited a portfolio of mostly nonperforming loans from FMBN and had excessive operating costs, did not play the expected role of market leader for PMIs. It was liquidated in 2004. FMBN suffered from impediments affecting the role of the NHF, both from cumbersome procedures in its PMI refinancing activity and from poor management that translated into recurrent operational deficits. The FMBN-NHF channel provided the equivalent of only $40 million in mortgages over 13 years (excluding developer loans). As part of a broader policy revision, FMBN's business model is being revised. FMBN should become a second-tier facility channeling capital market resources toward primary lenders, a perspective that became realistic with the establishment of fully funded pension funds in Nigeria.

---

* The oversight function was transferred to the Central Bank in 1997.

JMRC has had an impact in setting quality standards for loan origination and servicing and improving the lending terms. It became a catalyst and triggered the entry of new mortgage lenders. In all, eight banks are now active in the mortgage market and their supply of loans did much more than offset the withdrawal of the Housing Bank for Trade and Finance.

In Pakistan, while the housing bank HBFC was being overhauled, a conducive framework for lending for housing in general was established: an out-of-court foreclosure procedure was created (2001), credit reporting systems were developed for loans to individuals, tax incentives were devised for mortgage borrowers, and a strengthening of the real estate developer industry was promoted. Comforted by a noticeable improvement of the macroeconomic environment, in particular by a sharp fall in interest rates, commercial banks entered the market. In less than two years (2003–4), 20 lenders were active and together offered a higher volume of finance than the hitherto dominant HBFC.

In Korea, the evolution of the SHB was quite different. The Korea Housing Bank (KHB) operated on a commercial basis from the day of its creation in 1967 within a financial policy environment of strong directed credit as the only mortgage lender. A critical step took place in the 1970s, when the government agreed to separate social operations from the balance sheet of KHB and to finance the NHF from explicit fiscal resources; KHB was paid a fee to service the loans. KHB's charter changed from a specialized to commercial bank and became the Korea Housing and Commercial Bank (KH&CB) in 1997. The new charter, however, committed KH&CB to making no less than 50 percent of its loans to housing. The Ministry of Finance also maintained its power to appoint senior executives. In order to strengthen its performance by means of strategic investors, KH&CB became the first Korean bank to be listed on the New York Stock Exhange the same year. KH&CB was among the small minority of banks that weathered the 1997 financial crisis unscathed because it did not make loans to large business groups, or chaibols. It maintained a bad loan ratio of below 3 percent. In 2001, KH&CB had become the largest commercial bank in Korea through its merger with Kookmin Bank. Today, Kookmin Bank (the name the merged institution retained) maintains it quasi-monopolist dominance of the mortgage market and it remains the sole servicer of the NHF social lending. Together, the two portfolios represent 85 percent of the Korean mortgage market. Meanwhile, the new government-owned Korea Housing Finance Corporation started operating in 2004 as a secondary market institution that aims to diversify mortgage distribution channels and to lower the heavy dependence of the Korean market on ARM loans of very short maturities.

Conclusion: A Decision Tree for Policy Makers

One major problem with SHBs is that they apparently fill a vacuum immediately and provide loans for a few years before the risks and distortions embedded in the model start unfolding on a full scale. It is therefore critical that policy makers draw the lessons from the past and from other countries, and clearly define the goals they want to achieve before jumping to a solution that seems an easy answer in the short term, but tends to become a fiscal time bomb or an impediment to market development.

The question that is the root of many others is whether the government wants primarily to provide financial services itself, and replace the market, or develop the market as deeply as possible.

If the second option prevails, the next question is to determine what prevents the commercial sector from offering this service. If, as is usually the case, the answer lies with fundamental deficiencies in the market infrastructure and environment, the government's priority should be to focus on remedying such deficiencies. Establishing a state entity under such conditions will do little good, as the state-owned housing bank will encounter the same problems as commercial lenders (and more so given the difficulties of a government lender in controlling risk through underwriting and collections). Establishing a secured lending environment, providing access to adequate funding sources, and ensuring macroeconomic stability, in particular a decline of risks premiums included in interest rates, will likely trigger the growth of lending for housing.

If the main obstacles rather lie with the strategies of mainstream banks, which prefer other business lines and are not keen to invest in housing loans, then a government may want to support the emergence of "market makers" susceptible to having a catalytic effect on market development. This can take the form of specialized institutions as in India or Mexico, with indirect government support, or of second-tier institutions as in Jordan or Malaysia, along with a strategy of improving the legal and regulatory infrastructure. If the market failure mostly affects lower-income groups, the government may want to strengthen alternative lenders that "naturally" cater to their needs. It can also devise an assistance policy—direct demand subsidies, support to mortgage insurance or to savings for housing scheme—opened to any loan distribution channel, which can provide the required incentives for private institutions to enter new market segments.

If a new institution seems definitely needed to drive the market expansion or deepening, governments should prioritize the second-tier facility model. This model will be ineffective without a conducive environment, both in the primary mortgage market and on the capital market. Moreover, to be successful, it also requires good governance rules and a clear distinction between subsidies and corporate results.

It is only when none of the options of this decision tree are feasible that the SHB concept should be considered—and preferably not as an exclusive implementation tool of the development strategy. But many conditions must then be met: all of the above plus good governance principles, sunset clauses on regulatory or financial privileges, and a road map toward privatization. This is the best way to ensure that the institution is demand driven and has successfully established a new market.

CHAPTER 11

Housing Provident Funds

Loïc Chiquier

A common problem in emerging markets is high levels of inflation, which discourages savings combined with undeveloped capital markets. These problems conspire to limit any activities that would rely on the availability of long-term funds. A solution to this problem seen in a number of emerging markets is the creation of housing provident funds (HPFs). They are essentially long-term saving schemes that operate through mandatory contributions. While this can be an efficient and rapid way of raising long-term funds in environments where this would not otherwise be possible, it can also engender a number of costs. One of the main difficulties is in ensuring that the HPF does not distort market pricing through unrealistic and regressive subsidies. This chapter reviews some of the different models and structures of HPFs, as well as some issues that have arisen with their creation.

Description of HPF

HPFs are specialized financial institutions that collect mandatory savings from employees—from the public or private sector—expressed as a defined percentage of their salary. Sometimes the employers are also required to make additional proportional contributions (for example, one-to-one match in China). The HPF then manages these accrued long-term savings, which are often remunerated at a below-market yield. This permits the contributing members of the HPF to

- withdraw their accrued savings as a down payment for a housing investment (but they cannot otherwise withdraw their savings before retirement);
- receive long-term housing mortgage loans, usually at a preferential rate (either directly lent by the HPF or through another lending institution);
- benefit from retirement savings as additional income to the retirement system; and
- receive unemployment severance payment (in some cases).

The organization, products, and governance of HPFs are shaped to reflect their multiple functions. Although they act as deposit takers and lenders, they are not banks and are often not regulated as such (in terms of capital adequacy, provisioning, financial oversight, and so on). Although they provide retirement benefits, they are neither regulated as a pension fund or subject to investment limits and performance benchmarks. They are typically created through a specific law, or in some cases their existence is laid out in the constitution. Their activities and products are determined by law.

Subsidies

HPFs were often created when and where private lenders were not active in long-term housing lending, as a self-funded housing finance system capable of producing a sizeable amount of new housing loans. HPFs have been created in many emerging economies, including Mexico, Nigeria, Brazil, Jamaica, the Philippines, and China.

Although often plagued by financial inefficiencies and regressive cross-subsidies, their market shares in housing finance can be quite significant. They may even dominate residential markets (70 percent market share together for the HPFs in Mexico at the end of 2005), mainly as the result of the recurrent and quasi-tax nature of their collected mandatory savings. After reaching a cruising regime, the reflows from the portfolio can also be recycled into even more new loans.

In other cases (for example, the National Housing Trust in Nigeria), they fail to provide any sizeable funding to develop a critical mass in the housing finance system. This occurs because employees try to avoid paying their contributions when the interest rates on saving are negative in real terms, and the proportion of savers to borrowers is exceptionally low.

HPFs often finance favored population groups in preferential credit conditions, but not necessarily among the lower- or informal-income segments. HPFs are then exposed to considerable political pressure and interference from changing governments. Most of the time, this is to the detriment of their financial sustainability as lending institutions and pension funds, as seen, for example, in the Philippines (Filipino Development Housing Fund; PAG-IBIG) or Mexico (Fondo de Vivienda para los Trabajadores al Servicio del Estado; FOVISSTE]). In Mexico, the other large HPF (INFONAVIT) has been restructuring to improve its efficiency and governance.

Their implied level of *cross-subsidization* can be larger than any other state program of housing subsidies. It depends mainly on three core factors: (i) the proportion of contributing savers who will never receive a long-term housing loan (but have their savings under-remunerated to the detriment of their future pensions), (ii) the interest rate gap below market levels for the savings and credits, and (iii) the mortgage portfolio performance (the less performing, the more inefficient subsidies).

This *system of cross-subsidies is often socially regressive.* The proportion of borrowers to savers is low by arithmetic necessity, given the relatively large amount and long-term nature of housing loans (less for eligible home improvement purposes). This reality is not necessarily an issue, except if the loan interest rates are subsidized by the under-remunerated savings of the contributing members. Informal-income households also do not access these preferential credits as they are not formally employed. The problem of cross-subsidization is compounded when most of the credit subsidies benefit higher-income households that could have afforded private-market loans, and are actually funded by lower-income employees to the detriment of their retirement.

Even in the favorable case of an HFP refocusing its preferential housing lending to the underserved populations to minimize the regressive nature of cross-subsidies, it sacrifices its provident fund function to become an indirect *taxation and redistribution vehicle*, although (i) this role is often not integrated within the national housing policy of the government (given the HFP legal and corporate governance structure), and (ii) these *subsidies do not appear as on-budget fiscal expenditures* (inefficient but sometimes perceived as convenient by some governments exposed to tight fiscal constraints).

Governance

The multiple mandates and legal foundations of HPFs are often reflected through an inefficient corporate governance structure. The main body is a special council or board, composed of an excessive number of persons representing different stakeholders (several ministries, including labor, finances and housing, private construction and financial sectors, trade unions representing the employees, and so forth). This often results in a combination of a quasi-independence, poor accountability, and high degree of inertia in opposing strategic reforms. Once in operation they serve strong vested interests—developers, unions, public sector workers—which makes it difficult to change (for example, moving away from subsidization, even if detrimental to the lower-income savers).

Abuses and corruption are also encouraged by a lack of transparency; for example, part of the credit subsidies may be wrongly captured by developers when setting their sale prices, if households cannot freely choose their housing investment. The lending also suffers from administrative rigidities that conflict with industry standards and the nature of the market demand. A lack of transparency may affect the process of credit and home allocation. For example, many HPFs accept as housing investment only a home purchase (sometimes only a finished home built by a developer) versus a demand from poorer members for lower credit for renovation and repairs on their existing homes.

These funds can deter the rise of private mortgage markets, if new private lenders cannot compete against the HPF's preferential conditions. An uneven playing field may be created by undue legal and regulatory privileges, but also from the following strategic difference: no private lender can survive substantial defaults by relying on contributions from member wages or by paying a negative real return on savings (as the Mexican HPFs did during the 1990s). Sometimes, HPFs also enjoy the exclusive privilege to deduct loan payments directly from salaries (which is cheaper and safer), nor do they pay income taxes or have to reserve capital against unexpected losses.

Development of an HPF

Many variants exist, notably whether the HPF is a direct lender (as in Mexico and China) or not (as in Brazil or Singapore). But many HPF share some common features at a certain stage of their development:

- low-income savers cross-subsidize a smaller number of better-off borrowers;
- the accrued savings are not sufficiently remunerated for retirement needs;
- administration costs of HPF are high and the lending performance is poor;
- their presence may hinder the expansion of other private lenders.

A challenge in countries where private lenders enter the mortgage industry consists for the HPF in encouraging private lending for middle-income households rather than competing against them. This implies a need to revisit their own credit products (develop co-financing, let other lenders use the savings as down payment or guarantees), better target their borrowers, improve lending efficiency, narrow the interest rate gap with market rate conditions, and target the subsidy element only for the underserved groups. Such reforms have been initiated in Brazil by the Fundo de Garantia do Tempo de Serviço (FGTS) and in Mexico by INFONAVIT.

At a certain stage of their development, HPFs are confronted with a strategic choice between their functions as a pension fund, housing lender, and subsidy distributor:

If the priority consists in improving the retirement of members while private mortgage markets may expand, HPFs should optimize and diversify their investments rather than increase their market shares as a primary mortgage lender. The housing lending should be then separated from the provident fund operations, and the main activities focused on efficiently investing in a diversified way the savings through financial markets (including market-based refinancing of other mortgage lenders). This evolution of a separation between the savings and then lending—see Singapore—often represents the best scenario, when technically and politically feasible.

If the assigned priority mandate rather consists in facilitating housing finance for the underserved population, the HPF should revisit its credit policy to better target its loans. Should it lend to informal-sector workers who did not contribute through savings, strengthen all aspects of its lending operations, leverage other private lenders to serve members,[1] price its housing loans according to market realities, target subsidies in a transparent and effective way (ideally through lump-sum grants), or provide a complementary second-lien housing loan to the main mortgage credit, which is provided by another private lender (as developed in France)?

International Experience

China

The HPF was initially introduced as a pilot program in Shanghai in 1991 and later extended nationwide in 1995, in order to kick-start a housing finance system that could carry on the housing policy reform (for example, transform housing from welfare to commodity). HPF operations are now conducted through 320 management centers. The interest rates are regulated by the People's Bank of China, while the Ministry of Construction and Ministry of Finance are responsible for overseeing the scheme at the national level. At the local level, housing committees determine policies with the management centers. Commercial banks are appointed to handle the deposits, lending, and financial management.[2]

---

1. For example, by co-financing loans, as is now the case with INFONAVIT. But HPF savings can also be used as guarantees and down payments for other lenders.
2. In some cases, management centers also collect funds and provide financial supervision.

These savings earn a low interest rate. The participant's employer provides a one-for-one match to the employee's deposits. The employee can only use the funds for the purchase or major repairs of housing or to supplement retirement income. When purchasing housing, the member can withdraw the savings and obtain a loan at a preferential rate. Upon retirement, the employee can withdraw the account for other purposes.

By the end of 2005, HPF savings represented RM 626 billion collected from 63.3 million employees. Despite an RM 283 billion mortgage portfolio, their housing lending remains limited (versus 1.6 trillion mortgage portfolio held by commercial banks). Only 45 percent of collected savings has been provided as housing loans and only 8 percent of savers are housing borrowers. Fund loans have performed well, with only a 0.12 percent delinquency rate as of the end of 2005. These credits are not used very much by lower-income groups, but HPF rather competes with banks for upper-income borrowers. Despite preferential credit rates, their accessibility and impact remained limited. Over time, HPF lending has mainly benefited upper-income households or privileged employees, but did not help the many households that are unemployed or marginally employed. A total of 80 percent of HPF lending in Beijing went to the purchase of high-cost housing, while in Shanghai 44 percent of lent funds went to 4 percent of contributors. HPF lending is a regressive policy in which the lower end of the income distribution receives a limited benefit in the form of reduced-yield savings, helping to cross-subsidize the loans to upper-income HPF participants.

In addition, some HPFs act as inefficient lenders, for example, in processing loan applications when compared to the commercial banks. They are administratively managed, resulting in cumbersome procedures and market-unfriendly limitations. The loan amount is capped while housing prices keep increasing. There are reported cases of corruption and misused funds for other priorities of a local government, notably when the local management center supersedes banks in controlling all financial transactions.

The performance of China's HPFs leads to several important policy lessons:

- The HPFs were created as a means to create long-term mortgage markets at a time in which banks were absent from the market. Since then, most banks have been competing on mortgage lending, so the activities and market positioning of the HPF should be revisited accordingly (lower income, complementary funding, etc).

- HPF preferential lending fails to meet the affordability purpose, as its design favors higher-income workers. Most members will not receive a loan over their lifetime and are forced to save at below-market rates. The functions of subsidy and finance should be separated and subsidies better targeted.

- The HPFs are insufficiently diversified (most of their assets are in real estate loans from a particular area). The system should be more consolidated.

- HPFs are regulated by the Ministry of Construction, which has no expertise in financial regulation and which has a potential conflict of interest: the desire to develop housing as opposed to safe and sound lending. As a matter of safety and soundness, HPF activities should be regulated by a qualified financial regulator.

Singapore

Residents in Singapore are required to put a large proportion of disposable income into the Central Provident Fund (CPF). Virtually all employees pay as much as 35 percent of their gross income (for those 35 years of age or younger) into the CPF, which invests the savings in a diversified portfolio of domestic and international assets that earn a positive real return for participants. The CPF acts as a pension fund rather than as a housing lender.

A majority of housing finance is provided by the Housing Development Board (HDB), a government agency that develops, finances, and manages housing. HDB requires a 20 percent down payment for its loans, and households can borrow from the CPF for the down payment and amortization of their housing loan, but these funds must be repaid over time. The savings in the CPF are used for down payment and loan repayment but not for direct subsidized lending, which reduces the possible confusion of roles.

In the past, HDB provided both market rate and subsidized loans. The Ministry of Finance lends to HDB at the government borrowing rate and the HDB provides interest rate subsidies to households according to need. As of 2003, HDB no longer provides market rate loans—households are expected to obtain credit from banks. HDB continues to provide concessionary interest-rate mortgage loans for first-time flat buyers and current HDB borrowers who are upgrading from smaller flats (first-time buyers and married households with children receive priority). The subsidized and market-rate lending sectors are quite separate segments of the business. Borrowers obtaining market-rate credit from a bank can also use their CPF savings for their required down payment.

In addition, housing loans account for only a small fraction of CPF uses of funds, so the CPF can operate in an actuarially sound manner to provide the highest return for its participants, in keeping with international standards for pension fund management.

Mexico

There are two large HPFs, one for the employees of the private sector (INFONAVIT) and the other for public-sector employees (FOVISSTE). Both have been operating for more than 30 years. Both collect 5 percent of the salaries of employees through individual savings accounts (withheld at source by the employer). Both make direct mortgage residential loans to their members. The credits are quite subsidized in the case of FOVISSTE. Members may withdraw their savings to use as a down payment to purchase a house, together with a loan from either their HPF or from a private lender. Any savings remaining at retirement are available to supplement retirement income. INFONAVIT loans are linked to an index of wage inflation, to which a spread is added that varies by income category, cross-subsidizing borrowers in lower-income segments.

The two funds represent 70 percent of the Mexican mortgage market by the end of 2005 (INFONAVIT 60 percent, FOVISSTE 10 percent) despite a rapid growth of private-market lending by SOFOLs and banks. In particular, INFONAVIT went through several operational reforms that helped to increase its share of primary mortgage markets.[3]

---

3. From 49 percent in 2000 to 60 percent in 2005 in terms of outstanding balance. As a share of the new 2005 production of mortgage loans, INFONAVIT weighted 67 percent and 44 percent respectively in number of loans and in loan amounts.

Box 11.1. The Reforms of INFONAVIT in Mexico

INFONAVIT management implemented operational reforms during the last six years that have significantly improved the performance of INFONAVIT. The main blocks were to modernizing information and accounting systems, improving the procedures in mortgage origination and servicing, appointing external debt collectors, better tracking the evolution of employees who left their jobs (operational risk as one of the main reason of defaults), and creating new committees for risk management, auditing, and strategic policy.

By lending according to mortgage industry standards, these reforms enabled INFONAVIT to increase its lending, improve the cash flows, and pay a return on savings comparable to private pension funds (Afores). INFONAVIT has adopted international accounting standards and made itself subject to the financial regulator oversight—Comisión Nacional Bancaria y de Valores—and is now subject to all reporting and control rules of commercial banks. The default rate has been reduced to 8 percent. Its savings pay a positive net real yield (3.5 percent in 2005), close to the net yields of private pension funds in the last years. But on average since 1997, its yearly performance has been lower by 0.4 percent than the private Afores.

INFONAVIT has widened its cooperation with the private sector, providing its members with the ability to leverage their savings. Members may simultaneously originate the purchase of a house with one credit from INFONAVIT and another from a private lender. They may also use their INFONAVIT savings as a down payment for a loan originated by another lender.

In order to grow, INFONAVIT has also initiated a securitization program. This move requires credit policy reforms in favor of more transparency, advanced systems, rigorous improved standards, and market-based pricing. So far, securitization has been expensive through high over-collateralization ratios (between 18 and 23 percent). Any sizeable expansion would require more market-friendly and better-priced underlying loans.

INFONAVIT has been targeting its subsidized lending only to the underserved households. Between 2002 and 2005, 76 percent of its originated loans went to individuals earning 7 times the minimum wage or less, a segment that is lightly served by SOFOLs, and not at all by banks. This means less regressive cross-subsidization. Despite this, INFONAVIT only lends to about 20 percent of qualified participants, and the ratio of borrowers to savers remains low.

Both HPFs suffered from political influences and weak financial management for many years, which resulted in a poor performance both as lenders and as retirement plans. They were under pressure to provide subsidized housing loans to favored groups, and extensive forbearance to borrowers, with the same moral hazard issue as faced by any other public lender. Prior to 2000, both recorded default rates on mortgage loans in the excessive range of 30 to 40 percent. INFONAVIT paid negative real rates of return on savings during much of the 1980s and 1990s, while FOVISSTE built up a funding shortfall. Most members failed to receive a loan, and had not much left to collect at retirement.

These HPFs found it hard to reconcile their functions as housing lenders, subsidy distributors, and pension funds. They had to ration credits (by 2000 only one loan for seven savers at INFONAVIT), which remain accessible only by the formally employed minority. Despite governance reforms, the risk remains that future governments may return to politically influenced financial policies. They cannot represent the sole and maybe even the main solution to resolve urban housing shortages, or to extensively lend for affordable housing (they will soon reach a plateau level).

All these reforms correspond to major improvements, but have not resolved the internal conflicts between its roles as lender, pension fund, and subsidy provider. There is an inherent conflict between maximizing returns for savers and providing low-cost mortgage finance through cross-subsidies. Will the core functions as a housing lender and as pension fund require further separation?

FOVISSTE has made less progress than INFONAVIT, in terms of operational reforms and corporate governance. It is now developing new automated systems and streamlining its business processes, but more remains to be done: management reforms, external audit committees, basic data on the portfolio and its performance, oversight by Comisión Nacional Bancaria y de Valores, and international accounting standards. FOVISSTE also provides deeper rate subsidies than INFONAVIT, but its effect on the market is limited because of its restricted membership base.

Brazil

Most of the housing finance system remains funded by the FGTS, which operates as an HPF. In 2005, the FGTS provided R$5.5 billion of on-lent housing credits, plus R$1.2 billion of complementary up-front housing subsidies (448,000 loans, including 150,000 micro-consumer loans). In 2006, the FGTS should reach R$10 billion for housing credits and R$1 billion in subsidies.

The FGTS collects a levy of 8 percent of all formal private-sector salaries (including the employees from government-held companies). This total represents an impressive amount each year (4 percent of GDP). These contributions are credited to "accounts" of individual workers. Savings are remunerated at *tasa referencia* (reference rate) plus 3 percent, which is the minimum imposed by FGTS law but stands below inflation. By comparison, voluntary housing savings—SBPE system managed though most banks—are much better remunerated (yield higher by 3 percentage points), and short-term rates from Sistema Especial de Liquidação e Custodia are even higher.

Its performance as a pension fund has been poor, and its own administrative costs high. The savings become available to the worker in case of lay-off, retirement, or for application to housing expenditures. Although severance and retirement may be provided to only the contributing members working in the formal sector, housing loans may be granted to any eligible borrower, even if not contributing to the FGTS.

Part of the accrued savings are invested into treasury securities, while another part is invested into infrastructure loans and housing loans at a rate of return of *tasa referencia* + 6.2 percent (considerably below free-market mortgage rates). Every year, the council decides how much funding will go to housing loans (recently expanding but historically quite fluctuating and unstable contributions), as the fund is also subject to political pressure.

The FGTS does not directly extend mortgage loans but finances the Caixa Econômica Federal (Federal Housing Bank; CEF), a state-owned bank that is both the sole operator of the FGTS for originating and servicing housing loans, and the appointed management agent of the FGTS (part of this role consists of guaranteeing a return to the FGTS even if other lenders fail to perform). The spread charged by the CEF is 2.16 percent. The system is designed to pay back to the FGTS a fixed remuneration of *tasa referencia* + 6.16 percent, and discriminate credit rates across different borrowers (subsidized rates only for low-income ones).

This system has financed a rationed number of loans. A large part of the portfolio was non-performing when CEF needed to be recapitalized in 2000.[4]

The FGTS program has been gradually but steadily re-focused on the lower income groups with 77 percent of the number of loans going to households with incomes less than 5 times the minimum wage. In 2005, this movement was pursued with the FGTS stopping new lending to higher income groups (10 times the minimum income) and introducing upfront subsidies for lower income households (less than 5 times the minimum income).

The next challenge consists in broadening the distribution of these housing finance resources through to other competing lenders, which could distribute this attractive program (reduced credit risk by the upfront subsidy and the cheaper credit rate).

Philippines

PAG-IBIG is an HPF, which operates as a public corporation with its own board of trustees. Its mandates are multiple, including investing the collected savings into assets for retirement purposes, and directly lending for housing both to developers and to the employees-members (a retail portfolio of about a half-million households). The portfolio is highly subsidized (the less the loan amount, the cheaper the interest rate, which ranges between 6 and 12 percent). Special devices have been introduced to improve debt recovery (penalties for late payments, rent-to-own leasing, loan restructuring). PAG-IBIG is a public housing lender that leads the market. It is funded by the savings contributions (mandatory since 1994; between 1 and 2 percent of the wages for the employees according to their wage, and 2 percent for the employers). It has been tapping bond markets since 1997 to increase its funding capacity.

Its weaknesses lie within substandard financial reporting, weak asset liability management (increasing pressure for additional liquidity), technological gaps, high proportion of non-performing loans (NPLs), insuf-

---

4. Until 2001, a large number of nonperforming loans characterized the balance sheets of CEF and Banco de Brasil. The federal government absorbed those loans at a net cost of approximately 6 percent of GDP, three-quarters of which was due to the restructuring of CEF.

ficient delinquency management, and inequitable cross-subsidization between savers and borrowers. The more its lending is underperforming and cross-subsidized, the lower its performance as a provident fund for the taxed employees. Its subsidized lending also hampers the growth of private mortgage lending. These features suggest the need for strategic choices, depending on whether other sources for low-income housing finance may emerge, according to the level of macroeconomic stability, and the health of the mortgage finance system (historically plagued by inefficiencies and high risks in the Philippines), as well as the capacity to find mechanisms to lend to low-income households. Even if the case for such a special lending circuit based on mandatory savings is confirmed, the issues of default leakage and cross-subsidization need to be addressed.

Nigeria National Housing Fund

The National Housing Fund (NHF) was established in 1992 with the objective of facilitating the provision of houses for Nigerians at affordable prices, ensuring a constant supply of loans, and providing long-term loans to mortgage institutions for on-lending to contributors. Nigerians earning Naira (N)3,000 or more per year (about $24 per year) are required to contribute 2.5 percent of their monthly income to the fund. This is a very low threshold— it has not been revised since the inception of the system—which should result in including the near totality of the salaried workers in Nigeria. The fund could also receive voluntary contributions, thus allowing non-salaried workers to participate in it. In addition, commercial banks are theoretically required to invest 10 percent of their loans and advances, and insurance companies are to contribute 10 percent of their non-life funds and 20 percent of their life funds, but these provisions have not been enforced. Contributions earn a rate of interest of 2 percent. Loans are channeled through a specialized circuit comprising the Federal Mortgage Bank of Nigeria, which runs the fund, and a network of specialized institutions. Contributors, and only them, can request a loan after having contributed for at least six months. The amount of the loan is not related to the amount of contributions, but is subject to a ceiling of N5 million. Interest rate is set at 6 percent, well below market rates, which were 20 percent (all in cost) in early 2006.

The scheme has had little success. It disbursed a cumulative amount of N5 billion in 13 years in individual loans.[5] The number of beneficiaries were 5,250 at the end of 2005, compared to 2.8 million contributors—or a ratio of 540:1. NHF funds are effectively accessible mostly by high-middle-income groups, which can afford the mortgage payments on the loan amounts not covered by the NHF funds and can access bridge financing before NHF funds are allocated—a process that can take more than two years. Partly because of the low probability of benefiting the system, the actual number of contributors is moreover far below the theoretical scope—in the range of 12 million employees. Furthermore, it is said that diversions of contributions from their legal use take place.[6] Voluntary contributions are insignificant.

A new legislation has been drafted for NHF, which could partially remedy the flaws of the system in two key aspects. First, the fund would be given the structure of a trust, and administered by a board of trustees compelled to stronger accountability obligations than now. Second, the relationship between contributors and borrowers would be changed, possibly limiting the reverse subsidization mechanism: the wage level above which salaried workers would have to contribute would be raised to seven times the minimum wage, and NHF would be entitled to lend to noncontributing, low-income households. The law, however, would set interest rates at below the market level for both for savings and lending, thus giving a new legal comfort to a still potentially regressive subsidization scheme.

---

5. And N8 billion for developer finance.
6. Igbinoba 2005.

G21 O16
R21 P34
R31 G10
G28

Selected countries

CHAPTER 12

Mortgage Securities in Emerging Markets

Loïc Chiquier, Olivier Hassler, and Michael Lea

Despite its recognized economic and social importance, housing finance often remains underdeveloped in many emerging economies. Residential lending is typically small, poorly accessible, and depository based. Lenders remain vulnerable to significant credit, liquidity, and interest rate risks. As a result, housing finance is relatively expensive and often rationed. The importance of developing robust systems of housing finance is paramount as emerging-economy governments struggle to cope with population growth, rapid urbanization, and rising expectations from a growing middle class.

The capital markets in many economies provide an attractive and potentially large source of long-term funding for housing. Pension and insurance reform has created large and rapidly growing pools of funds. The advent of institutional investors has given rise to skills necessary to manage the complex risks associated with housing finance. The creation of mortgage-related securities (bonds, pass-throughs [PTs], and structured finance instruments) has provided the multiple instruments by which housing lenders can access these important sources of funds and better manage and allocate part of their risks.[1]

The use of mortgage-related securities to fund housing has a long and rich history in industrial countries. Mortgage bonds were first introduced in Europe in the late 18th century and are a major component of housing finance today (EMF 2005). Mortgage PT securities were introduced in the United States in the early 1970s and along with more complex structured finance instruments now fund more than 50 percent of outstanding debt in that country. Today, mortgage-related securities have been issued in almost all European and many Asian and Latin American countries.

There have been numerous attempts to develop mortgage securities to secure longer-term funding for housing in emerging economies. The view has been that such instruments can help lenders more efficiently mobilize domestic savings for housing, much as they do in industrial countries. In addition, mortgage securities are pursued to develop and diversify fixed-income markets as a complement to government bonds for institutional investors.

Despite the strong appeal of financing housing through the capital markets, there are significant barriers to the development of mortgage securities in emerging markets. Their success is dependent on many factors, starting with a proper legal and regulatory framework and liberalized financial sector, and including a developed primary mortgage market. Perhaps not surprisingly, the experience in developing mortgage securities in emerging markets has been mixed. This paper reviews that experience and explores the various policy issues related to this theme, including the supportive role of the state.

The organization of the chapter is as follows. First, the rationales for introducing mortgage securities to fund housing are reviewed. Second is a discussion of the many prerequisites that underlie successful introduction. Third, there is an exploration of the role that government can play in developing these instruments, from both a theoretical and functional perspective. Fourth is an examination of the experience of issuing mortgage securities in selected emerging markets, including a summary of the lessons learned from

---

1. For a comprehensive review of securitization activities in emerging markets, see *Merrill Lynch Guides to Emerging Mortgage and Consumer-Credit Markets, vols. I–III.* For detail on security types, see Davidson, Sanders, Wolff, and Ching 2003.

these experiences, both in general and with specific reference to the proper role of the government.

Why Are Mortgage Securities Important?

Mortgage securities can perform a number of valuable functions in emerging economies. Their introduction and use can improve housing affordability, increase the flow of funds to the housing sector, and better allocate the risks inherent in housing finance.

In economies with pools of contractual savings funds, mortgage securities can tap new funds for housing. Institutional investors (pension, insurance funds) with long-term liabilities are potentially important sources of funds for housing as they can manage the liquidity risk of housing loans more effectively than short-funded depository institutions. Investors that specialize in certain securities can broaden the types of loans and borrowers served by the primary market. Securities issued against mortgage pools may vary widely in their duration and credit quality, so different investors can select the securities that meet their particular preferences. An increase in the supply of funds can, all other things equal, reduce the relative cost of mortgage finance and improve accessibility to finance by the population.

The resulting increased liquidity of mortgages helps to reduce the risk for originators and their required risk premium. The ability to dispose of an asset within a reasonable time and value, a crucial factor for mobilizing long-term resources, is a service that capital markets, as opposed to banking systems, can provide. A frequently expressed reluctance of primary-market financial institutions to provide housing loans is a lack of long-term funds. This is not only a matter of availability of resources: deposit-taking institutions can be cash rich, but be rightly concerned by the management of their liquidity situation over a long period.[2] Access to the long-term funds mobilized by institutional investors can reduce the liquidity risk of making long-term housing

---

2. There is a degree of speciousness to this argument, however. In most countries, depository institutions have a core of long-term deposits. Although the contracts may be short term, they are typically rolled over and can fund long-term housing loans. An institution can provide a significant percentage of its loans for housing while accepting only a modest amount of liquidity risk. This statement frequently masks other reasons for not providing housing loans, including high transaction costs, high perceived credit risk, and so forth.

loans and lengthen the maturity of loans, thus improving affordability, particularly in low-interest-rate environments.

A third rationale for introducing mortgage securities is to increase competition in primary markets. The development of capital-market funding sources frees lenders from having to develop expensive retail funding sources (for example, branch networks) to mobilize funds. Securitization, for example, can allow small, thinly capitalized lenders who specialize in mortgage origination and servicing to enter the market. These lenders can increase competition in the market and can lower margins and introduce product and technology innovation into the market. The experience of Australia in the 1990s provides dramatic evidence of the power of capital-market-funded lenders to change a market (Gill 1997). The market entry of wholesale-funded specialist lenders led to a reduction of 200 basis points in mortgage spreads during the 1994–6 period. The subprime markets in the United Kingdom and United States were created by new entrant specialist lenders funded through securitization.

Increasing competition and specialization can in turn increase efficiency in the housing finance system. Greater specialization can lead to cost-savings and reduce spreads. The phenomenon of unbundling has been associated with development of secondary mortgage markets. As the functional components of the mortgage process are unbundled, specialists emerge and obtain market share through scale economies in processing, access to information, and technology and risk management.

Capital market funding can also help smooth housing cycles. Lenders relying on deposits may be subject to periodic outflows because of economic downturns or widening differentials between deposit and alternative investment rates (for example, if deposit rates are regulated). Access to alternative sources of funds through the capital markets may allow lenders to keep providing housing finance throughout the cycle.[3]

---

3. The subprime credit crunch of 2007 demonstrated that securitization can have destabilizing effects as well. A combination of rising default rates on U.S. subprime loans and falling house prices led to a panic among investors in subprime and other non-government backed mortgage securities as well as more complex mortgage-related securities (for example, collateralized debt obligations (CDOs)). Their refusal to hold or buy such securities not only shut off funding to the mortgage market but also destabilized the banking industry as trust in banks that held or lent against such securities disappeared. The interbank lending market was disrupted and overall bank lending declined, leading central banks in Europe and the United States to inject liquidity into the system in an attempt to stabilize the market.

Finally, there are general economic benefits to developing capital markets, including financial deepening, fostering economic growth, and improved stability of the financial system. The ability to spread risk and match maturities can stimulate investment and lower the cost of capital to lenders. Creating long-term assets can foster the development of contractual savings institutions by providing an attractive low-risk alternative to government debt.

What Are the Prerequisites for Issuing Mortgage Securities?

As part of the broader securities markets, mortgage securities also require a macroeconomic and fiscal environment conducive to the supply of good quality securities and demand for them, and a legal, regulatory, and institutional infrastructure capable of supporting efficient operation of the securities market.

Beyond the basics, there must be a demonstrable market need for the type of funding offered by the capital markets. It is almost always the case that capital market (wholesale) funding is more expensive than retail (typically deposit) funding on a debt-only, non-risk-adjusted basis.[4] Why would a mortgage lender look to the capital markets for funding? There are three main reasons:

- *The lender may be capital constrained,* as was the case of the Chartered Institute of Housing in Morocco during its restructuring period, or the Colombian Saving sand Loans after their crisis. In such circumstances, the all-in costs of wholesale funding may be less than retail funding, taking into account the high expense of equity capital, if the capital savings enabled by securitization (if the lender can get the assets off the balance sheet for risk-based capital purposes) can more than make up for the higher cost of debt. From a balance sheet and regulatory-capital-management perspective, however, the lower-

---

4. That is before consideration of the operating costs of raising funds through branch deposits. These costs are often ignored or understated, as lenders may view them as fixed or allocate them to other activities of the branch. The transaction costs of wholesale funding need also to be taken into account.

risk weight of residential mortgages may lead the lender to securitize other classes of assets.[5]

- *The lender may be liquidity constrained.* Wholesale funding may be cheaper than retail, particularly on the margin, where raising additional funds through retail sources may entail pricing up the stock of outstanding deposits. Lenders may want to diversify their funding sources as well. Even if wholesale funding is currently more expensive than retail, a lender may wish to create a wholesale funding channel to better manage liquidity and funding risk in the future. The more liquid the lender, however, the less likely they are going to ascribe a liquidity premium to mortgages. The lack of securitization in many Asian countries reflects the liquid conditions of the banks after the fiscal crisis. However, overdependence on wholesale finance, as in the use of specialst subprime lenders in the United States or the United Kingdom can lead to institutional failure in the event of a market disruption.

- *The lender may have cash-flow risk management needs.* For example, it may wish to offer products the characteristics of which are difficult to manage via traditional retail means, such as a long-term fixed-rate mortgage (FRM). On-balance-sheet funding of such loans entails significant cash-flow risk, both interest-rate risk if not match funded and prepayment risk if the borrower has that option. Lenders offering reviewable ARMs (a common emerging market mortgage instrument in which the lender adjusts the interest rate at its discretion) will have less need to fund these through wholesale sources, as they entail virtually no interest rate or prepayment risk. As observed in Hong Kong, liquid and performing banks found little appetite for securitizing their mortgage loans despite the active presence of a public secondary-mortgage company (Hong Kong Mortgage Corporation; HKMC). The countries with the greater proportion of funding coming from the wholesale markets (Denmark, Germany, United States) have high proportions of mortgage loans with extended fixed-interest periods (Mercer, Oliver, Wyman 2003). The objective of introducing FRMs for

5. For example, consumer loans with a 100 percent risk weight rather than residential mortgage loans with a 35 percent risk weight or even lower under the revised Basel Internal Risk Based Approach.

lower-income households in Korea is the main driver of the Korean Housing Finance Corporation's securitization activities.

To supply funds there must be a demonstrable investor demand for mortgage-related securities. Specifically, there must be a class of investors with an appetite and capacity for securities backed by mortgages. Often the demand comes from depository lenders. More importantly, the demand may come from institutional investors such as life insurance companies or pension funds. These investors will have long-term liabilities and thus seek longer-term assets to match their cash flow and investment needs.

When will investors be interested in mortgage-related securities? There are several prerequisites:

- *Mortgage securities must offer attractive risk-adjusted returns.* In most cases, institutional investors will look to mortgage securities as an alternative to government bonds that provide a benchmark yield, as they typically represent a default-risk-free, liquid-investment alternative. Investors will seek a premium over government bond yields to reflect credit risk, liquidity risk, and transaction costs of purchasing and managing the assets. When this premium is insufficient, as was the case in Russia for the mortgage loans purchased by the public secondary mortgage company (Agency For Housing Mortgage Lending, a sizeable development is unlikely to occur, beyond the inefficient scope of any mandatory investment. Any large-scale development of MBS markets in China is limited by the relatively low yield of mortgage loans (less than 6 percent); in addition, issuers may not be found among banks that do not face capital or liquidity constraints (given abundant and cheap core deposits). The premium required by investors may be reduced if credit enhancement (either by third parties or through structuring) is credible and if there is some market liquidity (for example, if there are market makers committed to trade at posted prices with acceptable bid-offer spreads). Likewise, mortgage securities can be an alternative to corporate bonds, offering greater security reflecting their collateral.
- *Investors must have a capacity for mortgage-related securities.* In markets in which governments are issuing debt excessively, the

capacity of institutional investors to purchase mortgage securities may be limited or nonexistent (that is, the government may crowd out other issuers). Capacity may also be related to the liability mix of the investors. If investors have short duration liabilities, they will seek short duration assets as a match. Investors may prefer short duration assets in volatile environments to minimize the price risk in their portfolios.

- *Investors must be able to invest in mortgage-related securities.* Investors must have the legislative and regulatory authority to invest in such assets, and the regulatory treatment (for example, for capital adequacy, liquidity and asset allocation purposes, eligibility for technical reserves) must be well defined. In many countries, such investment rules do not recognize the existence of specific mortgage securities.

Even if there are willing issuers and investors, there are a number of infrastructure requirements underlying the development of mortgage capital markets. Without going into detail regarding each of the requirements, issuance will depend on:

- *An adequate legal, tax, and accounting framework for securitization and secured bond issuance.* The accounting and tax treatment of mortgage securities for both issuers and investors must be clear and complete—in particular, for the creation of bankruptcy remote-issuance vehicles (Special Purpose Vehicles [SPVs], Special Purpose Corporations, Fonds Commun de Créances, Mutual Debt Funds, and so forth). Adequate disclosure of information on the collateral and the issuer is necessary to assess risk. Many countries have been struggling with such issues, such as Poland, China, and Thailand, although progress is being made on that front.
- *Facilities for lien registration.* Mortgage securities are backed by mortgage loans. There must be an accurate and timely recording of the lender's interest in the collateral. Recording of liens must involve modest cost as well.
- *Ability to enforce liens.* Because investors can be last-resort bearers of the credit risk attached to underlying mortgages, the enforceability of the lender's security interest is a major determinant of the attractive-

ness of mortgage-related securities. If liens are not enforceable, there is little to distinguish mortgage-related securities from those backed by unsecured assets.

- *Ability to transfer (assign) security interest.* In the case of securitization, there is a transfer of the lender's beneficial interest to the investor. The legal system must recognize and record the transfer and it should involve only a modest cost. In the case of mortgage bonds, the ability to transfer beneficial interest is important in the event of bankruptcy of the issuer.

- *Protection of investors against bankruptcy of originator or servicer.* The credibility of the legal provisions ensuring bondholders that the collateral backing their assets would stay out of the reach of other creditors in case of insolvency proceedings is of the essence. For securitization purposes, the concept of an SPV or other construct that isolates the collateral pool from the issuer or servicer is essential to obtain off-balance-sheet accounting and capital treatment for the issuer. The concept of a bankruptcy remote-issuance vehicle is critical for the development of securitization and is often lacking in country law, notably in civil code systems.

What Has Been the Experience in Emerging Markets?

There have been many examples of individual transactions by banks or creation of institutions as securities issuers in emerging markets (table 12.1).[6] These transactions range from simple mortgage bonds to complex pay-through securities. There have also been a number of mortgage-securities-issuing institutions created in emerging markets.

---

6. Mortgage bonds are bonds that are issuer obligations and issued against a mortgage collateral pool. Investors have a priority claim against the collateral in the event of issuer bankruptcy. Mortgage securities can be simple pass-through securities issued against a specific collateral pool subject to cash flow matching or pay-throughs that are multiple securities issued against a single collateral pool. Pay-throughs modify cash flows between borrowers and investors to meet the needs or requirements of investors typically by prioritizing the repayment of principal across securities. Conduits purchase mortgages (typically accepting the credit risk) and issued mortgage-backed securities. Liquidity facilities make collateralized loans to primary market lenders funded through bond issuance in the domestic capital markets. For more detail on the individual cases, see Chiquier, Hassler and Lea 2004.

Table 12.1. Capital Market Finance of Housing in Emerging Economies

Mortgage bonds	Structured finance (Asia, Africa)	Structure finance (Latin America, CEE)	Conduits	Liquidity facilities
Chile	China	Argentina	Argentina	India
Colombia	Hong Kong, China	Brazil	Brazil	Jordan
Czech Republic	Korea, Rep. of	Colombia	Colombia	Malaysia
Hungary	Malaysia	Chile	Hong Kong, China	Mexico
Kazakhstan	The Philippines	Mexico	Korea, Rep. of	South Africa
Latvia	Thailand	Panama	Trinidad	Trinidad
Poland	Morocco	Peru	Thailand	
	South Africa	Trinidad		
		Latvia		
		Russia		

Source: Chiquier, Hassler, and Lea 2004.

With a couple of exceptions, the percentage of funding obtained from the capital markets in emerging countries is low. Very early and for a long time, Chile has the highest percentage, mainly in the form of mortgage (covered) bonds. Hungary obtains over 60 percent of housing funding and the Czech Republic over half of its funds through mortgage bonds. Approximately 30 percent of funding comes through MBSs in Colombia.

There are several examples of successful introduction of mortgage securities in emerging markets, including mortgage bonds in Chile, the Czech Republic, and Hungary; MBSs in Colombia and Mexico, and liquidity-facility bond issuance in Jordan and Malaysia.[7,8]

Covered Bond Issuers

The oldest example of capital market funding of housing in an emerging country is the Chilean mortgage bond market. Covered bonds are the dominant fixed-income instrument in the market and enjoy widespread acceptance without having ever received government guarantees. The Letras de

7. The main criterion of success is repeat issuance of standardized securities, a significant share of funding for housing coming from the capital market, and secondary trading in these security instruments. An additional contributor to success is the ability to engender significant change in the primary market (for example, lengthening maturity, bringing new lenders to the market).

8. Although not reviewed in this chapter, the Home Mortgage Bank of Trinidad may also be considered a success. Home Mortgage Bank was created in 1985 along similar lines as Cagamas. It has a similar structure and prerequisites as Cagamas and is the major nongovernment bond issuer in the country. Recently it evolved through MBS issuance and introduction of primary mortgage insurance.

Crédito (Letters of Credit) were reintroduced in 1977 after the collapse of the Chilean S&L system. They benefited from the creation of private pension funds around the same time that provided a natural investor in the bonds. The Letras are issued by commercial banks and modeled after the Danish mortgage bond system with a full passthrough of principal and interest. Chilean mortgage bonds are general obligations of the issuer backed by preferential access to the collateral. They provided nearly 70 percent of mortgage funding through the late 1990s. More recently, their share of mortgage funding has dropped sharply (down to 39 percent in 2005) as a decline in interest rates created a wave of prepayments and a reduced yield for investors. Over half of mortgage funding now comes from bank deposits. The success of the Letras was followed by the introduction of Mutuos Hipotecaria Endosables (whole loan sales), which accounted for 20 percent of funding in 1999 before falling to 10 percent in 2005, and MBSs, which accounted for 6 percent of mortgage lending in 2005.[9]

By the criteria of issuance volume and share of total funding (over 50 percent in each country), covered mortgage bonds in the Czech Republic and Hungary can be considered a success. Both countries have passed robust legislation defining the instruments that allow access by the dominant lenders, mainly commercial banks (as direct issuers in Czech Republic and indirectly in Hungary).[10] In both cases, however, the bonds benefit from high subsidies that encourage their use. In Czech Republic, the bond interest is tax exempt. In Hungary, only mortgage banks (funded by covered bonds) can provide loans that qualify for a government program of interest rate subsidies, and most of the bonds have been issued by the mortgage banking subsidiaries of (OTP and FHB banks). The FHB mortgage bank issues bonds backed by the mortgage loans it has originated, but also backed by mortgage liens it has purchased from other commercial banks, which retain the loans and credit risk on their books. As such, the FHB acts as a centralized capital market funding source for other lenders that are not specialized or just have smaller portfolios (similar to a liquidity facility).

---

9. The Mutuos Hipotecarios Endosables are in particular issued by specialized originators.
10. Although mortgage banks have an 85 percent market share (2005), one of them, FHB, purchases the mortgage liens from partner commercial banks that retain all of the credit risk and therefore most of the margin.

MBS Issuers

MBSs were issued by several mortgage banks in Colombia in the 1990s but the volume of issuance accelerated after 1999 with the creation of Titularizadora Colombiana (TC) in 1999. By 2005, TC had securitized over 30 percent of the outstanding mortgage stock. The company's securitization program has facilitated the restructuring of the mortgage market and banking system. TC has issued securities backed by NPLs and recently issued a covered bond.

TC is a private conduit owned by the major mortgage lenders in Colombia (the International Finance Corporation [IFC] is also an investor). Its creation was prompted by a severe economic crisis combined with a portfolio mismatch that bankrupted the Corporaciones de Ahorro y Vivienda in 1998. Creating a new, well-capitalized intermediary to issue MBSs allowed these lenders to obtain needed funds from the capital markets at reasonable yields. Although the government has no ownership interest in TC, it provides tax exemption of interest on the securities. The government also provides—for an actuarial-based fee—timely payment guarantees on social housing loans securitized by the company (also available to other issuers).

TC issues structured securities backed by specific pools of mortgages. The securities are internally credit enhanced through a combination of subordination and excess interest with no external guarantees. They have been successful in placing relatively complex securities in the domestic capital as evidenced by the declining spreads associated with each issue, which fell from more than 5 percent to 2 percent from 2003 to 2006.

MBSs have been issued by both public- (INFONAVIT) and private-sector (SOFOLs) entities in Mexico. While more recent (the first securities were issued in 2004), the issuance volume has steadily increased (over $1.8 billion in 2006) and the range of security features and forms of credit enhancement (public, private, international financial institution) have expanded. Credit enhancement through partial mortgage insurance and security payment guarantees from a government development bank, the SHF, has been instrumental in developing the market.[11] SHF provides top loss mortgage insurance on individual loans covering up to 35 percent of exposure. Recently, SHF signed contracts with two U.S. private mortgage insurers to reinsure 70 per-

---

11. The SHF also functions as a liquidity facility, providing back-to-back loans to SOFOLs, funded through bond issuance.

cent of its risk. The companies will also enter the market as primary insurers in the future, with SHF gradually refocusing on social interest housing loans and special risks.

SHF also provides partial guarantees on MBSs, with the issuer taking a first loss (subordination or over-collateralization) position.[12] Through 2008, SHF had provided guarantees on 49 issues for more than $4.5 billion[13] SHF has encouraged private sector insurers and guarantors to enter the market. The private securitization market took off in 2007, with several SOFOLs issuing securities using internal credit enhancement or private guarantees. The largest SOFOL, Hipotecaria Su Casita, issued the first peso-denominated security and have sold portions of two issues in the United States. Starting in 2006, commercial banks began issuing MBSs, and the largest lender, INFO-NAVIT, has also had several issues without an explicit guarantee.

By some criteria, Banco Hipotecario SA (BHSA) in Argentina could be considered a success. BHSA was successful in tapping international markets through issuance of structured, pay-through securities. BHSA showed how structuring could improve the marketability of mortgage loans, allowing it to break the sovereign ceiling with its securities. Although BHSA securities were not guaranteed by the government, it was exempt from the gross proceeds tax on the sale of mortgages; however, BHSA only concluded five transactions before the devaluation crisis and therefore did not have the opportunity to show that it was a sustainable model. Forced pesofication of the bonds led to their default and demonstrated the risk of currency mismatch. Since the end of 2004, the bank has resumed issuing MBSs—for still short, but growing maturities—which are denominated in pesos and include innovative structured features. While BHSA accounts for one-third of the market, the Argentine mortgage market is very small—less than 3 percent of GDP. Only 6 percent of funding comes from the capital markets.

---

12. The *garantia de pago oportuno*, or timely payment guarantee, is a credit enhancement at the deal level of the structure. Sometimes referred to as a partial guarantee, the *garantia de pago oportuno* is similar to a credit line. If the trust does not have sufficient cash to make a given payment, the line of credit can be drawn to pay both interest and principal. Once the line of credit is repaid, it can be drawn down again, if the need arises. The fee to the provider of the *garantia de pago oportuno* is part of the expenses of the trust (see Crédit Suisse 2006).

13. Silva de Anzorena 2009.

Liquidity Facilities[14]

The largest and most successful liquidity facility has been Cagamas Berhad in Malaysia. It was created in 1985 when the banking system was in the midst of a liquidity crisis. Its objectives are to help lenders manage risk, expand mortgage markets, and develop private bond markets. Cagamas funded as much as 30 percent of the mortgage market in the 1990s and has been the largest private debt-security issuer in the country. Its refinancing activities have been mostly conducted through purchases with full recourse, although it has started to conduct securitization activities as well more recently. After the Asian financial crisis of 1997–8, banks have been liquid and have significantly reduced their refinancing of mortgage loans to Cagamas, with its market share falling to 10 percent. Cagamas has also pioneered the capital market funding of Islamic loans, which may be a role model for other Islamic countries.

The Central Bank is a minority owner of Cagamas but chairs its Board of Directors. This role has been providing comfort for private-sector investors through an implicit state guarantee and a prudential policy. In the past, Cagamas' loans and bonds received favored regulatory treatment, including a low-risk weighting, eligibility for the interbank market for its bonds, exemption from stamp duties for its purchases of mortgage loans, and an exemption from statutory reserves for the refinanced lenders in order to help them meet their imposed quotas of social housing loans. These preferences were eliminated in 2004.

Until 2004, all of Cagamas' purchases were for a fixed period (three to seven years) with full recourse to the originating bank. Its bond issues are "agency" debt, unsecured obligations of the corporation but in effect backed by its mortgage loan portfolio. It started to buy mortgages without recourse and issue mortgage pay-through securities in 2004, mainly to finance loans made to civil servants through a special program.

The Jordan Mortgage Refinance Corporation (JMRC, a liquidity facility) has funded 13 percent of the outstanding mortgage debt JRMC has encouraged more banks to lend and facilitated a lengthening of loan maturities. Its

---

14. See Hassler and Walley 2007.

volume of issuance accelerated in 2005 update?—the test will be whether it can sustain its success.

JMRC was founded in 1997 to expand competitive mortgage lending by offering refinancing of mortgage loans to banks. Its creation coincided with a financial deregulation of the state housing bank that opened up the market for other lenders. It refinances banks that provide a pledge of their mortgage loans (120 percent over-collateralized) and issues private bonds. Similar to Cagamas, the Central Bank of Jordan is a minority shareholder and board chair, and JMRC-refinanced loans and bonds receive favorable regulatory treatment. It has achieved relatively low spreads on its bonds because of their low perceived risk.

JMRC has had a catalytic effect on the mortgage market, which has grown to more than 11 percent of GDP. Borrowers have benefited from longer mortgage terms, lower rates, and higher LTVs. As with other liquidity facilities, JMRC's business fluctuates with the market and the relative liquidity of the banking system. JMRC is exploring the introduction of MBSs and Islamic finance.

There have been numerous less successful attempts at developing mortgage capital markets. Many fail to generate an ongoing flow of business (for example, MBSs issued by Colombia S&Ls and Philippine banks and the government pension fund, several securitization conduits [Cibrasec in Brazil, the Agency for Housing Mortgage Lending in Russia (until recently), the Secondary Mortgage Corporation in Thailand]) and cannot be regarded as successful (from a business perspective), at least to date. Initially successful issues by government-owned conduits in Hong Kong and Korea have not been sustained, as banks are reluctant to sell loans and the entities securitize loans primarily from special programs.[15]

There are various reasons for this lack of success, including a lack of investor acceptance, weak legal and regulatory framework, and securities being an overly expensive funding option. All the cases with limited results have attempted to use more complex security designs, usually pay-through

---

15. The Hong Kong Mortgage Corporation is a conduit owned by the government with an explicit guarantee for its securities. It has issued corporate bonds, PT, and structured securities. It has also developed a mortgage insurance program with private-sector reinsurance. The Korea Housing Finance Corporation is a 100 percent government-owned conduit (successor to an earlier public-private partnership, Komoco) that securitizes loans originated by the National Housing Fund.

structures. These instruments may be too complex for the markets in which they were introduced. There are a number of countries still in a take-off phase, including India, Morocco (through two large and successful mortgage securitizations piloted through a conduit to help the main housing bank Crédit Immobilier et Hotelier manage its liquidity needs), and South Africa. In these cases, there have been pilot issues after many long years of development. It remains to be seen whether they will be successful on a larger scale.

Although emerging market lenders have continued to tap the capital markets since the onset of the global capital markets crisis it is clear that the prospects for continued growth will be adversely affected.[16]

Safety and Soundness Regulation in Mortgage Capital Markets

Mortgage-Backed Securities

Securitization has broadened and deepened capital markets in many countries, and mortgage securitization in particular has improved access to housing finance and reduced its cost. Well-structured MBSs are attractive investments for pension funds and insurance companies. The securitization technology permits issuers to tailor cash flows to the needs of institutional investors. These advances represent a broadening in the market for risk, and depend on an understanding on the part of investors that acceptable risks exist with less than a triple-A rating.[17]

On the other hand, weak management of investments in securitization bonds has lead to a few spectacular bank failures (see box 8.5). Risks in securitization include credit risk from the collateral and from the structure of the securitization trust, liquidity risk for the servicer and investor, operational risk for loan servicers and bond administrators, legal and reputational risks for the issuer, and, in subordinated bonds, more leverage than appearances

---

16. For example, TC, Su Casita, and the Korean Housing Finance Agency have all issued MBSs in 2008, albeit at wider spreads than previous issues.
17. International Swaps and Derivatives Association comment to Basel Committee, January 2003.

might imply. Securitization has motivated new capital rules in the United States and Europe, and now under the Basel II Capital Accord.

Supervisors can encourage growth in the securitization market by setting ground rules for its operation. These include standards for disclosures in the issuing prospectus, risk-based capital requirements for issuers, guidelines for assessing the capacities of institutions to issue and administer securitizations, and capital rules for investments in securitization bonds, particularly subordinated bonds.

Central to understanding risk in securitization is the notion of "true sale." The pool of assets resides in an SPV that must exist legally separate from the issuer. There can be no possibility for the issuer to control the collateral or retrieve assets from the securitization pool after the collateral pool is transferred to the SPV.[18] In many countries, the notions of true sale and SPV require special legislation, or at least confirmation by the courts.

When regulators first look into securitization, they are often tempted to view potential risks in terms of the strength of the issuer; however, in a true securitization, the SPV stands alone as a legal entity. The value of a securitization depends upon the performance of the pool of collateral and the structure of the securitization itself. In turn, these factors have little to do with the performance of the issuer. The only influence that the issuer should have would be over the quality of servicing of the collateral pool.

Securitization transactions can be complex. In understanding the risks and rewards of a given transaction, supervisors should ask a series of basic questions: How does the issuer produce earnings on the transaction? In each transaction, how has the issuer added value, and where does the value appear? In each transaction, who ends up with risk, and how much do they hold? What is each bond class worth to the issuer or to investors? What will it be worth tomorrow? What are the terms of the securitization that determine the value of the bonds, given the performance of the collateral? The issuer should make the answers to these questions readily available to the market as a whole, and to regulators via the prospectus, financial reports, and conversations.

Most PT securitizations create two basic classes of bonds: senior and subordinated. The senior bonds have a priority of the principal and interest flows

---

18. Basel Committee 2004, 115.

from the collateral pool, and so receive a higher rating and fetch a better price from investors. But risk allocation through securitization is a zero-sum game. The lower risk to the senior bond investors is offset by the higher risk to the subordinate bond investors.

The cash flows and, as a result, the values of subordinate bonds are much more volatile than those of senior bonds. If a collateral pool prepays or defaults at rates higher than originally expected, the subordinate pool may receive less cash flow, and so have less value. The protection afforded the senior bond (as well as the value of the subordinate bond) will depend on the magnitude and cash flows of the underlying collateral. Thus the rating and valuation will depend on the accuracy of the forecasts of prepayment and default.

Because increased defaults can destroy the value of the subordinate pool, many structured finance underwriters look to the servicer to retain the subordinate bond. If the servicer buys the subordinated bond, it will have a significant incentive to service the collateral pool effectively, and make sure that the loans perform well so that the subordinated bond performs well. But then the transaction may not be off balance sheet.

Holding the subordinate bond on balance sheet is riskier than holding the senior bonds. As a result, there are extensive rules in international accounting standards (IAS) regarding the valuation of such securities, and capital rules increasingly address that risk as well. The Basel II framework provides a set of requirements for asset securitization that are based primarily on agency ratings, but with special exceptions for subordinated tranches.

Mortgage Bonds

Like securitization, mortgage bonds are created from the cash flows of a collateral pool; however, distinct from securitization, the collateral pool and resulting bonds remain on the issuer's balance sheet as assets and liabilities. Mortgage bonds permit issuers to match the terms of funding and assets, and to issue long-term liabilities at a lower cost than general obligation bonds. Mortgage bonds are attractive investments for pension funds and insurance companies. Mortgage bonds can be legally simpler than MBSs, and the lack of customization can contribute to their liquidity.

Mortgage bonds provide additional security over a general obligation bond of the lender, in that the cash flows of the collateral pool are pledged to support the bonds. The value of mortgage bonds remains linked directly to the financial strength of the issuing institution. The presence of the collateral pledge can raise the rating on the resultant bonds by one to four notches, depending upon circumstances.

In Europe, where mortgage bonds are a popular means of funding long-term FRMs, the collateral pool receives special protections in law.[19] The loans that make up the collateral pool and the resulting bonds are often recorded in an official register. In the event of issuer bankruptcy, the collateral pool is separated from the rest of the bankruptcy estate and made available to the bondholders under the management of a specially appointed manager. Rules govern the permissible assets that may be placed in the collateral pool, and they regulate the interest-rate risk possible in a mortgage bond by requiring complete matching between the collateral and the bonds.

Many emerging countries permit the issuance of mortgage bonds, but few have the extensive legal infrastructure that support mortgage bond markets in Nordic and other European countries. As a result, few countries outside of Europe have truly extensive markets in mortgage bonds.[20] Establishing a mortgage bond framework[21] implies at least amendments to the bankruptcy law to allow the ring fencing of collateral, asset quality norms, and matching rules between the bonds and the cover pools. In addition, regulators can promote transparency and growth of mortgage bond markets by setting minimum rules for prospectus disclosures and for disclosures regarding the performance of the collateral pool as time passes. Beyond disclosures, depending on the authority granted to them, supervisors may issue decrees to establish ring fencing of collateral, matching requirements, and collateral registers, or they can propose legislation to establish such legal protections.

---

19. Prime examples are Denmark and Germany.
20. Chile being one notable exception.
21. The Capital Markets Board of Turkey has created guidelines for mortgage bonds and MBSs. See www.cmb.gov.tr for a copy of the law passed in 2007.

Reporting for Secondary Market Instruments

Mortgage lending and securitization require faith in the long-term future of local capital markets, something that is missing in most emerging markets. While mortgages and MBSs extend to 10, 15, and 30 years, most emerging markets lack liquidity in the fixed-income market beyond one year. Aside from performance itself, one of the best ways to build credibility is to disclose detailed information about the collateral pools, securitization trusts, and the expected performance of bonds created in securitization structures. Such disclosures should begin at the time of issuance, and continue throughout the life of the securities.

MBS and mortgage-bond investors want to know about the expected and actual credit performance of the collateral that backs the securities. They want to know how the collateral pays off over time; how the pool evolves with regard to the original projections. This information is especially critical for MBS-subordinated bonds and interest-only bonds, the value of which is extremely sensitive to the performance of the collateral.

Investors also need to know about the management capabilities of issuers. Their systems, controls, and business processes need to be adequate to service the bonds for periods of 20 years and more.

MORTGAGE BONDS

A mortgage bond is an obligation of the issuing bank, with a collateral pledge in case the bank fails. As a result, institutional exposure is more important than collateral exposure. Investors want to know about the overall financial strength of the institution.

For the collateral, investors will want to know about expected prepayment and default rates, and performance over time versus those expectations. The issuer should specify if and how prepayment risks are passed to bond investors. In most countries, investors will prefer to see diversified residential occupancy loans versus risky non-standardized commercial property in the pool. The prospectus should disclose individual and pool LTV ceilings, valuation and matching principles, geographic diversification, and information on where and how the mortgage liens have been registered.

Many mortgage bond indentures enable the issuing bank to replace defaulted collateral. It is essential to disclose the amount and nature of eligible replacement assets, whether non-mortgage assets are permitted and which, and replacement procedures. The prospectus should describe any independent and permanent monitoring of the cover, the registration of cover assets, and the nature of the privilege that mortgage-bond holders enjoy in bankruptcy of the issuing institution.

SECURITIZATION REPORTING

Securitization is a means to allocate the risk and reward embedded in the pool of loans that make up the collateral. The securitization process cannot create more value than that which exists in the collateral pool. In fact, the costs of the transaction will consume some of the value. As a result, at the time of the transaction, the issuer should not see undue gains on sale of the senior class, nor on the sale and repurchase of retained subordinate tranches. An example of an undue gain or loss would be one that is out of line with market movements in interest rates that would create a market-to-market gain or loss on the assets transferred to the SPV.

The transfer to the SPV must qualify as a sale. Under IAS 39, there are two broad conditions for sale: 1) the transferor cannot reacquire assets, unless the asset is readily obtainable in market, or reacquisition is at fair value price; and 2) the transferee has the right to sell or pledge the asset. In assessing fair value, the best evidence is market price, but lenders are expected to use a model when there is no price available. It is then up to the auditor and regulator to accept the calculated fair value.

BASEL II CAPITAL REQUIREMENTS

Under Basel II, mortgage bonds are treated as other security investments, with risk weights set in terms of agency rating. In adopting Basel II, the EU plans to or does provide reduced-risk weights for mortgage bonds issued in countries that have demonstrably robust legal frameworks that support the bankruptcy remoteness of the mortgage bond collateral.

Table 12.2. Basel II Standardized Risk Weights for Long-Term Bonds

Rating	AAA to AA−	A+ to A−	BBB+ to BB−	BB+ to BB−	B+ and below or unrated
Risk weight	20%	50%	100%	350%	deduction

Source: Basel Committee on Banking Supervision 2004.

MBS investments are treated under the Basel II Securitization Framework, assigning risk weights in terms of rating-agency ratings, unless the issuer uses the IRB approach for the type of underlying collateral that is securitized.[22] So a mortgage lender that uses IRB for its retained loan portfolio would be required to use IRB for MBSs that it retains or purchases. Key issues have to do with the treatment of subordinated bonds and credit enhancements. This section briefly touches on those key issues, without reproducing all of the requirements.

In the standardized approach, risk weights are assigned by rating, as shown in table 12.2 for long-term bonds. As can be seen in the table, very low-rated bonds are deducted from capital. Since subordinated bonds often are issued at a very low rating or without a rating, they are often deducted from capital. Under the standardized approach, when a bank other than the issuer provides credit enhancements to a securitization, it has to calculate a capital requirement for that exposure. The capital requirement on the covered exposure is calculated as if the bank offering the enhancement were an investor in the securitization.

The IRB approach to securitization exposures is also guided by agency ratings, but it provides more categories of weights, and for unrated bonds, it enables banks that have internal rating systems to use them to establish risk weights for capital. In the words of the accord, "The risk weights depend on (i) the external rating grade or an available inferred rating, (ii) whether the credit rating (external or inferred) represents a long-term or a short-term credit rating, (iii) the granularity of the underlying pool, and (iv) the seniority of the position." Granularity refers to the number and size of assets in the collateral pool—more granular pools have a large number of small

---

22. Basel Committee 2004, 113 and 126. Basel II also provides the Supervisory Formula Approach to setting capital requirements for investments in asset-backed securities. The Supervisory Formula Approach uses the investor's estimation of risk to set capital levels. The Supervisory Formula Approach is complex and has strict requirements for the data and methodology to be used. Very few banks are expected to actually use the Supervisory Formula Approach.

loans. There are extensive conditions for the use of internally derived ratings, and they must be mapped to the ratings systems of external agencies.

The Role of the Credit Rating Agencies

The market for structured finance issues such as MBSs is largely driven by credit ratings, at least in part because of the complexity of securitization structures. In the early days of the structured finance market, issuers worked with rating agencies to establish rating criteria that would make structured credits comparable to traditional corporate issues in the eyes of investors. The dependence on ratings has persisted even though many institutional investors in developed markets state that they rely more on their own analysis than on ratings. Even when investors model cash flows accurately, it is difficult for them to anticipate changes in the collateral payment stream that may result from unexpected defaults or prepayments. A recent study found that downgrades of structured products had a stronger effect on structured bond prices than do downgrades on corporate bonds, and structured product downgrades are anticipated less by prices than are bond downgrades.[23]

Since securitization is a ratings-driven market, it is necessary to obtain a rating to make a public transaction possible. Rating-structured finance is a specialized function, and is dominated by the largest rating agencies. Many emerging countries lack rating agencies. In countries that have them, ratings of structured transactions such as mortgage securitizations are often carried out by teams of experts drawn from foreign offices that specialize in such transactions.

Given their central role in the development of capital markets, emerging country regulators should be aware of the transparency, methodology, and capabilities of rating agencies active in their markets. Particular attention should be paid to questionable practices such as nonpublic ratings and unsolicited ratings. Agencies should have rigorous and systematic rating methodologies, be independent of the firms they rate, have well-established systems to manage the conflicts of interest inherent in charging fees for ratings, and publish their rating methodologies.

---

23. Ammer and Clinton 2004, as cited in Committee on the Global Financial System 2005.

Rating agencies should have consistent and clear methodologies, particularly for mortgage bonds and for structured products such as MBSs. For each of these products, the intrinsic legal structure provides a vehicle for reducing subjectivity in the rating. Each has a pool of homogenous collateral, a historical base for estimating the future performance of the collateral, and an algorithm for assigning the collateral cash flows to the bonds. As a result, the rating agency depends less on subjective judgments about the quality of earnings going forward, and can instead look to the experience of like collateral to estimate expected defaults and prepayments.

Rating agencies have assumed a central role in developed capital markets with only limited regulation of their activities.[24] Their increasingly important role in international capital markets, contrasted with some notable failures to anticipate bond defaults, has raised questions about the role and oversight of rating agencies (one of the most recent failures being their rating Enron as a good risk until four days before it declared bankruptcy).[25] International regulatory bodies have also undertaken reviews of the role of rating agencies, generally with an eye to promoting transparency without imposing a detailed methodology for the rating process.

---

24. In 2006 a bill to overhaul the framework for registering and overseeing credit rating agencies was passed in the United States. The legislation removed the Securities and Exchange Commission (SEC) from the process of approving certain credit rating agencies as Nationally Recognized Statistical Rating Organizations. Instead, the SEC will register credit rating agencies that meet a new definition, and would oversee the companies through inspections, examinations, and enforcement. Principal objectives of the legislation were to enhance competition in the industry and to improve the transparency and consistency of the ratings methodology. There are currently five Nationally Recognized Statistical Rating Organizations: A.M. Best Company, Inc.; Dominion Bond Rating Service Limited; Fitch, Inc.; Moody's Investors Service, Inc.; and Standard & Poor's.

25. The ratings process has drawn extensive criticism in the 2007 subprime mortgage crisis. The rating agencies have been accused of being overly optimistic in their ratings based on over-reliance on models with limited historical data. More fundamentally, they have a conflict of interest as they are advisors in the design of structural finance products that they rate. For an analysis of the role that rating agencies played in the crisis see Mason and Rossner 2007.

Lessons Learned

The Basics

A country must have a sufficient legal, regulatory, and primary market infrastructure in place before mortgage securities can take hold. A good framework is a necessary but not a sufficient condition for success.

The sheer difficulty of developing infrastructure is one reason why there has been only limited success in introducing mortgage securities in emerging markets. The legal and regulatory complexities of mortgage securities and specialized institutions are formidable even in sophisticated developed economies. It is the case that many pieces of the puzzle have to be put into place before a picture emerges, and in a number of countries, the introduction of mortgage securities is still a work in progress.

It would be easy if setting up an appropriate legal and regulatory framework were sufficient to establish a market, but this is far from being the case. Many countries have devised a framework for securitization or covered bonds, but the time lapse between the creation of the legal infrastructure and the actual development of regular issues can be very long—as much as four and 10 years. The development of a satisfactory legal framework for mortgage securities is also often complex and time consuming (often requiring amendments in existing laws or new laws), notably in civil code legislative environments where the concept of a trust may be missing as a convenient, flexible, and bankruptcy-remote special vehicle to issue MBSs.

In rare cases, technical flaws in the framework explain the difficulty; for instance, Chile's securitization law in 1999 where SPVs had to buy portfolios before issuing securities, or in Poland where the securitization law did not permit sellers to hold any subordinated tranche, or in Thailand until the legal and regulatory framework for SPVs was improved. More often, exogenous obstacles stunt the actual use of a framework, however well designed. For instance, in Poland the length of the lien registration process that could take up to several months in Warsaw—before a more recent modernization effort—had been a strong impediment to the issuance of mortgage bonds. In India, the extension of securitization is hindered by the level of stamp duties on the assignment of financial assets (between 3 and 14 percent of the mortgage balance in many states).

The most difficult obstacles to overcome are often the ones that are anchored in local market conditions. For MBSs, a major hindrance is the lack of a "market" for credit risk. In most emerging economies, there are no insurers, guarantors, or investors ready to take over the risk from the lenders. In this case, MBS sellers must use internal credit enhancement tools, which are necessarily very expensive if high ratings are sought. Also, in the case of PT instruments, there are often few investors willing to buy the prepayment options embedded in the loans, which are very difficult to value in the absence of historical data and uncertainties about borrowers' behavior.[26] In many emerging markets, it is still difficult to lay off cash-flow risk. Investors will not accept long-term instruments or prepayment risk. Many issuers and investors do not have the necessary systems and capabilities to manage amortization and prepayment.

A simple and fundamental factor that can block the growth of mortgage securities is the lack of development of the primary market itself. Although the lack of long-term funding is an issue that can impede development, the growth path starts with the lending activity—even in the case of specialized institutions created to remedy the lack of interest of commercial banks.[27] For various reasons—the building up of a portfolio, name recognition, time needed to arrange issues, and, in the case of securitization, high issuance expenses—the volume of loans must first reach a critical mass before making efficient use of capital market instruments. It is unrealistic to expect to issue mortgage securities as long as overall market lending remains below a certain threshold.

---

26. The recent sharp reduction in the volume of mortgage bond issuance in Chile reflects the negative reaction by investors to a wave of unanticipated prepayments, the risk of which was underpriced.

27. It is a basic rule that specialized institutions rely on capital market for their funding, but at the start of their activity they typically use their equity or bridge financing from banks before tapping the capital market. The lack of bridge funding has slowed development of a private secondary market in Korea. Specialist mortgage companies have entered the market and successfully issued mortgage pay through securities. They have been very small scale and thus expensive, however. The mortgage companies have not been able to get significant amounts of reasonably priced warehouse funding, which has limited their ability to aggregate loans to create larger pools.

Market Demand

Potential issuers in many countries have not perceived a need for creating or issuing mortgage securities. The need for securitization has been low, as capital ratios have been improving in most countries, implying less need for off-balance-sheet finance. In recent years, most depositories have been liquid and not in need of significant new sources of funds. In most markets, deposit funding is significantly cheaper than capital market funding, providing a further obstacle to capital market funding. Lenders not pressed by liquidity or capital constraints such as liquid banks also tend to prefer retaining their high-quality mortgage loans on their balance sheets, and to access bond funding through a liquidity facility or by issuing their mortgage bonds, rather than taking the securitization road.

The structure of mortgage markets is also an obstacle in some countries. If a market is dominated by a few large, liquid depository institutions, it will be difficult to create a successful mortgage securities market. The large lenders, who may ration mortgage funds, do not need the funding and can underprice new competitors using wholesale funding. These lenders do not need mortgage securities to manage cash-flow risk either, as their main mortgage instrument is an ARM that can match funds with deposits.

There must also be a demand for such securities by investors. In part this is an infrastructure issue. They must have the authority to invest and be able to realize the benefits of a low-risk investment through risk-based capital treatment, reserve eligibility, and so forth. In addition, investors must understand and be able to manage the complex risks of mortgage securities. This requires a combination of disclosure and education at the least. Importantly, it requires a commitment on the part of issuers for regular issuance, as liquidity is a major characteristic in demand by investors. Government must play a role by leaving sufficient space for issuance. Excessive government debt issuance crowds out mortgage securities and does not give them a chance to take hold.

Simplicity

It is notable by our measure of success that simpler instruments and institutional designs have been more successful. Some of the most successful examples of mortgage capital market development came from covered bond issuance. These instruments are relatively simple—with credit enhancement from the balance sheet of the issuer. The more successful institution designs have been liquidity facilities rather than conduits.

It is a simple fact that there are limits to the complexity that can be imposed on emerging markets (Pollock 1994).[28] While there may be great appeal to securitization (and conduits that issue such securities), their complexity raises the cost of issuance and reduces liquidity. The instrument and issuer has to be tailored to the needs of the markets. This suggests the use of simpler product variants to facilitate investor acceptance and designs that will work in the current context. It is perhaps best to think of mortgage securities in an evolutionary context—starting with simple designs (for example, bullet bonds) that do not tax the infrastructure or investor capabilities and introducing more complex designs as the market develops. Of course, it ultimately depends on the market—complexity can be good if it meets the specific needs of investors but it can undermine liquidity and the development of a secondary market.

Although there may appear to be logical succession between mortgage bonds, a much older and a simpler instrument, and MBSs, the two instruments in fact meet different needs. There is no linkage in the timing of their respective development, and ideally, both instruments should be simultaneously available in a diversified market.

Securitization will remain a preferred road for mortgage lenders subject to balance sheet pressure, forcing them to better manage their scarce capital, or to better manage their liquidity and market risks, as seen in Morocco (housing bank in dire straits funding during a transition phase after a crisis); Mexico (non-depository lenders facing growing funding challenges as their portfolio is expanding beyond government funding limits); or Colombia (former S&Ls faced with restructuring problems and a significant exposure to market risks).

---

28. Excessive complexity is one of the root causes of the subprime crisis of 2007. Investment banks created derivative securities (collateralized debt obligation CDOs) by combining highly rated tranches with structured pay-through securities backed by subprime loans. The CDO tranches themselves were recombined into new CDOs. The underlying characteristics of the mortgage pools were poorly disclosed and investors relied too much on the ratings without looking at the origins of the securities.

It can be observed that there may be an excessive focus on institutional creation in advance of other fundamentals. Simply creating a secondary market institution will not create a market. For example, in Russia there was considerable technical assistance investment in the creation of the Agency for Housing Mortgage Lending (AHML). The creation of this institution in 1997 preceded the drafting of a mortgage law and development of a primary market, as well as of the needed legal and regulatory framework for mortgage securities. AHML did virtually no commercial business through its early life (through 2003). With the passage of a comprehensive package of legal and regulatory reforms affecting both primary and secondary mortgage markets in 2006, the role and activities of the agency became more significant. However, it provides for only 12 percent of outstanding lending, and a number of banks have also issued mortgage securities.

Development efforts in many emerging countries have focused on institution development, particularly conduits with government involvement. In many cases they may be ahead of their time (or solutions in search of a problem). Governments and technical assistance providers may need to spend more time and resources on infrastructure development to allow individual issues of mortgage bonds and securities before investing in institutions.

Role of Government

The success stories in this analysis all involved important government support. As emphasized repeatedly in this text, the government must provide a strong legal and regulatory infrastructure. It is no accident that the most successful emerging (for example, Chile and Malaysia) and developed (Australia, Denmark, United Kingdom, United States) market examples of mortgage security issuance are those countries with the strongest infrastructure.

In both Malaysia and Jordan, the government provided critical support in the form of seed capital by investing in a mortgage securities issuer and incentives through the regulatory treatment of the products and securities. In Chile, the Central Bank temporarily acted (for two years) as the main investor of mortgage bonds to help jump-start the market, and facilitated market development by creating institutional investors through pension reform. In Mexico, the government development bank SHF provided critical credit enhancement to early issues. Government support in Colombia took the form of tax incentives for investors and a temporary program of priced state guarantees, which may be turned off when not perceived as necessary once market investors have regained enough confidence in the MBS markets. All of these initiatives allowed institutions to come to market with more favorable financing terms than can be done by private-sector institutions alone. Government can also develop a secondary market in mortgage securities through liquidity support and reserve eligibility. Providing guidance on disclosure and standardization are additional important roles for government.

Credit enhancement through a government guarantee can be an important way to catalyze a market. It is difficult to get investors to accept (or price) the complex risks of mortgage securities. A government guarantee, whether implicit through ownership or explicit, eliminates one risk, allowing investors to focus on the others. But guarantees are dangerous as they can involve adverse selection and are detrimental to the government, and the government could end up with large contingent liabilities. Also, government support can create a monopoly that dominates a market and generates excess returns for its shareholders. Thus, a sunset provision should be considered in conjunction with government guarantees or financial support.[29]

The importance and risks of government guarantees has been amply demonstrated in the subprime mortgage crisis. Issuance of private label MBS has virtually disappeared in the United States with the only capital market funding being provided by the government-sponsored enterprises (Fannie Mae and Freddie Mac) and government agencies (Ginnie Mae). However, the combination of past accounting scandals, large losses from mortgage and subprime securities investments, and plummeting share prices have forced the U.S. government to make its support for the GSEs more explicit.

It is important to create a proper incentive structure in the design of secondary markets. For example, in the United States private mortgage insurance companies take the first loss on high LTV loans and lenders are subject to (credible) recourse by the GSEs in cases where loans are not originated to

---

29. An example of an ex ante sunset is the government guarantee given to Caisse de Refinancement Hypotecaire in France, which was withdrawn on schedule after three years. In the United States, the Student Loan Marketing Association (Sallie Mae) successfully dropped its government status in 1996.

agreed standards. Mexico has adopted a similar approach, requiring issuers to take a first loss position in front of the SHF guarantee. In theory, the risks can be better managed by the private sector, as it has an incentive to properly underwrite and price risk in order to maximize the value of the franchise. Inevitably, however, this approach creates economic rents for the institutions benefiting from the guarantee and can lead to greater risk for government (for example, through leveraging the guarantee) if not properly regulated and supervised. This has been the case with the U.S. GSEs, where critics point out that the model of implied guarantees privatizes profits and socializes risks and losses.

A critical function for government is to build the proper legal and regulatory framework. There must be proper safety and soundness regulation of issuers, and the framework must clearly define the structures, treatment of issuers (for example, true sale), and investors (authority and incentive to invest). Proper tax treatment is critical in developing mortgage securitization. First and foremost, there should not be double taxation of the security issuance vehicle. There should not be excessive stamp duty or taxes on the registration of securities or their transfer. In addition, regulation must eliminate artificial arbitrages.

Government support has drawbacks as well. Even if the government is a minority shareholder it typically wields majority influence. This could lead to inappropriate lending programs or investment, as is the case with many housing banks. Questions also arise as to how long the government needs to support securities issuers. For example, Cagamas was a monopoly provider of service. The government did remove its regulatory privileges after nearly 20 years of successful operation; however, it may be that the institution should be privatized or phased out in favor of direct-lender bond issuance. TC dominates the securitization market in part because of the tax exemption (but also because of the liquidity in its bonds and reputation). The tax exemption was initially due to be withdrawn in 2006 but was recently extended to 2009.

Selecting the right options for a given context may speed up the process. Selecting a model based on simplicity, type and number of primary market players, regional experiences, capital market infrastructure, and legal and regulatory infrastructure is key to market development. Blind replication of practices prevailing in developed markets should be avoided. Investors should be actively involved in the preparation of policy choices, as their skills and capacities are an important factor for the acceptance of instruments.

Selected countries

G21
R21 G22
R31 016
p34
G32

CHAPTER 13

Mortgage Insurance

Roger Blood

Mortgage default insurance (MI)[1] supports housing finance and macro-economic goals for a growing number of housing finance systems, both in mature and still-developing economies.

Starting with a historical perspective, this chapter will help public- and private-sector officials who may be considering whether MI may have some useful role to play in their country's housing markets, and, if so, what options for implementation may be more or less attractive to pursue.

Drawing upon examples from a number of diverse countries, we shall look in particular at prerequisite conditions for MI to succeed, key program features, regulatory and capital issues, credit-risk management tools, consumer issues, technology, forms of sponsorship, and options for public-private collaboration. The chapter ends with examples of adverse experience in several countries that may suggest ways to avoid similar pitfalls elsewhere.

---

1. Also known in certain countries as mortgage credit insurance, mortgage guaranty insurance, mortgage indemnity insurance, and lenders' mortgage insurance. This chapter's discussion of MI is directed at mortgage lending secured by individual, primarily owner-occupied, residential dwellings. Much more limited MI programs also have been used in several countries for income-producing residential and commercial properties.

Definition and Unique Features of MI

Stated simply, MI protects mortgage lenders and investors against loss by reason of borrower default. Such losses arise when the realizable value of the collateral property securing the mortgage is insufficient to repay in full the borrowers' outstanding debt.

Whether government or privately sponsored, MI has several unique features relative to other forms of insurance:

- The nature of the hazard covered—economic catastrophe.
- The long duration of the insured risk, that is, the full term or life of each mortgage loan.
- The unusually long cycle of risk, which follows general economic cycles.
- Risk performance that is uniquely dependent upon government economic policies.

Because of the long-term need to protect against economic catastrophe, MI requires special analytic and regulatory tools, even in countries where prerequisite conditions for MI are favorable.

Purposes of MI

MI can serve to meet a number of worthy public policy goals, including:

- expanding homeownership via lower down-payment financing, including to households of limited means;
- developing mortgage and capital markets by building investor confidence; and
- strengthening credit risk management in the banking system.

While the predominant reason given at present for individual countries' use of MI is to reduce the amount of cash required to buy a home, there are significant exceptions, both now and historically. One of the leading objectives of public MI programs both in the United States and Canada four decades ago was to set improved physical standards for new and existing housing. While that goal has largely been achieved in these countries, it is one that should not be overlooked in less affluent areas. In some economies where lenders are reluctant to make any home mortgage loans, MI can be used to jump-start the process. Government-sponsored MI in particular may be directed at unserved or underserved market segments defined in ways other than just inability to accumulate cash savings.

Some developing countries faced with serious market impediments, mainly relating to foreclosure proceedings and collateral recovery, have considered introducing MI so that lenders might avoid these problems by shifting collateral recovery risks and costs to a third-party insurer, at least until needed market reforms are implemented. MI is not well suited to solving this particular problem.

Compared with direct subsidies, publicly sponsored MI may be a more efficient, off-budget policy tool for expanding residential mortgage markets, but only where an emerging economy's underlying primary market mechanisms are already working reasonably well.

Countries that Have MI Today

MI in some form is available for residential lenders in over two dozen countries (see table 13.1). Most of these programs are government sponsored and are of fairly recent origin.

The following discussion focuses mainly on programs that have insurance like features, such as risk-based premiums and capital reserves. Where public sponsorship is involved, a government's ability to structure and run its MI program according to long-established insurance and commercial principles has been, and will continue to be, a key success factor, both for long-term viability and for achieving social and public policy objectives.

Prerequisite Conditions for MI Success

In order for mortgage default insurance to help a country advance toward its macroeconomic and housing policy goals, its primary housing markets

Table 13.1. Selected Countries with MI Programs, 2008

Country	Year of origin	Sponsorship
Algeria	2000	Public
Australia	1965	Private*
Belgium		Public (regional government)
Canada	1954 and 1963	Public and private
Colombia	2004	Public
Finland	mid-1990s	Public
France	1993	Public-private combination
Guatemala	1961	Public
Hong Kong, China	1999	Public-private reinsurance
Iceland		Public
India	ongoing project	Public-private combination
Ireland	1999	Private
Israel	1998	Private
Italy	2003	Private
Kazakhstan	2004	Public
Latvia	**	Public
Lithuania	1999	Public
Mali	1998	Public-private combination
Mexico	2004 and 2007	Public and private
Morocco	2004	Public
New Zealand	1997 and 2004	Private and public
Netherlands	1957	Public-private combination
Peru	1999	Public
The Philippines	1950	Public
Portugal	2003	Private
South Africa	1989	NGO/private reinsurance
Spain	2002	Private
Sweden	1992	Public and private
United Kingdom	pre-1970	Private
United States	1934, 1956, and 1987	Federal, private, and state
West Bank and Gaza	2000	Public

Sources: MI program surveys conducted by author.
* Initial public sponsor, privatized in 1997. Competing private firms began in the 1970s.

first must function reasonably well. Otherwise, not only will the cost of MI be excessive, its presence might actually mask the urgent need for primary market reforms.

Table 13.2 provides a checklist of prerequisite conditions for MI success.

Each factor above should be examined for any specific shortcoming that would impede the ability of MI to function as intended, or would raise its cost prohibitively. Some of these factors (for example, collateral recovery) are more critical than others (for example, industry associations).

An added consideration, thought not an absolute prerequisite, is a country's geographical size and diversity. "The law of large numbers" and the need to diversify risk are universal underpinnings for all insurance lines, including MI. A large, populous country having many far-flung urban and regional markets, such as the United States or India, can better avail itself of MI's potential benefits than can a geographically compact nation with one or two dominant urban centers. The latter type of country, when contemplating MI, will face both greater overall risks and diseconomies of scale.

Experience across numerous countries suggests that the threshold of initial feasibility for government to offer MI is lower than for private enterprise. For example, a private firm will need a proper regulatory framework and some mortgage experience (actuarial) data in order to launch MI in a country where none has existed theretofore, whereas a public start-up program may not require so rigorous a foundation. Accordingly, where private MI exists

Table 13.2. MI Prerequisite Conditions for Success

Regulation and legal	Primary mortgage market
• Laws and judicial system (esp. foreclosure, collateral recovery) • Mortgage and title registration • Bank/lending regulation • Insurance regulation • Mortgage insurance regulation	• Banks' lending and loan servicing practices • Insurance product acceptance • Transaction costs (transfer, regulation) • Property taxation • Property valuation/appraisal practices • Condominium governance and maintenance • Industry associations, standards (lenders, builders, sales agents)
Information	Other
• Housing markets, sales price information • Borrower credit information (credit bureau) • Standard definitions—residential lending • Mortgage portfolio experience/performance • Pricing model data requirements	• Economic policies fostering stability, personal savings • Government, political support • Citizens' attitudes toward homeownership, debt repayment

Source: Author's own research.

today, almost invariably a publicly sponsored program has preceded it (for example, United States, Canada, and Australia).

Even emerging economies that appear to meet prerequisite conditions for adopting MI should not view MI as a panacea. Table 13.1 shows that most of the numerous MI programs operating in developing markets are of recent origin and have not undergone the test of time and economic stress.

Key Program Characteristics

Among the many variables that drive the risk of home mortgage default and loss, loan-to-value (LTV) ratio (a proxy for borrower equity) has predominated, both historically and across international boundaries (table 13.3). So strong is this correlation that some emerging economies—and historically even the United States—have imposed regulatory LTV limits on bank lending or loans eligible to back mortgage securities.

Countries that offer MI use it predominantly to induce lenders to make higher-risk, higher-LTV-ratio loans, thereby reducing the amount of cash savings that borrowers must accumulate to purchase their first home. Maximum LTV ratio—insured versus uninsured—in any given country, is, therefore, the first MI program feature to consider.

Table 13.3. LTV Correlates Strongly with Default Risk and Losses

	Six-country averages indexed to 75.01 to 80 percent LTV *	
LTV ranges (percent)	Default probability	Loss severity
50.01–60	0.26	0.15
60.01–65	0.62	0.40
65.01–70	0.73	0.63
70.01–75	0.84	0.83
75.01–80	**1.00**	**1.00**
80.01–85	1.20	1.15
85.01–90	1.48	1.29
90.01–95	1.88	1.41
95.01–98	2.31	1.46
98.01–100	2.69	1.52

Source: Fitch IBCA 1998. Model assumptions applied to BBB-rated MBS.
* Australia, Germany, Netherlands, Spain, United Kingdom, and United States

In most countries, at the time MI is initiated, mortgage lenders generally are willing to lend without insurance up to some benchmark LTV ratio, beyond which they feel overexposed to loss in the event of borrower default. While this LTV benchmark varies from country to country and also may increase over time, the introduction of MI covering at least the top layer of risk exposure above the lenders' benchmark LTV can induce lenders to raise their top LTV up to the insurer's higher limit. Insured LTV limits, likewise, will vary from country to country, and tend to increase over time as satisfactory experience unfolds.

A reasonable "rule of thumb" where MI is new to a market may be initially to set the maximum insurable LTV at a level where it reduces the required borrower down payment by one-half. Hong Kong and Kazakhstan, for example, used MI to cut the minimum borrower down payment from 30 percent without MI to 15 percent insured. U.S. private insurers originally introduced MI that lowered minimum down payments from 20 percent to 10 percent. Israel's new MI program permitted borrowers to buy homes with 20 percent down, compared with 40 percent previously. Once a successful underwriting record could be demonstrated, the United States and Hong Kong programs, for example, then further reduced their minimum down payments—the United States in several increments over 30 years. Until now, some 100 percent of LTV loans are insurable.

Individual Loan Coverage

How much coverage against losses should MI provide for individual home loans? Two principles should apply in making this important decision regarding program design: (1) to avoid "moral hazard"[2] and to control catastrophic losses, the MI provider should share some risk with the originating lender; and (2) the lender's likely collateral recovery under adverse conditions should be estimated and need not be insured. Where MI is used as credit enhancement for MBSs, the amount of loan level coverage needs to fulfill rating agency requirements. Further, if a country's risk-based capital

---

2. "Moral hazard" refers to a party that acquires insurance cover whose behavior changes as a result of the curtailed exposure to loss in such a way as to increase the risk that is being insured.

regulations (discussed further below) bestow a lender benefit on those who use qualified MI, the amount of coverage must be sufficient to earn such favorable treatment.

Admittedly, some MI programs that provide 100 percent loan-level coverage, both government and private, have succeeded. Among these are the Federal Housing Authority (United States) and public and private MI programs in Canada and Australia; however, many others, both old and new, have benefited from risk sharing ("coinsurance") with their lender-policyholders. These include the U.S. private and state-level public insurers, as well as programs in Hong Kong, South Africa, Israel, and Lithuania (the latter of which changed its program from 100 to 25 percent coverage in 2002). New MI programs in Kazakhstan and Mexico also are designed with partial (top-down) loan coverage.

Premium Rates

Establishing an MI premium rate structure appropriate to any national market entails several considerations. Most important, of course, is to set rates at a level that are both sufficient to cover future losses, including under severe economic stress, but not so high as to impair affordability.

In most countries with newly developing mortgage markets, there is little or no usable mortgage performance history to provide the type of data required to project, even roughly, future default frequency and loss severity. Where policy makers conclude that MI will bring near-term benefits to a country's housing and mortgage markets, they need not await the time when such data becomes available. As long as the national economy and financial and housing markets show reasonable stability, a suitable MI premium can be adopted to enable a government-sponsored program to get under way. The initial MI premium should be set conservatively (it can always be reduced later on), based upon benchmark foreign-experience data, adjusted to reflect potentially higher risks and volatility associated with the domestic market. This approach recently was used in Kazakhstan and, to a lesser degree, in Mexico, where some local data existed, but was insufficiently robust for rate-making purposes.

Elaborate pricing models are not needed to create a public MI program. It will normally suffice to apply conservative rates at the outset, with later refinements as experience develops. This data then can also be held out to attract private, including foreign, MI risk capital.

The inclination (unique to a government-sponsored MI program) to set premium rates at levels insufficient to cover future losses—in order to improve affordability—should be resisted. Rather than risk the future insolvency of a public MI fund, given the political and fiscal pain such a failure would cause, it is far better to target transparent needs-based subsidies—including MI premium subsidies—to work in conjunction with an actuarially sound MI fund. An example of this enlightened approach is found in Lithuania, where many of the less-indebted middle-income country's borrowers are income qualified to receive separately budgeted MI premium subsidies, thereby boosting affordability.

The major variables that determine default frequency or loss given default (severity) also drive premium rates, including, most notably, the following:

- Loan-to-value ratio
- Loan term
- Percent of insurance coverage (for programs that offer different coverages)
- Type of mortgage instrument (for example, fixed versus variable rate or payment)
- Owner-occupation versus investor-owned rental unit

A detailed exposition of MI pricing methodology is beyond the scope of this chapter. We shall note only that MI pricing does entail economic stress modeling to ensure the buildup and retention of capital reserves sufficient to withstand abnormally high default and loss rates associated with severe national economic adversity.

A second programmatic pricing decision to be made, after overall rate adequacy and risk classifications have been established, is how to structure the actual MI premium payment. The lender, as beneficiary, purchases the MI coverage, but—one way or another—the cost of the MI coverage must be passed through to the borrower (who also "benefits" by making a lower down payment). Among the premium payment options are the following:

- Add the cost of MI to the loan interest rate
- Charge MI as a separate add-on cost, monthly or annually
- Charge the full cost of MI as an up-front lump sum, due at loan closing
- Add the full up-front MI premium charge to the initial loan amount, thereby financing the cost over the loan life (but also increasing the initial LTV ratio)

Each of these options has advantages and disadvantages with varying degrees of transparency. In a developed market, the ideal is for the MI provider to offer as many payment options as the market may have reason to use. For a start-up situation in a less-developed market, the up-front lump sum charge, "capitalized" as part of the beginning loan amount, may be preferable. It is the most affordable for the borrower; it provides maximum funding to the insurer's loss reserves; and it is administratively simple. Whatever payment options may be offered, the lender should clearly disclose this cost to the consumer.

Eligible Loans

All MI programs, both public and private, define and restrict what is an insurable loan. Limits can relate to property type (for example, individual dwelling units versus entire apartment buildings); loan purpose (for example, home purchase versus home construction or improvement); or mortgage instrument terms (for example, fully amortizing loans versus loans with lump sum due dates) and first lien mortgages versus junior or subordinated loans. Table 13.4 below reveals some variety among country MI programs regarding types of insurable residential loans.

As discussed in the "lessons learned" section later in this chapter, efforts to extend MI beyond the insurance of mortgage loans secured by individual, mainly owner-occupied dwelling units—even to financings that on the surface seem quite closely related—has sometimes failed at considerable cost.

Table 13.4. Insurable Loans, Selected Countries

Country	Program	Insurable loan feature	Remarks
Algeria	SGCI	Individual dwelling units only	
Australia	Private MI		
Canada	CMHC	All residential, including construction loans and rental apartments, retirement homes	Also guarantees mortgage securities
Estonia	Kredex	Home purchase or renovation	
Guatemala	FHA	Single homes, construction loans	
Hong Kong, China	HKMC	New, individual dwelling units	
Kazakhstan	KMGF		
Mali	FGHM	Single homes only	Market has no condominiums
Netherlands	NHG	Home purchase loans only	
The Philippines	HGC	Single homes, multifamily development, and construction loans; long-term leases	Also guarantees mortgage securities
South Africa	HLGC	Loans secured by home, pension fund balance; also lease-purchase	Special program for borrowers with AIDS
Sweden	BKN	Owner-occupied, co-op, rental	New, rehab apartments only
United States	FHA-MMIF (federal)	1-to-4-family properties only; amortizing loans only	Separate program for rental housing
United States	Private MI	1-to-4-family properties only; completed construction only	Subject to strict "monoline" regulation
United States	Mass MIF (state)	1-to-4-family owner-occupied properties only	

Source: Author's own research.

Underwriting Method

Another key feature of all MI programs relates to the method by which risks are assumed, which typically will be stipulated contractually with the insured lender. This program feature entails not only risk management, but also marketing, information technology, and cost-efficiency aspects, each of which needs to be weighed and balanced in designing and implementing an MI program.

There are basically four types of underwriting methods available to an MI provider:

- Substantial participation with the insured lender in the direct under-writing of the loan
- Underwriting review and prior approval of loan documentation generated by the lender
- Electronic data transfer and "automated underwriting," (AU) using experience-based decision model, with human review of "marginal" cases identified by the "AU" decision program
- Authority to bind the MI coverage on individual loans delegated to the lender subject to the lender's compliance with agreed-upon standards and procedures and periodic reporting

Few, if any, examples of the first of the above methods is found today, although the U.S. government's FHA program operated in this fashion for many years, even to the extent that the entire property valuation process was run by the FHA independent of the lender. This alternative, though perhaps the safest, is simply too cumbersome and costly to be accepted in any competitive marketplace.

Review underwriting of individual loan documents—either selected documents or the full loan package—strikes a balance between the need to screen risks adequately versus cost and efficiency concerns. Such "review underwriting" was for many years the dominant process for MI underwriting in most advanced markets, including the United States, Canada, and Australia—first via mail, later by fax. The process worked successfully, with same- or next-day response meeting market needs.

Automated underwriting now has largely supplanted MI review of loan documents in most advanced markets where credit and loan experience databases are sufficiently rich to validate the decision models that underpin automated underwriting systems. The efficiency of this underwriting method has reduced MI costs considerably, with no apparent weakening of risk management until the market turmoil that started in 2007, which generated high delinquencies in insured portfolios such as the "Alt A" segment (borrowers with decent credit records but undocumented income), or 100 percent LTV loans with no borrower equity. In the United States, another strong impetus for this advance has been the dominant role of Fannie Mae and Freddie Mac both as providers of MBS capital to insured lenders, but also as standard setters for all mortgage-market participants in terms of both automated underwriting and information technology.

Underwriting authority delegated by the MI provider to the lender is a common, though far from universal, practice in both developing and advanced markets. Among the programs outside North America that employ delegated underwriting are the National Housing Credit Guarantee Board (BKN) in Sweden and Home Loan Guaranty Company (HLGC) in South Africa, while Hong Kong is just beginning to test it out. The simplicity and efficiency of this method of risk assumption makes it appear a very attractive option for both the lender and the MI provider; however, this approach also entails three potential disadvantages:

First, the MI that delegates its underwriting function to the insured lender may find that it has assumed greater risks than anticipated.

Second, the "value added" that secondary mortgage investors may perceive from an independent third-party review of pooled mortgage loans by the insurer may be diluted.

Third, the lender who assumes delegated underwriting authority may find later that the insurer will find "technical violations" of the delegated underwriting agreement as an excuse to deny the payment of claims. The potential for such contention can increase with the frequency of claims submitted.

One reasonable approach to delegated underwriting can be for the MI provider to award this benefit to individual insured lenders that demonstrate their commitment and ability to produce quality loans. Of course, the supporting technology needs to be in place to assure timely monitoring, and regular on-site compliance audits are essential.

In any event, the underwriting method(s) employed over time in any country should balance the inevitable needs for adequate information and control, prompt and cost-efficient service, and technology platforms available to both the MI provider and its users.

Public MI programs typically—though not always—have incorporated additional program features that emphasize their social and public policy goals, as discussed in further detail in the following section.

Meeting Social Objectives

Government MI programs in particular need to justify themselves, not only in terms of being financially self-sustaining but in also stimulating more homeownership and lending opportunities. Usually they are also expected to serve a targeted segment of the population that may otherwise not have access to home financing. In developing economies such groups most often include both lower-income families and the "informal sector," where non-salary incomes tend to be irregular and hard to document. Government-sponsored MI, though not a direct housing subsidy, should not be expected to serve the very wealthy or to help finance luxury housing.

Typically, there are three simple means, one or more of which government MI uses to target its benefits to low-, moderate- and middle-income households. These methods are insurable limits expressed in terms of (1) loan amount, (2) home price, or (3) household income. Of these, household income limits tend to be the most restrictive, while loan amount limits are the most permissive. Even with insurable loan limits, for example, a wealthy borrower could still purchase a very expensive home.

While social goals for most public MI programs may be most directly addressed with some form of household income limits for eligible loans, as noted above conditions in developing markets may not permit many borrower incomes to be reliably documented. Of the above-noted targeting methods, loan amount is the most easily verified. Any such limit, however, ought to reach well up into the middle of the market so as to create a broad base of demand and to include a relatively low-risk segment of the market in order to strengthen credit risk management. As a practical matter, any public MI program with household income limits probably does not need either insurable loan or home price ceilings.

Any subsidies associated with a public MI program are best designed to be both transparent and distinct. That is, separately budgeted funds may be used to subsidize lower-income borrowers' MI premiums, to directly subsidize a portion of the required cash deposit, or even to temporarily "buy down" or subsidize the borrower's interest payments. But the MI program's premium rates should be fully loaded, and reserves fully funded, to cover all future losses and ongoing program costs. Such precautions will help to avoid the political backlash that might well accompany future calls for the government to "bail out" a depleted MI fund facing large immediate and future claims obligations.

Lithuania's MI program is unusual in this regard. About one-half of insured borrowers—those below a set income threshold—currently benefit from significant MI premium subsidies. In the United States, lower-income borrowers covered under the Commonwealth of Massachusetts' MI program receive a 20 percent MI premium discount, but this benefit is achieved via an internal cross-subsidy from higher-income borrowers covered under the program. The Philippines' Home Guaranty Corporation program employs similar cross-subsidies to support qualified "social housing."

Another type of subsidy—cross-subsidies—can play a useful role in some countries' MI programs. Rather than classifying premium rates according to variations in credit risk, some countries intentionally cross-subsidize among classes of insured borrowers, either by applying a uniform rate (historical policy of the FHA in the United States) or by applying lower rates to higher-risk classes (the Philippines). In both instances, the public-purpose goal is to secure for borrowers of lesser means access to home financing on terms at least equal to the rest of the market.

To the extent that premiums are cross-subsidized or other means are employed to serve borrowers at the lower end of the income spectrum, to compensate for the added risk and remain viable, the public MI must adopt suitable alternative underwriting and risk management standards (for example, rigorous homeownership and credit counseling).

Special MI Products for Mortgage-Backed Securities (MBS)/Structured Finance

For the primary home mortgage market, nearly all MI programs provide, that is, "certify," coverage for individual home loans, most often with partial risk coverage. Although 100 percent coverage tends to use insurance capital inefficiently and is susceptible to moral hazard, such coverage does translate easily from the primary to the secondary and MBS market, where investors have no appetite for assuming unfamiliar risks. Modern-era MI programs that provide primary lenders less than 100 percent loan-level coverage can provide two types of companion products when the need arises to satisfy MBS investors, as well as rating agencies upon whom such investors will rely.

Mortgage Pool Insurance

Mortgage pool insurance provides a specially designed second-tier MI coverage for institutional MBS investors who are unfamiliar with mortgage risks and who wish to rely on investment ratings, including third-party credit enhancements. Mortgage pool insurance typically provides 100 percent cover for individual defaults in an MBS mortgage pool. Pool coverage, however, is subject to a stipulated aggregate loss limit for the overall pool. Normally, the rating agency, using stress-test modeling, will establish the pool policy's required aggregate loss limit ("stop loss"), a percentage that will depend upon both the risk characteristics of the particular mortgage pool and the desired rating for the security that is backed by the insured loan pool.

Timely Payment and Cash-flow Protection

Timely payment and cash-flow protection often will be needed on an investment-grade-rated MBS issue as an adjunct to mortgage default insurance. Security holders expect not only ultimate recovery of their mortgage principal, but also timely repayment of principal and interest according to the payment schedule provided in the offering document. If a number of insured loans in the mortgage pool fall into arrears, a temporary cash-flow shortfall will develop that is not acceptable to the security holder. While a variety of structured financing techniques exist to address such shortfalls (for example, lender obligation to advance payments owed by delinquent borrowers, special reserve funds), a timely payment guaranty from a government-backed or highly rated private third-party insurer has become an MBS mainstay in several countries.

The largest, and most well-known, MBS timely payment guaranty program is the Government National Mortgage Association (Ginnie Mae) in the United States, which is used in tandem with pools of loans insured by the

FHA and guaranteed by the Department of Veterans Affairs. The Ginnie Mae cash-flow guaranty, which backs up the loan servicer's obligation to advance out-of-pocket all payments due on delinquent loans, is provided for an added annual fee of six basis points. These insured advances are recovered later when the underlying FHA or Department of Veterans Affairs claim payment is made, or when the delinquent borrower brings the loan current.

Timely payment guarantees are provided in some other countries with active MBS markets, including Australia, where all MBS and all MI are private. In Australia, for a nominal premium, private "AA"-rated MI providers offer timely payment guarantees of up to 24 months for pooled loans that back highly rated MBS issues.

In short, as some countries' primary mortgage markets mature to include securitization, primary MI also can and should evolve, mainly in two respects that will satisfy non-mortgage investors' needs: first, to eliminate most loan-level credit risk; second, to protect not only against ultimate loss of capital following borrower default and collateral recovery, but also against interruption of mortgage pools' scheduled cash flows from borrowers' periodic loan repayments.

Credit Risk Management

Although they have little control over external forces affecting risk, including macroeconomic policies of the national government, public and private MI providers alike have at their disposal a powerful array of credit risk management tools. Most of the risk management tools noted below can be put in place during a program's planning and design and start-up phases.

Regulatory Issues

Regulatory concerns mainly, though not exclusively, relate to privately sponsored MI programs. These concerns fall into two basic categories:

- Rules directly governing how an MI program will operate
- Rules governing how banks and secondary investors use MI

Table 13.5. Credit Risk Management Tools

Risk management tool	Example
Rules and incentives to prevent adverse selection of risk by insured lenders	Seek reduced risk-based capital for high-LTV-ratio insured loans
Share risk exposure with originating insured lenders	Partial, rather than 100%, loan-level coverage
Share risk exposure with qualified third parties	Quota share loan-level or excess-of-loss portfolio-level reinsurance
Employ risk-based pricing based upon economic risk modeling and proper risk classification	Charge higher premiums for rate-indexed loans, based on simulated volatility
Define clearly both risks covered and risks excluded	Do not "second-guess" a lender's underwriting to deny a claim. Exclude fraud or material misrepresentation from coverage
Define clearly insurable loan types	Maximum LTV ratio; first liens; completed properties; single dwelling units
Define master-policy (lender contract) terms and conditions meticulously and clearly	Describe clearly all lender actions needed to sustain coverage, submit claims
Define clear eligibility and performance standards for originators and administrators of insured loans	Insured lenders must have their own regulators; administrators of insured loans must have adequate IT platform; apply sanctions against substandard loan administrators
Require adequate information reporting, internal and external, to monitor significant risks	Design and maintain a loan-level database capable of tracking significant risk factors and concentrations; invest early and wisely in information technology
Maintain effective loan underwriting methods, approval criteria	Review each individual insured loan document package until alternative methods are proven to be reliable; publish and adhere to approval criteria
Diversify risks geographically	In a large country, maintain a physical presence in all key regions; in a small country, if private MI, seek to write MI in multiple countries
Maintain effective local and regional housing market intelligence	Establish independent "human intelligence" on major builder-developers; deploy underwriting and quality control staff in regional facilities
Invest in comprehensive, proven methods of quality control, including fraud detection	Employ qualified internal and external operational auditors
Control excessive or adverse risk concentrations	Limit, by various means, aggregate risk assumed in very large projects
Employ conservative loss-reserving methods	Track and analyze delinquent loan behavior patterns and reserve accordingly
Manage defaults and pending claims aggressively and mitigate losses creatively	Offer incentives to defaulting borrowers to convey property title voluntarily
Shield the entire operation from political influence	Strictly limit staff dealings with elected politicians on business matters; structure board with strong private-sector representation

Source: Author's own analysis.

Key regulator concerns regarding MI behavior, taking account of its unique features noted earlier, should include the following:

- Maintaining adequate capital reserves relative to total risk exposure, including ability to survive economic catastrophe
- Segregating this unique form of insurance from other insurance lines
- Controlling conflicts of interest and maintaining underwriting independence between the mortgage insurer and the insured lender
- Defining classes of insurable loans
- Defining insurable lenders (for example, regulated lenders only)
- Requiring suitable loss provisioning on delinquent and foreclosed loans
- Ensuring adequate, but not excessive rates; nondiscriminatory rates; disclosures
- Requiring appropriate examinations and actuarial audits
- Restricting excessive risk concentrations
- Ensuring sufficient liquidity; avoiding risky, illiquid, or other inappropriate investments
- Applying appropriate standards and reserve requirements for potential reinsurers

The most comprehensive MI regulation is found in the United States, where all insurance is regulated by the individual states. The National Association of (state) Insurance Commissioners has promulgated a "Model Act" for mortgage guaranty insurance that provides a useful and comprehensive reference point for undertaking MI anywhere in the world. Some markets, for example, Hong Kong, Canada, Australia, and Israel, have enacted individual regulatory provisions similar to some of those appearing in the U.S. Model Act, such as the monoline restriction, special MI contingency reserve, and stringent risk-to-capital ratio limits, while not adopting the entire Act. One alternative to having a comprehensive MI law is to adopt a more abbreviated regulation under which the regulator then issues an MI insurance license based upon its approval of, and the insurer's adherence to, a detailed business plan. Canada, for example, operates in this fashion.

Although not regulated in the same sense as private MI providers, the most soundly conceived government-sponsored MI programs are those that operate under rules similar to those governing private insurance programs. Most important are the rules requiring actuarial soundness, including premium rates and reserving formulas. Less important for government programs are the rules relating to conflict-of-interest and consumer protection.

Public MI programs that have, since the early 1990s, benefited from stringent rules include, most notably, the FHA's Mutual Mortgage Insurance Fund (MMIF) and the Canada Mortgage and Housing Corporation's MI fund. As described in the final section of this chapter, each of these programs encountered solvency challenges in the late 1980s. As a result of their financial stress, each was subjected to stringent new rules and required to operate under more rigorous commercial principles; each is stronger today as a result.

Some developing countries that have, or are contemplating, a public MI program do not yet have any legal or regulatory provision for a mortgage-insurance type of fund. Mexico and Mali are examples where the MI fund has been established, at least temporarily, as a special type of banking institution. Although the risks of home mortgage lending and mortgage insurance are similar in some ways, the MI fund does need insurance-specific rules, for example, for segregated capital accounts, actuarially based premiums, and rules for catastrophic loss reserves and loss provisioning that are different than for banks. In short, while private MI may require more extensive regulation than a public provider, the public MI must be subject to effective core regulations requiring a prudential, commercially based activity. The final section of this chapter discusses historical MI failures in several countries; weak regulation or supervision often was a contributing factor.

Because MI risks embody both insurance and real estate lending traits, its ideal regulator in a national government probably is of the type where all major financial institutions (banking, insurance, securities) are consolidated under a single authority, for example, Sweden (Swedish Financial Supervisory Authority), the United Kingdom (Financial Services Authority), Canada (Office of the Superintendent of Financial Institutions), and Australia (Prudential Regulatory Authority), rather than under fragmented authorities, most notably the United States. As MBS activities have grown, along with the influence of the Basel Accords, over risk-based capital, this type of regulatory framework for MI becomes even more advantageous. As noted further in the following section, a unified and coordinated financial-institutions regulator can minimize lender opportunities to engage in unhealthy "regulatory capital arbitrage."

Finally, consideration should be given to what rules governing MI should be statutory versus what should be established by ministerial regulation. In short, rules that are rarely in need of change are better enshrined by law; those that may evolve with changing market conditions are better left to the regulator's discretion.

Bank Risk-Based Capital Rules

In gauging the outlook for MI in any country, banking regulation can be at least as important as insurance regulation. Of course, the MI provider needs its policyholders to be financial stable and competent lenders. More specifically, however, how banks' risk-based capital regulations are implemented under the Basel Accords in any given country can directly influence—positively or negatively—prospects for MI success.

It may be only a small overstatement to say, "There is no natural market demand for MI." In fact, left to their own devices over time, private lenders may be inclined to retain for themselves (while possibly underestimating) whatever risk premium the market may be willing to pay for making higher LTV-ratio home loans. Even where MI is seen as a tool to jump-start a dysfunctional or reluctant private-lending market, natural demand for MI may not be sustained over time, or lenders may adversely select for insurance protection only those loan applications they perceive to be inferior risks.

For the public-purpose objectives of MI to work well—reaching underserved market segments, extending affordable homeownership, and fortifying credit risk management system-wide—regulated banks need a broad-based incentive to use MI in a way that averts adverse risk selection. Experience in some countries shows that the risk-based capital weightings judiciously applied to home mortgages can be used to achieve these ends.

As noted earlier and illustrated in table 13.3, LTV ratio is the predominant variable, over both time and geography, which drives default risk on home loans. High LTV (low borrower equity) loans in any given environment produce much higher default and loss rates than lower LTV loans.[3]

In deciding how, and whether, to grant favorable risk weightings on residential mortgages, it makes sense for a central bank to recognize this dramatic inverse relationship between borrower equity and risk, first by setting a sensible LTV cap on home loans eligible for favorable capital treatment. If domestic mortgage experience data is lacking, this important decision can be well grounded in rich international experience tying borrower equity to mortgage risk.

Then, to advance the above-noted public policy goals associated with the use of MI, it also makes sense for a central bank to recognize—consistent with Basel—the added insurance-sector capital support of MI serving to offset the higher credit risks of high LTV lending. Without qualified MI credit enhancement,[4] home loans exceeding the set LTV benchmark should not be risk weighted any more favorably than a commercial mortgage.

Countries whose banking regulators currently assign a reduced-risk weight for home mortgages exceeding a designated LTV ratio but covered by private MI coverage include the United States (90 percent LTV); Australia, Italy (80 percent LTV); and Israel (60 percent LTV).

Finally, financial-sector regulators operating under emerging Basel II rules need to guard against "risk arbitrage" by primary lenders. Credit-risk-based capital rules need to be consistent, particularly among direct primary lenders, mortgage holders under various forms of structured financings and securitization, and mortgage insurers as third-party credit enhancers. The rules should not provide any incentive for perverse lender behavior, that is, to undertake transactions that allocate, shift, or substantially increase credit risks solely to exploit inconsistency in risk-based capital rules.

---

3. Overall loss rates are computed as default frequency × loss severity. Table 13.3, shows expected losses on 98–100 percent LTV loans to be more than four times the expected losses on 75–80 percent LTV loans. Recent empirical studies suggest that several variables, including credit scores, rival LTV as predictors of borrower default. These indicators, however, relate more to early borrower credit failure than long-term mortgage loss incidence.
4. MI that is government backed or that has been assigned a high investment rating for claims-paying capacity. Also, loan coverage that reduces lender exposure to an LTV level that is considered safe without MI.

Consumer Issues

Several issues related to consumers (borrowers) have arisen in countries having the most extended MI experience, including:

- Definition of beneficiary
- Subrogation rights[5]
- Refund of unearned premiums

Issues relating to who is the beneficiary and what are (or what should be) the rights of subrogation under the MI policy are somewhat related, so we shall discuss them together.

The MI provider always issues its policy (typically in the form of a "master policy") to the insured lender. Then, the lender, upon the payment of the MI premium and some form of underwriting review, receives certification that individual loans submitted for insurance are covered under its master policy. The question regarding who is the beneficiary has arisen largely because the premium charge ultimately is borne by the borrower. This question elevated into a heated consumer issue in several countries mainly when MI providers, upon the payment of claims—especially under depressed market conditions—have pursued dispossessed borrowers to pay off their remaining debt after the mortgaged home has been resold.

Problems arising from mortgage insurers seeking recourse against defaulted borrowers have arisen mainly in the United Kingdom, Australia, and New Zealand and, to a lesser extent, in the United States. In Australia and New Zealand, the issue was effectively clarified going forward by changing the name of the product from mortgage insurance (MI) to *lenders* mortgage insurance (LMI).

For those who may be structuring a new MI program—public or private—this question merits thoughtful attention and a balanced approach. One middle-ground approach used in the United States has been to exempt bona fide owner-occupant borrowers from mortgage insurer recourse (except

---

5. "Subrogation" is an insurance term referring to the right of the insurer, upon the payment of a claim, to "step into the shoes" of the insured and assert any rights the insured may have had to recover losses from a third party. In the case of MI, this means the MI assumes the lender's rights to pursue the defaulting borrower for any unpaid debt outstanding after resale of the collateral property.

where any such borrower acted deceitfully). The argument can be made that one who borrows for investment purposes, that is, to rent out the dwelling unit, rather than live in it, is party to a commercial transaction who has not lost his or her home. Such a defaulting borrower should remain liable to pay any remaining debt after the pledged collateral has been resold.[6]

Under MI programs where the entire premium is prepaid—often 3 to 4 percent of the total loan amount—a consumer protection question can arise with respect to a program's provisions for partial refund of premium paid in the event that the insured loan terminates much earlier than expected. Some such refund provision should apply, at least over the early years of the loan. Some programs, including in the United States and in Israel, have offered the choice of a nonrefundable premium at a discounted rate compared with the refundable MI premium option.

In recent years, so-called "captive insurance" has gained ground among MI users in several developing markets. Insured lenders have formed MI affiliates or subsidiaries expressly designed to capture a share of the total MI premium through various risk-sharing arrangements, for example, reinsurance. Consumer concerns regarding this practice may arise to the extent that the lender's profit motive may result in the cost of MI being higher than it otherwise might be, or MI might be required on loans that would otherwise be made uninsured.

Finally, in some countries, an attractive consumer benefit has been appended to some existing MI programs. In mid-2004, two leading private MI firms, as well as the state-sponsored Massachusetts Mortgage Insurance Fund, announced the addition of "mortgage payment protection" coverage to their standard MI programs. For no additional premium payment, borrowers who become involuntary unemployed can have six to nine monthly mortgage payments made directly by the insurer to the lender on their behalf. Similar, though not identical, mortgage payment protection programs have existed for some years in France and the United Kingdom.

---

6. A corollary to this observation is that only borrowers who are personally liable for repayment under their mortgage loan agreement should be eligible for MI.

Information Technology

For the two key reasons of managing risk and controlling costs, the public or private MI provider must pay keen attention to applicable and specialized information technology.

All insurance lines rely heavily on statistical data. MI's information needs are especially demanding. As noted earlier, MI needs three basic types of data: (1) housing market and home price data, (2) borrower income and credit data, and (3) home mortgage performance data. In most developing markets, for a number of reasons, such information is more difficult to obtain than, say, data needed to write auto, homeowner, or life insurance. More often than not, mortgage performance data of the character and duration needed by MI does not even exist at the outset.

For a public or private insurer to be financially self-sustaining it needs to operate under the "law of large numbers," which means gathering and managing large amounts of external and internal data, and doing so efficiently.

In the most advanced markets, MI providers are electronically connected to their insured lenders, credit reporting bureaus, and property information databases. They rely on large mortgage performance databases to validate their automated underwriting decision models. Massive credit history databases and predictor models now generate Fair, Isaac and Company (FICO) and related loan-scoring systems to support both MI underwriting and pricing. Drawing on huge property transaction databases, automated valuations are even beginning to supplant individual home appraisal reports. Property and mortgage registry systems are being converted to electronic form, able to provide MIs and other market players with near-instantaneous reporting. Behavioral models now are being used to guide MI claims-servicing personnel on the use of their time and resources.

Government MI programs in particular need to "keep up" with private lenders for the sake of both risk management and marketing. In the United States, for example, lagging legislation and underinvestment in technology has proved costly to the FHA's MMIF, both in terms of market share and loss management. By contrast, the CMHC has stayed "ahead of the technology curve"; for example, with its EMILI automated underwriting system and electronic lender interface for both issuing new insurance certificates and for processing claims.

Table 13.6. Advantages and Disadvantages of Public and Private MI Schemes

Public MI advantages	Private MI advantages
• Zero or minimal regulatory capital • Ability to impose uniform standards • Better able to cover catastrophic risk • More inclined to serve small market • More inclined to operate in untested primary market • No requirement to pay taxes or produce a return on invested capital	• Credit risk management expertise • Cost and operational efficiency • Investment in technology • Ability to spread risk across international borders • Product design/marketing responsiveness • Free from political influence

Source: Author's own analysis.

Sweden's BKN is another MI program notable for its leading-edge investment in information technology, which has paid off in terms of extremely low operating costs relative to outstanding guarantees. Automated processes include lender registration of new loan guarantees issued as part of its "delegated underwriting" system, and the electronic linking of BKN's database with a national database of property registrations.

Most developing markets are not prepared to take full advantage of these information technologies. But, any business or strategic planning for starting a public or private MI should consider these things as they relate to local market conditions and its anticipated rate of development. At a minimum, with respect to IT, the MI provider should keep up—and ideally remain a bit ahead of—the lenders it serves.

Whatever the state of a market's IT development, any MI sponsor will have a vital interest in promoting standardized and robust loan-level mortgage data collection by lenders and loan administrators, including detailed loan characteristics at origination and loan-performance detail from origination to termination.

Public-Private MI Partnerships

As noted earlier, most countries' MI programs today are government sponsored. Yet, many public officials where government MI already exists or is planned also want to attract private MI risk capital in support of their public policy objectives.

Government and private MI bring advantages and disadvantages, respectively, to the marketplace, most notably those shown in table 13.6.

Not surprisingly, policy makers seek to devise constructive public-private MI partnership arrangements that can realize "the best of both worlds." Following are a number of such arrangements that are currently in use or in active planning.

Public MI Provider Supported by Private Reinsurer(s)

This partnership device is used in a number of countries, including the following:

- *The United States*—The State of Massachusetts' MI fund reinsures a quota share 90 percent of its credit risk with a large U.S. MI firm, thereby adding geographic diversification and writing capacity.
- *Hong Kong*—The HKMC presently reinsures 80 percent of its MI risk with four highly rated private reinsurers—two domestic and two United States–based.
- *Mexico*—Private reinsurance with one or more U.S.-based MI firms (initially 50 percent quota share) is a core component anticipated by Mexico's revised public MI program, currently being launched by the Socieded Hipotecaria Federal (SHF).
- *South Africa*—The Home Loan Guarantee Company (HLGC) (a nongovernmental organization originally capitalized by the South African government) has for some years relied upon a U.K. reinsurer for capital support and added writing capacity. Unlike the government insurers noted above, HLGC also depends upon its foreign reinsurer for the investment-grade rating that has made its guarantee viable with domestic lending institutions.

Advantages of the government MI and private reinsurer partnership arrangement include the following:

- The up-front guarantee, issued by a government agency, serves to minimize—or even eliminate—insured lenders' risk-based capital weighting under Basel rules that strongly favor government-backed loans. In many countries this has proved a major incentive for banks to engage in low-down-payment residential lending.
- The government MI program may be subject to added market discipline, especially in terms of pricing and screening of risks. The public agency can benefit from the reinsurers' knowledge and experience regarding, for example, marketing and product design.
- If a small country, the government MI can effectively diversify its risk beyond national boundaries.
- The reinsurer can familiarize itself with a new or emerging national market without having to invest so heavily in establishing its own direct writing capability.
- The government program's writing capacity—therefore, its mission achievement—can be greatly expanded without requiring a corresponding increase in capital or contingent risk.

Caveats applicable to this particular arrangement include the following:

- The reinsurer should thoroughly understand the MI business in country-specific terms
- The private reinsurer should be an active risk management and marketing partner, not just a financial partner for the government MI
- The government program should not become vulnerable to any sudden reinsurer withdrawal from the market
- Ultimate catastrophic risk coverage is left to the private partner, rather than the government

Government Backup for Private MI Provider

This type of partnership arrangement has worked well in Canada for many years. Canada has one public MI (CMHC) and one private MI (Genworth, formerly GE Canada). Under a catastrophic form of "reinsurance" arrangement, the private MI has paid about 10 percent of its annual premium into a special reserve fund, and, in return, its policyholders are covered up to 90 percent on any claim that the private MI might ever fail to pay as a result of future insolvency. This special arrangement helps to place the competing public and private MI providers in Canada on a relatively "level playing field." Of particular value, the 90 percent backup coverage translates into 90 percent risk-based capital relief under the Basel bank capital agreements.

The Homeownership Guarantee Fund, the Netherlands' quasi-private MI program, also operates with a form of catastrophic government backup. In the event the Homeownership Guarantee Fund were unable to pay its claims, the national government and the municipalities are obliged to step in on a 50–50 basis and cover the fund's entire deficit in the form of interest-free loans. This government backup translates into a zero risk-based capital weighting for insured home mortgage lenders in the Netherlands—as noted, a strong incentive for banks to make such loans.

Of the above two MI partnership models in which the public and private player respectively assumes risk in a primary or secondary role, given the above noted advantages of each, which alternative is preferable?

While the answer will depend somewhat on a country's individual circumstances, including its stage of mortgage market development, a sovereign government should be better suited to filling a backup position that includes assuming ultimate catastrophic (systemic) risk; a private MI provider, in turn, ought to be better suited to providing direct primary lender and market interface and assuming the risks that are most measurable and predictable. As a practical matter, drawing a bright-line distinction between these two types of risk can be a difficult exercise.

So, one may ask, why is the more preferable of these two basic alternatives the one less frequently found in practice? Among the likely answers are: First, if the primary market is not well developed, private MI providers will be reluctant to engage in direct underwriting and market interface; they will prefer to negotiate reinsurance arrangements that assure reasonable control of risks and costs and opportunity for profit. Second, in a developing market, the government may be in a better position to impose rules and terms for the type of program that will meet its perceived public policy objectives.

A note of caution: While government might appear ideally suited to assume catastrophic MI risk, experience shows this not always to be the case, as illustrated later in this chapter. A sovereign government under fiscal duress may not always fulfill its obligations when they are presented, whereas a triple-A-rated private MI will have rigorously stress-tested capital reserves dedicated to payment of claims at depression levels, and an enforceable obligation to do so.

These two alternatives for allocating risk between public and private MI partners need not be mutually exclusive. A working blending of the two may be found in a form of "mezzanine" coverage used elsewhere by private reinsurance firms. Under such an arrangement, the public MI would assume both a limited first-tier risk *and* ultimate systemic risk, while the private carrier would assume a middle, or mezzanine, layer of risk. In the private sector, the reinsurer's liability may be triggered when the loss ratio in a given year reaches a threshold percentage; the reinsurer's liability is exhausted, in turn, when the loss ratio for that period reaches and exceeds a second, much higher, trigger point.[7]

Government-Sponsored Enterprises (GSEs), Privately Insured[8]

Unique to the United States, this MI public-private partnership bears mention, if not imitation. Fannie Mae, Freddie Mac, and the Federal Home Loan Banks—all formerly government entities—are today federally chartered, privately owned special-purpose enterprises whose core mission includes providing capital market access for primary home mortgage lenders. Together, these three GSEs fund over two-thirds of all U.S. home mortgage loans. In their own right, they guarantee, for a fee, repayment of the mortgage pools they buy and securitize. As hybrid entities, the GSE boards include both private- and public-sector officials. Although privately owned, they receive

7. The applicable period for establishing the loss-ratio triggers may be either the year in which losses occur or the year during which the risk was originated, the latter being known as "book of business" risk.
8. This discussion describes the recent pre-crisis structure of the three U.S. housing finance GSEs. In late 2008 two these quasi-government enterprises—Fannie Mae and Freddie Mac—facing severe portfolio losses and technical insolvency—were ordered into conservatorship by their federal regulator and infused with massive infusions of "bailout" capital by the national government. The U.S. Congress will eventually determine whether their future sponsorship will be public, quasi-public, or private.

special government benefits and are subject to some social targeting of their financing activities. All three GSE's partner with domestic private mortgage insurers—two by statutory mandate and one voluntarily—by relying on private MI risk capital to cover top-layer credit risks on their securitized high LTV loans.

Whichever of the above public-private partnership models may be adopted, the national government should properly account for its net state exposure (contingent liabilities net of reserves and reinsurance) as part of its total public debt.

The matter of public-private MI partnership should be viewed dynamically, that is, in terms of possible sequencing of optimal arrangements as a country's mortgage market develops and matures. The nature of this sequence normally should be toward progressively more private assumption of MI risk, subject only to continued fulfillment of core social objectives. Such a progression, tracking with overall market maturation, might go through the following stages:

STAGE ONE: Government MI as sole provider

STAGE TWO: Government MI with private reinsurer(s)

STATE THREE: Adoption of "sunset provision" for government provider

STAGE FOUR: Possible entry of private MI provider(s) in tandem with government

STAGE FIVE: Sale of minority ownership in government provider to private partner(s)

STAGE SIX: Ceding of controlling or 100 percent interest in government provider to private MI investor (that is, partial or full privatization, with exercise of sunset provision) with government assumption and retention of catastrophic (systemic) risk; also, possible reinsurance of higher-risk loans meeting targeted social goals.

Public-Private MI Competition

Several advanced markets—notably the United States, Canada, and Australia—have experience with competing public and private MI programs.

In each instance, public MI preceded private MI. While this configuration evolved, rather than being an explicit public policy decision, both regulators and customers may derive certain benefits from it:

- Premium rate and service competition helps both the market and the regulator.
- While restraining monopolistic behavior by a single public or private provider, the government-sponsored MI program can continue to target "down market" or other underserved markets (for example, rural housing, low-income, informal sector) that a for-profit MI may find less attractive.

To endure, this type of public-private competition requires a conscious balancing act by politicians and regulators. The government insurer will have inherent financial and market advantages (for example, no taxes, no required investor returns, less stringent regulation, minimal risk-based capital weight for lenders). Yet, the competitive playing field must be kept reasonably level in law and regulation. Despite periodic grumbling, the United States and Canada have, for the most part, maintained such a balance. While the private MI share of Canada's market is considerably smaller than in the United States, the Canadian government, as noted above, has continued its capital backup for the private provider, thereby helping to ensure that Canada's MI market remains competitive.

Australia has gone a different route; in 1997 the national government withdrew from the MI market, selling its once dominant public MI entity outright to a foreign-owned private MI firm. In New Zealand, by contrast, a pilot, publicly sponsored MI program was begun in 2003 with a single lender. Targeted at low-income, mostly rural and small-town borrowers, it does not for now appear to be competing directly with the two established commercial MI providers. Market expansion by either the public or private programs, however, could result in direct competition.

Despite the perceived advantages of sustaining competing public and private MI in some developed markets, this probably is not a model for a developing economy to emulate. Any of the previously referenced public-private MI partnerships probably would be preferable.

Table 13.7. MI Program Reversals and Resolutions—Selected Cases

United States

PROBLEM: For about 20 years up until 1996, the FHA allowed insured lenders to receive a 100% claim payment on many delinquent loans without having to foreclose prior to submitting the claim. Instead, the lender would simply assign ownership of the delinquent mortgage to the FHA. Only borrowers who were delinquent "through no fault of their own" and who were determined to have a "good chance of bringing their loan current" could have their loans transferred from the lender to the government MI. Then, a 1995 study concluded that FHA's Assignment Program had cost the MI fund an extra $1.5 billion and that about 2/3 of all loans assigned to FHA ended up in foreclosure anyway. The government's effort to help distressed borrowers or save money by servicing delinquent loans in lieu of private lenders was a costly failure.

RESOLUTION: The FHA Assignment Program was terminated in 1996. Since then, improved techniques for helping delinquent borrowers resolve their problems and for mitigating MI losses have produced dramatic positive results.

Canada

PROBLEM: Following two severe regional recessions in the 1980s, the government-sponsored CMHC's reserves became depleted to the point where it had to seek additional funding from the federal treasury. Funds needed to pay claims were advanced by the government to CMHC in the form of a loan. Prior to this event, CMHC's claims reserves had been funded based upon year-to-year loss projections.

RESOLUTION: Federal legislation was passed requiring that CMHC be run according to commercial insurance principles, including actuarially based premium rates and capital reserves. These reforms were implemented, including increased premium rates.

PROBLEM: The remaining private MI firm in the 1980s suffered severe claims losses in the country's major energy-producing province. These losses were aggravated by a provincial foreclosure law prohibiting lender or MI recourse against defaulting borrowers, regardless of ability to pay. Many borrowers simply "walked away" from homes whose resale values had fallen well below the outstanding mortgage balance. The competing government MI, exempt from provincial law, retained full recourse rights.

RESOLUTION: After an extended effort, an agreement appears to have been reached to establish a "level playing field" between the public and private MI providers, including recourse rights for both only on loans over 75% LTV, with clear borrower disclosure required.

United Kingdom

PROBLEM: In the 1980s, economic weakness and the bursting of a home price "bubble" in the London area and several other markets caused MI carriers to face massive claims and losses, resulting in the failure of one leading insurer and nonpayment of many claims by others. Poorly written insurance contracts resulted in widespread misunderstandings and disputes between insurers and lenders. "Mortgage indemnity" insurance experienced a severe and lingering loss of credibility.

RESOLUTION: Program reforms, including reduced coverages, clarified contract terms, greater risk sharing, and higher prices. Formation by some lenders—reluctant to continue using third-party insurers—of affiliated "captive MI" companies. Eventual entry of new international MI providers. Unfortunately, the commingling of MI with other homeowner-related coverages continues and MI regulation has not been strengthened.

The Philippines

PROBLEM: After 50 years of ongoing operations, the government-sponsored MI in recent years experienced heavy claims and losses and a depleted balance sheet. Lacking capital, it temporarily suspended writing new coverage, while awaiting a substantial capital infusion from the government. Although economic instability was a contributing factor, the severest losses were caused by defaults on large-scale development-related loans.

RESOLUTION: Despite the program's full government guaranty, many claims went unpaid during the program's suspension. Although claims gradually are being honored—partly in cash and partly with government credits and paper, many prior claims remain unpaid, still awaiting requested legislative appropriations. The insuring activities that caused such high claims have been terminated.

continued

Table 13.7. MI Program Reversals and Resolutions—Selected Cases *(continued)*

Sweden	
PROBLEM: The public MI fund paid out losses amounting to over US$1.1 billion on risks that it underwrote during the early 1990s. These claims were mostly from loans secured by rental apartments, and, to a lesser extent, cooperative projects. Causes of widespread defaults included cost-based valuations that proved too high relative to market values, exacerbated by deep recession and the absence of borrowers' personal liability on non-owner-occupied loans, along with higher taxation and reduced subsidies for the housing in question. Even during the several years when so many insured loans went bad, the MI program's loans on owner-occupied homes suffered minimal claims.	RESOLUTION: Program regulations were changed, including severe restrictions on guaranty amount as percent of property valuation. Economic conditions improved. MI losses on loans insured since 1994 have been miniscule, but so also has new business volume.

Mexico	
PROBLEM: FOVI, the predecessor to SHF, the current public MI agency, provided its insured lenders with a 50-50 "pari passu" credit guaranty scheme during the 1990s under which the underwriting was delegated to the originating lender. For years, the program paid almost no claims. The reason: conditions for submitting a valid claim, including required documentation that the loan had been originated in accord with program requirements, were so stringent that lenders were unable to recover under the guaranty when borrowers failed to repay.	RESOLUTION: SHF, under its recently reformed MI program for new originations, also has revised and relaxed requirements for receiving claim reimbursement for defaulted loans under the old FOVI credit guaranty program. Establishing credibility for Mexico's new public MI program is being done in part by restoring the old program's credibility.

Source: Author's own research.

Lessons Learned

This chapter began by relating the 1930s debacle of an entire MI industry in the United States. Learning from that experience, both public and private MI providers have operated more soundly over recent decades than they might have otherwise.[9]

Over the past few decades, a number of MI programs and providers have suffered significant, though less dramatic, reversals. From each of these, however, something of value might be gleaned for an MI program operating at a later time and in a different country. Table 13.7 provides a number of such experiences, including inferences that may be drawn.

Some useful inferences that may be drawn from these international MI experiences include the following:

9. While the MI industry largely avoided assuming the risks and devastating losses caused by subprime lending, it has experienced severe and growing losses from the Alt-A market segment, as well as on negatively amortizing "Option ARM" and 100 percent LTV loans.

- The success or failure of an MI program in a developing market cannot be judged until it has faced and survived a major economic downturn. Very few emerging economies have to date reached a point where their current MI programs either have encountered economic adversity or have registered a major impact on the markets they serve.

- The closer that an MI program adheres to its main mission of supporting homeownership—that is, insuring loans secured by individual owner-occupied dwelling units—the more stability it is likely to demonstrate in times of adversity.

- MI pricing must be actuarially based and maintained at levels that will be self-sustaining over the long term. A false sense of well-being that prevails in upward-trending markets should not be the basis for reducing MI tariffs.

- Though generally not required to make a profit or pay taxes, a public MI should adhere to established commercial and insurance principles.

- The terms of MI coverage should be established clearly when a loan is first insured so that loss reimbursement at the time of claim is predictable and prompt, barring fraud.

- Default risks covered by MI need to be shared with originating lenders in such a way that lenders face some contingent risk exposure on loans not properly underwritten or serviced.

- Foreclosure laws need to permit recourse against defaulting borrowers who are able to repay their debt. MI providers need to have at least some limited ability to assume a lender's recourse rights after the payment of a claim.

- A sovereign MI guaranty may not be fully reliable, despite the favorable capital treatment it bestows upon lenders. Even government-backed programs need to have sufficient dedicated capital reserves and cautious screening of the type of risks to be insured.

- Collateral recovery as a condition for claim payment is highly advisable. If the collateral property cannot be recovered in a reasonably predictable time frame, then the benefit of the mortgage being a high-quality secured asset, whereby loss exposure can be mitigated, is lost to the MI provider.

Conclusion

Mortgage default insurance can be a useful supporting component of a developing housing finance system, especially in reaching aspiring first-time home buyers who have difficulty saving the large down payment needed to qualify for an uninsured bank loan.

While potentially valuable, MI is not a panacea. Some developing economies may view public MI as a way to jump-start home mortgage lending without having to implement painful primary market reforms. Others may see MI as a costless way to subsidize homeownership for low-income or other socially needy families. Any such MI initiatives should be avoided; their true costs may be deferred or concealed for some years, but will eventually emerge at a most unwanted time.

Public MI should not become a vehicle for dumping bad contingent risks on the government. Enduring social benefits of a public MI will only materialize if the program operates under key insurance and risk management principles. This worthy goal, in turn, is unlikely to be realized unless the public MI is subject to strong, commercially oriented regulation and supervision.

Many developing countries will find it difficult to induce a private-sector MI firm to enter their market as a primary provider. Lack of historical mortgage performance data and other market information, impediments relating to collateral recovery and mortgage and title transfers, and limited business-volume prospects often present a level of uncertainty and perceived risk that will deter early entry by a private firm.

This does not mean a lack of interest; however, housing finance officials may need to chart an alternative course of action to make MI a reality and to eventually attract private risk capital. The government may need to assume the role of initial MI sponsor, at least as a model or pilot to demonstrate its viability. As part of a larger plan and effort to grow the housing finance sector, such a step can pay dividends beyond simply proving that it can be done. Properly positioned and supported, MI can serve as a market catalyst, not only for increasing loan volume, but helping to set standards that will raise the home mortgage's investment quality for banks and secondary investors alike.

This chapter has offered an international blend of historical experience, program information, suggestions, and caveats about MI, all for the purpose of giving some insight and help to those who are facing decisions regarding whether to go ahead with MI, or having already decided, how to go about it.

Chapter 14

Residential Rental Housing Finance

David Le Blanc, with major contributions
from Richard Green and Claude Taffin

Introduction

Recent years have witnessed the fast development of residential mortgage markets all over the world. In countries such as India, China, Turkey, Mexico, and Morocco, the introduction of market-friendly reforms has permitted the private mortgage sector to start expanding rapidly.

By contrast, rental housing remains underdeveloped and underfinanced in many emerging economies. An inhospitable environment facing the rental sector is directly reflected in the large portion of the housing stock that is outside the bounds of formality. Without alternatives to buying a formal dwelling, which is often unaffordable to a large portion of the income distribution, households resort to informal housing, be it owned or rented. Thus, in many countries a large informal rental market exists, in which the landlords are mostly individuals, not firms. The financing of this rental stock is overwhelmingly based on equity.[1] By contrast, in developed countries a number of financing options for rental housing has developed over the years.

---

1. In parallel, there may exist a small rental segment at the higher end of the market, owned by private investors and operated by professional firms, and aimed at housing more wealthy

In many countries, the rental sector houses the youngest and poorest parts of the population. In emerging economies, many renters would not be able to buy property, even if mortgage finance were more developed. The challenge facing policy makers is thus to provide affordable rental housing opportunities for these categories. One of the tools that can be used to achieve this is rental subsidies. These subsidies must navigate between two conflicting goals: they have to enable the supply of affordable rental housing for low-income households, while at the same time not discourage investment in rental housing; for example, maintaining attractive risk-adjusted returns for rental investors. Developed countries have put in place various types of rental subsidies, either for the sector as a whole in order to stimulate investment, or more targeted to middle- and low-income households. The main issue with these subsidies is that they are usually fiscally expensive, and therefore may seem beyond the reach of most countries, which face at the same time more pent-up housing demands and less favorable macroeconomic conditions.

The main objective of this chapter is to take stock of the various ways by which residential rental housing in emerging economies could be financed and subsidized in order to enable the provision of affordable rental accommodation for middle- and low-income families.

The Rental Sector in Housing Policy

The Importance of Enabling a Vibrant Rental Sector

Enabling the development of a healthy formal rental-housing sector is important for a number of reasons:

First, the rental sector is a natural outlet for households that do not have sufficient income to afford buying a home, or that have not saved enough to meet down-payment requirements for ownership. Young adults and the poorer fractions of the population fit into these categories. In countries where the private rental market is small or declining, the interim role played by the rental stock is missing, and one sees young adults living longer with their parents.

---

categories of the population including young professionals.

Second, vibrant rental markets are key to active resale markets and flexible labor markets. Mostly because of transaction costs, ownership entails high mobility costs, which can penalize mobility. Ownership can thus provide negative incentives to relocate closer to jobs (mobility trap). In contrast, mobility within the rental sector entails relatively low fixed costs, which can be seen as an advantage in societies going through rapid changes in the structure and localization of employment. This would characterize most transition countries (see World Bank 2005).

Third, a robust rental sector is needed to give households a larger choice for asset investment. In most countries, housing as an asset has the two drawbacks of being indivisible and relatively illiquid, which affects the way households can manage their portfolios. As a tenure choice, rental may allow households to avoid overinvestment in housing, compared to other assets. As an investment, rental housing generates a source of income that complements other income sources. In many developing countries it can also be a substitute for nonexistent pension systems, thus being a critical element of welfare improvement for the elderly (UN-Habitat 2003).

Lastly, affordable rental markets make it easier for households to accumulate down payment funds and thus promote mortgage markets, increase the value of housing assets, and facilitate the fluidity of resale housing markets. The importance of a functioning formal rental market is all the more crucial when the mortgage market is not fully developed, because access to ownership is more difficult. Usually, as mortgage markets develop, LTV limits tend to increase, which facilitates access to homeownership by households at early stages of the life cycle (for example, with low savings but high future income streams). In parallel, credit providers tend to serve more families in lower-income brackets, thus allowing a greater portion of the middle- and low-income population to access homeownership. Before these favorable outcomes are realized, though, rental markets have an important role to play in the life cycle of most families.[2]

---

2. A manifestation of the need for rental markets in undeveloped financial systems is the existence of intermediate systems between ownership and rental. Residential leasing is one such system. *Antichresis*, by which landlords basically raise equity from tenants in exchange for a limited time of rental without payments, is very popular in some Latin American countries. The *Chonsei* system in Korea is another well-known example. Such practices are obviously made easier by the absence of low-down-payment mortgages, and would probably tend to disappear when the mortgage market expands.

Imbalance between Rental and Homeownership

Despite compelling reasons for enabling a vibrant rental sector, the rental sector has received, at best, limited attention in many developed countries and emerging economies, in comparison to homeownership.[3]

Support of homeownership has emerged from different perspectives depending on the regions and historical contexts. Homeownership has been actively supported by many governments on the grounds that it promotes citizenship, essentially by giving a stake to individuals in the society. This paradigm is characteristic of the United States which subsidizes homeownership through the tax system (deductibility of mortgage interest and property taxes, non-taxation of imputed rent, virtual non-taxation of capital gains) and the financial system (lower cost finance through support of government-sponsored enterprises). Ownership of one's home has been seen as providing many social and economic benefits, including in particular the free usage of the space allowing families to set up businesses or income-generating activities within the premises. Homeownership is also thought to provide neighborhood externalities through maintenance and improvements. For example, promoting homeownership has been an explicit policy choice in most countries of Latin America. Transition economies constitute a special case, in the sense that high ownership rates mainly result from mass privatization of the housing stock undertaken in the post-Soviet era (see World Bank, 2005).

In many countries, the stated or implicit preference of the government for ownership has resulted in an uneven playing field between the two main tenure modes and ownership often benefits from more favorable tax regimes and subsidies. A result of this imbalance is that in many countries, rental housing is considered as an unprofitable and risky investment. It is not uncommon to see private investment in the sector stopping for whole periods of time, up to a point where the size of the sector decreases. This happened, for example, in the United Kingdom after drastic rent controls were put in place in the aftermath of World War II.

As argued above, the role of rental markets is potentially greater in countries still at earlier stages of mortgage-market development. What often happens in those countries, though, is that formal rental markets are weak or

3. For a complete discussion on this issue, see UN-Habitat (2003).

virtually nonexistent. As families need shelter whatever the circumstances, these countries witness the development of informal rental and ownership markets in all kinds of forms, often resulting in economically and socially suboptimal outcomes.

Overall, this is all the more regrettable, as no sustainable alternative to public rental housing has yet emerged in many developing countries. Public rental housing played a major role in the 1960s and 1970s in almost every region of the world, but has steadily declined since. Plus, the bulk of subsidies to households have been shifted to sustaining homeownership. Private-sector tenants receive little help of any kind. As a consequence, some entire segments of the poor populations have been mostly left out of the subsidy system.[4]

Rental Housing as an Investment

Rental investment can basically be decomposed in a series of cash flows. The first cash flow consists in an initial investment in a property (development), including land costs, construction costs, financial costs, "soft" costs such as fees, and taxes. After completion of the units, the project generates a series of periodic cash flows reflecting on one hand the collection of rents from the dwellers, and on the other hand the operation and maintenance costs as well as the taxes incurred by the landlord. After the end of the exploitation phase, the property can be sold by the owner, which generates a positive cash flow and is generally subject to tax.

This sequence of cash flows determines the net present value and the internal rate of return of the rental project. Net operating income, defined as the difference between rents and operating and maintenance costs, is the key element considered by financiers when considering whether to provide financing for a rental project.[5] The one positive component of net operating

---

4. For example, the rental market still houses between 20 and 40 percent of households in Argentina, Brazil, Chile, Mexico, and Peru, and data show that the homeownership rate among the poorest households (first quintile) has declined in all those countries during the last decade (World Bank 2004). In other regions of the world the rental sector is by far the dominant tenure status for the poor; yet a negligible proportion of housing subsidies is reaching them.
5. The availability of ways of financing involving leverage is of the utmost importance, especially for institutional investors.

income, the rent, is of course a critical element of the profitability of a rental project.

Other elements impacting the net operating income relate to the various costs borne by the landlord during the rental period. The main costs relate to the following:

- Management of the building—this comprises physical management of the structure, tax and administrative management, and commercial management, including minimizing the vacancy periods.
- Maintenance of the building—in many countries this item can become problematic, as the division of responsibilities between landlords and tenant relative to maintenance are not clearly defined.
- Taxes and fees—there are two components to this item: taxes and fees applying to the structure, which can in part be paid by the renters, and taxes on rental income which are paid by the landlord.

Looking at the structure of these costs, it appears that management costs, and to a lesser extent maintenance costs, allow for economies of scale. Thus, higher returns can potentially be achieved for multifamily buildings than for single rental houses. In order to achieve these economies of scale, however, two conditions must be met:

- Financing must be available—the size at which economies of scale are maximized is significant; thus, investments of the appropriate size will necessitate leverage.
- Professional real estate management capacities must exist.

These two conditions are often not met in emerging economies.

Most of the cash flows generated by a rental project are uncertain. Thus, the decision of the investor to invest or not in rental housing is dictated not only by return considerations, but also by risk considerations. The main uncertainties that distinguish rental investment from homeownership investment concern the collection of rents, which constitute the bulk of the positive cash flows generated by the project. In addition to rent payment risk, risks peculiar to rental versus ownership include the following:

- Vacancy risk, stemming from the fact that the probability that a given unit in the project will be vacant and may remain vacant for a long time, is not known;
- Eviction risk, meaning that evicting a delinquent renter involves costs and may prove difficult, whether because the judiciary system tends to interpret the texts in favor of tenants, or because the execution of judiciary decisions against tenants is not enforced;
- Disposal of the asset, in the sense that the law may restrict the landlord from using the dwelling units as he or she wishes (for example, to renovate, remodel, sell or destroy the unit).

These risks are influenced or directly governed by the legal and regulatory framework that regulates relations between tenants and landlords. When this framework is perceived as too coercive by landlords, the latter stop investing in formal rental housing, and, when alternative investments are missing, which is frequently the case in emerging economies, informal rental develops.

The Challenges of Developing Rental Housing in Emerging Economies

The development of rental markets in emerging economies is hindered by many constraints that do not specifically relate to the lack of finance for rental housing. These bottlenecks can be classified into two main categories. The first category includes adverse macroeconomic conditions and inappropriate regulatory environments applying to housing construction (building codes, housing standards) in general.

In some countries, macroeconomic fundamentals do not permit the two sides of the market to match. A fairly common case is the combination of low incomes and high interest rates, which generates a basic affordability problem. Household income is very low, and a small fraction of households could afford to pay the rent of a minimal-size dwelling as defined legally. The problem is compounded in a high-interest-rate environment, because the opportunity cost of investing in rental housing is high. As a consequence, at the required level of financial return, there is no demand for the minimum-standard product developers are allowed to construct. Or, conversely, current rent levels are not attractive enough to generate new investment. This has been the case in Brazil, for example, because of consistently high interest rates.

Minimal habitability standards are often set too high by the national housing policy. Unrealistically set minimal habitability standards are potentially a stumbling block to affordability policies, both in the ownership and rental sectors. In some countries, the construction costs of the "minimal unit" (that is, a unit having the minimal characteristics deemed to necessary to provide "decent" shelter) are far above the means of a large portion of the income distribution. This means that, either large subsidies will have to be provided in order to make standard housing units affordable to everyone, or some portion of the population will have to be housed in units not matching minimum habitability standards. Mobilizing enough (direct or indirect) subsidies to house all households in standard units often just proves to be unsustainable. As governments cannot explicitly recognize the necessity to lower minimal standards, there will be room for a large informal or substandard rental sector.

The existence of a repressed rental demand for units smaller than the minimum standards is visible in many big cities of the world where low-income workers choose to live close to jobs in substandard rental tenements, where they usually pay high rents. The so-called *tugurios* in Lima and the *cortiços* in Brazil are Latin American examples; collective rental accommodation in Dhaka, Bangladesh, is another example. A common feature of informal rental products in Dhaka and São Paulo is that they are reportedly very profitable. Thus, it is probable that there would be both social gains and a profitable niche for private-sector involvement, were the governments willing to accept to lower standards to include similar types of dwelling units.

The second category of obstacles includes other factors related to the environment of the rental sector, and specifically:

- the legal and regulatory framework governing the landlord-tenant relationship,
- rent control, and
- the tax system applying to rental housing.

Box 14.1. Returns on Formal Rental Housing in São Paulo, Brazil

In many cities comparable to São Paulo, the rental sector would be a natural outlet for low-income housing demand. A survey done for the municipality of São Paulo in the central districts of the city in 2004 showed that the rental stock has been in constant decline, going from 60 percent of dwellings in 1980 to 22 percent. This can be associated with low returns on rental investment in general. Data from the survey showed that average gross returns ranged from 7.6 to 14.4 percent, depending on the type of units. When adjusted for maintenance costs, vacancy, and nonpayment risks, these returns are far lower than those of other types of investments (in 2006 the current yield of government securities wass around 18 percent).

Generally speaking, in many countries, government policies in these domains tend to depress returns (often by increasing the costs associated to rental operation), while at the same time increasing risks of rental invest-ment. When the overall environment of the rental sector is perceived as too coercive by potential investors, private investment in formal rental housing stops. This may provide a rationale for the government to start providing rental housing directly but, in turn, the existence of an important public rental sector may hinder the development of the private rental market.

Rights of Landlords and Tenants

Many of the cash flows determining the returns on a rental investment are inherently uncertain. The risks associated with the income streams associ-ated to a rental property are influenced or directly governed by the legal and regulatory framework that governs relations between tenants and landlords. Many governments like to present themselves as the defenders of tenants, versus landlords, and impose stringent conditions on the scope of rental con-tracts, as well as on their execution. Examples include the following:

- imposing minimal durations for lease contracts and legal limitations to the yearly increase in rents,
- imposing strict conditions to recovery of the dwelling by the landlord,
- systematic interpretation of the texts by the judiciary system in favor of the tenants, and
- reluctance or refusal of the executive branch to enforce court decisions of eviction against defaulting tenants.

All these circumstances basically increase the rental risk faced by investors. This type of problem has plagued countries as diverse as Egypt, India, France, and Morocco. In addition, the political sensitivity of these issues makes changing the legal framework a real challenge that cannot be tackled frequently.

Rent Control

The introduction of rent controls used to be a standard measure even in market economies if rents in the private rental market were considered too high from a political standpoint. A famous example is the rent freezing introduced in several European countries during the First World War, which was maintained for decades thereafter. As a consequence, the private rented stock almost disappeared in the United Kingdom and suffered from lack of maintenance and underinvestment in France, which eventually built up the political pressure for mass production of public rental housing in the post-World War II period.

The economic effects of rent control have been analyzed extensively.[6] Economists traditionally distinguish "first generation" rent controls, which basically freeze the rents to their current nominal level, from "second generation" rent control, which apply milder constraints. A particular sort of second-generation rent control is tenancy rent control, whereby initial rents are set freely (for example, the rent can be freely adjusted whenever a new

---

6. See, for example, Arnott and Johnston 1981, Arnott 1995, Basu and Emerson 2000 and 2003, Fallis and Smith 1984 and 1985, Glaeser and Luttmer 2003, Gyourko and Linneman 1989, and Igarashi and Arnott 2000.

tenant moves in), but the progression of the rent for the duration of the lease is fixed or capped by an index.[7]

First-generation rent control, when imposed on the existing housing stock, constitutes a forced, uncompensated transfer from the landlord to the tenant. In some countries (for example, Egypt), the controlled unit can pass to the heirs of the sitting tenant with no or minimal adjustment of the rent, in which case the unit itself is practically transferred to the tenant, while all the costs and liabilities remain on the owner's shoulders. This has resulted almost universally in high vacancy rates (owners prefer to leave their units empty than to rent them out), absence of maintenance, absence of rehabilitation and upgrading of the controlled stock (in some cases going up to the collapse of buildings), as well as low residential mobility. Illegal subletting and increased key money charges are also common practices in the rent-controlled sector, as in public rental housing (see for example, Arnott and Anas 1992 for the Swedish case). The main other effect of rent control is to deter any new investment in the rental sector. Egypt and France after World War II offer extreme examples of the negative effects of rent control.

Evidence on second-generation rent controls is more mixed. While it may have positive effects in cases where landlords may have some monopoly power (Igarashi and Arnott 2000), it is nonetheless thought that such systems penalize frequent movers (in practice, mostly young people), because landlords factor in the fact that the rent is fixed for the duration of the lease into the initial rent (see Basu and Emerson 2000 for a discussion on India on this aspect).

To summarize, countries that have imposed hard types of rent control have witnessed a dwindling of the rental sector. Unsatisfied rental demand, as well as investors' money, has been carried over to the informal housing sector, with precise outcomes depending on the countries.[8] It is now widely accepted that the best remedy against situations of scarcity and high prices in the private rental market is comprehensive housing market deregulation and, where appropriate, introduction of explicit public subsidies.

---

7. For example, this form of rent control is the prevailing regime in France, and is also prevalent in India.
8. In developing countries, informal housing has played a role of adjustment between demand and (insufficient) formal supply. In transition countries, where the stock was already produced and impossible to hide, many ingenious ways of circumventing rent controls have been devised, with the same motives of escaping the administration.

It often proves difficult, however, to shift from a system in which implicit subsidies are paid to tenants by landlords, to one in which subsidies must be paid for up-front by the government.[9] Countries wanting to phase out rent control have often proceeded gradually. Usually, rent control on the existing stock is maintained, while new construction is exempted from it. This creates a dual rental market, with very low rents in the rent-controlled segment, and very high rents for uncontrolled units. This can be seen in Egypt and Lebanon.

Unfavorable Tax Regimes

In many countries, the stated preference of the government for ownership versus rental as a tenure status has translated into a favorable tax treatment for homeowners. By contrast, rental housing often offers limited tax advantages compared to other types of investments. The asymmetry between rental and ownership for tax purposes is often visible in the form of the following:

- Favorable tax treatment of capital for developers, such as accelerated amortization, exemption of construction tax, etc. For example, in Morocco, considerable tax breaks are granted to developers constructing social housing (defined as units with value under an MDH 200,000 [US$24,000] ceiling) for ownership; these advantages are not available for rental programs.
- Tax advantages to homeowners such as income tax deductibility of mortgage interest (India, Mexico), temporary exemption of property tax, and more favorable local taxes.

For individual investors, the proportion of gross rental income that can be deducted for income tax purposes is often not sufficient to cover the real management and maintenance costs, or the provisions for amortization of rental investment are not as attractive as those applying to other forms of capital investment.

---

9. Rent control can be a highly inequitable form of income redistribution as well. As it is unit based at opposed to individual or household based and not means tested higher income individuals or households frequently benefit.

As a result of these tax policies, the choice between rental and ownership from the point of view of both investors and households is biased, because the cost of capital is lower for ownership than for rental.[10]

Social Rental Housing

Historically, social rental housing in developed countries may be seen as the outcome of a situation where the housing conditions of the poor were seen as unacceptable or generating too many negative externalities (notably in terms of health conditions and crime), and private finance was not available for production on a significant scale. Countries wanting to implement social housing programs thus had to find low-cost resources to finance them. In a country like France, specialized financial circuits allowing for subsidized resources for lending to social housing companies were put in place.

In the version that was widely developed in socialist economies, in the United States and in Western Europe after the Second World War, most units produced under the system were managed by the government (local or central) or by companies controlled by the government. Units were allocated to households selected according to more or less transparent criteria. Generally, rents were set with no or few references to market rents.

This model of housing production and management has generated many economic and social issues. Therefore, over time, developed countries have adjusted their social rental programs. Although the degree and speed of change has differed across countries, some general patterns can be identified:

- There is a general tendency to disengage government at all levels from the ownership of rental properties and from direct management of social units. A well-known example is the policy of privatization of the municipal housing stock in the United Kingdom, through a right-to-buy scheme or the transfer to housing associations.

---

10. This issue has been thoroughly investigated in the United States. See for example Poterba 1980, Hendershott 1980, Hendershott and Shilling 1982, Hendershott and Ling 1984, DiPasquale 1989, and DiPasquale and Wheaton 1992.

- Rents in the public-rental sector are more often set in reference to private rents—be it through "fair market rents" (United States), rents found in comparable units in the neighborhood (United Kingdom), etc.
- Governments and regulators tend to introduce competition in the attribution of subsidies and off-market (low-cost) financing, by promoting competitive biddings and yardstick competition (for example, in the United States for tax-exempt bonds or projects financed by the housing tax credit, and the United Kingdom for additional financing for rehabilitation).

There is also a general trend toward using market-based funding for public rental housing, made possible by the development and liberalization of the financial sector in the 1980s. Macroeconomic stability and decreasing interest rates after the introduction of the Euro further encouraged social landlords to turn to market finance. For example, the Housing Finance and Development Centre of Finland (ARA) uses modern financial-market instruments, including securitization. France and Austria are now the only countries in the Euro zone that still use a state subsidiary to finance the social rental sector.

Specific intermediaries, however, are often needed to help smaller investors access capital markets and secure guaranteed loans (for example, in Finland, the Netherlands, and the United Kingdom).

In the 1960s and 1970s, many developing countries replicated the basic public rental model with even less success. Reasons for failure included, among others:[11] (i) units built at too-high standards and unaffordable to low-income residents, even with low rents; (ii) lack of basic commercial concerns, resulting in construction of public units in places where there was no demand for them; (iii) politically driven attribution of units or implicit encouragement by politicians not to pay the rents; (iv) exacerbated social problems resulting from the absence of basic infrastructure, water and sanitation, jobs, and services in the neighborhoods of the public compounds, resulting in economic segregation of the residents; and (v) lax management practices, resulting in low rent collection and financial stress for the public companies,

---

11. For a discussion on this point, see UN-Habitat (2003) and Villoria Siegert (2004), and references therein.

and eventually in lack of resources for operation and maintenance, then for new production.

This lack of sustainability has led to the scaling down or abandonment of public rental programs in many countries. Public rental housing has been abandoned in most Latin American countries, with the notable exception of Brazil, which has developed a residential leasing program (Programa de Arrendamento Residencial [Residential Leasing Program; PAR]). Poland has also been an exception, with the creation of a special fund for municipal rental housing. Both programs, however, are currently facing sustainability problems. The experience of these two countries is discussed in the section on country examples.

Some Market Financing Models for Rental Housing

This section briefly outlines various financing strategies relying on the market that can be applied to rental housing, from the least to the most sophisticated financially. Obstacles relevant to emerging economies are also discussed.

All-Equity Based

This model is prevalent in many developing countries where access to financial market is limited, and rental housing is perceived as too risky by institutional investors. This could be a valid description of the context prevailing in Morocco, for example. Households already owning a dwelling (formal or informal) having saved enough cash decide to add one floor to their house (or to build another house in the neighborhood) in order to rent it out, after comparing the return they get from this investment to the returns they could get on alternative investments (the set of which may be fairly limited, especially for non-banked households).

Compared to institutional investors, individual landlords often largely escape the tax system, both during the production phase and the exploitation phase, which increases the return on the investment. They also are able to enjoy a closer relationship with their tenants, which confers the following advantages: (i) usually, there is only one tenant household, which avoids contagion problems; (ii) the landlord may install individual meters for water and electricity or at least individual connections, which he may cut in case of nonpayment of the rent; this, along with the risk to the neighborhood reputation of the tenant, lowers the risk of nonpayment; (iii) very often there is no formal lease contract, which allows the landlord to bypass legal and judicial difficulties in case of problems. For all these reasons, the returns to individual landlords can be higher than those of institutional investors and explain why the latter are absent from the rental sector.

This strategy has obvious drawbacks:

- the invested money is not leveraged;
- because of the (varying) degree of informality of the process, the constructed dwellings largely escape the tax system, but also the benefit system—renters are difficult to identify and be provided benefits;
- the investment is very illiquid, especially in the case of a floor in the landlord's home;
- there is no diversification of risks.

There are many variants to this case. In Saudi Arabia, some real estate companies are beginning to invest in multifamily rental apartments, based mostly on own equity. At the same time, these companies are actively paving the way for alternative ways of funding projects (bank loans or direct tapping of capital markets).

Real Estate Investment Trusts (REIT)

A more sophisticated form of rental investment consists in investment funds (whose legal nature and structure can vary depending on the country), whose purpose is investment in rental housing. The prototype of such funds is the U.S. equity real estate investment trust (equity REIT). The funds raise equity from investors, and then buy, develop, or manage the rental properties directly. The basic concept of these structures is to allow the pooling of equity for investment in rental projects in a tax-efficient manner. Simply stated, an equity REIT serves as a conduit through which income is passed, in the form of dividends, from a real estate portfolio to shareholders. If certain conditions are met the income that is passed through is not taxed at the REIT level. Such vehicles provide liquidity to the rental equity market, both because individual investors can invest in shares with low unit value compared to a physical investment in rental housing, and because shares can be traded on a secondary market.

North America has well-established REITs. Australia, Japan, Singapore, Hong Kong, New Zealand, and South Korea also have well-established, or newly formed, REITs. In the EU, four countries (Belgium, France, Greece, and the Netherlands) have clear tax-efficient REIT structures in operation, while Italy utilizes a hybrid structure. The two largest economies in the region, Germany and the United Kingdom, introduced tax-transparent REITs in 2007. Two other European countries, Russia and Turkey, also have existing REIT structures.

Compared to the individual investor model described above, the advantages of real estate investment funds such as REIT or the French Société Civile de Placement Immobilier (Real Estate Investment Trust; SCPI) are the following:

- net returns are potentially higher because of professional rental management and economies of scale;
- risks are reduced because the portfolio of the fund consists in multiple properties, which can be located in different regions or parts of the cities, and thus, rental and geographic risks are mitigated;
- there is no "indivisibility effect" (no minimum investment required), which is good in terms of portfolio composition for individual investors;
- the investment is more liquid.

Of course, appropriate regulation, especially in terms of accounting, prudential rules, and consumer information, has to be set up by the regulating authority in order to avoid misuses of investors' funds. In France, SCPI are submitted to regulations that closely resemble those of other financial products, in terms of governance, accounting, and disclosure of information. SCPI owners also benefit from the tax incentives applying to individuals investing in new rental housing.

Usually, commercial rental investment is more profitable than residential housing, which in turn is more profitable than social rental housing. Thus, private investors attracted by those structures will not necessarily be interested in social housing investments, unless additional tax advantages are granted to social projects. Examples of equity REITs used to finance social housing exist, however. A prominent example of such a REIT is the Community Development Trust based in New York, the primary goal of which is to preserve and increase the stock of affordable housing through long-term equity investments and mortgage lending. This privately held REIT invests in affordable housing in more than 20 states and has attracted private investors who are currently receiving a yield of nearly 5 percent per annum.

Bank-Supplied Credit for Residential Rental Investment

Lending for rental housing investment is essentially long term. Therefore, all the potential issues associated with long-term lending by banks (liquidity and interest rate risks, instruments for matching asset and liability durations, existence of a demand for long-term paper) are relevant and should not be underestimated. These issues, however, are not specific to rental investment lending, and we refer the reader to other chapters of this book for a thorough discussion. In this chapter, we start from the premise that banks do lend long term to other sectors, for example, mortgage lending for homeownership. What, then, are the obstacles that could prevent lending for residential investment?

The provision of loans to investors eager to undertake residential rental projects relies on the willingness of the banks to engage in this activity, as well as their getting sufficient know-how in this kind of product. The two conditions can be problematic in specific countries.

First, in many countries (including developed countries), residential rental housing is perceived as less profitable and more risky than commercial rental.[12] Thus, banks will tend to engage first in commercial lending.

Second, lending for residential rental housing is very different from retail lending for ownership. Multifamily housing financing is a complicated venture, involving a whole range of stakeholders. In addition, unlike

---

12. The reasons for high risks in the residential rental market have been elaborated on in the previous section. For example, the capacity of enforcing the lease contracts may be low. Low forecasted returns can be the consequence of legal caps to rent increases, low household incomes, or high maintenance costs.

Box 14.2. Underwriting Criteria for Multifamily Rental Loans

Contrary to owner-occupied loan underwriting, which involves evaluating the borrower as much as the property, underwriting residential rental loans is closer in spirit to underwriting business loans and relies heavily on the examination of the cash flows generated by the project. Although the assessment of the risk of rental loans will include commercial criteria such as market need, zoning, architectural merits, availability of community resources, etc., lenders will typically focus on three ratios when underwriting income properties:

- Loan-to-value, similar to mortgage lending for ownership;
- Debt coverage ratio (defined as net operating income over debt service), and
- Breakeven ratio (debt service + operating expenses over gross operating income). Breakeven measures the amount of vacancy the property is able to sustain without incurring negative operating income.

In the United States, there are some commonly accepted benchmarks for these ratios. For example, a debt coverage ratio of 1.20 or more is necessary to get a mortgage. In the case of replacement of credit enhancement facility, credit providers or enhancers also typically require that the property has performed well in terms of occupancy rates over a specified period prior to closing.

single-family construction, no standardized debt instruments or financing process exists and multiple funding sources are common. As a business line, it is closer to project finance, as it relies heavily on the examination of the cash flows generated by each particular project. As such, it is less subject to automated procedures of loan approvals and other refinements that have facilitated mortgage lending in many countries. This implies that lending for multifamily housing will generally be done by a specific department in the financial institution, comprising specific profiles of staff and using specific models for assessing the risks of the projects. For all theses reasons, some banks choose not to develop this activity.

Finally, lack of information on rental markets and on housing markets in general can be detrimental to the development of a lending activity to multi-family housing. The assessment of the financial viability and profitability of a rental project relies heavily on projections of future rents, operating expenses, and real estate prices. The first two parameters determine the sequence of net operating income streams, while the second drives the behavior of the investor's net equity in the project. A lack of information on the housing market as a whole, which is common in developing countries, thus translates into difficulties in projecting key financial parameters over the life cycle of the project. This results in the price of credit being higher to compensate for the higher perceived risks and, secondly, banks will be less inclined to develop specific products for rental investment.

Capital Market Financing

In a rental investment project, at least two kinds of cash flows can be used for the purpose of structuring financing instruments: the repayments of a mortgage taken on the project, and the cash flows (net rents) generated directly by the project. Consequently, there are different avenues for tapping capital markets: Examples include the following:

- issuance of bonds or securities backed by the mortgages made by banks or other lenders for rental investment (residential commercial mortgage-backed securities);
- direct financing of the rental project on capital markets by bonds, with or without backing from a non-bank intermediary (used in the United Kingdom for the financing of social housing);
- issuance of bonds by local governments, the proceeds of which are lent to rental projects (municipal tax-exempt bonds in the United States).

The first type of bond is a particular kind of mortgage bond or MBS. The second case is closer to methods used for the financing of infrastructure, whereby the bond yields are directly based on the future income streams generated by the project. In the third case, what the investor is buying is the municipality's (or its affiliate's) signature, not directly the individual project owner's quality.

COMMERCIAL MORTGAGE-BACKED SECURITIES

Lenders can access the capital market through securitization of the mortgages provided to rental investors. In the case of rental housing, the associated products are called (multifamily) commercial mortgage-backed securities.[13] In the United States, GSEs such as Freddie Mac purchase multifamily rental loans for securitization. In Europe, some social housing entities have been using transactions similar to commercial mortgage-backed securities to sell some of their portfolio loans. The best known example is the Fennica transactions of ARA (which is the Housing Fund of Finland) (see box 14.3).

Box 14.3. Securitization of Multifamily Rental Loans and Social Housing Loans

In the United States, Freddie Mac buys rental loans for securitization. The products ("Multifamily PCs") are secured by structures with five or more units designed principally for residential use, with terms generally ranging from five to 30 years. They offer the Freddie Mac guarantee of timely payment of interest and full and final payment of scheduled principal. Generally, Freddie Mac requires the following of all mortgages it purchases:

- be secured by properties with occupancy rates of at least 90 percent for the three months prior to loan closing and as of the loan closing date,
- have debt coverage ratios of at least 1.25 for the first mortgage and 1.15 for the first mortgage and any subordinate mortgages, and
- have LTV ratios not exceeding 80 percent for the first mortgage or 85 percent for the combined first and subordinate mortgages.

(continued)

---

13. Commercial mortgage-backed securities are similar to MBSs but backed by loans secured with commercial rather than residential property. Commercial property includes multifamily, retail, office, etc.

Box 14.3. Securitization of Multifamily Rental Loans and Social Housing Loans (*continued*)

Social housing is provided throughout Europe, and there are a number of examples of the use of securitization for funding purposes in a wide range of methods in quite a few countries.

- In Sweden, through the *Framtiden* issues made between 1995 and 2001, the city of Gothenburg sold a number of portfolios of loans to multifamily housing companies that provide low-cost rental houses for families to an SPV, which raised funds in the asset-backed capital markets.
- Similarly, in Finland through the *Fennica* issues, funds have been raised in the asset-backed capital markets by the sale of loans made by ARA subsidized by another agency of the Republic of Finland to social housing borrowers for the purchase or construction of multifamily rental housing.
- In Belgium, this is also the case with the Atrium and Eve issues, where loans made to social housing companies for the provision of low-cost single-family housing were securitized; and in the Netherlands with the Colonnade and Dutch Housing Association Finance issues going back to 1997, which financed the securitization of loans to Dutch housing associations guaranteed by a specially established state entity.

DIRECT TAPPING OF CAPITAL MARKETS

Securitization of rents is a technique that can be compared to the securitization of mortgages. Future flows of rents from a given project and for a limited period of time are sold to an investor, like future loan repayments. The default risk is also transferred to the investor. Investors and rating agencies will be interested by the potential for the project, as measured by the expected evolution of rents (and allowances when applicable) and vacancy rates.

Since the introduction of securitization in the United Kingdom, securitizations of social housing receivables have been completed by housing associations and other Registered Social Landlords (RSLs). While the biggest housing associations have gone to the market on their own, The Housing Finance Corporation Limited (THFC) has played an increasing role as a provider of funds for RSLs that will not or cannot do the same. THFC issues bonds on behalf of its client RSLs. Before the financial crisis, 30-year bullet (interest-only) structure bonds issued by THFC on behalf of RSLs achieved margins under 100 basis points under the treasury-bond rates for similar durations, with a AA rating.

The motives of social lenders in the United Kingdom to use rent securitization (as opposed to secured financing) are not so much capital efficiency or bad credit conditions;[14] for most RSLs, banking credit remains the most asset-efficient source, based on current asset-cover ratios being achieved. Rather, the demand stems from the potentially loan-capital-intensive nature of RSL development activity and the need to underpin the supply of assured investment funds for supporting a long-term business.[15]

Credit Enhancements and Insurance Products

A number of financial products aim at rendering the investment in residential rental housing more attractive. A distinction can be made between:

- insurance products devised to insure the cash flows produced by the property to the landlord,
- credit enhancement products applying to individual mortgages (aimed at primary lenders), and
- credit enhancement products applying to the bonds issued to finance the investment (aiming at achieving a triple-A rating for the bonds).

Among the first category, one finds insurance for rental payment for landlords (timely payment or nonpayment). In Europe, insurance companies

---

14. There is no equivalent to the Basel capital adequacy regime for housing associations. Equally, the sector has an extremely good credit track record.
15. Undiversified social lenders are (arguably) countercyclical businesses, whereas wholesale bank funding tends to be cyclical. Hence, measures to diversify funding to include elements of capital markets funding, as well as bank and building society funding, should be considered prudent.

offer this kind of product to landlords through real estate agencies. Subsidized versions of this product also exist (for example, LocaPass in France, financed out of the "1 percent levy").

In the second category, mortgage insurance is the most popular product. Mortgage insurance insures lenders against loss on mortgage defaults. In so doing, it makes capital more readily available to developers. In the United States, HUD provides mortgage insurance for profit and non-profit sponsors in Section 221(d)(3) and Section 221(d)(4) for the construction or rehabilitation of rental and cooperative housing for moderate income groups. The program allows for long-term mortgages (up to 40 years) that can be financed through Government National Mortgage Association MBSs.

In Europe, local and central governments have often played a role in guaranteeing loans made to social housing institutions. Guarantees are still offered by local governments to public housing projects (France)[16] or by mutual funds to social housing projects (France, United Kingdom, the Netherlands). In Slovakia, the state guarantees loans for the construction of rental apartments for lower-income groups in order to provide incentives to the use of private finance. In the Netherlands, a complex system of guarantees for social housing loans has been put in place, in which the state and municipalities play the role of last-resort guarantor on top of other guarantees.

Alternative or additional securities can be provided to the lender by securing reserve funds that can be tapped in the event of late payments or default. Recent loans to housing associations in the United Kingdom were secured by mortgages on social housing properties and cash reserves in favor of the issuer and bond trustee. In the event of default, the bond trustee will have the right to collect the rents and manage the secured property.

Bond enhancement products provide security for the bondholders and impact the bond rating. A higher rating translates into a more favorable bond interest rate and ultimately a lower mortgage rate. These products are distinct from mortgage insurance in that they typically do not look at the quality of individual credits within a pool. Rather, they provide additional security on top of what is already provided by, for example, mortgage insurance. In the

---

16. In return, there is a reservation of 20 percent of the units financed with the guaranteed loan.

> **Box 14.4. Bond Enhancement Products for Multifamily Rental Housing**
>
> Credit enhancement products used for securities based on multifamily housing are of the same kind as those existing for other types of mortgage securities. In particular, they include the following:
>
> - guarantee of payment of mortgage principal and interest that is used to pay the bond investors;
> - liquidity facility, aimed at meeting the scheduled cash flows in the event the borrower is not able to meet its commitments; and
> - principal reserve fund, particularly in the case of variable rate bonds. Principal payments may be made to a principal reserve fund held by the trustee rather than directly amortizing the bonds. Payments made to a principal reserve fund will accumulate. At the maturity of the bonds, the funds accumulated in the principal reserve fund will be paid to the bondholders. Alternatively, they can be used to redeem bonds.

United States, all bond-financed mortgages issued under tax-exempt bond-financed programs must be credit enhanced.[17]

Country Examples

This section discusses examples of programs of public support to the financing of rental housing financing from selected developed countries and emerging economies. The choice of the countries and programs is aimed at illustrating the variety of the subsidies used and the diversity of public-private partnership arrangements through which they are implemented. The examples also try to highlight the difficulties and pitfalls embedded in public support programs.

---

17. Eligible credit enhancers include banks, mortgage insurance companies, bond insurers, the FHA, Fannie Mae, Freddie Mac, and Ginnie Mae. The difficulties of bond insurers and mortgage insurance companies in the financial crisis have led to a virtual cessation in private sector credit enhancement.

The Low-Income Housing Tax Credit (LIHTC) in the United States

Affordable rental housing in the United States is provided through a combination of federal and state programs, very often with supplementary financing or subsidies from other institutions (NGOs, local governments).[18] Each state has its own housing finance agency, whose goal is to provide affordable housing opportunities for low-income families throughout the state. State agencies review and select projects for financing on federal programs, based on transparent criteria.[19] Federal subsidies are rationed and awarded through competition between projects. Housing finance agencies usually also have their own programs, which can complement federal programs (in some cases, a development becomes eligible for state credits once the housing finance agency has approved an application for federal credits. If a development does not receive federal credits, it cannot receive state credits).

The two main federal programs directed at affordable rental housing are embedded in the Tax Code:

- LIHTC is a 10-year tax credit granted to investors investing in affordable rental equity. Housing tax credits can either be syndicated to generate part of the required equity or be utilized directly to offset the borrower's tax payments.
- Tax-exempt bonds for multifamily rental housing financing are bonds issued by local governments for special government purposes, including the production of affordable rental housing.

The purpose of the federal LIHTC program is to create a financial incentive (in the form of tax credits) for private investors (both profit and non-profit) to invest in the development of low-income rental housing. The

---

18. Apart from subsidies to the production of affordable rental housing, the United States also has an important federal program of direct subsidies to renter households (Section 8 vouchers). This program has been analyzed in a number of papers to which we refer the reader (for example, Crews Cutts and Olsen 2002).

19. In addition to evaluating applications for credits, the housing finance agencies monitor housing credit properties to ensure that rents are maintained at the agreed levels, that tenants' incomes do not exceed the allowable limits, and that the apartments are well maintained.

developer sells the tax credits to a private investor (both individuals and corporations) through a process know as "syndication." A "syndicator" is an organization that helps set up a partnership between the developer and the private investor to cooperate on tax-credit projects. The developer is typically the general partner, while the private investor is a limited partner. The development capital thus raised will be paid through the syndicator's equity fund in stages, which are subject to negotiation.[20]

The private investor benefits by using the tax credits to reduce its annual tax liability each year during 10 years. The tax credit is an actual dollar-for-dollar reduction in the amount of taxes due to the tax authorities. As a partner and co-owner of the project, the investor enjoys other tax advantages, such as accelerated depreciation on the buildings and passive losses.

During the period 1995–2005, 1,100,000 housing units have been constructed under the program, and their financing, design, and target populations have varied significantly according to state and local needs and preferences. On average, an additional 110,000 units are created each year, representing approximately 30 percent of all multifamily housing construction annually. The program has proven successful at both creating affordable housing and providing good returns on investments. Competition for tax credits has increased as investors have become more familiar with the program. For example, the amount of private investment raised per dollar of tax credit rose from $0.47 when the program was originated in 1987 to $0.62 by 1996. As investors have become more comfortable with the program's minimal risk level, the returns they require in order to invest in an LIHTC property has fallen from an internal rate of return of 28.7 in 1987 to 18.2 by 1994 (assuming an eight-year pay-in) (Cummings and DiPasquale 1998).

Brazil: the Residential Leasing Program (PAR)

Brazil offers a good example of a country in which the legal framework governing the relations between tenants and landlords are judged well balanced,

---

20. A typical payment schedule would be 30 percent upon formation of the partnership, 40 percent upon completion of construction, and 30 percent upon completion of occupancy. Therefore, the developer will need to secure predevelopment loans, construction loans, and "bridge" loans to finance the development until tax-credit payments are received.

but where adverse macroeconomic conditions have prevented private rental markets to develop during the recent years.

The PAR constitutes an attempt by the Brazilian federal government to introduce a residential leasing program aimed at reaching low- and middle-income groups. The PAR is targeted at households with income between four and six minimum salaries. Beneficiary households rent their units and have a buy option after 15 years. The program applies to newly constructed units and to renovated units as well.

The PAR is managed by the main public housing bank, CEF. Municipalities play a key role in the program.[21] They negotiate with CEF on the location of the program and the counterpart funding that will be brought by the municipality (usually in the form of land provided for the construction of buildings, or through the donation of municipal residential buildings to be renovated); they participate in the design of the construction or rehabilitation program (approval by CEF is needed). They propose a list of beneficiaries of the program to CEF, which then screens applications and makes the final selection of beneficiaries.

It can be estimated that the value of the financial subsidy embedded in the PAR corresponds to 55 percent of the unit value; however, the total subsidy rate is higher, because some costs are not included in the value of the unit used for rent calculation, such as the value of the land donated by the municipality when applicable, the value of infrastructure built and not included in the unit price, the value of exemptions of local taxes, etc. Overall subsidy rates for the PAR can be estimated to be around 70 percent of the total unit value.

The PAR is considered in Brazil as a successful example of cooperation between municipalities and actors from other government levels. Since the inception of the program in 1999, 160,000 housing units had been constructed or renovated and 75,000 were under construction at the end of 2006.

However, the PAR illustrates the difficulties faced by governments wanting to deliver finished housing units meeting minimal quality criteria to low-income households who could not afford them otherwise. Because of very high subsidy rates, the financial balance of the program has been put at risk,

21. PAR also works with associations (very often cooperatives gathering members of professional corporations). The cooperative usually provides the land and selects the applicants.

despite the existence of low-cost resources from the provident fund FGTS. Maintaining such a high level of subsidies is simply not sustainable in the long run.

Poland: the TBS Experience

Private residential rental markets are currently underdeveloped and underfi-nanced in Poland. Among other factors, this can be attributed to unfavorable legal and tax environments.

The National Housing Fund (KFM) is a public rental program that has financed, between its inception in 1996 and the end of 2005, the comple-tion of 61,600 new rental units for moderate income tenants (an additional 11,800 dwellings were under construction at the end of 2005). The program has been steadily growing in size, with production in 2004 staying at 9,100 dwellings, but in 2005 declined to 8,000 dwellings.

The Fund is directly administered by the state bank, Bank Gospodarstwa Kra-jowego (Bank of the National Economy) through long-term credits extended to nonprofit landlord organizations (TBS). No fee or margin is applied (but the bank's treasury may commercially invest the budgetary allocations before disbursement). The repayment performance of this subsidized long-term port-folio until 2004 was excellent, partly because of subsidized credit rates.

The main operators and borrowers are non-profit associations (TBS) championed by municipalities, and some rental cooperatives and sometimes even private developers (in total about 450 institutions by the end of 2004). The applied rents must cover the credit repayment and all maintenance and renovation costs, and should not exceed 4 percent of the replacement invest-ment value. The KFM also finances infrastructure loans directly to munici-palities, but this activity is still relatively marginal in size.

The rental associations or cooperatives are required to provide 30 per-cent equity, the fund financing up to 70 percent of the project. This down payment may be derived from the tenants, who as a result consider them-selves as quasi-owners and are selected through this qualification. This situation may end up running against targeting goals[22] and create problems for housing allocations.[23]

The program does not target low-income tenants in particular. The KFM does not control the declared incomes, as this responsibility is delegated to the TBS and the sponsoring municipality according to its own local housing policy, but anecdotal evidence suggests little follow-up monitoring and evaluation.

This experience is unique in transition economies. The KFM was designed at a time of high market interest rates, a depressed construction cycle, and a moribund public rental sector. After ten years of operations and important changes in the economy and housing markets, the following assessment could be made.

The funding of the KFM depends excessively on budgetary grants from the national housing budget. As repayment inflows from the long-term loans are marginal, any expansion is affected by planned budgetary cuts. Out of PLN5.3 billion of credits disbursed by the KFM until 2005, about PLN3.2 billion, or 60 percent, has been funded by government budget grants. The rest was mainly funded by long-term public debt contracted after 2002 from two multilateral institutions in order to keep expanding the program.

This vulnerability would be reduced if KFM loans were less subsidized. Narrowing the gap with market conditions seems increasingly needed for the next generation of KFM loans that would not target lower-income tenants. Co-financing and refinancing with commercial banks, as well as issuing domestic bonds, should be considered to relieve the pressure of budgetary funding. In order to bridge its funding needs, the KFM is currently considering refinancing by selling its current portfolio for a 20-year period to mortgage banks. It is also paying for the interest rate differential with the requested market rate, including a margin for the purchasing banks.

---

22. Households that provide a large down payment may not receive subsidies through low rents funded by subsidized credits.
23. Many of these households will not become legal owners when their incomes increase.

Conclusions

As mentioned in the introduction, rental financing in most developing countries is still in an emerging state. Although it can be argued that the circumstances vary a lot across developing countries, most often the reasons behind this lag can be found among the following main obstacles and bottlenecks.

In many countries, the environment remains hostile to a thriving private rental sector. In many emerging economies, some stumbling blocks remain for the development of formal rental markets, relating to the inadequateness of the legal and judiciary framework and to adverse macro-economic conditions. Such an adverse environment may in turn result in the absence of financial-sector involvement or absence of investors' demand for rental products or derivatives.

Among all the possible ways to finance rental housing, banking credit is likely to develop first in many countries, because the banking and financial infrastructure is already in place. It requires specialized lines of product that do not necessarily exist, however, even in countries where the banking system is fairly developed. Rental finance is a complex enterprise. Financing apartment communities—both existing buildings and new construction—is more complex than single-family financing, because of the greater diversity of properties and the perceived higher risk associated with apartments. In addition, unlike single-family construction, no standardized debt instruments or financing process exists and multiple funding needs and multiple funding sources are common. Affordable housing adds to this the need for additional subsidies or "gap financing" to bridge the shortfall between available debt and equity.

In the context of most emerging economies, helping the low-income populations through rental subsidies is challenging on many grounds. Making rental housing affordable amounts to finding ways to design "smart" subsidies in order to attract private capital toward rental housing. Rental subsidies, however, pose special challenges when compared to ownership subsidies. They tend to be fiscally expensive, and their implementation faces information problems. As a result, it is difficult to target the neediest populations.

The public sector alone cannot solve the housing problems of low-income households. More and more often, interventions on rental housing markets occur through public-private partnerships, by which different levels of government participate in various forms to the financing of the units located in their jurisdictions, together with private entities. The diversity of these partnerships across countries also suggests that there is no single best (one-size-fits-all) choice of partnerships in financing affordable rental housing. Rather, the solutions chosen should depend on the institutional context of the country (for example, the degree of executive and financial autonomy of local governments); on the tax system; on the development of the financial and capital markets; and on the fraction of the population that is targeted (private involvement is higher for middle-income households than for low-income households).

Selected countries
G21 O16
R21 E43
R31

CHAPTER 15

Housing Microfinance

*Franck Daphnis, with contributions from
the World Bank Housing Finance Group*

The Rise of Housing Microfinance

A home is the most important asset most people will ever own. Yet, access to housing finance is limited in most emerging economies, as residential mortgage lenders do not finance the housing needs of the poor, when exposed to large cash-flow and credit risks. Low-income households often lack the income to afford a market-rate mortgage for a completed house that meets common quality standards,[1] and lending remains limited to upper- and middle-income households with steady and verifiable incomes. Only in a few countries such as Mexico or Malaysia have mortgage lenders reached down to finance moderate- or median-income households. Beyond lending markets, most large-scale programs of housing subsidies have fallen far short of achieving their social objectives.

---

1. Rental may offer standard quality housing for the lowest-income groups. In emerging markets, squatting, land invasions, and informal rentals have emerged as responses to deficient formal housing markets.

As a result of these and other factors, the main funding sources for low-income households to acquire housing, besides their own savings, have been trade credit or neighborhood moneylenders at expensive credit terms (10 to 20 percent or more per month).

In this context, microfinance institutions (MFIs) have observed that some of their clients use micro-enterprise loans to improve their housing conditions[2] as a supplement or alternative to saving. Many client homes serve as both the micro entrepreneur's shelter and place of work. As a result, some MFIs have expanded their range of microfinance loans from enterprise lending to personal asset building (housing). The resulting housing microfinance (HMF) products are short-term, cash-flow-based loans for renovation and incremental construction purposes.

Micro loans can be useful for low-income households that have acquired a plot of land, but lack formal title, and that lack access to formal financial systems. By borrowing small amounts for successive short periods of time, such a household can finance discrete upgrades to a progressively self-built structure, such as an improved roof, a cement floor, or connections to municipal services. The short maturity of each loan suits the volatility of informal incomes. The lack of a mortgage lien is attractive to the poor who do not wish to put their most important asset at risk to secure a larger and longer-term loan, or who do not want to pay for additional fees to register a mortgage.

The development of HMF shows that economically active poor people can finance some of their housing needs incrementally and affordably and under conditions that allow the lender to cover all associated costs. HMF clients and traditional mortgage borrowers should in principle travel in different circles. If an individual is able to obtain a mortgage loan, that individual is bankable and can get a mortgage loan or a personal loan for home improvement purposes at a credit rate lower than what MFIs offer. At the same time, the HMF market (current and potential), comprises individuals with a demonstrable capacity to repay, albeit one that only MFIs recognize at the present time.

If ever supplied at a larger scale, HMF could play an important role in helping to provide an answer to the "qualitative" housing deficits,[3] and com-

2. Many microenterprises are located in the entrepreneur's home. See Ferguson and Haider 2000.
3. Qualitative deficits refer to the prevalence of substandard housing units. Quantitative deficits refer to the lack of sufficient units to house the population at an acceptable standard of space per inhabitant.

plement conventional mortgage markets that remain bordered by an "access frontier"—as developed by D. Porteous and FinMark—with the example in figure 15.1 of the Government and Banking Association charter target group in South Africa.[4]

The potential reach of HMF may be found among those who do not qualify under current banking criteria but would pay for a higher credit rate for a HMF loan. They are in the "current market" development zone of residential mortgage markets.

The emergence of HMF, its rise and financial performance (in terms of risk-adjusted profitability) in several countries has shown that innovative solutions can stretch traditional paradigms and offer effective finance alternatives to the poor. It is still early in the extension of microfinance to housing, however, and success has not yet been replicated on any significant scale beyond a few countries. While HMF has the potential to reach a sizeable proportion of households in countries with thriving microfinance

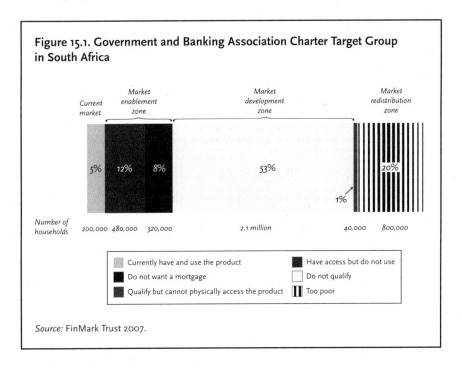

Figure 15.1. Government and Banking Association Charter Target Group in South Africa

Source: FinMark Trust 2007.

4. Definition paraphrased from Melzer 2006.

industries, HMF portfolios worldwide remain tiny relative to GDP or total bank assets. Other factors limiting HMF expansion include high rates and the reality that HMF is primarily a means of financing home improvement rather than new construction.

Still, the growth of HMF is relatively recent, and much remains to be done to document its successes and shortfalls, standardize its methods, and disseminate best practices. To date, there has not been much rigorous investigation of the potential size of HMF markets.

An Overview of Housing Microfinance[5]

HMF reaches clients who lack access to formal financial institutions and who cannot afford the payment on a mortgage loan, which would be large enough to finance a completed house situated on serviced urban land sold at market prices. Low income households generally earn informal and irregular incomes. In many emerging markets, the majority of the urban poor lack access to formal financial services. Mortgage lenders generally prefer to lend in larger amounts to upper and middle-income households that have larger, steady, and verifiable incomes and that hold the promise of consuming other financial services.

Rapid urbanization and the slow pace of development of urban services (water, sewage, energy) have raised the price of serviced and registered urban land in many countries beyond the reach of low income households. As a result, land invasions and gray markets in unregistered land have sprung up as a solution for poor households in need of shelter. Most of these households progressively build and improve their house as they can. They save in the form of building materials, accumulating until a new stage of construction is feasible. As governments recognize such settlements, formalize title, and retrofit services, the value of the occupied land acts as a subsidy element for the household.

Housing microfinance applies microfinance principles to the delivery of loans for house improvement or renovation for households that have obtained land. HMF typically comprises small loans (usually from $500 to $5,000) of

---

5. Definitions in this section are based on Daphnis and Ferguson 2004.

limited maturity (from six months to three years) generally without collateral. Though large by microfinance standards, HMF loans are small when compared to most mortgage loans. In Peru, HMF loans average approximately $1,000, while subsidized MiVivienda mortgage loans reach $30,000.

As with enterprise microfinance, the short maturity and relatively small size helps to control credit risk—the borrower has an incentive to repay the loan to receive another one. The microfinance methodology applies with financial and operational costs covered through interest and fees, a thorough knowledge of neighborhoods, additional guarantees from family members, and frequent contacts with the borrower. Most HMF clients have a good record of repaying previous enterprise microfinance loans.

HMF is often delivered with technical assistance to ensure the durability of the resulting construction. HMF typically serves micro-entrepreneurs and low income salaried employees. HMF is mainly used to finance progressive improvements to an existing dwelling or for the incremental construction of a home, rather the acquisition or construction of a complete new home. HMF loans may help borrowers purchase land, build sanitary amenities (latrines, sewer hookup), and in rare cases, can be pooled for the financing or partial financing of community infrastructure.[6]

A variety of institution types offer HMF loans, including: MFIs, non-microenterprise lending NGOs with a housing focus (such as Fundación Habitat y Vivienda, A.C. in Mexico), financial cooperatives (such as those affiliated with the Guatemalan Federal Credit Union), commercial banks involved with microfinance (for example, BancoSol in Bolivia, and specialized microfinance banks such as Tameer Bank in Pakistan), or traditional commercial banks (such as Crédit Libanais and Jammal Trust Bank in Lebanon).

Potential Size of HMF Markets: The Cases of Peru and Guatemala

HMF has reached relatively large scale in Peru. The success of HMF in Peru appears to result from three major factors: 1) the historical pattern of

---

6. SEWA Bank's Parivartan loan in India is a well-documented example for such pooling of HMF loans.

urbanization by low-income households, 2) the presence of a well-developed enterprise microfinance industry, and 3) the promotion of HMF by a market leader, MiBanco.

HMF suits the needs of the millions of Peruvian households that progressively built houses on lots acquired either in the gray market or through land invasions over the past four decades. More than 1.2 million of these households have benefited in recent years from title formalization programs. As these households have achieved security in their titles, they have a greater incentive to invest in improving their homes.[7] Most of these structures do not meet building codes, however, and so are not eligible for registration. Without a registered structure, the title to the lot is not sufficient to serve as collateral for a mortgage. Also, many of these lower-income households are reluctant to place their most important asset at risk to secure a mortgage. A series of micro credits to upgrade a house often suits circumstances and preferences better than a single, longer-term mortgage, even when the resulting HMF credit rate may exceed the mortgage credit rate.

Micro finance lenders in Peru operate in a regulated but relatively liberal environment, with the ability to freely design products to meet the needs of clients without limits on interest rates or fees. MiBanco has evolved from its nonprofit roots to become a profitable bank serving hundreds of thousands of clients, and has included HMF within its range of products. HMF now represents 15 percent of MiBanco's lending portfolio, and is expected to increase by 15 percent per year to reach a projected $348 million by 2011.[8] HMF is also estimated to represent at least 10 percent of all micro lending beyond MiBanco, and most non-bank MFIs (cajas and edpymes) plan to launch HMF products.[9]

Based on projections, HMF loans in Peru could amount to $700 million by 2011, or 20 to 30 percent of all microfinance lending. Given the average

---

7. Research shows that possession of formal title results in greater investments in the structure as well as improved social outcomes for affected families. See, for instance, Galiani and Schargrodsky 2006.
8. In Bolivia, a similar growth pattern has been observed, though the main lender BancoSol has decided to cap its total housing portfolio at 35 percent given the overwhelming demand from clients and the institution's desire to maintain a core focus on the enterprise lending market.
9. Assuming HMF portfolio share of 10 percent and a growth rate of 6 percent (observed current assets rate of growth), nonbank MFIs could potentially see their HMF portfolio rise to $214 million by 2011.

HMF loan size,[10] up to 7 percent of all households (460,000) could access HMF loans by 2011.

The case of Peru shows that under the right set of circumstances, HMF can be an effective tool in helping many lower-income households. Yet, it should be stressed that other countries remain far from reaching that scale, and that even in Peru the HMF portfolio represents less than 1 percent of GDP. By comparison, total bank loans now correspond to 15 percent of GDP.[11] The country's housing deficit is estimated at 1.3 million units, with an estimated 90,000 new homes required each year to ensure that the deficit does not increase.[12] HMF—despite the fertile ground found in Peru, the strides made over the past years, and the growth forecast—does not present a stand-alone solution to the country's housing problem.

Many countries are attempting to scale up their HMF system, but they face structural obstacles. For example, in Guatemala, HMF lenders (MFIs, cooperatives, NGOs) work successfully in the lower-income housing market, at commercial terms and with low defaults (less than 3 percent). Loan interest rates stand between 20 and 25 percent, loan maturities between one and three years, and the average loan amount is between $600 and $700.[13] But, in the absence of a specific legal or regulatory framework, the microfinance industry as a whole remains at a very small scale in Guatemala. While a few MFIs have risen to some local prominence, none have yet achieved the relative scale of MiBanco in Peru. The industry now makes 15 percent of all microfinance loans in Guatemala and one-third of the credits are made by cooperatives. HMF finances about 20 percent of the demand for home improvements and basic service provision. The demand is large and growing, but HMF lenders are constrained by their ability to raise funds. Most providers would like to secure commercial bank financing to continue their operations. Bank lending to HMF providers has doubled in the past 10 years, but is less than 2 percent of overall mortgage lending, which itself is less than 10 percent of overall lending. The Government of Guatemala is con-

10. HMF loan of $3,000 (currently, the average loan size in Peru for microfinance is $1,364, but housing loans should rise on average, reflecting a worldwide trend) and an average balance outstanding of $1,500.

11. Total mortgage loans correspond to 2 percent of GDP; total microfinance loans correspond to 2.5 percent of GDP.

12. Information culled from various sources, including the MiVivienda staff and Apoyo Consulting.

13. Analistas Financieros Internationales 2007.

sidering creating a fund that would partially guarantee loans from banks to HMF lenders for community upgrading and home improvement programs for families below the median-income level, where most of the problem of inadequate housing is concentrated.

Financial Performance of HMF

Although worldwide performance indicators on HMF portfolios are scarce, some comparisons can be made.[14] Table 15.1 presents the results from a regional survey from six MFI affiliated with Acción International and operating in Latin America.

HMF represents a relatively small percentage of their overall portfolio— with MiBanco and BancoSol as the two exceptions. Beyond the lenders listed in table 15.1, returns on equity in the 25 percent range or higher are not uncommon for large MFIs offering HMF in places such as Morocco (Al Amana, Zakoura, and the Foundation for Local Development and Partnership) or Pakistan (projected return on equity [ROE] for Tameer Bank in 2008).

HMF loans tend to perform better, from a portfolio-at-risk standpoint, than micro-enterprise lending, although the clientele and the guarantee requirements are nearly the same. In the case of Peru, microcredit portfolios in general perform better than banking-sector lending as a whole. Further, the data shows that HMF is usually priced somewhat lower than micro-enterprise lending, perhaps reflecting a perceived reduced risk. There is no specific return on assets (ROA) and ROE data for HMF, as most lenders are not able or willing to segregate return on a product-by-product basis. HMF lenders interviewed in Peru and Bolivia stated that rates of return were either on par with, or higher than, the traditional banking sector. The Banco de Crédito in Peru stated that its microfinance portfolio was the most profitable in the bank, along with the credit card business.

---

14. For older data, see Escobar and Merrill 2004.

Table 15.1. HMF Performance Indicators for Six MFIs in Latin America

	Mibanco (Peru)	BancoSol (Bolivia)	Banco Solidario (Ecuador)	FAMA (Nicaragua)	Integral (El Salvador)	El Comercio (Paraguay)
Loan portfolio (US$)						
Total institution	$207 m	$130 m	$207 m	$20 m	$17 m	$13 m
Mortgages	$4 m	n/a	$17 m	n/a	$0.5 m	n.a
HMF	$27 m	$45 m	$12 m	$2 m	n/a	$0.7 m
Proportion HMF/loans	12.8%	34.6%	5.7%	10.6%	n/a	5.4%
Maximum term (months)	60	60	36	n/a	48	24
Security of HMF loans	Co-signer	Co-signer or collateral for loans up to $6,000; mortgages for loans above $6,000	Co-signer	Mortgages and collateral	n/a	Collateral or personal co-signer
Interest rate (effective) monthly						
Total institution	2.63%	2.19%	1.10%	0.00%	2.15%	5.00%
HMF	3.06%	1.80%	1.70%	2.56%	n/a	2.72%
Estimated ROA (total institution)	14.10%	2.21%	1.85%	8.46%	3.64%	6.15%
Estimated ROE (total institution)	73.80%	19.35%	23.25%	21.55%	19.95%	28.74
Portfolio at risk > 30 days						
Total institution	1.26%	3.34%	4.17%	1.73%	11.48%	4.44%
HMF	1.24%	2.51%	n/a	3.20%	n/a	2.00%

Source: Acción International Survey 2002.
n/a = not available

Other Opportunities for Housing Microfinance

Questions frequently arise regarding HMF's potential role in relation to two commonly cited methods for serving the shelter needs of low-income households: (1) government-funded housing subsidies and (2) commercially viable banking services.

Limited Potential for Linking HMF and Housing Subsidies

Even in countries where HMF fills part of the financing gap of low-income families, public subsidies remain an important tool for improving the living conditions of the poor. Subsidies have historically taken many forms, the more successful of which include down-payment vouchers and slum upgrading programs.

In theory, MFIs could be seen as ideal institutions to better target and distribute subsidies, thanks to their track record in understanding the financial capacities of poor households, and because of their extensive branch networks and deployed staff in communities not typically served by traditional financial institutions.

But, the microfinance community has long opposed the concept of subsidies because of (i) its strategic drive toward "financial sustainability,"[15] and (ii) the inherent conflicts between qualifying an individual for a subsidy and assessing their capacity to repay a loan. On the one hand, to qualify for a housing subsidy, the individual has to demonstrate financial need and inadequate shelter. On the other hand, to qualify for a loan, the borrower wants to present the best financial picture possible. Successful MFIs strive to build a culture of loan underwriting and repayment by maintaining a strong network of loan officers who interview and visit their clients, assess their character and business prospects, reconstruct their cash flows, assess their credit risk, and collect payments. While the net financial picture of many poor families could

---

15. A consensus has emerged that while start-up support, operational grants, and portfolio guarantees are often necessary to help MFIs grow, interest rate subsidies and cash grants are conceptually anathema.

justify both a subsidy and a micro loan, it is difficult to build a corporate culture at the MFI that supports both types of operations simultaneously.

In the few instances where the cohabitation of HMF and subsidies has been documented, results are not encouraging. The Swedish International Development Agency (SIDA) supported MFIs in Costa Rica, Honduras, Guatemala, Nicaragua, and El Salvador throughout the 1990s, in an attempt to combine hybrid HMF and subsidy products. A 2004 SIDA-sponsored evaluation offered the following conclusion:

> Political considerations, bureaucratic inefficiencies, and financial mismanagement contributed to the fact that no SIDA program mixing HMF and housing subsidies is able to access the subsidies with which they were designed to work. As a result, supported MFIs have had to adjust their program design to offer their clients pure credit programs in lieu of the credit/subsidy mix several of these programs initially envisioned.[16]

In South Africa, one of the best-known examples of widespread use of capital subsidies for housing,[17] efforts to develop so-called "mezzanine" loan products, enabling qualifying families to supplement subsidies with small incremental loans, have so far failed to achieve results at any significant scale.[18] In Pakistan, Tameer Bank also experienced less-than-robust growth for its subsidy-linked housing microfinance loan,[19] while other products have turned Tameer into one of the fastest-growing banks in the country.

The difficulty is reduced if the client meets the income or housing criteria for the subsidy and produces evidence of sufficient cash flow to sup-

---

16. Daphnis and Faulhaber 2004, 74.
17. With the delivery of approximately 2 million housing subsidies for new home construction since 1994.
18. CHF International, working in the Eastern Cape, notably attempted to develop such a loan product through its CEBI affiliate in the late 1990s and early 2000s. PELIP, a SIDA-supported housing finance institution, also unsuccessfully sought to offer HMFs linked to subsidies during the same period. The Kuyasa Fund has also developed an HMF loan that clients can use as a "top-off" to subsidies. Though Kuyasa hopes to expand the product, total outreach has been limited to 2,500 clients.
19. Tameer offers a three-year, $1,700 home improvement loan to qualifying families who have participated in a government-funded relocation project in Karachi through which the government provided beneficiary families with land, titling documentations, and the foundations for a new home.

port the repayment of a HMF loan. Even so, as documented in the case of the Foundation for Rural and Urban Housing Development, problems emerge in instances where the same MFI manages both the need-based subsidy and the demand-driven loan, as the subsidy amount is inversely related to the credit amount (the proportion of subsidy would decrease as income rises, the proportion of the credit component would increase). The Foundation for Rural and Urban Housing Development product was similar to others experimented by SIDA throughout Central America in the 1990s, with little success. The Foundation for Rural and Urban Housing Development's experiment reached a similar fate, with a portfolio-at-risk exceeding 60 percent.

Key observations from the SIDA report include the following:

> Worldwide experience of credit and subsidy suggests that, while they can coexist alongside one another, two basic rules should apply:

> The credit provider and the subsidy provider should, preferably, be two different organizations. MFIs should focus on understanding, finding, and qualifying potential clients with a sufficient enough income to afford a housing microfinance loan. Subsidy providers should focus on understanding, finding, and qualifying potential beneficiaries whose income or economic and social circumstances are such that they would qualify for a subsidy.

> Subsidy and credit should not be mixed as part of a single package. This is not to say that one household could not be the benefit of a subsidy at one point in time and of a loan at another. It means that loan eligibility should be independent from the availability of a subsidy (in case, as is unfortunately often the case, the subsidy does not materialize or dries up over time).

> [With respect to HMF with direct subsidies to clients], HMF programs can be designed to work alongside subsidy programs, so long as loan disbursements are not dependent on subsidies disbursements [...] It is not advisable for the HMF retailer to also be the organization making the decisions on loan subsidies.

These experiences suggest MFIs should steer clear of simultaneously offering credit lines and subsidies to the same client through the same loan officer. Although in theory an MFI could find a way to create a "firewall" between the credit assessment and the subsidy qualification, in practice it will be difficult for the MFI to manage both processes.

Linkages between Commercial Banks and Housing Microfinance

The example of Banco de Crédito in Peru suggests that HMF can constitute a lucrative line of business for banks, at least for those which invest in the capacity to deliver HMF loans, including product development, specialized human resource acquisition and training, and adjustment to traditional delivery channels. The potential for HMF to become incorporated into the operations of banks is rather a function of these banks' interest in developing an overall microfinance portfolio, than a specific interest in HMF. The investment required to develop an HMF product is minimal if the bank already supplies individual micro-enterprise loans to its clients—especially if the bank provides no construction assistance with the HMF loan.

In many countries like Guatemala or Morocco, commercial banks have indirectly supported the development of HMF industry by providing some market-priced refinancing credit lines to the MFI in order to develop this new range of products. This banking activity is based on the overall financial strength of the MFI institutions, rather than on the quality of their unsecured HMF portfolio.

At present, banks have pursued three main avenues in directly developing microfinance windows that would also accommodate HMF. First is the servicing model, whereby an MFI helps the bank to service the microfinance portfolios of commercial banks (for example, the Access to Microfinance and Enhanced Enterprise Niches program in Lebanon teaming up with the Jammal Trust Bank and Crédit Libanais). Second is bank "downscaling," whereby an established commercial bank sets up a microfinance unit within the bank itself to manage its microfinance portfolio (such as Banque du Caire in Egypt). Last is the creation of stand-alone subsidiaries that are themselves regulated microfinance institutions (such as Sogesol and Microcredit

National in Haiti, owned by SogeBank and UniBank, the two largest banks in the country).

In the foreseeable future, it seems reasonable to expect that housing will be part of the second wave of products commercial banks develop subsequent to their entry into the microfinance market, with micro-enterprise lending continuing to provide the entry point into the market. Donors and governments interested in promoting HMF as a banking product would be well advised to focus their efforts on banks that have already become familiar with enterprise microfinance services.

Other forms of partnerships between banks and MFI can be developed to extend the scope of products accessible to lower-income households, from HMF loans to mortgage loans, according to the size of the housing investment, loan amount, and term. Banks and MFI can combine their respective strengths to deliver HMF and mortgage loans, not just distinct products by distinct institutions.

In Morocco, two MFI foundations (Zakoura and El Amana) are already active in providing small HMF loans to their clients mostly for existing housing improvement purposes. But, part of their creditworthy clients want to acquire new homes through a special subsidized program, which require former slum dwellers to contract larger and longer-term mortgage loans, although small compared to average bank mortgage practice and foremost among an unbanked population. Both foundations signed an agreement with a prominent private commercial bank, Banque Marocaine du Commerce Extérieur (Morocco), in order to commercialize and underwrite Banque Marocaine du Commerce Extérieur mortgage loans for low-income, non-salaried clients (service provided on a fixed-fee basis). The Banque Marocaine du Commerce Extérieur reduces its exposure through a credit-risk-sharing arrangement mechanism with a public guarantee fund, Fogarim. At a later stage, some MFIs are expected to seek the long-term funding and expertise— and modify their organization and procedures—in order to directly originate mortgage loans. Some MFIs (including MiBanco and BancoSol) have been already offering mortgages to their clients, as part of their diversification strategy.

The Limitations of Housing Microfinance

Wherever micro-enterprise lending thrives—in countries as disparate as Indonesia, Morocco, Kenya, or Mexico—clients also make use of borrowed funds to finance housing improvements. The microfinance industry acknowledges this phenomenon and has a term for it: "fungibility." Households may borrow for the stated purpose of acquiring a specific fixed asset and use the money toward another end, including housing rehabilitation. It is nevertheless fair to observe that HMF, marketed as an explicit service through MFIs or other microfinance lenders, constitutes an emerging product and that the promise for scale and impact has yet to fully materialize on a widespread basis.

Market Size

Even in the most favorable circumstances it is difficult to envision more than 10 percent of any country's households to access HMF loans. In some cases, this could amount to several million customers and contribute to significant reductions in national qualitative housing deficits. Two important cautionary notes should accompany this observation. First, and as evidenced in the case of Peru, a number of prerequisites must be in place in order to achieve this market penetration, including a large and profitable microfinance industry, a supportive enabling environment, and an institutional champion. In countries meeting these conditions and where demand for incremental housing finance exists, it is reasonable to expect that the examples of MiBanco and BancoSol would be emulated. Second, the small size of HMF loans implies that even with a deep market penetration, HMF loans will weight a small percentage of the total financial sector, even if the size of HMF markets grows along with broader microfinance. The projection for HMF in Peru (1 percent of GDP within five years) remains a goal to which no other country has come close.[20]

---

20. To the degree that large commercial banks such as ICICI in India prepare to enter the urban housing microfinance market on a national scale, it is possible that this 1 percent threshold will be exceeded in the long term.

Pricing and Access

Prevailing HMF credit rates—for example, 37 percent on a yearly base charged by MiBanco—constitute an impediment to scaling beyond traditional microfinance markets, as these rates tend to be several times higher than traditional consumer or mortgage loans of banks. High interest rates represent the price of access to non-collateralized lending for a riskier clientele that generally lack alternatives.

MFIs justify high rates in terms of the need to cover higher financial and operational costs, as well as in some cases to return a profit to their shareholders. The higher credit risk of unsecured loans to borrowers that lack resources, the costs of more labor intensive microfinance underwriting and servicing, the smaller economies of scale relative to traditional banking, and the lack of access to institutional funding constitute the prime factors underlying MFI's pricing. Though efficiency gains have been observed as the industry grows, the average operating cost ratio for profitable MFIs was

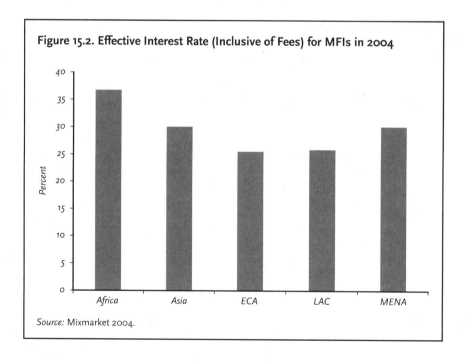

Figure 15.2. Effective Interest Rate (Inclusive of Fees) for MFIs in 2004

Source: Mixmarket 2004.

still 12 percent in 2004 and 27 percent for unprofitable MFIs.[21] Other factors behind high-interest rates include (i) insufficient competition in most HMF markets in the initial stage, and (ii) the lack of infrastructure platforms to reduce transaction costs (for example, such as that built by Cemex's Patrimonio Hoy program in Mexico to have building material suppliers accept a standardized credit card to simplify the disbursement of HMF loans).

As banks enter microfinance and as competition increases, interest rates charged may decrease. It is also possible to envision a transition phase, however, in many countries where the supply of HMF would grow more slowly and still at high-interest rates. This could occur if a few dominant HMF lenders prefer to extract greater consumer surplus on fewer loans rather than diverting scarce resources from their highly profitable and fast-growing core business. This would be the case if HMF is seen as risky and complex in comparison to enterprise microfinance. In such cases, competition can be facilitated by external funding or guarantees supplied to competing HMF lenders.

More broadly, it is unlikely that HMF interest rates will ever fall to the same level as those charged for consumer or mortgage loans by banks. The risks and costs are different. This reality should be recognized by policy makers, who may otherwise apply counterproductive social and political pressure against higher lending rates for lower-income households, notably when subsidies are also provided, or when the government shares credit risk with lenders (for example, the guarantee fund Fogarim in Morocco).

The fact that HMF rates are high has raised issues of consumer protection—and in some countries the loans may even run afoul of usury laws. The best solutions for reducing HMF rates, however, lie in competition and reduced risk rather than in regulatory limits on interest rates. Where such limits have been introduced, low-income borrowers are left with informal moneylenders that charge much more than MFIs. For example, Colombia has imposed a limit of 11 percent on the real interest rate, including fees that may be charged for all social housing loans. Since the resulting nominal rate is inadequate to compensate for cost and risk, HMF is not available in

---

21. *Micro-banking Bulletin* Issue No 12, April 2006. http://www.mixmarket.org/medialibrary/mixmarket/MBB12_2006.pdf.

Colombia. Lenders need to be able to charge prices for their services that reflect the risks and costs that they bear.

Beyond a certain point, the level of income does not represent the main barrier for a bank, but rather the lack of income documentation, instability of income, and the lack of housing collateral. These are themes better mastered by MFIs for the economically active poor. So, a typical microfinance borrower that is able to repay a $1,500 loan within 18 months, may as well repay a $15,000 loan over a longer 20-year period if either banks or MFIs made such a product available.[22]

Whether regulated financial institutions can develop mortgage products that actually reach out to a majority of these potential clients in the near future remains doubtful, in light of land tenure issues, the inadequacy of foreclosure and asset transfer regulations, and the informality of income irregularity. HMF thus represents an important complementary part of the "market development" zone for mortgage lending.

Refinancing and Other Microfinance Limitations

The examples of MiBanco in Peru, BancoSol in Bolivia, and the Foundation for Local Development and Partnership in Morocco suggest that the growth of housing microfinance can be swift once the product is aggressively marketed to a microfinance clientele. Limitations inherent in the microfinance model as it currently exists, however, may prove constraining in the long term. The limitations include, notably:

REFINANCING

The ability of MFIs to finance themselves over the long run ranks high among the challenges facing the microfinance community. Regulated microfinance

---

22. An unlikely occurrence as noted elsewhere. Commercial banks may view this client as an unacceptable risk because he or she probably lives in an informal settlement, offers no tangible collateral and his or her income cannot be properly documented. Furthermore, current income may be too unstable to support a long-term repayment obligation, particularly if the products on offer do not feature payment flexibility. An MFI that is able to document the income through its know-how, would still be unlikely to extend a loan beyond three or four years, as short repayment periods are a key element in the MFI risk management strategy.

banks such as MiBanco in Peru, BancoSol in Bolivia, and Tameer bank in
Pakistan, while a growing phenomenon, remain the exception rather than
the norm in the world of microfinance. More often than not, non-bank organizations ranging from foundations, to NGOs, to special associations dominate national microfinance markets. Regulators, legitimately, often preclude
them from mobilizing savings from clients. Though MFIs have devised ingenious methods to work around these constraints,[23] increased regulation of
the industry will mean that the cheapest and most desirable form of portfolio
financing (deposits and savings accounts) is not an option for many HMF
lenders. Equity financing is also not a sustainable funding, which leaves grant
funding and debt financing as the prevalent funding sources. In the case of
non-regulated institutions, such debt comes at a market-base price (regular
retail credit rate plus the cost of credit enhancements). As MFIs grow in size
and profitability and eventually undergo the transformation into regulated
financial institutions capable of capturing savings, acquiring debt at interbank rates, or accessing capital markets, the refinancing burden will logi-
cally ease. For most MFIs around the world, even in thriving markets such
as Morocco, this has yet to become a reality and as a result, documented
demand for HMF continues to go underserved.[24]

SPECIFICITY OF MICROFINANCE METHODOLOGY

If one solution to the challenge of microfinance portfolio financing lies
in MFIs becoming regulated and being able to access cheaper sources of
financing, an alternative option has been for regulated institutions to go
"down market" and serve traditional microfinance clients through any of the
three models described previously. All three show that large regulated institutions can leverage their position and their access to capital to enter the
microfinance market. These successful examples also suggest that they will

---

23. For instance, MFIs in Yemen collect compulsory cash "collateral" payments from clients
that are reimbursed when the loan reaches maturity. This practice is common in the Yemeni
microfinance community even though the central bank prohibits MFIs from offering savings
accounts to clients.
24. The Foundation for Local Development and Partnership in Morocco reported this lack of
financing options as the major reason behind its decision to hold off on expanding its HMF
portfolio, despite exploding demand since the institution began offering the product in 2005.

only do so with the support of rigorous and often complex organizational arrangements. The successful delivery of microfinance services cannot be improvised. It is dependent on a commitment to a microfinance "culture" and to methods for client origination and follow-up, line staff management, and field-based work that can differ significantly from the established practices of more traditional banks. This required level of commitment (and to a certain extent, the inability to relate) to a different management culture and mode of operation explains, in large part, why commercial banks have yet to rush and embrace the microfinance world, despite the promise of high returns and expanding market share.

Potential to Contribute to Entrenchment of Informality

Housing microfinance often provides financial access to clients who do not formally own the land on which their dwelling is built. The HMF literature puts forth the concept of land "security," rather than proper ownership as an operative criterion for MFIs in deciding whether it is acceptable to approve an HMF loan.[25] Practicality dictates flexibility on ownership criterion, as many MFI clients do not actually own the land they occupy, often living in informal or precarious settlements. By lending to such clients, though, MFIs may play an inadvertent role in the entrenchment of informal housing. In some cases, such as with the Inter-American Development Bank in Central America in the mid-1990s, donors have attempted to link HMF loans to land regularization programs. Such programs, however, have a limited impact and have not held the promise of large-scale replication.

Conclusion

Microfinance has an important role to play in the context of a comprehensive country-level housing finance strategy. HMF should be the key product

---

25. Land security for housing microfinance exists when (1) a client has the use of the property when the loan is made, (2) the MFI determines that the client will not be forced to vacate the property during the time it takes to repay the loan, and (3) that determination is supported by customary practices. See Daphnis and Tilock (2001).

when poor and low-income-earning families seek to improve the condition of their existing homes. Within the broader spectrum of housing finance, the comparative advantage of HMF consists of helping poor and low-income-earning households to access home improvement and incremental construction finance. Provided clients possess a minimal capacity to repay a loan under microfinance conditions, HMF potentially offers a reliable, if incremental, path toward transforming a ramshackle dwelling into a livable home. HMF is not the "silver bullet" that will solve the challenge of universal access to homes and is not a suitable solution for large-scale, non-subsidized, new home constructions, the provision of which remains the major challenge in many of the countries where HMF thrives. Policy makers should therefore not promote HMF as the primary solution for filling quantitative housing shortages, even if HMF can play a vital role in reducing qualitative shortages. HMF is not a substitute for affordable long-term mortgages. Rather, the specific promise of HMF is that it may provide reliable financing to those who do not qualify for a mortgage, but are solvent enough to borrow in order to improve the quality of their existing dwelling.

As MFIs grow and as HMF develops into a mainstream microfinance service, the HMF industry faces scaling-up issues as long as commercial banks express no appetite for such products (although, as the BCP example shows, this mindset is beginning to evolve).

HMF can work alongside housing subsidies programs, but it is advisable that the provision of microfinance loans and of cash subsidies be separated from one another.

CHAPTER 16

Housing Finance Subsidies

Marja C. Hoek-Smit

Housing plays a special role in the social and political dialogue in most societies.[1] It is often the largest single category of household expense, and the housing sector is a large part of the economy. Housing is also a major component in creating stable and healthy communities and a very visible indicator of social conditions. These economic and social characteristics of the housing sector are the reason that almost all societies intervene in housing markets through an array of policies intended to increase housing consumption by various groups. This chapter focuses on one category of government intervention in housing markets—subsidies related to housing finance, that is, the way in which the housing asset is being paid for. Housing finance subsidies can be applied to reduce equity contributions and improve availability and lower cost of debt for construction, sale, and resale of housing in the ownership

---

1. This chapter uses parts of unpublished materials for a forthcoming book on housing finance subsidies produced by Marja C. Hoek-Smit and Douglas Diamond commissioned under a collaborative agreement between the World Bank Housing Finance Group and the International Housing Finance Program, Wharton School, University of Pennsylvania.

and investment markets. Of all forms of housing subsidies,[2] housing finance subsidies are among the most prevalent policy tools and are currently much discussed in the context of overall reforms of housing finance systems.

The current period of macroeconomic stability, sustained economic growth, and lower interest rates in a growing number of developing and emerging market economies has caused governments to take a look at the existing housing subsidy policies and program, which were often designed during periods of turbulent macroeconomic conditions that prevented the development of financial systems in general and housing finance in particular. Much progress has been made by many governments in improving the conditions for financial sector development[3] and in strengthening the legal infrastructure for housing finance. Some examples include improved land-titling and property registration systems and transferability of titles; greater enforceability of contracts, including foreclosure procedures; and reforms in judicial systems that are frequently strongly biased in favor of the underdog.[4] Such macroeconomic and legal improvements have increased the interest of the private sector in expanding the scale and extent of its mortgage and consumer lending for housing. Current subsidy systems are often not well aligned. These changing circumstances and the expansion of formal housing markets to lower-middle income groups have been disappointing in many countries. In addition, most such subsidies are linked to mortgage finance and are not accessible for low-income households.

Major structural problems in the sector remain in many countries, often because of the large role of government-owned housing finance institu-

---

2. The universe of possible subsidies is quite large. It includes production subsidies (for example, land and infrastructure, reduced standards), tax subsidies (for example, property tax abatement, mortgage interest deductions), capital expense subsidies (for example, reduced interest rates, investor guarantees), operating expense subsidies (for example, for public rental housing, heat and utility subsidies), and general housing-expense subsidies (for example, housing allowances, up-front cash grants). Price controls are yet another form of housing "subsidy" through regulatory controls.

3. A recent IMF study showed the importance of structural reforms for the financial sector as a whole in terms of benefits for growth and stability, drawing on a large sample of countries (Kose, Prasad, Rogoff, and Wei 2006).

4. Comparative data for European countries compiled by MacLennan, Muellbauer, and Stephens (1999) indicate that asymmetries in market structure, institutions, and tax policies affect the degree of competition in the housing finance system and the related extension of housing finance more than relative income levels and have far-reaching implications on macroeconomic policy. Other studies show that micro-level housing finance policies have a greater impact on (formal) homeownership rates than the income level of countries in their sample (Chiuri and Jappeli 2003).

tions. Central banks and finance ministries are under pressure to commercialize or privatize the many state-supported or state-owned housing finance systems. They are also under pressure to curb the deep institutional and nontransparent subsidies that have often led to unanticipated liabilities to the state in the past and have hindered private market entry into the sector. Structural reforms have proven difficult because of current subsidized housing finance institutions' fear that they will lose their privileges,[5] in addition to the lingering perception by governments (housing ministries, in particular) that the state is more efficient in allocating scarce housing credit to large segments of society. Indeed, the risk that governments will unexpectedly change the rules and regulations to which private lenders have to comply is still a major reason why banks are reluctant to enter. High real interest rates, or lingering volatility in inflation, are generally continuing to limit housing affordability and long-term lending in several countries (for example, Brazil, Turkey, Indonesia). Private lenders are reluctant to expand their lending operations to underserved markets that are considered more risky, because the mechanisms to deal with those risks are inadequate. It is indeed uncommon that households below the 70th or 60th percentile of the income distribution or those employed in the informal sector have access to mortgage finance, and frequently not more than 10 or 20 percent of housing transactions uses finance (Angel 2000). Additionally, constraints in the land market and land-development sector have driven up prices of housing in many countries and contribute to the limited scale of formal housing supply, while demand is growing because of decreasing interest rates, increasing real incomes, and growing urban populations. Without elastic land and housing supply, improvements in housing finance merely generate price effects (Mayo 1993).[6]

Many governments in emerging market and developing economies therefore face a fourfold challenge in expanding housing finance systems downmarket and the related reform of their housing subsidy policy. They have to (1) reform subsidized state housing finance institutions as a prerequisite to

---

5. This phenomenon has been observed by Rajan and Zingales 2003, for the financial sector in general.
6. The World Bank in its 1993 programmatic shelter paper, "Enabling Housing Markets to Work," undertook the last available comprehensive review of land conversion and servicing multipliers globally (Mayo and Angel 1993). The analysis revealed inefficiencies of the supply processes in much of the developing world.

creating a more competitive and efficient housing finance system, (2) provide institutional incentives (mostly regulatory, but also subsidy incentives) to strengthen the private housing-finance sector and stimulate efficient lending without exposing the state to excessive risk or moral hazard, (3) reform household subsidies to improve their targeting to well-defined segments of the housing market and specific underserved groups of household, and (4) improve real-side institutions and subsidies and regulatory environments to allow expansion of down-market housing supply. These transformations require that consumer subsidies, now flowing through state-owned lending or land development institutions and often implicit and poorly targeted, be rationalized.

This chapter intends to assist that process by providing the context for such broad analyses. It will focus on finance subsidies and only flag the importance of reforms of real side subsidies and regulations. It discusses separately the different subsidies to address constraints in the housing-finance system and subsidies that assist individual households to access finance and pay for better housing. Specific subsidy programs are briefly discussed in boxes in the text and are elaborated in a separate volume on housing finance subsidies by the same authors to be published by the World Bank and the Wharton International Housing Finance Program. The chapter starts out with a discussion of how to frame a subsidy policy.

Where to Start?
Linking Housing Problems to Subsidy Policy

Analyzing the Causes of the Housing Problems

Unlike advanced economies whose housing systems and housing finance institutions have evolved gradually over an entire century and whose policy issues usually involve only modest incremental changes in existing systems, emerging market economies also have to deal with fundamental questions such as property rights, public regulations, and structural problems in the housing finance sector, while under political pressure to do something about housing conditions of a large proportion of urban households that are perceived as unacceptable. The multitude and depth of problems can feel overwhelming to policy makers. All too often the response is to embark on ill-advised attempts to adopt practices from other countries that may be inappropriate to solve the housing problems in the country. Another frequent reaction is to request more subsidies for the housing sector, while in reality the subsidies to the housing sector are already high in most emerging market countries, but are hidden and are not allocated efficiently and equitably.

What is needed in many countries is an in-depth, broad-scaled inquiry into the nature, breadth, and causes of their housing problems and a similar wide-ranging review of existing subsidy programs, their depth, and current beneficiary groups and their performance. Based on such diagnostic analysis government can define long-term policy goals and medium- and short-term programmatic actions—a road map—to achieve greater private-sector participation and address housing problems of those population segments that cannot yet be served by market forces, even with government incentives. The complexity of that process makes it necessary to have high-level political and administrative commitment for a multiyear and multifaceted reform program.

Such straightforward exercises would create, within a short time, the general basis for initial housing policy analysis because pertinent housing issues will be out in the open and can be discussed at various levels of government and among government and private-sector agents in the housing market. It will show the gaps in access to formal housing and housing programs for different income and employment groups that may not have been realized by policy makers because of the hidden nature of many subsidies. Examples of countries that have recently implemented such exercises and have followed up through a medium-term strategic plan for the sector are Latvia, South Africa, and Thailand, and several countries have recently engaged in such processes, for example, Brazil, Mexico, Peru, Colombia, Korea, Indonesia, Vietnam, and Morocco.

The outcome of such broad-based housing-sector analysis would ideally be the identification of specific market segments for different types of housing and housing-finance products and their frontiers, that is, the margin beyond which specific demand and supply constraints limit expansion of and access to these markets. The following are the usual broad market segments to which government interventions may most fruitfully be directed and the areas where expansion of opportunities is most likely:

- Middle- and lower-middle-income market segment (typically upward from the 40th or 50th percentile of the income distribution) where household incomes would be adequate to obtain formal moderate-income housing, but most live in unauthorized or substandard formal housing. The frontier for expanding the formal housing market downward for this segment is not so much constrained by low incomes, although that is certainly part of it, but by lack of access to finance related to informal employment, lack of wealth or savings, uncertain collateral because of poor land registration and cadastre systems, alternative types of property rights or neighborhood risk factors, inefficiencies and incompleteness of housing finance markets, and the related lack of appropriate housing products delivered by the market. In some countries, housing-finance-linked subsidy programs allow households at the top of this income bracket to obtain formal-sector new housing. But regulatory constraints on the real side and controls on rental markets often form barriers to expansion of formal housing for the unassisted part of this market segment, and upward mobility out of unauthorized or substandard formal housing is limited.
- Low-income or perceived high-risk segments of the market where households live in substandard housing or substandard neighborhoods with limited access to services. These are typically households below the 40th percentile of the income distribution or households that are considered not creditworthy, such as informally or self-employed households, or households whose collateral is considered inappropriate for lien-based mortgage lending. Housing subsidies for this segment are often limited to selected upgrading programs. Formal housing markets seldom deliver new housing for this segment and the challenge is to provide effective government incentives to bring more households into the formal housing sector. The frontier for expansion of formal, healthful low-income housing is often two-dimensional: 1) the frontier for improvement of existing housing conditions is confined by lack of infrastructure, formally registered property rights, inadequate regulations, and lack of access to consumer or microcredit for home improvement; 2) the frontier for new low-income housing is constrained mostly by a combination of low incomes and a lack of access to appropriate financial instruments,

Table 16.1. **Potential Access to Housing Finance in Mexico, 2006**

Households in the formal economy	6% have no access to mortgage finance and limited access to microfinance	16% have access to subsidized mortgage finance	25% have access to subsidized and market mortgage finance
Households in the informal economy	24% have no access to mortgage finance and limited access to microfinance	17% have limited access to mortgage finance	12% have access to market mortgage finance
Monthly income	Less than US$420	US$420–840	More than US$840

Source: CONAVI.

and nonfunctioning land markets, regulatory issues, and poor permitting procedures that drive up the price of housing unnecessarily. Microfinance lending, even if it is available, will not be the solution for large-scale development of new housing for this market segment because of its rate structure, but it can play an important role in progressive housing models. Expansion and strengthening of existing credit cooperatives or mutual credit unions may, however, be relevant for the top end of this segment.

The relative proportion of households in each category will differ in each country, and so will the specific causes of the housing problems.[7] Table 16.1 shows a simple assessment of the proportion of households in Mexico that would potentially qualify for a mortgage based on income, available house products, and interest rates for that market niche.

This example shows that 47 percent of households would not be able to access mortgage finance because incomes are too low or insecure, or house prices of "acceptable" collateral or interest rates price households out of the market. Without mortgage-linked subsidies to formal-sector employees that pay into the labor tax funds this figure would be even higher. Yet Mexico is a middle-income country where the mortgage sector is developing rapidly and nominal interest rates have come down to the 10 percent level. It is therefore not surprising that in many emerging market economies with less favorable income and finance-sector conditions 60 to 70 percent of new households

---

7. For example, in transition economies, the second market segment may not exist or it may be in the form of substandard condominiums or rental units (or mixed rental-ownership buildings) for which it is difficult to attract improvement loans.

Table 16.2. Affordable Loan/House Price Scenario

Urban households		Urban household expenditure percentile								
	10th	20th	30th	40th	50th	60th	70th	80th	90th
Monthly income, based on expenditures *	310	450	351	610	770	840	1,085	1,285	1,775
Borrowing capacity	10%	15%	20%	20%	20%	20%	20%	20%	20%
Monthly payment capacity	31	68	102	122	154	168	217	257	355
Term	2	5	7	15	15	15	15	15	15
Interest rate–nominal	30%	30%	20%	17%	17%	17%	17%	17%	17%
Affordable loan	554	2,086	4,593	7,927	10,006	10,916	14,100	16,699	23,067
Savings effort/down payment	10%	10%	20%	20%	30%	30%	50%	50%	50%
Afford with loan alone	554	2,086	4,593	7,927	10,006	10,916	14,100	16,699	23,067
Afford with down payment	616	2,318	5,742	9,909	14,295	15,594	28,200	33,398	46,134

Source: Author's calculations.
* in U.S. dollars

Box 16.1. Example of Income and Finance Affordability

The stylized "affordability" distribution of a fairly typical emerging market country shown in table 16.2 calculates the house price that households at each income decile can afford if they use either mortgage credit or consumer or microcredit at nominal market rates. At the time this calculation was made, the lowest-priced house in the formal urban housing market in a city approximately 40 km outside one of the main metropolitan areas was $25,000 and could only be afforded by the 75th percentile of the income distribution and only with a 50 percent down payment. Supply of this type of house at a national level was only a tiny fraction of the yearly increase in the number of households in the 70th percentile group alone. As a consequence, only a small part of the requirement for new housing each year can be fulfilled through the construction of standard private-sector-provided houses and the subsequent filtering up of lower-income households (for example, up from the 40th or 50th percentile) into the vacated houses. *
This situation puts strong pressure on government to provide high subsidies for middle-income households.

   The bottom half of the income distribution has no access to adequate new market-provided housing nor can it finance the purchase of existing housing. Access to credit was minimal for households below the 40th percentile. The country had small upgrading programs and deeply subsidized but small (relative to urban household growth) government-funded new housing programs, and most low-income households have no choice other than to self-construct houses in unauthorized settlements. Several attempts by the federal government to subsidize developers and lenders to construct and finance a $10,000 house, based on the premise that households were to access housing finance to complement these up-front subsidies, were thwarted because lenders would not provide loans to this segment. Such programs ended in providing free houses for the lucky few and no expansion of the lower-income housing market.

---

* The concept of filtering is used to describe the process by which successively lower-income households move gradually into better-quality existing housing when supply of new housing allows those with relatively higher incomes to move into standard new housing.

coming into the market each year cannot afford to pay for the lowest-cost house produced in the formal sector.

The example in box 16.1 shows a hypothetical housing affordability analysis based on income and different types of debt finance with different loan terms and interest rates for different market segments. In this example, nominal (and, importantly, real) interest rates are much higher, loan terms are shorter, and down-payment requirements are higher than in the Mexico example, and as a consequence housing affordability is lower. Such a gap in affordability cannot possibly be filled by household subsidies in typical emerging market countries.

Successful approaches to expand the frontiers of different housing market segments must deal with critical supply bottlenecks on the real side and in the housing finance sector to create an upward filtering of households into better-quality formal housing appropriate for each income level. While normal market forces will gradually expand these frontiers, well-targeted regulatory or subsidy actions are often necessary to accelerate this process.

Subsidies and Other Types of Government Intervention

So far the concept of a subsidy has been defined loosely. Subsidies are incentives to change behavior either of consumers or lenders and producers of housing to achieve specific goals and objectives (box 16.2). While this is an inclusive definition of subsidies, the focus in this chapter is on two types of subsidy interventions: (i) modifying regulatory or legal policy related to housing finance to shift market activity in certain ways to reach social or eco-

---

Box 16.2. Defining Subsidies

Subsidies are often perceived as giving or receiving something for free. That notion is misleading. From a broad perspective, "a subsidy is an incentive provided by government to enable and persuade a certain class of producers or consumers to do something they would not otherwise do, by lowering the opportunity cost or otherwise increasing the potential benefit of doing so" (adapted from the U.S. Congress [1969]).

nomic goals, and (ii) expending financial resources (both through budgetary allocation and fiscal policies) or taking risks to support desired behavior or address specific market failures (for example, externalities). For example, a government may establish a liquidity facility to increase the efficiency of certain segments of the mortgage market or to make the mortgage market more attractive relative to other segments of the financial system.

Subsidies can be difficult to identify, however, because of the hidden nature of some subsidies, particularly in the housing finance sector. For example, the creation of a government mortgage-insurance program ostensibly run on full market principles may imbed deep subsidies either because administration costs are not accounted for, initial capital is provided by government at no cost, or the presence of catastrophic risk being borne by the government is ignored.

Because subsidies can be costly and distorting, they should be a policy of last resort, after or in conjunction with other policy steps that are low cost. Much has been written about the enabling policies required for housing markets to work well (Mayo 1983; Angel 2001).

Some critical measures to improve identified housing problems may not be related to housing directly, but may involve macroeconomic or fiscal measures to improve the stability of the financial system or the overall income distribution. There may be a need for policies to improve the business climate in certain areas or to adjust labor laws to encourage more people to obtain formal-sector employment, which may have a positive impact on housing investments. But other problems require housing or housing finance-sector policies to support the demand side or the supply side of the market. Many potentially important regulatory and institutional improvements in the housing finance sector have been discussed in previous chapters.

In this connection, it is important to emphasize the negative effects of *inappropriate government regulations and institutions* on market outcomes. For example, unnecessarily strict building, planning, and subdivision standards, poor property rights and registration systems, excessive government involvement in the urban land or housing finance sectors, rent control, and other policy or regulatory bottlenecks may frustrate the efforts of the market to serve all portions of the population. The highest priority for government action under these circumstances is to remove or adjust such institutional and regulatory bottlenecks before any subsidies are considered that compensate for poor market outcomes.

The challenge for central government is that most such policies and regulations on the real side are in the political realm of local government, which is often under political pressure *not* to allow low-income developments. Furthermore, it often has limited analytical capacities to assess the impact of poor regulations and development procedures. Benefits of reform of nontransparent systems are frequently limited or even negative for local-level parties, which makes it difficult to change such systems. It often requires central-government subsidy incentives for local governments to undertake the necessary enabling policies (see also Mayo 1999).

Paradoxically then, it often takes strong central government incentives to unblock local-level housing markets for lower-income households, whether through sticks (conditional withholding of housing-related subsidies and transfers) or carrots (through capacity building, support to local land and property institutions or subsidies for the development of residential serviced plots for low-income households). The challenge for both local and central government is to make sure that all parts of the supply chain work sequentially for different market segments (for example, improving the supply process for each market segment before finance-system and household subsidies are used to expand demand).

Why Subsidize Housing?

The debate over the efficacy of government interventions in the housing sector is too often clouded by confusion over their objectives. There needs to be clarity about the public purpose of government intervention and the value of achieving various housing goals to society at large. The question of why housing should be subsidized can best be understood by perceiving better housing as a means of achieving higher-level societal goals. Two broad goals are usually involved, explicitly or implicitly, in the political discussions about subsidy intervention in the housing sector. These are the following:

- Improving public health, justice, and fairness
- Improving market efficiency

The first of these reasons for subsidy intervention relates to housing conditions directly and focuses on promoting welfare in society through the housing sector. The second reason focuses on expanding housing opportunities by pricing and allocating costs and risks in the housing and housing-finance sector more optimally, for example, through subsidizing the provision of inputs that are underprovided by private markets and addressing externalities created by market operations. These broad goals need, of course, to be specified in considerable detail. For example, measures to address housing inequality in society may focus particularly on increasing home-ownership and, even more specifically, on overcoming constraints faced by first-time homeowners in buying a house. Specific market and household constraints need to be identified that prevent lenders or developers to serve the targeted population group in order to develop an effective package of regulatory and subsidy measures. A framework for such detailing will be discussed for each of the main types of subsidies: (1) subsidies to the housing finance system, (2) subsidies to investors in rental housing, and (3) subsidies to households directly.

Subsidies and the Expansion of Housing Finance Systems

Housing Finance Sector Problems, Causes, and Subsidies

Constraints to the efficient growth of housing finance systems, whether for mortgage or non-collateralized lending, vary widely across countries and among mortgage finance and other types of housing finance.[8] Apart from the broad macro-economic problems discussed above, there are at least three general categories of constraints in the expansion of housing finance systems:

- System imperfections resulting from market-concentration problems or lack of a level playing field among financial institutions, or the exis-

---

8. Imperfections such as asymmetric information, incompleteness of markets and moral hazard are endemic in housing finance systems and make it necessary to accept that second-best solutions to those assumed by theories of complete and competitive financial-market models are all one can aspire to. Allen and Gale (2001) discuss such trade-offs for financial systems in general.

tence of powerful gatekeepers resisting innovation and new entries into the market.

- Constraints in funding markets to deal with liquidity or interest rate risks, thereby truncating lending options and possibly leading to destabilization of the housing finance system.
- Lending market failures or incompleteness because of lack of credit and property market information, high risk of loss given default because of poor foreclosure systems, lack of mechanisms to deal effectively with credit risk, lack of consumer protection, and high transaction costs of lending prevent suppliers of credit from profitably serving all or a large portion of the housing market.

How can government intervention, and specifically subsidies, help overcome such constraints? There are four general types of subsidies to housing finance systems: (1) subsidies to research, information collection, or education programs; (2) provision of below-market funds for housing loans or insurance schemes; (3) direct government provision or risk sharing in financial intermediation at the retail or secondary market level; and (4) regulatory controls on prices or credit allocations for housing finance.[9]

Specific incentives will of course depend on the existing housing finance system and the quality of the infrastructure in each country, as well as on the type of housing finance system the country is moving toward, for example, a system based on capital market funding through securitization or mortgage bonds, or a predominantly deposit-based system where non-bank financial institutions do not play a major role. Since subsidies are prone to misuse, in particular in the hands of powerful interest groups that control their delivery, the choice of subsidies will also depend to a large degree on their relative advantage to contain misallocation and moral hazard for government.

Table 16.3 gives a summary of the main constraints in the housing finance sector and the types of subsidy that have frequently been applied,

---

9. By the definition used here, a government intervention to improve the housing finance system is a subsidy even if government is compensated on the basis of some accepted measurement of suitable rate of return, because the intervention lowers the opportunity costs for the lenders, whether these are private or state sponsored. The all-in impact of the subsidies on financial intermediation will, of course, depend on the differential between the rate of compensation to government and the presumed "market" rate to deliver the service.

Table 16.3. Examples of System Subsidies

Housing finance system constraints	Possible subsidy measures	Issues
1. Market structure and vested interests		
State or incumbent lenders limit new entry, innovation and price competition	• Remove subsidy and other privileges from state lending institutions • Support (short-term) alternative types of lenders, for example, through liquidity funding, capacity building • Increase competition through liberalization of the financial sector and removal of hidden subsidies • *Remove price controls (for example, caps on interest rates for micro loans or mortgage loans)*	• Vested interests resist removal of subsidies • Usually requires additional regulation of such lenders • *Interest rate controls often decrease volume of lending to targeted groups.*
2. Funding constraints and risks *		
Limited or costly equity funding	• *Provide equity capital for (part) state-owned housing lenders, w/o dividend obligations* • Provide equity for non-profit financial institutions that on-lend for social rental housing	• *Partial or full state control can lead to operational inefficiencies, reduced competition and excessive risk-taking.*
Limited access to or high costs of funds for lending	• *Subsidize cost of funds through government credit lines, special tax funds, or debt funds for social rental or ownership housing* • *Tax subsidies for funds channeled to housing finance (for example, bonds, savings)* • Public guarantees for lenders to access funds (public-private partnership) • Cash subsidies to the cost of funding for housing finance • Subsidized cash-flow guarantees for debt funds channeled to housing lenders	• *This class of subsidies is often provided through special government-sponsored institutions, adding to the cost of the subsidies and likely inefficiencies in the marketplace.* • Subsidizing ways to assist private lenders to access debt or capital markets carries less risk (see also below)
Liquidity risk	• Access to (part) government-sponsored liquidity facility (or secondary mortgage market) for all or a certain class of mortgage/microfinance lenders	• May be structured as joint public-private venture limiting government risk or political misuse
Interest rate risk or prepayment risk	• *Shift (part of) funding risks to government-sponsored agency* • Provide cash flow insurance or tax benefits for private mortgage or micro-loan securitizations	• *Combines moral hazard with potentially large government risk. Risk can be decreased if limited to cap on ARMs or other shared-risk arrangements* • Effective if insurance fee reflects real risk to government. Tax benefits are less transparent and should be phased out when market permits.
3. Lending risks and costs (in underserved markets)		
Credit risk or collateral risk for mortgage lending	• Subsidize information collection and research on property and credit markets • Pay for premium of private mortgage insurance (household subsidy) • Pay for borrower education • *Shift (part) credit risk to a (part) state-sponsored entity* • Provide (part) guarantees for social rental housing loans	Additional government actions needed: • Facilitate credit bureau • Allow payroll deduction • Improve foreclosure methods • Use community negotiations in case of defaults • Neighborhood investment plan to mitigate collateral risk Requires private sector to: • Invest in user-friendly servicing system

(continued)

Table 16.3. Examples of System Subsidies *(continued)*

Housing finance system constraints	Possible subsidy measures	Issues
Credit risk related to construction lending	• Link household subsidies to housing developments to ensure market for housing production • Provide (part) guarantees for construction loands	• *Developer may capture a portion of the subsidy* • *Highly risky; requires safeguards on quality of construction, etc.*
High transaction costs for loan origination and servicing	• Subsidize transaction cost of lenders for selected borrowers through cash payment or compensation for higher interest rate (can also be structured as part of a household subsidy)	Prerequisite: • Improved underwriting and servicing methods

Source: Author's own analysis.
Note: The italicized text indicates subsidies that have often induced high costs to systems or governments and should be avoided at all costs.
* Sovereign and exchange rate risk are not considered in this table.

or may be considered being applied, to overcome the causes or effects of such constraints.

Housing Finance Subsidies, Market Structure, and Vested Interests

When one or a few large lenders with vested interests gain excessive power over the housing finance sector and unduly influence the pricing of loans or types of loan products made available and market segments served, or prevent new entries and innovations, there is likely to be higher than necessary costs of lending and inappropriate limitations on access to loans. These structural and political problems can occur in both public and private sectors.

PUBLIC-SECTOR-INDUCED STRUCTURAL PROBLEMS IN HOUSING FINANCE

Structural and anti-competitiveness problems frequently arise because of the subsidization of specific state-owned institutions or by regulatory or political barriers to entry induced by these institutions.

Many countries have state housing-finance funds or banks, state conduits in the secondary market, state-mortgage insurance companies, or state micro-lending institutions. These institutions were established mostly during times that conditions were not suitable for the participation of the private sector in housing finance, or because the state needed to take on specific functions that would improve market performance. Such institutions usually have tax, funding, or risk-bearing advantages and do not have the same concerns about return on equity (ROE) to the owners as do private institutions. It is difficult for private lenders, insurers, or guarantors to compete in the market segments dominated by such state institutions or programs. They also often hinder innovations in the sector, for example, in the development of risk mitigation measures, since their risk profile is different than that of private new entries. The first priority, and a prerequisite to the creation of a more competitive and effective housing finance system, is the elimination of the (often hidden) subsidies to state housing finance institutions or, alternatively, to provide access to these subsidies by all qualified actors in the sector or reorient these subsidies to leverage private sector participation.

This is not an easy task, particularly when these institutions are the largest sources of funds for housing finance and have powerful constituencies. Many other emerging economies are analyzing or trying out alternative options to dissolve, break up, or change the function of state housing finance institutions (for example, Korea and Peru dismantled their special funds, and Indonesia, Mexico, and to a more limited extent, Brazil and Nigeria are seeking reforms in their state housing finance institutions).

When new public institutions are considered to provide financial intermediation functions that the private sector will not yet find profitable to deliver (for example, mortgage insurance, accessing capital markets), an exit or sunset provision should be included to prevent these institutions from turning into gatekeepers that will dissuade private-sector entry later.

Private-sector-induced Anti-competition Problems in Housing Finance

In some countries, the private housing finance industry itself may engage in anti-competitive behavior (for example, price setting, collusion not to enter in certain submarkets, lobbying to prevent entry by other types of financial institutions into housing finance). There is often a lack of clear rules guiding market conduct and structure (for example, no disclosure standards, competition rules). Government's first priority should be to improve such regulatory measures. Regulators, however, frequently use *price controls and credit allocation requirements* to reach social goals for housing finance under these conditions (for example, ceilings on interest rates, whether for mortgage or micro loans, quotas for lending to special groups or special sectors).[10] This approach can create an undesirable system of hidden subsidies, which may be more costly than the anticompetitive behavior that the regulations are intended to address. Repealing such controls and replacing them with positive subsidy incentives to lower the cost of providing housing finance services to underserved markets generally yields better results.

Housing Finance Subsidies to Alleviate Funding Constraints

In developing and emerging market economies, capital markets are often not well developed or are dominated by government debt. This situation is changing rapidly, however, because of innovations in voluntary savings systems, among other things.

Governments may want to channel a larger share of these longer-term savings into housing, through improvement of the housing finance system, either for the sake of the overall efficiency and stability of the financial system or to serve social goals. For example, even if a country has vibrant primary lending institutions, these may be limited in scale by lack of stable funding, or the system as a whole may not have appropriate markets for managing funding risks such as liquidity risk, interest rate risk, and prepayment risk. If so, interest rates will be higher and more volatile, loan terms will be shorter than they otherwise would be, and appetite for FRMs will be low.

Hypothetically, private investors might create institutional arrangements to best manage these risks. For example, Mexican non-bank financial institutions (SOFOLs) have successfully tapped capital markets to increase their

---

10. Malaysia has gone one step further and mandated a certain amount of below-market lending to lower-income households, which is partly cross-subsidized from lending to higher-income households. South Africa has also considered mandating lending at lower-income levels, funded by cross-subsidization if necessary.

funding options. For a variety of reasons, however, this is not happening in many countries: investors are often distrustful toward investing in mortgages or mortgage-backed bonds, yield curves on these investments may not be as attractive as for government or other comparable paper, and cash flows are less predictable.

The government could, under these circumstances, support interventions (which are subsidies even if not usually called that) to improve access to capital markets and hence increase funding options and manage the risks related to long-term lending. For example, it may establish a liquidity facility or a secondary market institution or provide cash-flow guarantees or tax incentives for mortgage securities. Such measures are not only important for expanding mortgage lending, but may be particularly relevant for the expansion of microfinance systems when funding through a deposit base is either limited or not an option since most such institutions are non-banks.

The state may also seek to reduce funding constraints and risks not just to improve markets, but for the explicit purpose of reaching social goals. It may provide subsidized equity funding, lines of credit, or other funding advantages to (state-owned) primary market lenders with the explicit purpose of providing below-market loans to specific categories of borrowers or investors in social or private moderate-income rental or ownership housing. These latter institutional subsidies are often accompanied by equity investments and tax write-offs on interest costs, indirectly reducing the cost of rental housing for lower-income groups. Such systems are often put in place with assistance from international development institutions; however, the costs and distortions imbedded in such special non-market funding systems have to be carefully assessed for their long-term impact on the sector. They often do more damage than good. Since such subsidies were not originally designed to serve equity purposes, they are often inefficient in reaching distributional goals because of their often high hidden costs to the financial systems and the economy, as well as poor targeting. Policy makers need to carefully assess alternative ways to reach distributional goals; for example, through transparent household subsidies.

Subsidies to Address Lending Risks and High Transaction Costs

An increasingly accepted subsidy objective for housing finance is to provide incentives to agents in either the primary or secondary markets to expand into sections of the housing finance market that are underserved because of political or practical difficulties in pricing differentially for risks and uncertainties (which often cannot be insured in this type of market) or high transaction costs.

The first priority for government is to improve, jointly with the private sector, the regulations, institutions, and information infrastructure that affect the workings of the mortgage or consumer and micro-lending sectors (for example, appropriate standards, property registration systems and cadastres, information and research on the housing sector, a credit information system and credit bureaus, improved foreclosure methods, reform of usury laws, and improved underwriting and servicing methods by the industry). It may also share some of the lending risks or pay for high origination and servicing costs. Ideally, once the risks in serving these markets are better understood and controlled and the transaction costs are reduced, government can decrease or phase out such support.

INFORMATION AND RESEARCH

Information collection and research is needed for the efficient working of the housing market, but is often not gathered if any one private entity cannot capture the benefits. Examples of such useful "public good" data and research topics include comprehensive property information, consolidated credit information across financial institutions (for use in credit scoring or development of mortgage default insurance or securitization markets), research in standardization of mortgage procedures, new credit instruments, reasons for default, default trends and the scale of and reasons for losses after default occurs, trends in house prices, and so on. The rewards from developing expertise within the industry on housing and housing finance issues are extremely high, given the huge amount of resources that most governments and societies invest in the housing sector.

CREDIT RISKS

The most basic lending risk is credit risk and is often the main reason for the reluctance of the private sector to enter underserved markets. Interventions that share the credit risks can improve the overall efficiency and stability of the system, and can also be designed to fulfill social goals.

One proven positive intervention is subsidizing the establishment of a credit information system or a credit bureau. Government can go a step further and support the establishment of private credit insurance, share some risk in a public-private insurance scheme, or even establish its own credit insurance system, though that bears higher moral hazard risks.

The type of credit insurance program will differ depending on the mix of goals set by government. For example, insurance may be "market priced" or "below-market priced"; it may be universal or applied to targeted households; it may cover only part of the risk or take on all of the risk, or it may be designed for long-term mortgage credit or shorter-term microcredit. Government may also consider paying for the mortgage insurance premium for selected households rather than sharing in the credit risk directly. These alternative options are currently debated by SHF in Mexico. A major issue to consider is that, whenever the state takes on risk itself, there may be problems with moral hazard; for example, participants will be prone to commit fraud or take on excessive risks. The design of the administrative and control systems is therefore as equally important as the insurance system itself.

One proven method to decrease credit risk is to educate borrowers before they get a loan, not just on the rights and duties of borrowing, but also in home maintenance. Government can subsidize such education. The effectiveness of this method has been shown in the United States (Hirad and Zorn 2001) and South Africa (HLGC, personal communication). South Africa's HLGC and Mexico's SOFOLs have proven as well that user-friendly servicing systems that pay immediate and personal attention when a borrower misses a payment are critical to reduce losses when a default occurs.

If the goal is to expand lending into marginal neighborhoods, a partial mitigation of the credit risk will seldom be sufficient in emerging markets. Much broader infrastructure and institutional support is often required to alleviate neighborhood or condominium risk effects on the value of the collateral.[11]

A special type of credit risk and related subsidies are related to development and construction lending. This type of short-term lending is relatively risky because of the frequent construction delays, difficulty in enforcing quality controls, uncertain collateral value of unfinished construction projects, and sensitivity to macroeconomic cycles or risks in the sale and transfer process to end users. Lenders are often reluctant to make such loans and will only do so with special guarantees. Government may develop special measures to overcome this constraint for construction of socially important housing, perhaps by paying for guarantees offered through private guarantors, by establishing institutions that guarantee construction quality controls (South Africa), or by taking on (part) of the risk by itself or jointly with private or international development institutions, with the necessary safeguards to protect against moral hazard.

TRANSACTION COSTS

The main reason for housing submarkets being underserved by lenders, aside from credit risk, is related to costs relative to profit of certain customer segments or loan products. Household income verification may be more cumbersome because of a larger proportion of self-employed households in those markets, loans are smaller and therefore the origination fee is either inadequate for the lender or excessive for the borrower, and servicing of loans is costly relative to the size of the loan. Government may decide to compensate lenders directly for these higher transaction costs to bring financial institutions into those markets, at least for an initial period. Colombia used this method successfully and phased it out when lenders had gained experience in servicing more risky markets.

---

11. The single-most-important barrier to lending in low-income markets is the uncertainty of neighborhood factors that are critical in determining house-value movements. Lenders may require additional equity investments by third parties and agreements on an investment plan by local government before entering into low-income markets or neighborhood improvement ventures. In the United States, the FHA insurance program was effective in stimulating investments in underserved neighborhoods, even without additional community support.

The resistance of mainstream mortgage finance institutions to incur setup costs to reach lower-income, higher-risk customers, even with subsidies, has led to the conclusion that it may be more cost effective to target this type of government support toward community-based or smaller mutual housing-finance institutions. These lenders already have better information systems in place to deal with less conventional customers since they work at the community level.

Problems with Subsiding a Housing Finance System

The previous discussion showed in general terms that system subsidies can play an important role in overcoming the inefficiencies or instability of housing finance systems, but it also noted that they have frequently created new problems. These poor outcomes are often the result of poor subsidy design that underestimated the total costs of the subsidy, because such costs were not made transparent or did not take into account the extent or type of private sector response. Overly deep intrusions into the housing finance market have also created strong distortions elsewhere in the growth of the financial system. The key to avoiding this is to have political commitments to remove these interventions over time (which may prove hard to do) or induce markets to eventually take over the functions provided by the subsidy programs.

Probably a bigger source of problems derives from a lack of clarity in the purpose of subsidy. Some housing-finance-system subsidies focus on the improvement of the stability and efficiency of the housing finance system, while others are purposely introduced to seek distributional goals, for example, providing housing finance services at below-market prices to lower the cost of housing (usually through either funding of financial services, direct provision, risk sharing, or regulation). Some aim to do both. Even when intended to simply increase efficiency, many system subsidies serve equity goals through the "back door" when the pricing of original efficiency-oriented subsidies is not adjusted or the subsidy is not phased out when no longer needed to improve the private market. (A good example of this is the implicit government guarantee of the secondary market entities in the United States.) Even the subsidy mechanism is often the same irrespective of the goal. The distinction between market efficiency and equity goals is, therefore, important mostly in the way system interventions are priced, adjusted, and phased out over time when the market can take on the risks and costs covered by the subsidy.

But, if social goals are the primary purpose for initiating subsidies to the housing finance system, the long-term and hidden cost of these types of subsidy and their redistributive effects would need to be compared with alternative subsidies provided directly to households. It will often turn out that both their cost efficiency and equity outcomes are second best to using transparent household subsidies, such as up-front grants in the form of down payments, land grants or savings-linked grants, payment for up-front mortgage insurance premiums, and interest-payment buy-down subsidies.

Subsidies for the Financing of Rental Housing

The Rental Market

A sound rental sector is important for labor mobility and to accommodate those who do not want or are unable to become homeowners (for example, older and young households, or low-income households). The market for rental housing is in some ways more complex than that for home ownership. First, it is a two-level market involving investors and tenants who are different entities. Second, there are different types of investors—private formal and informal landlords, nonprofit or public entities—with very different motivations and constraints and serving different market niches.

Private rental markets provide the bulk of rental housing in most emerging market economies. Little is known about these markets, however, because much of the rental activity is informal, specifically for the lower-income end of the market and in low-income countries. While informal rentals fill an important gap in the housing market, they give tenants little security and the quality of housing is often poor. Reasons for failures or inefficiencies in private rental markets appear to be related to (1) poor taxation and regulatory systems that discourage investment in rental housing,[12] (2) lenders'

---

12. Tax codes often favor ownership tenure. Preferable tax should be tenure neutral to allow the supply of housing to be driven by preferences.

constraints in dealing with the particular risks of lending to rental investors, and (3) a mismatch between tenant incomes and the cost of providing formal rental housing in the lower-income segments.

The direct provision of public rental housing is, in most countries, limited to civil servants' housing and has proven in most countries to be an inefficient model for the provision of housing to the general public. In some countries, it has been used for a short time to deal with massive low-income housing needs. But, these schemes are mostly phased out when markets are sufficiently developed to take over, and only a small public housing stock is maintained for the lowest income groups. In some countries, particularly in Europe, nonprofit housing associations provide the bulk of "affordable" rental housing. Subsidies to nonprofit institutions whether through finance, production grants, and operational costs have generally been deep. These are for that reason difficult to implement in emerging markets. In addition, the wisdom of high levels of rental supply-side subsidies to accommodate households that would have been able to become homeowners with a similar or lower level of public expenditure can be questioned in the light of the often negative wealth effects for such households. It is critical that objectives for government subsidies to specific segments of the rental sector be spelled out clearly.

Rental Sector Regulations, Taxation, and Subsidies

Rental housing in most emerging market economies is subject to a plethora of regulations and taxes often related to the political sense that tenants need protection from landlords. Rent control laws and rigid tenant protection regulations were introduced in many countries and have resulted in a severe lack of investment in rental housing. Other regulations, such as high building standards for multifamily housing, double value-added tax (VAT), and high taxation of rental income prevent private investors in the low- and middle-income market from formalizing their rental business. They equally prevent institutional investors from entering the market. If the aim is to attract more investors to the formal rental sector and increase supply of rental units, the first requirement is to remove rent control and unduly restrictive regulations and taxes.

It is unlikely, however, that such measures will be sufficient to incentivize the real low-income informal rental market into compliance, at least in countries with a relatively fast-growing low-income urban population (for example, most African countries). The main constraint in the low-income segment remains the mismatch between incomes and the cost of formal rental housing, both investment and operation cost, and enforcement of even relaxed standards may make such markets unfeasible. Also, in this segment landlords are mostly natural persons, often living on the premises or in the neighborhood, and it is customary to have non-written leases and face-to-face relationships between owners and tenants.[13] Conflicts are therefore settled more easily. Nor would formalization of the low-income sector expand the fiscal base since most small-scale landlords do not file income taxes. A rental policy for the low-income sector in such high-urban-growth countries is therefore best focused on the general improvement of urban infrastructure and neighborhood services, which would improve the quality of life of low-income renters more than almost any other government measures.[14] Improved inspection and compliance with basic sanitation and safety codes would make a difference in housing quality as well. In addition, access to microfinance can assist landlords in improving low-income rental housing and sanitation.

For investors interested in the middle- and lower-middle-income rental market (or the low-income market in transition economies) regulatory facilitation and removal of double taxation may be a necessary incentive to enter the formal rental market. It may, however, not be sufficient. Lack of access to finance and the mismatch between incomes and the financing and maintenance costs of formal rental housing may require additional subsidy incentives to reach priority households according to government policy. Government subsidies may have to complement regulatory change. The level of subsidy required will depend to a large degree on the building standards, land market efficiency, and regulatory constraints applied to this sector. For example, in Thailand development and building standards for rental and

13. See Melzer (2006) for South Africa, Hoek-Smit (1998) for surveys in Sri Lanka and East and Southern Africa, and Huchzenmeyer (2006) for Kenya (2006).
14. Some middle-income countries have implemented programs for small direct-income transfers to low-income groups, conditioned upon keeping children in the household in school, but not linked to specific types of spending. Housing voucher programs are impossible to administer in these markets.

ownership housing were lowered in the 1980s (for example, unit size of 20 square meters) to allow an increase in affordable housing supply without additional subsidies.

Subsidies to the Rental Sector

If it is a government priority to increase the private or nonprofit supply of middle and lower-middle rental housing or to make it more affordable, there are three broad alternative approaches for subsidization: On the supply side there are (1) investor subsidies and (2) production subsidies. Supply-side subsidies often differ for nonprofit and private investors (for example, non-profit's tax-exempt status make tax subsidies unfeasible) and for different types of private investors (individuals and corporations).[15] A third class of subsidy is the rental allowances to individual households. These demand-side subsidies will be discussed briefly in the section "Housing Finance Subsidies to Households," but they are often not feasible in emerging market economies because of housing market conditions and information require-ments. In most industrial nations, formal private or nonprofit rental housing remains unaffordable for low-income households, even with different layers of supply-side subsidies. For this reason, most Western European countries and the United States still require housing allowances to low-income tenants to bridge the affordability gap in such projects.

The main supply-side subsidies that help pay for rental housing are briefly summarized:

SUBSIDIES LINKED TO DEBT FINANCE

Most rental finance subsidies consist of interest rate subsidies and credit risk guarantees. Debt-related subsidies are of particular importance to social landlords, as they have little own funds to invest, and up-front subsidies are usually small. In the past, many governments developed separate funds to provide below-market finance for social housing, sometimes using below-

---

15. Subsidized rental housing becomes social rental when the subsidy is accompanied by restrictions attached to that unit.

market interest-rate loans, which hide the true cost of the subsidy and often include other hidden subsidies. For example, in some transition economies, the state provides below-market-rate housing loans by establishing a public fund to promote rental housing construction and purchase. Some examples of such funds are the Housing Fund of Slovenia, the State Fund of Housing Development of the Slovak Republic, and the National Housing Fund in Poland. The United States has special loan funds operating at the state level.

This situation is changing, however, and increasingly Western European countries use market-based funding for social rental housing, made possible by the development and liberalization of the financial sector in the 1980s. France and Austria are now the only countries in the Euro zone that use a state subsidiary to finance the social rented sector.

Private sector lending for social rented housing by commercial banks or specialized lenders poses a number of problems, however: (i) such loans are (very) long term, often more than 30 years, making it difficult to raise matching funds; (ii) in some countries, the LTV ratio of such loans is typically high, since investors want to keep equity low; and (iii) loans are difficult to appraise since the value of the property is often impacted by the fact that it is impossible to evict defaulting tenants, and, in case of foreclosure, the only potential buyers are other social landlords. These factors increase the risk premium. As in Western Europe and the United States, when part of the rent is paid for through individual housing allowances, and the risk is spread over a number of properties, the risk of such loans is often overestimated. Where, however, the loss given default is high, the probability of default is low. An alternative security to the lender for such loans is the future rent stream. Recent loans to housing associations in the United Kingdom were secured by mortgages on social housing properties and cash reserves in favor of the issuer and bond trustee. In the event of nonpayment, the bond trustee will have the right to collect the rents and manage the secured property.

Because of the complex risk profiles of such loans, credit guarantees are sometimes used, at least for private investor loans. Some countries use special types of guarantees offered by the state (Slovakia), local authorities (France), or mutual housing funds (France, United Kingdom, the Netherlands). Such guarantees are frequently underpriced and may have very high future costs to the state, increasing the ultimate subsidy amount.

Subsidies Linked to Equity Investments

Equity subsidies assist social housing investors to decrease debt funding, and therefore lower the repayment burden. Subsidies toward equity can be provided through direct grants or through tax credits for private equity investors in either private-rental or nonprofit-rental housing projects. The U.S. Low-Income Housing Tax Credit (LIHTC) is the most prominent of these programs.

Production Subsidies

Such subsidies can take various forms: (i) the provision of land for free or at a below-market price by the state or local authorities (the cost of which is often not appraised at market value), and (ii) up-front grants for a proportion of the total land and construction cost, tax subsidies such as VAT exemption, or reduced tax rate on construction.

Up-front land or cash grants are the most transparent and are therefore generally preferred over other forms of subsidies to raise equity or reduce debt burdens. The downside of up-front production subsidies is, however, that they can be captured more easily by the builder or the developer, who may not translate these subsidies into lower rents in the future. Debt or certain equity-linked subsidies disbursed over time can be monitored and ended if the investor does not comply with rental agreements.

Operating and Maintenance Subsidies

Operating and maintenance subsidies tend to be avoided, as they consist of long-term commitments that cannot easily be anticipated. Income or property tax rebates or exemptions, VAT on renovation or improvement, VAT on interest payments, taxation of rental income, or depreciation concessions, however, are frequently used mechanisms to alleviate the mismatch between rental income and operating (and debt repayment) costs during the leasing phase.

Tax Subsidies

Tax subsidies feature prominently in the development and leasing phase of private or mixed non-profit-private rental housing. A characteristic of tax subsidies to private landlords is that, in most cases, the depth of the subsidy depends on the income of the beneficiary landlord, either directly through the scale of income taxes (for example, when applied to rental income or capital gains) or indirectly through the value of the property (in the case of property tax, wealth tax, transfer tax on inheritance). For subsidies linked to income taxes, landlords must fall into the taxable income bracket to benefit from the subsidy. As a consequence, most such subsidies will not benefit poorer households and may therefore be socially regressive. Another issue is their lack of transparency, since the size of the subsidy is often not known.[16] Since tax subsidies do not appear on the budget, they are often politically irresistible and difficult to change or eliminate when no longer needed. Furthermore, in emerging economies, tax subsidies on private rental housing may not be attractive because of income tax avoidances and non-written customary leases in the targeted segment of the market.

Rental Voucher Schemes

Rental voucher schemes are in operation in a number of countries (in particular, United States or France; also experimented with in Poland) where eligible low-income tenants receive subsidies in the form of vouchers that must be spent on housing, in particular to pay for the difference between market and contractual rents. The motivation behind subsidizing the demand side is to foster a competitive private-rental market, where in theory the supply would respond to the increased demand the voucher scheme creates. Such schemes may be implemented to accompany any rental deregulation reform. In practice, these schemes have been subject to a number of administrative and fiscal problems, including abuses by ineligible tenants, disincentives to become owners for those who could afford it, and significant fiscal costs in the longer run for the sponsoring public entities.

---

16. Some programs such as the LIHTC in the United States allocate specific amounts of tax subsidies per year.

Project Finance for Ownership Housing

Several of the subsidies mentioned here for rental multifamily projects can equally be applied to the development of low-income-ownership housing projects by private or nonprofit developers. In several countries, production grants, low-interest loans, and tax credits are part of the broader low-income housing subsidy package for single-tenure or mixed-ownership and rental developments. In fact, most so-called "demand-side" subsidies to beneficiary owners are simply production grants to developers (see the section "Housing Finance Subsidies to Households"). The same concerns about transparency and efficiency of such supply-side subsidies apply as they do for the rental production subsidies, with the main concern being how much of the subsidy is in fact translated into lower housing prices, rather than increasing developer profit or paying for transaction costs.

Public-Private Partnerships for the Provision of Affordable Rental Housing

Delivering affordable rental housing can entail deep subsidies (depending on the country, total subsidies in social-rental housing projects can easily reach 40 or 50 percent of project value). Usually, these subsidies cannot be provided by only one level of government. Indeed, a sound conclusion that has emerged through the years is that the public sector alone cannot solve the housing problems of low-income households.

In most, if not all, countries, subsidies to affordable rental housing and, more generally, rental housing finance involve partnerships between different government levels, as well as between the government and the private sector. Attractive tax and subsidy packages are combined with contributions (for example, in the form of land or equity, or guarantees) from various levels of government. Municipalities often play a pivotal role in those partnerships. First, they are the government level most interested in providing adequate shelter to their constituencies. Second, they are often willing to play the role of investors or providers of guarantees.

In emerging economies, efficient partnerships in the delivery of affordable housing are often difficult to put in place. Brazil presents a good example of difficulties in cooperation through different levels of governments for the provision of affordable housing.[17] Because of the specificities of the relations between the three levels of government, coordination between them has been a challenge both in terms of financial resources and in terms of leadership. As a result, the use of public assets or money to finance affordable housing may be suboptimal from the social point of view, even though it corresponds to the profit-maximizing (or loss-minimizing) behavior of individual partners. This may arise because of accounting incentives (for example, direct spending shows on municipal budgets, whereas land grants do not), inadequate management (for example, it can be optimal to give out a small grant complementing another layer of subsidies rather than making a bigger loan that will not be recovered), or political incentives (pouring small subsidies across already financed or subsidized projects allows individual institutions to claim the delivery of more units).

Making Rental Subsidies Work

In summary, the best policy in situations of scarcity of low-income rental housing and high rents in emerging market economies is comprehensive housing-market deregulation, and, if necessary, the introduction of select production or investor subsidies to stimulate the flow of new housing to the market where a proven gap remains. Such subsidies could be designed to gradually move the formal rental market to lower-income segments. The most efficient and equitable on-budget subsidies are arguably the ones that are linked to private-sector loans, transparently priced (for example, interest buy-downs, credit guarantees), and preferably through multiyear allocations with requirements to maintain "affordable" rent levels. Such subsidies, however, will not benefit informal investors in low-income housing, unless regulatory adjustments make it financially feasible for this sector to be "formalized."

---

17. Although the Federal Residential Leasing Program, the PAR, can be considered an exception in the sense that it has achieved a reasonable degree of cooperation between municipalities and the main operator of the program, the Federal Housing Bank (CEF).

Housing Finance Subsidies to Households

Household Problems and Subsidies

Household subsidies are intended to increase the willingness and the capacity of beneficiary households to consume better quality housing or to become homeowners through cash or in-kind grants or expanding their ability to obtain a housing loan or the maximum size of that loan.[18]

Individual household subsidies were introduced in many countries as a reaction to the gross misuse and inefficiencies of supply-side subsidies to developers. One of the major advantages of household subsidies is that they can be much more refined in targeting and better monitored than most supply-side subsidies if they are designed as explicit, direct subsidies. They are therefore often preferred when the objective is to improve *fairness and justice* in society through housing. Unfortunately, the political process that ultimately approves such subsidy programs frequently has unclear or multiple goals and confuses targeting. Implementation of household subsidies may also be hampered by lack of detailed information necessary to select targeted beneficiaries and by political interference. As a result, most countries have multiple programs of household subsidies—on-budget and off-budget—that provide vastly different levels of support to households in the same income brackets, while often excluding the most deserving households. Such outcomes are particularly prevalent when subsidies are linked to mortgage finance in countries where most of the population has no access to such finance.

Vaguely defined, household subsidies are sometimes used to improve general housing consumption in society without taking specific goals into account, or to stimulate growth in the construction sector. Such unclear goals give rise to broad-based general subsidies such as tax subsidies for loan repayments or broad interest rate subsidies available to the majority of households with mortgage loans. Expected outcomes of such subsidies are unclear and hard to evaluate. When such subsidies are tax subsidies or do not

---

18. While household subsidies may use the housing finance system as a distribution channel, if they are subsidizing individual households, and not the system itself, they are treated here as household subsidies.

appear on the budget for other reasons, they are often inefficient, particularly in emerging market economies, and can be extremely inequitable.

A premise of the approach to subsidy design and reform proposed here is that details matter a lot and that the only way to get the details right is to start from a clear definition of housing problems for different segments of the housing sector and specific objectives for a subsidy policy. The usual general goal of household subsidies is either a social equity one involving promoting the housing consumption of certain socially meritorious groups, or a political stability goal involving higher homeownership levels. The constraints faced by households usually differ for the different housing market segments discussed in the section "Linking Housing Problems to Subsidy Policy" above, and household subsidies should be tailored accordingly. Some of those constraints are outlined as follows.

Middle- or lower-middle-income households:

  i. Their incomes are too low relative to the cost of housing or the cost of borrowing to obtain a house in the formal market, whether existing or new, rental or ownership, and of a quality considered appropriate given the income level and societal values in their country.
 ii. They may have difficulty accessing long-term finance needed to own a formal-sector house because
     a. they cannot save for the down payment while still paying a large proportion of their income for rent (a particular problem for first-time homeowners),
     b. their income may be too variable for carrying a regular housing loan (whether mortgage or non-secured),
     c. they may only be able to afford a house in a neighborhood or building where future house values are highly uncertain (for example, areas subject to redlining) or where property rights are not clear (that is, informal settlements, multifamily units with mixed ownership and rental units, or a weak condominium law), or
     d. they may simply lack experience dealing with financial institutions or home maintenance, or fear long-term housing debt or debt in general.

Low-income households:[19]

- they cannot purchase new (but modest) formal-sector housing because of a combination of inappropriate standards, non-functioning land markets, low incomes, and lack of access to appropriate financial instruments;
- their incomes are too low to improve existing informal-sector housing conditions and they lack access to microcredit, infrastructure, or formally registered property rights;
- they may lack affordable, decent rental options.

The housing markets of different income categories are interrelated. In countries where serious housing problems exist for both lower-middle and low income groups, government interventions focused on low-income housing solutions have proven to be ineffective only since middle-income groups will capture the subsidies meant for low-income households. Equally, when relatively higher-income formal market solutions are stimulated by government interventions, some lower-income households may benefit by upward filtering through the resale market. But, this process will be inadequate to improve the housing conditions of the poor, particularly when urban growth rates are still high.

There are five main types of household subsidies that are frequently used in this context: (1) direct payments, either up front (to lower the loan amount, the closing costs, the down payment, or the insurance premium, or in the form of a capital grant for land) or on a monthly basis; (2) subsidies tied to savings programs; (3) interest rate or interest payment subsidies, including interest subsidies tied to appreciation of the property; (4) tax subsidies tied to mortgage payments or real estate taxation; and (5) payment for education programs or community support activities.

Table 16.4 summarizes households' housing problems and the types of household finance subsidies that might be or have frequently been applied to alleviate them. In the following sections we briefly discuss the different issues that arise in developing subsidies to address each of the constraints. Subsidy

---

19. The low-income constraints may not exist in transition economies and middle-income countries, where the low-income groups may face constraints similar to those discussed for lower-middle-income households.

Table 16.4. Examples of Housing Finance Subsidies to Households

Household constraints	Possible subsidy support	Issues
A. Lower-middle-income households that can access formal housing markets		
1. Income constraints relative to house prices or interest rates		
Low income relative to lowest formal-sector house price, cost of finance, or both	• Contribution toward loan amount or cash grant • Partial coverage of monthly payments or interest due (buy-down) • Reduce VAT (often double taxation) • *Interest rate subsidies* • *Tax subsidies for loan repayments*	• *Interest rate subsidies are often insufficient and regressive* • *Tax subsidies are regressive, nontransparent, and mostly ineffective* • *Both involve nontransparent future costs*
2. Lack of access to credit to purchase new or existing housing		
Savings constraints	• Support with closing and titling costs • Contribution toward owner's down payment and equity with or without savings requirement • Payment for mortgage insurance (to raise maximum LTV ratio) • Borrower education • *Soft second loan*	Requires: • Access to savings facilities • Savings programs linked to subsidy programs • *The concept of turning a deferred loan into a grant or a loan is difficult to implement*
Employment volatility	• Blocked deposit available for temporary "missed payments" (insufficient for conditions of chronic high unemployment) • Borrower education	Requires: • Flexible mortgage, line of credit • User-friendly servicing and institutional delivery capacity • Community-support organizations and funds
Lack of property title, maintenance, and housing risk (including condo-minium or mixed rental and ownership)	• Contribution toward owner's equity (lower LTV) • Community and condominium home-repair fund • Home-maintenance education or service for first-time homeowners and condominium support	• Support for title registration • Community and condominium support organizations are critical for success in risky neighborhoods, buildings • May need improved law on sectional title
Neighborhood risk (major reason for lack of resale finance in low-income neighborhoods)	• Disclosure requirements; consumer protection against discrimination • Local government agreement on investment plan for infrastructure and services in selected neighborhoods	• Involves interventions primarily through legal or government systems, not individual subsidies
B. Low-income households that cannot access mainstream formal markets		
3. Income constraints relative to formal housing options		
Poorly functioning land and finance markets for new formal, low-income housing	• Grants in kind (serviced lots and core house) to household and developer • Support to community-based organizations to assist progressive construction • Cash payment to micro-lenders to assist targeted borrowers with home construction and inspection • Funding "missed payment" accounts • *Interest rate subsidies*	• Government has to provide off-site infrastructure, facilitate permitting process, and set affordable standards • *Subsidies on interest rates in this submarket can prevent its expansion*
Weak incentives for upgrading of informal housing	• Grants (possibly linked to private micro-lending options) for home improvement and expansion to complement upgrading programs	• Requires comprehensive upgrading strategy, including service provision, property registration

Source: Author's own analysis.

mechanisms in italics have proven to be more problematic in relation to their efficiency, equity, or transparency outcomes.

Lower-Middle Income Households

SUBSIDIES TO HELP HOUSEHOLDS PAY FOR STANDARD HOUSING

Most household subsidies are used simply to help specific beneficiary groups to increase their housing purchasing power and obtain a house produced in the formal market. Many such subsidies are linked to debt finance, helping households to take on a larger loan than they would otherwise be able to (for example, income tax deductions of interest payments, reductions in interest rates for mortgage loans), or a grant to bring down the loan amount and thus monthly payments. Other such subsidies assist households directly in paying for the acquisition or improvement of their homes without a link to credit. Examples of the latter are cash grants to first-time (formal-sector) home-owners, who are responsible for buying their own home.

If the goal, however, is to improve equity in society in an emerging market economy, the use of household subsidies that are an integral part of a housing loan is seldom optimal or even effective. For example, income tax deductions of interest payments or a broad-based interest rate subsidy for mortgage loans tend to be both regressive and ineffective. These subsidies increase with the amount of the loan and benefit those who can afford larger loans more than those with smaller loans. They typically do not expand the frontier of the formal housing market by much.

Moreover, in some countries where borrowing is primarily displacing use of internal (extended family) sources of finance, borrowed amounts may increase, but not housing consumption. They are also inefficient in other ways. When tax and interest rate subsidies are granted to the middle class as well, their total costs can be extremely high, particularly relative to the benefits. For example, in the United States the income tax losses from the deduction of interest payments on mortgages are equal to 2.7 percent of the federal budget,[20] and Hungary's interest-rate and tax subsidies (if correctly

20. While it may seem small initially, deductions of interest payments from taxes can quickly become very costly when a country industrializes and a larger proportion of its labor force files income tax returns in the higher tax brackets.

calculated) reached about 5 percent of central government consumption. In addition, tax subsidies are not transparent, nor are most interest subsidies; Interest rate subsidies, however, can be structured in such a way that all future costs are recognized in the current year (for example, the buy-down).

- *Up-front grant programs for home-ownership.* Up-front grants are mostly applied toward the down payment of a loan. They use more equitable targeting mechanisms than tax subsidies or interest rate subsidies. For example, the up-front cash-grant subsidy system in Chile, while open to roughly two-thirds of all households, uses a point system for the allocation of subsidies that causes the subsidy to decrease with higher income and prioritizes households on the basis of need. Expenses per household for cash grant programs and housing allowance programs, however, are relatively high if a fairly high minimum housing standard is set for participants and the use of complementary debt finance is low. Both of these problems are the main constraints in the South African up-front subsidy program. These programs are often expensive to administer as well. The transfer efficiency—the effects of the subsidy on the actual production and consumption of houses—is generally considered to be much higher for up-front grant programs, especially compared to interest-rate deductions from income tax, and in particular for moderate-income households. These programs often require additional support to improve access to finance to work efficiently (see examples on system subsidies in table 16.4.

  Up-front grants are on-budget in their entirety and costs are therefore known. This makes them less favored politically. They can be evaluated more readily, however, and are in general more frequently adjusted. This also means that they are more readily phased out; for example, when donor funding is stopped or the budget needs tightening. Such was the fate of up-front grants in Costa Rica.

  Another issue with up-front grants is that when housing supply for the targeted market is dependent on the subsidy—that is, when there is no market yet—up-front grants are often provided to developers directly rather then to households to find their own house in the marketplace. They mostly are used as production grants, with all the potential shortcomings of supply-side subsidies.

Subsidies to Increase Access to Mortgage Finance

Another category of subsidies explicitly addresses constraints on accessing credit to become homeowners in the formal sector. Such subsidies are usually more efficient than general household subsidies to increase affordability since they:

- focus explicitly on households "at the margin" who cannot become homeowners without the subsidy and credit,
- leverage households' own resources, and
- provide incentives for the housing finance system to expand down-market.

These advantages, however, assume that the housing market and the housing finance system are reasonably efficient. If this is not the case, such subsidies are merely compensating for the shortcomings of these systems. Interventions to make the housing finance system more efficient should precede or complement household subsidy programs that intend to use the housing finance system.[21] Finding the right combination of household subsidies and subsidies to the housing finance system to expand lending to subsidy beneficiaries is a major challenge in many middle-income countries, including in South Africa and Mexico.

When there is a possibility that lenders will expand their lending to moderate-income households, the key question becomes what types of subsidy will be most effective in making households with acceptable credit records good borrowers. This choice depends critically on the analysis of specific constraints faced by moderate-income households in acquiring a loan—for example, savings constraints, volatility of income or employment, or high

---

21. Many governments are tempted to do the lending for this "non-qualifying" group, taking all the credit risk themselves. This leads nearly invariably to large loan losses, since governments are poor at collecting on defaulted loans.

collateral risk. These constraints will differ in different developing, emerging, or transition economies and for different submarkets within countries.

- *Savings constraints.* Studies in several countries have shown that the main hurdle for expanding moderate-income homeownership is for households to save enough money to pay for the down payment, title and closing costs, or an up-front premium for mortgage insurance.[22] Direct grants to alleviate this burden and assist in the payment for any or all of those expenses may be an effective way to expand the formal housing sector for households at the margin. Payments for mortgage insurance have several additional benefits; they generally lower the down-payment requirement and make the loan more attractive for the lender. Such up-front grants may be complemented by a required savings program to assist households to save for some of the equity in the house. Such savings programs are most efficient if they are part of an open financial system and do not lock the borrower into a closed system that sets interest rates for savings and lending administratively, and issuance of the loan depends on availability of funds in the system.

  Another, more complex way to lower the savings requirement is to extend a second mortgage loan that may be interest free and will need to be paid back after the first loan is paid off and only if the house has appreciated in value. While a second mortgage loan is potentially a more efficient subsidy than an outright grant, the conditionality of paying it back has been fraught with misunderstandings in the context of housing markets in emerging market economies.[23]

- *Employment and earnings volatility.* In general, self-employed or informally employed borrowers have a higher credit risk even if they qualify for a mortgage or consumer loan on the basis of their

---

22. Research has shown that the savings constraint is one of the most important deterrents to moderate-income households becoming homeowners (Linneman and Wachter 1989 for the United States). This may not apply in all markets, however. Also, if households have difficulty saving, the best way for government to be of assistance may not necessarily be to replace down payments with subsidies, but to provide better incentives for households to save.
23. For example, Costa Rica was forced to abandon the soft second-loan structure of their up-front subsidy.

expected cash flow from income. In many developing and emerging market economies, the majority of actively employed people work in the informal sector (for example, in Indonesia, this number is 74 percent, in Mexico more than 60 percent; and in most African countries this figure is even higher). It is important for formal housing-market expansion that mechanisms are found to facilitate lending to the most creditworthy households in this group.

The private market can accommodate this situation to some extent. Lenders may develop flexible mortgage instruments and servicing systems to accommodate such customers. They may do research on their portfolios to gain a better understanding of the risk profile of this group and price for the risk. They may require higher down payments or a "blocked" savings account that can be accessed when payments will be missed.

This sort of behavior can be supported in several ways. One type of transparent and up-front subsidy that could be applied for this type of borrower is a contribution to such a blocked deposit account. Such "payment insurance" scheme may also be usefully applied to consumer lending for housing that may be more appropriate for this group. Another subsidy that has proven particularly effective is supporting borrower education.

- *Housing and neighborhood risk.* There is another constraint facing moderate-income households in obtaining a loan that has to do with the housing collateral. The risk that the value of the collateral *decreases* over time and will be insufficient to pay the loan balance in case the loan defaults is considered greater in low- and moderate-income neighborhoods, and lenders are less likely to make loans in such areas. This type of credit constraint affects resale markets in such areas and becomes a vicious cycle. For example, when few loans are made, there is a weaker resale market and more fragmentary house-value information, resulting in higher defaults and costs to assess properties and thus even fewer loans.

  Mortgage insurance may be used to cover credit risk, but household subsidies may be necessary to decrease this type of collateral risk and to attract lenders and insurers to these markets. Subsidizing a larger part of the equity of the house is one way of increasing the lenders' comfort level. This may, however, be expensive. It has proven to be beneficial to complement insurance programs with subsidies for home-maintenance education of first-time homeowners, and, in cases of condominium ownership, support to set up a repair fund for the initial years and a condominium or neighborhood organization. These types of subsidies are in between system subsidies and household subsidies. Local governments play an important role in maintaining neighborhood value as well.

Low-Income Households: Subsidies When Housing Supply Markets Do Not Work

In low-income countries or lower-middle-income countries with highly skewed income distributions, a large proportion of households cannot aspire to solve their housing problems through formal housing markets. Incomes are simply too low relative to prices of serviced land and a standard formal house. Incremental construction is often not permitted nor is it profitable for private developers to produce core housing. In addition, appropriate types of debt finance are not available. Government has to play a more direct role to increase general housing consumption for the low-income segment in order to address concerns of public health and inequity in society. Improving land registration systems, regulations for subdivisions, planning and construction, and permitting procedures are the first things government has to do, in particular local government, to expand formal construction and attract private developers to this market. Subsidies are almost always necessary also, however.

- *Grants in the form of serviced land with or without a core house.* Such grants can be disbursed either to households or, more likely, to developers. Households can then use their own resources, including debt finance, to complete the house over time.

- *Home-improvement grants as a complement to upgrading schemes, including for rental extensions[24] of the house.* Such grants can be applied independent from debt finance and can therefore reach households that do not qualify for a loan, not even for microcredit, or in situations where microfinance is not yet available. Short- to medium-term microfinance loans, however, are now provided by private microfinance institutions in many countries, albeit not always for housing or at a scale relevant to address housing problems. These lenders may have to be assisted to develop housing credit products and reach scale. System subsidies in the form of liquidity support or technical assistance may help this sector to expand. If transaction costs are too high for micro-lenders to participate in this market, subsidies in the form of a fixed amount per household to defray the cost of guiding and supervising housing loan disbursement and recovery may be considered. Alternatively, financing "missed payments" accounts may be appropriate. Frequently, however, subsidies provided through government microfinance lenders, or donor assistance to nonprofit or private micro-lenders, are in the form of subsidized interest rates or internally cross-subsidized housing loans, making them affordable to the poor. Such subsidies limit the overall number of loans that can be made and have the additional disadvantage of preventing a strong private microfinance sector from developing.

  Another role for government is to encourage the establishment of community-based support systems to acquire building materials in bulk, provide some quality control, and assist in the development of community savings and counseling programs to help households that are currently not good credit risks to become so.

---

24. Rental housing for low-income households in low-income countries is best delivered through private small-scale investors who build additional rooms or floors. Formal-sector-built rental housing requires deep subsidies linked to finance, land, and construction and can be prohibitively expensive.

Conclusions

The liberalization and development of financial systems has deeply touched the housing finance sector in many emerging market economies and has created a momentum for reform in many countries. A growing demand for urban middle- and lower-income housing has fueled the urgency for the expansion of housing finance systems. One area of critical rethinking, and a frequent bottleneck in system expansion, is the system of housing finance subsidies. These are by far the most prevalent housing subsidies across all countries, but they are frequently not recognized as such. Many finance subsidies have had a negative impact on the development of housing finance markets and have a mixed record in reaching social goals. Indeed, goals and specific objectives are often not well defined. This situation leads to poor subsidy design.

Policy makers need to develop a strategic plan with a winning combination of incentives for mortgage systems and for households that are creditworthy and could access a mortgage with the right incentives—*moving mortgage credit down-market*. Even if finance is available, however, it is often the case that the land regulatory system makes it unprofitable or unfeasible for private developers to serve middle-income markets. Another part of this plan is to assist low-income households in accessing serviced land with core housing provisions or provide title and services to existing residential areas and strengthen the private and nonprofit microfinance sector (including the savings side) to expand household ability to expand their house over time—*moving savings facilities and non-collateralized credit upmarket and to scale*. When credit strategies work, *household subsidies* can decrease and be shifted to improved neighborhood and infrastructure services. Only then will the housing assets of lower-income people become "live assets."

This chapter has provided a framework to assist in such analyses. It made the point that only when systems work well for the majority of people can household subsidies be efficiently applied. It gave an overview of the broad categories of subsidy interventions and delivery mechanisms for each category of subsidy. There are, no doubt, many more variants one could choose to include. The aim is, however, to discuss the most prevalent "old generation" housing-finance subsidies and the gradual reforms and alternatives that may be considered in the current context of growing awareness of the need for transparency in financial markets, sound risk management in financial institutions, and the need to redress growing housing inequities in many emerging and advanced economies.

Bibliography

Abiad, Abdul, and Ashoka Mody. 2005. "Financial Reform: What Shakes It? What Shapes It?" *Economic Issues* 35.

Akerlof, George. 1970. "The Market for Lemons: Quality Uncertainty and the Market Mechanism." *Quarterly Journal of Economics* 84: 488–500.

Allen, Franklin, and Douglas Gale. 2001. *Comparing Financial Systems.* Cambridge, Massachusetts: The MIT Press.

Allen, Franklin, and Richard Herring. 2001. "Banking Regulation versus Securities Market Regulation." Working Paper Series, Wharton School, University of Pennsylvania, July 11.

Ammer, John Matthew, and Nathanael Clinton. 2004. "Good News Is No News? The Impact of Credit Rating Changes on the Pricing of Asset-Backed Securities." FRB International Finance Discussion Paper No. 809, July. Available at Social Science Research Network, www.federalreserve.gov/pubs/ifdp/2004/809/ifdp809.pdf.

Analistas Financieros Internacionales. 2007. "Diagnóstico del Mercado de Financiamento de la Vivienda, Guatemala." February.

Angel, Shlomo. 2000. *Housing Policy Matters: A Global Analysis.* New York: Oxford University Press.

Arnott, Richard. 1995. "Time for Revisionism on Rent Control?" *Journal of Economic Perspectives* 9: 99–120.

———. 2003. "Tenancy Rent Control." *Swedish Economic Policy Review* 10: 80–121.

Arnott, Richard, and Nigel Johnston. 1981. *Rent Control and Options for Decontrol in Ontario*. Toronto, Ontario, Canada: Ontario Economic Council, University of Toronto Press.

Ashcraft, Adam B., and Til Schuermann, 2007. *Understanding the Securitization of Subprime Mortgage Credit*. Federal Reserve Bank of New York.

Association of Corporate Treasurers (United Kingdom), Association for Financial Professionals (United States), Association Française de Tresoriers D'Entreprise (France). 2004. *Exposure Draft: Code of Standard Practices for Participants in the Credit Process*.

Association of German Mortgage Banks. 2004. *The Pfandbrief, Europe's Biggest Bond Market: 2004 Facts and Figures*. Berlin.

Babatz, Guillermo. 2006. "The Mexican Mortgage Market: Evolution, Strategy, and Expectations for the Future." Paper presented at the World Bank Conference on Housing Finance in Emerging Markets, Washington, D.C., March.

———. 2007. "Housing Finance in Mexico: Evolution, Strategy, and Challenges Ahead." International Housing Finance Program University of Pennsylvania, Philadelphia.

Banco Central de la República, Argentina. 2005. "Marco Normativo." July.

Banco Hipotecario (Argentina). 2002. Annual Report.

Bank for International Settlements (BIS). 1998. "Sound Practices for Loan Accounting, Credit Risk Disclosure and Related Matters," Consultative paper. Bank for International Settlements, Basel, Switzerland, October.

———. 2000. "Credit Ratings and Complementary Sources of Credit Quality Information." Working paper. Bank for International Settlements, Basle, Switzerland, August.

———. 2004. "International Convergence of Capital Measurement and Capital Standards: A Revised Framework." Bank for International Settlements, Basel, Switzerland, June.

Barker, Kate. 2004. *Delivering Stability: Securing our future housing needs*. London: HM Treasury.

Barth, James R. 2006. *Rethinking Bank Regulation and Supervision: Till Angels Govern.* New York: Cambridge University Press.

Barth, James R., Gerard Caprio, and Ross Levine. 2001. "Bank Regulation and Supervision: What Works Best." World Bank Policy Working Paper 2725. November.

Basel Committee on Banking Supervision. 1997. "Core Principles for Banking Supervision." September. Bank for International Settlements, Basel Switzerland.

Basel Committee on Banking Supervision. 2004. "Basel II: International Convergence of Capital Measurement and Capital Standards: a Revised Framework." Bank for International Settlements, Basel Switzerland. June.

Basu, Kaushik and Patrick Munro Emerson. 2000. "The Economics of Tenancy Rent Control." *Economic Journal* 110: 939–62.

———. 2003. "Efficiency Pricing, Tenancy Rent Control, and Monopolistic Landlords." *Económica* 70: 223–32.

Batchvarov, Alexander, Chinatsu Hani, Joyce Liang, and James Martin. 2007. *Merrill Lynch Guide to Emerging Mortgage and Consumer-Credit Markets: Volume 1 Asia and Australia.* Merrill Lynch, London.

Batchyvarov, Alexander, William Davies, Altynay Davietova, Flavio Rusconi, James Martin, and Sabine Winkler. 2007. *Merrill Lynch Guide to Emerging Mortgage and Consumer-Credit Markets: Volume 2 Central and Eastern Europe, Middle East and Africa.* Merrill Lynch, London.

Batchvarov, Alexander and Magda Guillen. 2007. *Merrill Lynch Guide to Emerging Mortgage and Consumer-Credit Markets: Volume 3 Latin America.* Merrill Lynch, London.

Bates, Mark, David Dale Johnson, and Jan Brzeski. 1999. "Property Valuation and Appraisal: U.S. Information Systems and Recommendations for Poland." Available at www.ceemortgagefinance.org.

Bentham, Jeremy. 1789. *Introduction to the Principles of Morals and Legislation: Utilitarianism and Other Essays.* London: Penguin Classics.

Berndt, Holger, Joachim Degner, Hartwig Hamm, and Andreas Zehnder. 1994. "Die Bausparkassen–Bausparfinanzierung und Bausparförderung." In *Taschenbücher für Geld*, Bank Börse, Bd. 5. Frankfurt am Main: Fritz Knapp Verlag.

Bernstein, Steven. 1996. "Mexican Autofinanciamientos: A New Source of Housing Finance." *Housing Finance International* 11(2).

BIS (Bank for International Settlements). 2006. *Enhancing Corporate Governance for Banking Organizations.* February.

Blood, Roger. 2003. "Key Policy and Regulatory Issues for Credit Insurance and Guarantee Schemes." Paper presented at the World Bank Conference on Housing Finance in Emerging Markets, Washington, D.C., March.

Bohacek, Zoran. 2003. "Developing Credit Bureaus: the Croatian Experience." Croatian Banks Association. Available on http://www.ceemortgagefinance.org/pdfs/03_Bohacek_5-04.pdf.

Boleat, Mark. 1985. *National Housing Finance Systems: A Comparative Study.* London: Croom Helm.

Börsch-Supan, Axel, and Konrad Stahl. 1991. "Do Savings Programs Dedicated to Homeownership Increase Personal Savings? An Analysis of the West German Bausparkassen System." *Journal of Public Economics* 44.

Brown, Warren. 2003. "Building the Homes of the Poor—One Brick at a Time: Housing Improvement Lending at Mibanco." *Acción's InSight Series,* No. 4. Available at SSRN: http://ssrn.com/abstract=771637.

Brzeski, W. Jan, Hans Joachim Dübel, and Ellen Hamilton. 2006. "Rental Choice and Housing Policy Realignment in Transition: Post-Privatization Challenges in the Europe and Central Asia Region." World Bank Policy Research Working Paper. No. 3884. April 14.

Buckley, Robert M., and Jerry Kalarickal, eds. 2005. "Thirty Years of World Bank Shelter Lending—What Have We Learned?" *Directions in Development Infrastructure.* Washington, D.C.: The World Bank.

Building Societies Association. 2005. http://www.bsa.org.uk/.

Butler, Stephen. 2003. "Enforcement of Mortgage Rights in Housing Finance." Paper presented at the World Bank Conference on Housing Finance in Emerging Economies: Policy and Regulatory Challenges, Washington, D.C., March.

———. 2006. "Broadening Mortgage Markets by Attending to Legal Fundamentals." Lecture notes for the Wharton International Housing Finance Program, University of Pennsylvania.

Cagamas Berhad. 2002. *Annual Report.* Kuala Lumpur. www.cagamas.com .my

———. 2003. *Annual Report.* Kuala Lumpur. www.cagamas.com.my

Calem, Paul S., and Michael LaCour-Little. 2004. "Risk-Based Capital Requirements for Mortgage Loans." *Journal of Banking and Finance* 28: 647–72.

Calhoun, Charles. 2001. "Property Valuation Methods and Data in the United States." *Housing Finance International* 16(2).

———. 2003. "Property Valuation Models and Housing Price Indices for the Provinces of Thailand: 1992–2000." *Housing Finance International* 17(3).

Calomaris, Charles. 2000. *U.S. Bank Deregulation in Historical Perspective.* Cambridge, U.K.: Cambridge University Press.

———. 2006. *U.S. Bank Deregulation in Historical Perspective.* Cambridge, U.K.: Cambridge University Press.

Caprio, Gerard, and Patrick Honohan. 2004. "Can the Unsophisticated Market Provide Discipline?" World Bank Policy Research Working Paper 3364, August.

Caprio, Gerard, Jonathan L. Fiechter, Robert E. Litan, and Michael Pomerleano, eds. 2004. *The Future of State-Owned Financial Institutions.* Brookings Institution Press.

Cardenas, Mauricio, and Alejandro Badel. 2003. "La crisis de financiamiento hipotecario en Colombia: Causas y consecuencias." Mimeo, Titularizadora Colombiana.

Carmichael, Jeffrey, and Michael Pomerleano. 2002. *The Development and Regulation of Non-Bank Financial Institutions.* Washington, D.C.: The World Bank.

Carstens, Agustín. 2004. "Opportunities for Emerging and Developing Countries in International Standard Setting: An IMF Perspective." Speech at the Fourth Annual IMF/World Bank/Federal Reserve Seminar Basel II—The International Banking System at the Crossroads, Washington D.C., June 2.

Chami, Ralph, Moshin S. Khan, and Sunil Sharma. 2003. "Emerging Issues in Banking Regulation." IMF Working Paper WP/03/101, May.

Chiquier, Loïc, Jacek Laszek, and Michael Lea. 1998. *Analysis of Contract Savings for Housing Systems in Poland.* Warsaw: The Urban Institute Consortium for USAID.

Chiquier, Loïc, Olivier Hassler, and Michael Lea. 2004. "Mortgage Securities in Emerging Markets." World Bank Policy Research Working Paper #3370, August.

Chiquier, Loïc. 1998. "Dual Index Mortgages: Lessons from International Experience and Conditions of Development in Poland." In *Housing Finance International* 13(1): 8–23.

———. 2001. *Secondary Mortgage Facilities: A Case Study of Malaysia's Cagamas Berhad*. Washington, D.C.: The World Bank, March.

Chiuri, Maria Concetta, and Tullio Jappelli. 2003. "Financial Market Imperfections and Homeownership: A Comparative Study." *European Economic Review* 47: 857–75.

Cho, Man. 2007. "180 Years' Evolution of the U.S. Mortgage Banking System: Lessons for Emerging Mortgage Markets." *International Real Estate Review*, Spring.

Clauretie, Terrence M., and Thomas N. Herzog. 1990. "The Effect of State Foreclosure Laws on Loan Losses: Evidence from the Mortgage Insurance Industry." *Journal of Money, Credit and Banking* 22(2): 221–33.

Coady, David P., and Rebecca L. Harris. 2004. "Evaluating Transfer Programmes within General Equilibrium Framework." *The Economic Journal* 114 (October): 778–99.

COFOPRI (Organismo de Formalización de Propiedad Informal; Agency for Formalization of Informal Property). 2005. "Perú: país de propietarios." Lima, Peru.

Colton, Kent. 2002. *Housing Finance in the United States—The Transformation of the U.S. Housing Finance System*. Cambridge, MA: Joint Center for Housing Studies at Harvard University.

Committee of Inquiry into the Australian Financial System. 1981. "Australian Financial System: Final Report of the Committee of Inquiry." Canberra: AGPS, Chair: J. K. Campbell, 332.0994/14 Law, Wol, Arch, Bus, U, RL Parliamentary Paper: 208/1981 (Aust.) September.

Committee on the Global Financial System. 2005. "The Role of Ratings in Structured Finance: Issues and Implications." Bank for International Settlements, January.

CONAVI (Comisión Nacional de Vivienda). Various years. Government of Mexico. www.conavi.gob.mx.

Cooter, Ronald 1982. "The Cost of Coase." *Journal of Legal Studies* 11: 1–29.

Credit Suisse. 2006. "Mexico's Residential Mortgage-Backed Securities: An Overview of the Market". *Fixed Income Research*. September. www .credit-suisse.com/researchandanalytics.

Crews Cutts, Amy, and Edgar O. Olsen. 2002. "Are Section 8 Housing Subsidies Too High?" *Journal of Housing Economics* 11(3)(September): 214–43.

Cristini, Marcella, and Ramiro Moya. 2004. "Las instituciones del financiamiento de la vivienda en Argentina." Working paper no. 498. Washington, D.C.: Research Department, Inter-American Development Bank.

Cummings, Jean L., and Denise DiPasquale. 1998. *Building Affordable Rental Housing: An Analysis of the Low-Income Housing Tax Credit*. Boston, MA: City Research, 46.

Daphnis, Franck, and Bruce Ferguson, eds. 2004. *Housing Microfinance: A Guide to Practice*. Kumarian Press.

Daphnis, Franck, and Ingrid Faulhaber. 2004. *Housing Microfinance: Policy Recommendations for SIDA's Programs*. Stockholm: SIDA.

Daphnis, Franck, and Kimberly Tilock. 2001. *So You Want to Do Housing Microfinance?* Silver Spring, MD: Community Housing Foundation International.

Davidson, Andrew, Anthony Sanders, Lan-Ling Wolff, and Anne Ching. 2003. *Securitization: Structuring and Investment Analysis*. John Wiley. New Jersey.

de Soto, Hernando. 2000. *The Mystery of Capital*. New York: Basic Books.

Deaton, Angus, and John Muellbauer. 1980. *Economics and Consumer Behavior*. Cambridge University Press.

Demyanyk, Yulia, and Otto Van Hemert. 2007. "Understanding the Subprime Mortgage Crisis." Federal Reserve Bank of New York.

Deng, Yongheng, Andrey Pavlov, and Lihong Yang. 2004. "Spatial Heterogeneity in Mortgage Terminations by Refinance, Sale, and Default." LUSK Center for Real Estate, Working Paper 2004-1003.

Deng, Yongheng, John Quigley, and Robert Van Order. 2000. "Mortgage Terminations, Heterogeneity, and the Exercise of Mortgage Options." *Econometrica* 68 (2): 275–308.

Department of the Treasury. 2003. "Enhancing Disclosure in the Mortgage-Backed Securities Markets, Staff Report." Washington, D.C.: Office of Federal Housing Enterprise Oversight, Securities and Exchange Commission, January.

Department of the Treasury and the Reserve Bank of Australia. 2003. "Globalization: the Role of Institution Building in the Financial Sector. G20 Case Study: An Australian perspective." September.

Diamond, Douglas. 1998. "The Current Operations of the Bauspar Systems in the Czech Republic, Hungary and Slovakia." Study commissioned by USAID. San Diego.

———. 1999. "Do Bausparkassen Make Sense in Transition Countries?" *European Mortgage Review* 21. Council of Mortgage Lenders. London.

Diamond, Douglas, and Michael Lea. 1992. "Housing Finance in Developed Countries: An International Comparison of Efficiency." *Journal of Housing Research* 3(1): 1–271.

Diamond, Douglas, and Michael Lea. 1993. "The Decline of Special Circuits in Developed Country Housing Finance." *Housing Policy Debate* 3(3): 747–78.

Diamond, Douglas B. 1999. *The Transition in Housing Finance in Central Europe and Russia: 1989–1999.* Washington, D.C.: The Urban Institute.

Diamond, Douglas B., and Marja C. Hoek-Smit. 2000. "Unblocking Finance for Affordable Housing." Report for the National Housing Finance Corporation of South Africa, International Housing Finance Program, Wharton School, University of Pennsylvania.

DiPasquale, Denise, and William Wheaton. 1992. "The Cost of Capital, Tax Reform, and the Future of the Rental Housing Market." *Journal of Urban Economics* 31(3): 337–59. May.

DiPasquale, Denise. 1989. "Homeowner Deductions and First Time Homebuyers." Joint Center for Housing Studies of Harvard University, Working Paper W89-2. Boston MA.

———. 1999. "Why Don't We Know More About Housing Supply?" *Journal of Real Estate Finance and Economics* 18(1): 9–23.

DiPasquale, Denise., and Jean L. Cummings. 1992. "Financing Multifamily Rental Housing: The Changing Role of Lenders and Investors." *Housing Policy Debate* 3(1): 91.

Djankov, Simeon, Rafael La Porta, Florencio Lopez-de-Silanes, and Andrei Shleifer. 2002. "Courts: The Lex Mundi Project." NBER Working Paper Series, Working Paper 8890.

Dübel, Achim. 2000. "Separating Homeownership Subsidies from Finance: Traditional Mortgage Market Policies, Recent Reform Experiences and Lessons for Subsidy Reform." Land and Real Estate Initiative Research Papers, Background Series #14. Washington, D.C.: The World Bank.

———. 2006. "Mortgage Instruments and Market Risk Management." Presentation for the IFC Turkey Housing Finance Workshop, Istanbul.

———. 2003. "Financial, Fiscal, and Housing Policy Aspects of Contract Savings for Housing (CSH) in Transition Countries—the Cases of Czech Republic and Slovakia." Study commissioned by the Financial Sector Development Department of the World Bank. Washington, D.C.

Dübel, Achim, and Michael Lea. 2000. "Micro- and Macroeconomic Consequences of Residential Mortgage Prepayment. Evidence from the Denmark, France, Germany, the United Kingdom, and the United States." Schriftenreihe des Verbandes Deutscher Hypothekenbanken. Frankfurt: Fritz Knapp Verlag. 149–290.

Dübel, Achim, Michael Lea, and Reinhard Welter. 1997. "Study on Mortgage Credit in the European Economic Area Structure of the Sector and Application of the Rules in the Directives 87/102 and 90/88." Study commissioned by the Commission of the European Communities (DG XXIV). Brussels.

EBRD (European Bank for Reconstruction and Development). 2007. Mortgage Loan Minimum Standards Manual. London.

Edwards, Julian. 2003. "The Implementation of the UN Guidelines for Consumer Protection." Speech held before the Unctad Trade Commission.

Escobar, Alejandro, and Sally Merrill. 2004. "Housing Microfinance: The State of the Practice." In Housing Microfinance: A Guide to Practice, ed. Franck Daphnis and Bruce Ferguson. Kumarian Press.

European Mortgage Federation. 2001. Mortgage Banks and Mortgage Bonds in Europe, 3rd ed., Brussels.

———. 2002. "Efficiency of Mortgage Collateral in the European Union." European Mortgage Federation, Brussels.

———. 2002. "Developments in Property Valuation." No. 13, at www.hypo .org.

———. 2003. "The Protection of the Mortgage Borrower in the European Union." European Mortgage Federation, Brussels.

———. 2007. *A Review of European Mortgage and Housing Markets.* Brussels: Hypostat.

Fabozzi, Frank J., Chuck Ramsey, and Michael Marz. 2000. *Handbook of Non-Agency Mortgage-Backed Securities,* 2nd ed., McGraw-Hill.

Fabozzi, Frank, ed. 2001. *The Handbook of Mortgage Backed Securities.* McGraw-Hill.

Fallis, George, and Lawrence B. Smith. 1984. "Uncontrolled Prices in a Controlled Market: The Case of Rent Controls." *American Economic Review* 74(1): 193–200.

———. 1985. "Price Effects of Rent Control on Controlled and Uncontrolled Rental Housing in Toronto: A Hedonic Index Approach." *Canadian Journal of Economics* 18(3): 652–9.

Federal Deposit Insurance Corporation. 2004. Assessing the Banking Industry's Exposure to an Implicit Government Guarantee of GSEs. March.

Federal Reserve. 1998. *12 Code of Federal Regulations (CFR) 208.50 Subpart E—Real Estate Lending and Appraisal Standards,* July 13.

———. 2005. *Interagency Guidance on Nontraditional Mortgage Products. Docket No. OP-1246,* December 20.

Ferguson, Bruce. 2004. "The Key Importance of Housing Microfinance." In *Housing Microfinance: A Guide to Practice,* eds. Franck Daphnis and Bruce Ferguson. Bloomfield, CT: Kumarian Press.

Ferguson, Bruce, and Elinor Haider. 2000. "Mainstreaming Microfinance of Housing." *Housing Finance International.* September.

Field, Erica, and Maximo Torero. 2006. "Do Property Titles Increase Credit Access Among the Urban Poor?" Manuscript.

Field, Erica. 2002. *Urban Property Rights and Labor Supply in Peru.* Princeton, NJ: Department of Economics, Princeton University.

Financial Services Authority. 2006. *Financial Risk Outlook 2006.* London.

FinMark Trust. 2007. "Access to Housing Finance in the Financial Sector Charter Target Market." www.finmark.org.za.

Fitch Ratings. 2002. *As the Dust Settles: Current Performance of Argentine Structured Finance.* April.

Follain, James R., Patric H. Hendershott, and David C. Ling. 1987. "Understanding the Real Estate Provisions of Tax Reform: Motivation and Impacts." *National Tax Journal* 40(3): 363–72.

Franklin, Allen, and Douglas Gale. 2001. *Comparing Financial Systems.* Cambridge, MA: The MIT Press.

Fratzscher, Oliver. 2004. "Basel II: The International Banking System at the Crossroads." World Bank presentation, June 3.

Freixas, Xavier, and Jean Charles Rochet. 1998. *The Microeconomics of Banking.* Cambridge, MA: The MIT Press.

Friedman, Joseph, Emmanuel Jimenez, and Mayo Stephen. 1988. "The Demand for Tenure Security in Developing Countries." *Journal of Development Economics* 29: 185–98.

Galal, Ahmed, and Omar Razzaz. 2001. "Reforming Land and Real Estate Markets." World Bank Policy Research Working Paper 2616. Washington, D.C.

Galiani, Sebastian, and Ernesto Schargrodsky. 2006. "Property Rights for the Poor: Effects of Land Titling." Mimeo. Buenos Aires: University San Andres, March.

Gandelman, Eduardo, and Nestor Gandelman. 2004, "Los efectos del sector público en le financiamiento de la vivienda: el mercado hipotecario de Uruguay." Working Paper no.503, Research Department, Inter-American Development Bank, Washington, D.C.

Gautier, Maryse, Olivier Hassler, Mila Freire, Cynthia Goytia, Nora Clichevski, Marcela Cristini, and Ramiro Moya. 2006. "Review of Argentina's Housing Sector: Options for Affordable Housing Policy." Policy Research Working Paper. World Bank: Washington, D.C.

Gilbert, Alan, and UN Human Settlements Program. 2003. *Rental Housing: An Essential Option for the Urban Poor in Developing Countries.* UN Habitat, January 1.

Gill, Anthony. 1997. "Housing Finance and the Secondary Mortgage Market in Australia." *Housing Finance International* 12(2).

Glaeser, Edward, and Erzo Luttmer. 2003. "The Misallocation of Housing under Rent Control." *American Economic Review* 93: 1027–46.

Glaeser, Edward, and Joseph Gyourko. 2003. "The Impact of Building Restrictions on Housing Affordability, Policies to Promote Affordable Housing." *Economic Policy Review* 9(2): 21–39.

Glaeser, Edward, Joseph Gyourko, and Raven Saks. 2005. "Why Have House Prices Gone Up?" NBER Working Paper 11129.

Goldsmith, Richard, 1984. *Comparative National Balance Sheets: A Study of Twenty Countries, 1688–1979*. Chicago: University of Chicago Press.

Gramlich, Edward M. 2007. *Subprime Mortgages, America's Latest Boom and Bust*. Washington, D.C.: Urban Institute Press.

Gurenko, Eugene, and Rodney Lester. 2004. *Rapid Onset Natural Disasters: The Role of Financing in Effective Risk Management*. Washington, D.C.: The World Bank, April.

Guttentag, Jack. 2002. "Making Mandatory Mortgage Disclosure Effective: Some Guidelines." *Housing Finance International* 17(2): 37-40.

———. 2004. "Protection of Mortgage Borrowers in the U.S." Annual Conference of the International Union of Housing Finance Institutions, Conference Booklet. Brussels.

Gyourko, Joseph, and Peter Linneman. 1989. "Equity and Efficiency Aspect of Rent Control: an Empirical Study of New York City." *Journal of Urban Economics* 26: 54–74.

Hassler, Olivier, 2003. "Mortgage Bonds: Best Usage and Best Practice." Paper.

Hassler, Olivier and Simon Walley. 2007. "Mortgage Liquidity Facilities." *Housing Finance International*. December.

Hendershott, Patric H. 1980. "Real User Costs and the Demand for Single Family Housing." Brookings Papers, 2.

———. 1990. "The Tax Reform Act of 1986 and Real Estate." In *Building Foundations: Housing and Federal Policy*, eds. Denise DiPasquale and Langley C. Keyes, 241-63, Philadelphia: University of Pennsylvania Press.

Hendershott, Patric H. and David C. Ling. 1984. "Trading and the Tax Shelter Value of Depreciable Real Estate." *National Tax Journal* 37(2): 213–24.

Hendershott, P. H. and James D. Shilling. 1982. "The Economics of Tenure Choice, 1955–1979." In *Research in Real Estate, vol. 1*, ed. C. F. Sirmans. Greenwich, CT: Jai Press.

Herring, Richard, and Susan Wachter. 1999, "Real Estate Booms and Banking Busts: An International Perspective," Wharton Financial Institutions Center Working Paper 99-27.

Hilber, Paul, Qin Lei, and Lisbeth Zacho. 2001. "Real Estate Market Developments and Financial Sector Soundness." IMF Working Paper, September.

Hirad, Abdighani, and Peter M. Zorn. 2001. *A Little Knowledge Is A Good Thing: Emperical Evidence of the Effectiveness of Pre-Purchase Home-Ownership Counseling.* Washington, D.C.: Freddie Mac.

Hoek-Smit, Marja C. 1982. "Improvement Strategies for Lower-Income Urban Settlements in Kenya." In *The Residential Circumstances of the Urban Poor in Developing Countries: Housing Conditions and Improvement Strategies.* New York: Praeger Special Studies.

———. 2001. "Home Ownership Assistance Programs for Thailand: A Feasibility Study." Prepared for the Ministry of Finance and the Government Housing Bank, Government of Thailand and the World Bank.

———. 2002. *Implementing Indonesia's New Housing Policy: The Way Forward, Findings, and Recommendations of the Technical Assistance Project— Policy Development For Enabling the Housing Market to Work in Indonesia.* Washington, D.C.: The World Bank.

———. 2003. "Subsidizing Housing or Housing Finance?" Paper for International Housing Conference on the occasion of the 50th anniversary of the Hong Kong Housing Authority, February 2004.

———. 2004. "Making Sense of the Universe of Housing Subsidies." Paper prepared for the Housing Credit Conference, Dubna, Russia, February. International Housing Finance Program, Wharton School, University of Pennsylvania.

Hoek-Smit, Marja C., and Douglas Diamond. 2003. "The Design and Implementation of Subsidies for Housing Finance." Paper prepared for the World Bank Seminar on Housing Finance, March 10–13, 2003.

———. 2003. "Subsidizing Housing Finance." *Housing Finance International* 18(3): 3–13.

Hoek-Smit, Marja C., and Jasper J. Hoek. 1998. "Property Rights and Investment in Housing in Botswana, Tanzania, and Swaziland." Unpublished manuscript.

Homeownership Alliance. 2004. "America's Home Forecast: The Next Decade for Housing and Mortgage Finance." Washington, D.C.

Hong Kong Mortgage Corporation. 2002. *Annual Report.*

Igarashi, Masahiro, and Richard Arnott. 2000. "Rent Control, Mismatch Costs, and Search Efficiency." *Regional Science and Urban Economics* 30(3): 249–88.

Igbinoba, Roland. 2005. "Housing Finance in Nigeria: Past, Present, and Future." Report for the FMO.

International Monetary Fund. 2004. "The Global House Price Boom." *World Economic Outlook*, Chapter 2, Washington, D.C.

International Valuation Standards Committee. 2003. *International Valuation Standards. Sixth Edition.*

———. 2005. *International Valuation Standards. Seventh Edition.*

Jacobides, Michael. 2001. "Mortgage Banking Unbundling: Profit." In Mortgage Banking, Mortgage Bankers Association of America. January: 28–40.

Jaffee, Dwight and Bertrand Renaud. 1996. "Strategies to Develop Mortgage Markets in Transition Countries." World Bank Policy Research Working Paper, No. 1,697, December.

Jappeli, Tullio, and Luigi Pistaferri. 2002. "Tax Incentives for Household Saving and Borrowing." Working Paper No. 83, Centre for Studies in Economics and Finance, University of Salerno.

Jimenez, Emmanuel. 1984. "Tenure Security and Urban Squatting." *Review of Economics and Statistics* 66: 556–67.

Kose, M. Ayhan, Eswar S. Prasad, Kenneth Rogoff, and Shang-Jin Wei. 2006. "Financial Globalization: A Reappraisal." IMF Working Paper 06/189, Washington, D.C.

Krahnen, Jan Pieter, and Martin Weber. 2000. "Generally Accepted Rating Principles: A Primer." *Journal of Banking and Finance*, February 14.

Kritayanavaj, Ballobh. 2002. "Financing Affordable Homeownership in Thailand: Roles of the Government Housing Bank Since the Economic Crisis." *Housing Finance International* 17(2): 15–25.

La Porta, Rafael, Florencio Lopez-de-Silanes, Andrei Shleifer, and Robert Vishny. 1998. "Law and Finance." *Journal of Political Economy* 106: 1113–55.

Ladekarl, Jeppe. 2001. *Enhancing Market Liquidity for Mortgage Securities.* Washington, D.C.: The World Bank.

Lambert, Annik. 2004. "Consumer Protection in the European Union." Annual Conference of the International Union of Housing Finance Institutions, Conference Booklet. Brussels.

Laurin, Alain, and Giovanni Majnoni. 2003. "Bank Loan Classification and Provisioning Practices in Selected Developed and Emerging Countries." World Bank Working Papers, Washington, D.C.

Lea, Michael, and Bertand Renaud. 1995. "Contractual Savings for Housing: How Suitable are They for Transitional Economies?" World Bank Policy Research Working Paper No. 1516. Washington, D.C.

Lea, Michael. 1999. "Models of Secondary Mortgage Market Development." In *New Directions in Asian Housing Finance*, ed. M. Watanabe. International Finance Corporation. Washington, D.C. 14–49.

Lea, Michael, and Steven Bernstein. 1996. "Housing Finance in an Inflationary Economy: The Experience of Mexico." *Journal of Housing Economics* 5(1).

———. 2001. *The International Housing Finance Sourcebook 2000.* Chicago: International Union of Housing Finance Institutions, Chicago.

Loutskina, Elena. 2005. "Does Securitization Affect Bank Lending: Evidence from Bank Responses to Funding Shocks." Mimeo, Boston College, May.

Low, Simon, Achim Dübel, and Matthew Sebag-Montefiore. 2003. "Study on the Financial Integration of European Mortgage Markets." Study commissioned by the European Mortgage Federation to Mercer Oliver Wyman. Brussels.

MacLennan, Duncan, John Muellbauer, and Mark Stephens. 2000. "Asymmetries in Housing and Financial Market Institutions and EMU." In *Readings in Macroeconomics*, ed. Tim Jenkinson, 74–98. Oxford, UK: Oxford University Press.

Malpezzi, Stephen, and Stephen K. Mayo. 1997. "Getting Housing Incentives Right: A Case Study of the Effects of Regulation, Taxe,s and Subsidies on Housing Supply in Malaysia." *Land Economics* 73(3): 372–91.

Market Intelligence Strategy Center. 2005. http://www.marketintelligence .com.au.

Masciandaro, Donato. 2001. "In Offense of Usury Laws: Microfoundations of Illegal Credit Contracts." *European Journal of Law and Economics* 12(3).

Mason, David. 2004. *From Building and Loans to Bail Out: A History of the American Savings and Loan Industry 1831–1995*. Cambridge, UK: Cambridge University Press

Mason, Joseph and Josh Rossner. 2007. Where Did the Risk Go? How Misapplied Bond Ratings Cause Mortgage-backed Securities and Collateralized Debt Obligation Market Disruptions." Available at http://ssrn.com, May 14.

Mathey, Kosta. 1990. "An Appraisal of Sandinista Housing Policies." In *Latin American Perspectives* 17(3): 76–99.

Mayo, Stephen K., and David Gross. 1987. "Sites and Services—and Subsidies: The Economics of Low-Cost Housing in Developing Countries." *The World Bank Economic Review* 1(2): 301–35.

Mayo, Stephen K. 1993. "Housing, Enabling Markets to Work—with Technical Supplements." A World Bank Policy Paper, The World Bank, Washington, D.C.

———. 1999. "Subsidies in Housing." Paper prepared for the Sustainable Development Department Technical Paper Series, Inter-American Development Bank, Washington, D.C.

Melzer, Illana. 2006. *How Low Can You Go? Charting the Housing Finance Access Frontier: A Review of Recent Demand and Supply Data*. South Africa: FinMark Trust, April 25.

Mercer Oliver Wyman. 2003. *Study on the Financial Integration of European Mortgage Markets*. Brussels: European Mortgage Federation.

Miles, David. 2004. *The UK Mortgage Market: Taking a Longer View. Final Report and Recommendations*. London: HM Treasury.

Mills, Edwin S. 1986. "Has the United States Over-invested in Housing?" *Journal of the American Real Estate and Urban Economics Association* 15(1): 601–16.

Mitchell, Janet, and Ingo Fender. 2005. "Structured Finance: Complexity, Risks, and the Use of Ratings." *BIS Quarterly Review*, Bank of International Settlements, June.

Mixmarket. Various years. *The Microbanking Bulletin*. www.themix.org/microbanking-bulletin/microbanking-bulletin.

———. Various years. "Benchmarks and Trend Lines." http://www.themix .org/mbb/overview/benchmarks

Moody's Investors Service Banking System. 2004. *Outlook.* October.

Moore, Michael. 1989. *Roger & Me.* New York: Warner Bros.

Mortgage Bankers Association. 2007. "Characteristics of Outstanding Residential Mortgage Debt: 2006." Research Data Note, January.

———. 2007. "National Delinquency Survey, Third Quarter 2007." Mortgage Bankers Association of America. Washington, D.C.

Murray, Michael P. 1999. "Subsidized and Unsubsidized Housing Stocks 1935 to 1987: Crowding Out and Co-integration." *The Journal of Real Estate Finance and Economics* 18(1): 107–24.

Nabarro, Rupert, and Tony Key. 2003. "Performance Measurement and Real Estate Lending Risk." BIS Papers #21.

National Housing Bank of India. 2002. *Asset-Liability Guidelines.* June.

OECD (Organisation for Economic Co-operation and Development). 1996. *Consumer Policy in OECD Countries.* Paris.

———. 2004. *Principles of Corporate Governance.* April.

———. 2005. *Economic Outlook* 78. December.

Office of the Comptroller of the Currency. 1999. "Interagency Guidelines for Real Estate Lending Policies, Treatment of High LTV Residential Real Estate Loans," October 13.

Ozay, Ferhan. 2006. "Turkish Catastrophe Insurance Pool: An Innovative Model for CAT-Exposed Countries." Presented at the Southeast Europe Mortgage Finance Conference, February 28.

Palla, Ken. 2000. "The Potential of Scoring in International Mortgage Lending." *Housing Finance International* 14(3): 14–20.

Peek, Joe, and James A. Wilcox. 2006. "Housing, Credit Constraints, and Macro Stability: The Secondary Mortgage Market and Reduced Cyclicality of Residential Investment." *American Economic Review* 96(2).

Pence, Karen M. 2006. "Foreclosing on Opportunity: State Laws and Mortgage Credit." Pollock, Alex. 1994. "Simplicity versus Complexity in the Evolution of Housing Finance Systems,. *Housing Finance International* (8)3: 11–14.

Pollock, Alex. 1999. "A New Housing Finance Option in the US: MPF vs. MBS." *Housing Finance International* (13)3: 3–8.

Poterba, James. 1980. "Inflation, Income Taxes, and Owner-Occupied Housing." NBER Paper 533.

Poveda, Raimundo. 2000. "Reform of the System of Insolvency Provisions." Speech given at the APD, Madrid, January 18.

Powell, Andrew. 2004. "Basel II and Developing Countries: Sailing through the Sea of Standards." Washington, D.C.: World Bank Policy Research Working Paper 3387, September. Presented at the World Bank Conference on Housing Finance in Emerging Markets: Policy and Regulatory Challenge, March 10–13.

Quigley, John M., and Steven Raphael. 2004. "Is Housing Unaffordable? Why Isn't It More Affordable?" *Journal of Economic Perspectives* 18(1): 191–214.

Ragachan, S. 2003. "Alternative Dispute Resolution Mechanisms: Criteria for Appraising Efficacy." Paper presented at the Asian Conference on Consumer Protection, Competition Policy, and Law. Kuala Lumpur.

Rajan, Raghuram G., and Luigi Zingales. 2003. "The Great Reversals: The Politics of Financial Development in the Twentieth Century." *Journal of Financial Economics* 69: 5–50.

Ratcliff, Richard. 1949. *Urban Land Economics*. McGraw Hill.

Rawls, John. 1971. *A Theory of Justice*. Cambridge, MA: Harvard University Press.

Razzaz, Omar. 1993. "Examining Property Rights and Investment in Informal Setttlements: The Case of Jordan." In *Land Economics*, November.

RealKredit Danmark. 2007. *Danish Mortgage Bonds*.

Realty Times. 2004. http://www.realtytimes.com/.

Reifner, Udo. 2001. "The Future of Consumer Education and Consumer Information in a Market Economy." In *Consumer Law in the Information Society*, ed. Thomas Wilhelmsson, Salla Tuominen, and Heli Tuomola. Den Haag: Kluwer Law International.

Renaud, Bertrand, Ming Zhang, and Stefan Koeberle. 1998. "How the Real Estate Boom Undid Financial Institutions: What Can Be Done Now?", In *Competitiveness and Sustainable Economic Recovery in Thailand, Volume II*, ed. Johanna Witte and Stefan Koeberle, 103–51. Bangkok:

National Economic and Social Development Board and World Bank Thailand Office.

Renaud, Bertrand. 1999. "The Financing of Social Housing in Integrating Financial Markets: A View from Developing Countries." *Urban Studies* 36(4): 755–73.

Rischke, Carl G. 1998. "German Bausparkassen: Instrument for Creating Homeownership in the Transformation Countries." *Housing Finance International* 13(2): 8–14.

Rust, Kecia. 2006. *ACCESShousing* 1. April.

———. 2008. "Challenges to Housing and Housing Finance Affordability in South Africa." Presentation at the World Bank/IFC Global Conference on Housing Finance in Emerging Markets, Washington, D.C. May.

Saunders, Margot, and Alys Cohen. 2004. "Federal Regulation of Consumer Credit: The Cause or the Cure for Predatory Lending?" Joint Center for Housing Studies, Harvard University. Working Paper Series, BABC 04-21.

Securities and Exchange Commission. 2003. "Concept Release: Rating Agencies and the Use of Credit Ratings under the Federal Securities Laws." Release Nos. 33-8236; 34-47972; File No. S7-12-03, June.

Seraj, Toufiq M. 2003. "Solving Housing Problems through Private Sector Development." In *Water and Sanitation for Cities*, Dhaka: Bangladesh Institute of Planners, Centre for Urban Studies.

Shiller, Robert J. 2007. "Understanding Recent Trends in House Prices and Home Ownership." Mimeo for the 2007 Jackson Hole Symposium, Kansas City Fed.

Shleifer, Andrei. 1998. "State versus Private Ownership." *Journal of Economic Perspectives* 12: 133–50.

Silva de Anzoreana, Maria Paloma. 2009. "Mortgage Market in Mexico." Presentation at the World Bank/IFC FPD Forum, February. rru.world bank.org/FPDForum/sessions.apx.

Sinai, Todd, and Joel Waldfogel. 2002. "Do Low-Income Housing Subsidies Increase Housing Consumption?" NBER Working Paper, No. 8709, January.

Stanton, Thomas. 2002. *Government Sponsored Enterprises*. Washington, D.C.: AEI Press.

Stiglitz, Joseph. 2000. "The Contributions of Economics of Information to 20th Century Economics." *Quarterly Journal of Economics* 115: 1441–78.

Sungard Bankware Erisk. 2002. *Case Study: First National Bank of Keystone.* Available at http://www.sungard.com/bancware.default.aspx?id=4867.

Susin, Scott. 2001. "Rent Vouchers and the Price of Low-Income Housing." *Journal of Public Economics* 83: 109–52.

Titulizadora Colombiana. 2006. Presented at the World Bank Global Housing Finance Conference. March.

U.S. Departments of Housing and Urban Development and Treasury. 2000. "Curbing Predatory Home Mortgage Lending: A Joint Report." Washington, D.C.

UN-Habitat. 2003. *Rental housing: An essential option for the urban poor in developing countries.* HS/695/03 E. UN-Habitat: Nairobi.

U.S. Securities and Exchange Commission. 2003. "Report on the Role and Function of Credit Rating Agencies in the Operation of the Securities Markets." Washington, D.C., January.

———. 2003 and 2008. "Proposed Rules for Nationally Recognized Statistical Ratings Organizations. Washington, D.C. www.sec.gov/rules/proposed/338705fr.pdf and www.sec.gov/rules/proposed/2008/34-57967.pdf

———. 2005. "Definition of Nationally Recognized Statistical Rating Organization: Proposed Rule." 17 CFR part 240, April 27. www.sec.gov/rules/proposed/33-8570fr.pdf.

van Greuning, Hennie, and Sonja Bratanovic. 2003. *Analyzing Banking Risk: A Framework for Assessing Corporate Governance and Financial Risk Management.* Washington, D.C.: The World Bank.

Van Horne, James C. 1973. *Financial Market Rates and Flow.* 2nd edition. Englewood Cliffs, NJ: Prentice Hall.

Van Order, Robert. 2003. "Public Policy and Secondary Mortgage Markets: Lessons from U.S. Experience." Freddie Mac. Presented at the World Bank Global Housing Finance Conference, March.

Villoria Siegert, Nelliana. 2004. "What to Do with Public Rental Housing? Challenges and Options." Inter-American Development Bank, Washington, D.C., February.

Vittas, Dimitri. 1995. "Thrift Deposit Institutions in Europe and the United States." World Bank Policy Research Working Paper No. 1540. World Bank. Washington, D.C.

Vorms, Bernard. 1993. "The Expression of the Annual Percentage Rate of Charge in the Field of Mortgage Credit." Study commissioned by the Directorate-General XXIV (Consumer Protection) of the European Commission, Brussels.

Wheaton, William C. 1999. "Real Estate 'Cycles': Some Fundamentals." *Real Estate Economics* 27(2): 209–30.

Wiener Katz, Avery, ed. 1998. "Foundations of the Economic Approach to Law." *Interdisciplinary Readers in Law*. Oxford, UK: Oxford University Press.

World Bank. 2004. *Islamic Republic of Iran: Housing Sector Strategy.* Washington D.C.: World Bank.

———. 1993. "Housing: Enabling Markets to Work." Housing Policy Paper, Washington, D.C.: World Bank.

———. 2004. "The Urban Poor in Latin America." Report No 30465, Finance, Private Sector, and Infrastructure Management unit, Latin America and the Caribbean Region, The World Bank, Washington, D.C.

———. 2005. "Rental Choice and Housing Policy Realignment in Transition: Post-Privatization Challenges in the Europe and Central Asia Region, Infrastructure Department, Europe and Central Asia region." Washington, D.C.: The World Bank, December.

You, Seung-Dong 2003. "Establishing a New Government-Sponsored Enterprise, the Korean National Mortgage Corporation." *Housing Finance International* 18(2): 25–34.

Contributors

Roger Blood is a Senior Associate with Oliver Wyman and occasional independent consultant on mortgage default insurance for the World Bank. He has worked in the mortgage default insurance field for 40 years, including fourteen years as a risk management executive for a U.S.-based mortgage insurance firm. Since 1990 Mr. Blood has performed MI-related consulting assignments in fifteen countries. Mr. Blood served as senior vice president–risk management for a U.S.-based mortgage insurance firm. His responsibilities included product development, underwriting and claims management, pricing, and related regulatory matters. Mr. Blood has worked with Mortgage Insurance Companies of America, the U.S. mortgage insurance industry trade association, since its founding in 1973. He also served on the Fannie Mae Advisory Board, Southeast Region. As a consultant, Mr. Blood has performed mortgage-default insurance-related assignments for government and private clients in Argentina, Canada, the Dominican Republic, India, Israel, Kenya, Mexico, New Zealand, Poland, Thailand, Russia, the United Kingdom, and the United States. Mr. Blood holds an MBA degree from Wharton. He has published articles on mortgage risk and insurance and has co-authored a book entitled *The Private Insurance of Home Mortgages*.

Robert M. Buckley is an advisor with the Finance Economics & Urban Department of the World Bank. He has worked in more than 45 countries, helping to develop projects and undertaking studies. Robert has published widely; some recent studies are: *Thirty Years of World Bank Shelter Lending: What Have We Learned* (2006), *The World Bank Annual Review of Development Effectiveness* (1999), and *Housing Finance in Developing Countries* (1997); some recent articles: "Mortgage Credit Risk in EU Countries: Constraints on Exploiting the Single Currency Market," *European Journal of Law and Economics* (2006); and "Housing Policy in Developing Countries: Conjectures and Refutations," *World Bank Research Observer* (2005). Prior to joining the World Bank, Robert taught at the Wharton School and Syracuse University, and also worked at the United States Department of Housing and Urban Development, where he was Chief Economist.

Stephen B. Butler is an attorney who specializes in the legal and economic issues of land and property markets in developing and transitional economies. His main fields of work include housing and urban development, housing finance and development of private sector land and housing markets through law reform and institutional development. Since 1992 he has worked with the World Bank and other international institutions on land reform and land administration projects in Russia, Belarus, Kazakhstan, Ukraine, Georgia, Serbia, Croatia, Romania, Moldova, Macedonia, Bosnia-Herzegovina, Belize, Bangladesh, Nigeria, and Sierra Leone. He has worked with the International Finance Corporation on addressing administrative barriers to development of urban real property markets in Vietnam, Russia, Georgia, Latvia and Macedonia, focusing on business access to land and building permits. A significant part of his work has been on development of mortgage markets and secondary mortgage market institutions, and he has participated in development of laws on mortgage and mortgage securities and creation of secondary mortgage market institutions in Russia, Ukraine, Turkey, Armenia, Azerbaijan, Mongolia, Egypt, Tanzania, Rwanda, Slovenia, and the Palestinian Territories. Prior to beginning his work in international development Mr. Butler was a practicing attorney and housing development executive in the United States. He holds a law degree from New York University and a Masters Degree in Public Policy Analysis from Princeton University's Woodrow Wilson School of Public and International Affairs.

Loïc Chiquier is the manager of the unit in charge of insurance, housing finance, and pension funds within the Financial and Private Sector Development Vice Presidency of the World Bank. Mr. Chiquier has extensive experience in housing and urban policy issues, development of primary and secondary mortgage markets, reform of housing finance institutions, low-income housing policy instruments, mortgage credit guarantees, legal and regulatory environment, and so forth. His country work experience includes Algeria, Brazil, Colombia, Egypt, Iran, Ivory Coast, Jordan, Mexico, Morocco, Nigeria, Peru, Ukraine, and Russia. Prior to joining the World Bank, Mr. Chiquier worked as advisor for housing finance reforms to the Government of Poland, and as Head of Crédit Foncier International (subsidiary of a French bank providing international technical assistance) and director for Eastern Europe of this bank. Mr. Chiquier holds degrees from Ecole Polytechnique, France; diplôme d'études approfondies of Macroeconomic Analysis and Policy from Ecole Normale Supérieure; and master's degrees in finance from Ecole Nationale des Ponts et Chaussees and in international relations from the Institut des Sciences Politiques de Paris.

Franck Daphnis is currently the   President/CEO of the Development Innovations Group (DIG). His professional experience has focused on housing finance, microfinance, urban development, operations management, housing and infrastructure rehabilitation, municipal services cost recovery, and urban environmental management. Mr. Daphnis has authored and edited two books on housing finance, including *Housing Microfinance: A Guide to Practice* (Kumarian Press, January 2004.)

Douglas Diamond has spent 20 years as a full-time independent consultant specializing in housing and housing finance issues in developing countries. He has worked in all parts of the world, including extensively in European countries transitioning from communism, including Armenia, Estonia, Hungary, Kazakhstan, Lithuania, Poland, Russia, Slovakia, and Ukraine; in Africa (Ghana, South Africa, Tanzania); Asia (India, Indonesia, Pakistan, Sri Lanka, Mongolia, Vietnam); the Middle East (Egypt, Israel, Jordan, Saudi Arabia, Gaza and West Bank); Latin America (Brazil, Chile, Suriname); and the Caribbean (Barbados). His expertise derives from this wide range of experience in developing countries and from long involvement in all aspects of

U.S. housing research, including as a policy analyst at HUD and professor of economics. He holds a Ph.D. in economics from the University of Chicago.

Hans-Joachim Dübel is an independent international consultant based in Berlin and founder of the financial sector policy think tank Finpolconsult.de. In this function, he provides economic analysis and advice on the legal, regulatory, fiscal, and social aspects of global financial sector development, with a special focus on mortgage finance. His clients include international organizations, governments, trade associations, and the private sector. Achim also has broad international work experience in Europe, North America, transition countries, Latin America, Asia, and Africa. Achim was on the staff of the Financial Sector Development Department of the World Bank in Washington, D.C., as a senior financial economist from 1998 to 2000. In this position he advised emerging economies on mortgage and capital-market policy issues. From 1991 to 1998, he worked for empirica, an economic think tank based in Bonn and Berlin, as a senior economist focusing on mortgage finance, housing and urban development policy, and regional economic development; and evaluating large commercial real-estate investment projects.

Achim has been an advisor for the Association of German Mortgage Banks (now Pfandbrief Banks) on international regulatory affairs since 1993. In this function he undertook in 1995 the first econometric-model-based, commercial credit-risk analysis outside the United States that contributed to the change in regulatory approach in banking toward risk-based capital requirements. In 1997, he published the first internationally comparative analysis of mortgage prepayment risk. In 2003, Achim co-authored the Mercer, Oliver, Wyman study on financial integration in the EU for the European Mortgage Federation. He also advised in 2005 on the London Economics Study for the EU Commission on the efficiency of European mortgage markets.

Britt Gwinner is the Principal Housing Finance Specialist for Latin America and the Caribbean for the International Finance Corporation. Prior to this position, Mr. Gwinner served as Lead Housing Finance Specialist for the World Bank, and he also worked in financial risk management, primarily in terms of asset-liability and capital management for the World Bank's balance sheet. Before joining the World Bank, he participated in the development of risk based capital requirements for Fannie Mae, Freddie Mac, and the Federal Home Loan Banks. Mr. Gwinner has worked as a financial consultant for Fortune 500 companies and the U.S. federal government. Mr. Gwinner is a Chartered Financial Analyst, he holds an MBA in finance and a Masters in Public Policy from the University of Chicago, and a Bachelors degree in Political Science from the George Washington University.

Olivier Hassler is the Housing Finance Program Coordinator of the World Bank. He holds a master's degree in economics and the Diploma of the Institut d'Etudes Politiques de Paris, and worked for a long time for a financial institution specializing in mortgage finance, especially for lower-income households. He was mainly in charge of the funding and capital-markets operation of the company. He also had responsibilities in regulatory issues and in real estate portfolio management. He joined the World Bank in 2001 as a senior housing finance specialist. He has carried out missions or studies in numerous countries in South Asia, Africa, Middle East and North Africa, and Latin America.

Marja Hoek-Smit is the director of the International Housing Finance Program of the Wharton School Zell/Lurie Real Estate Center, and an adjunct associate professor in the Wharton Real Estate Department and Department of City and Regional Planning of the University of Pennsylvania. Her work focuses on housing and housing finance policies, particularly for low-income groups; housing demand and affordability analysis; the development of monitoring and evaluation systems for urban housing programs; and training in housing finance, housing market development, and urban development.

She has consulted with clients including the World Bank, International Monetary Fund, United States Agency for International Development, the United Nations, the Inter-American Development Bank, and directly for several governments and private financial institutions. Recent consulting activities include the development of a comprehensive housing strategy and subsidy system for the Government of Indonesia; urban housing market studies in Thailand, South Africa, Botswana, and Tanzania; the development of participatory approaches for urban and housing development for the governments of Sri Lanka, Indonesia, and South Africa; and the analysis and design of alternative housing finance and subsidy programs for the governments of Brazil, Mexico, Indonesia, Barbados, Trinidad and Tobago, and Suriname. She has also prepared national strategies for housing finance training for the governments of Pakistan and India.

David Le Blanc is an economist. He is currently working in the Division for Sustainable Development in the United Nations Secretariat in New York. He conducts analytical policy work or review work on topics related to sustainable development, to inform the Commission on Sustainable Development. His domains of work while at the UN have been water subsidies, sustainable agriculture, and sustainable consumption and production. He is currently Editor for *Natural Resources Forum—A United Nations Sustainable Development Journal*, a peer-reviewed Journal published by the Division for Sustainable Development. Prior to joining the United Nations, David worked for 3 years at the World Bank as Senior Economist in the Urban and Housing finance groups. During that period he worked in different countries in North Africa, the Middle East, Latin America and Asia. His work at the Bank included policy projects related to the housing sector, technical assistance on housing subsidies, and analytical work related to informal housing and housing subsidies. Earlier in his career, David worked at the French Statistical Institute (INSEE) both as a statistician and as an economist. From 1994 to 1997 he was Head of regional studies in the regional branch of INSEE in Lyons. During 1997–2000 he was Head of the National Housing Survey. He then joined CREST, Paris as a research fellow and worked on issues related to housing, housing subsidies, generational transfers, and child care. David holds diplomas from Ecole Polytechnique, Paris, Ecole Nationale de la Statistique et de líAdministration Economique, Paris, and a MSc in Stochastic Modeling Applied to Finance from Paris VII University.

Michael Lea has over 26 years of financial services experience, including more than 18 years of international experience in 30 countries spanning six continents. He has provided advice on the creation of market-based housing-finance institutions, products, and systems as a consultant to international development agencies, government-sponsored enterprises, trade groups, regulatory agencies, and major private-sector financial institutions in Europe, the United States, and emerging markets.

Dr. Lea has held a number of key positions with influential housing finance institutions. He has served as executive vice president for global markets at

Countrywide Financial Corporation, president of Cardiff Consulting Services Inc., senior vice president for finance and capital markets at the Imperial Corporation of America, and chief economist of Freddie Mac. He also served as a staff member for the President's Commission on Housing and was a Brookings Institution economic policy fellow at the U.S. Department of Housing and Urban Development.

Dr. Lea is an internationally known authority on housing and mortgage finance. He has published over 70 articles and book chapters, organized several conferences, and made numerous presentations to government agencies, multilateral institutions, trade groups, and academic and professional organizations. He has taught at Cornell University; the University of California, San Diego; San Diego State University; and the Wharton International Housing Finance Program at the University of Pennsylvania. He received his Ph.D. in economics from the University of North Carolina, Chapel Hill.

Bertrand Renaud is an internationally known expert with extensive experience in housing and housing finance issues in emerging and advanced markets. He has worked in some 40 countries that cover the full range of housing and development from the most basic stage to the most advanced system. He began his professional career as a specialist of urban development in Asia. He then joined the team of four experts who wrote the seminal urban strategy paper for the World Bank when that institution began focusing on urban development issues. In the early 1980s, he was appointed the first head of urban affairs at the Organisation for Economic Co-operation and Development (OECD) when industrial countries were confronted with the need to comprehensively rethink their urban policies. Upon his return to the World Bank, Dr. Renaud promoted housing finance activities as a key component of the urban agenda. He became advisor in the Financial Development Department of the World Bank when financial sector development became a core component of the development agenda in the early 1990s. There, he has provided policy advice to governments on strategic, operational, and technical issues of financial reforms for over a decade. He has also actively participated in or reviewed major World Bank operations. Dr. Renaud continues to advise government institutions and private groups in various part of the world.

Dr. Renaud's work has often taken place in periods of important changes in national housing systems when governments wanted to evaluate their options in terms of legal and regulatory infrastructure, institutions, and instruments, as well as their economic and social impacts. He led the first World Bank mission to China on urban reforms in 1988. His work on Russia's urban reform options was internationally recognized with the award of the 1995 Donald Robertson Memorial Prize in the United Kingdom. Throughout his career, he has maintained a continuing interest in Asia urban development. Dr. Renaud has taught and done research in major universities in Asia, the United States, and Europe, including the Massachusetts Institute of Technology, Hong Kong University, and Seoul National University. He has published extensively. His recent books include *Markets at Work: The Dynamics of the Residential Real Estate Market in Hong Kong* (HKU Press, 1997) and *Asia's Financial Crisis and the Role of Real Estate* (M.E. Sharpe, 2000). One of his latest articles appears in *Asset Price Bubbles* (MIT Press, 2003).

Dr. Renaud received Ph.D. and MS degrees from the University of California at Berkeley, and the degree of Ingépinieur INA in Paris, France.

Claude Taffin joined the World Bank in May 2008 as a senior housing finance specialist. He was the chief economist of "l'Union Sociale pour l'Habitat," the umbrella organization of French Social Housing Associations (Hlm). He had previously occupied a similar position at Credit Foncier, a specialist mortgage lender. He was first a statistician in charge of housing at the National Institute of Statistics and Economic Studies (INSEE). As a consultant for the World Bank, he worked in China, Iran, Ivory Coast, Jordan, Morocco and Poland.

Claude Taffin holds degrees from Ecole Polytechnique and Ecole Nationale de la Statistique et de l'Administration Economique (France).